Historical Traumas
AMONG ARMENIAN, KURDISH, AND TURKISH PEOPLE
OF ANATOLIA

Dedication
For my grandparents
Ilhami & Aynur
Ahmet & Nermin

Historical Traumas

AMONG ARMENIAN, KURDISH, AND TURKISH PEOPLE
OF ANATOLIA

A TRANSDISCIPLINARY PERSPECTIVE
TOWARD RECONCILIATION

NERMIN SOYALP

sussex
ACADEMIC
PRESS
Brighton • Chicago • Toronto

Copyright © Nermin Soyalp, 2022.

The right of Nermin Soyalp to be identified as Author of this work has been asserted in accordance with the Copyright, Designs and Patents Act 1988.

2 4 6 8 10 9 7 5 3 1

First published in Great Britain in 2022 by
SUSSEX ACADEMIC PRESS
PO Box 139, Eastbourne BN24 9BP

Distributed in North America by
SUSSEX ACADEMIC PRESS
Independent Publishers Group
814 N. Franklin Street
Chicago, IL 60610

All rights reserved. Except for the quotation of short passages for the purposes of criticism and review, no part of this publication may be reproduced, stored in a retrieval system, or transmitted, in any form or by any means, electronic, mechanical, photocopying, recording or otherwise, without the prior permission of the publisher.

British Library Cataloguing in Publication Data
A CIP catalogue record for this book is available from the British Library.

Library of Congress Cataloging-in-Publication Datf
To be applied For.

Hardcover ISBN 978-1-78976-085-9

Typeset & designed by Sussex Academic Press, Brighton & Eastbourne.
Printed by TJ IBooks Ltd, Padstow, Cornwall.

Contents

Foreword by Fatma Müge Göçek	viii
Preface	xi
Acknowledgments	xiii
Cover Design Credits and Symbolism	xv

Introduction	1
An Inter-Generational Story at the Fall of the Ottoman Empire	4
War and Trauma	8
Imagining New Identities in a New Republic	
Hidden and Oppressed Histories	9
Transgenerational Trauma	10
Revealing the Transgenerational Traumas of Anatolians	11
Epistemologies of Ignorance, Privilege, Suppression, and Oppression	13
Overview of the Book	14
Personal Background	15

1
Trauma and Its Psycho-Social Consequences	21
Psychological Trauma	22
Studies of Psychological Trauma in Turkey	24
Thinking About the Socio-Cultural Context of Trauma in Turkey	31
Collective Trauma	32
Cultural Trauma	34
Transgenerational Trauma	37
Healing Transmission of Trauma at a Personal Level	39
Healing Transmission of Trauma at a Systemic Level	41
Understanding Perpetrator Motives from a Psycho-Social Lens	44

2
A History of Collective Traumas: The Decline and the Fall of the Ottoman Empire	49
The Ottoman Empire	50
Anatolia	53
Armenians/Armenian Plateau	53
Kurds/Kurdistan	55

Nomadism/Transhumance	56
Millet System	56
The Hamidiye Massacres of 1894–1896	58
The Young Turk Revolution 1908	61
The Balkan Wars of 1912–1913	62
Committee of Union and Progress (CUP or Unionists) Takeover in 1913	64
The Armenian Genocide of 1915–1917	65
Transgenerational Aspect of Armenian Genocide	71
The Turkish War of Independence of 1919–1923	74
The Greco-Turkish War of 1920–1922	76
The Consequences of the New Nation's Turkification agenda	81

3
The Collective Traumas After the Formation of the Republic of Turkey

	83
Sheikh Said Rebellion of 1925	85
The Dersim Massacres of 1937–1939	89
Transgenerational Aspect of Dersim 38	96
Twenty Kur'a Military Service and the Wealth and Revenue Taxes of the 1940s	99
Twenty Kur'a (Mandatory) Military Service	99
The Wealth and Revenue Taxes of the 1940s	100
The Pogroms of September 6–7, 1955	104

4
The Inheritance of Military Ideologies and Its Consequences

	112
Military Coup (May 27, 1960)	112
Military Coup (March 12, 1971)	113
Military Coup (September 12, 1980)	113
The 1980 Coup: Before and After	114
Coup Reflections: Past and Present	115
The Diyarbakır Military Prison of 1980–1984 Torture	116
Partiya Karkerên Kurdistanê (PKK)	122
Effect on Families	123
Ongoing Strife Under Civilian Rule	124
Combat Trauma	128
Civilians Caught Between PKK and the Turkish Military	132
Village Guards	134
Forced Displacement of Kurds	137
Violence Against Alevis	143
Maraş Massacre	144

Sivas Massacre	144
Gazi Neighborhood Massacre	144
Large-Scale Military Intervention in Tunceli (Dersim)	145
Chaldiran War	146
Looking Back from the 21st Century	147

5
Epistemologies of Ignorance of Turkishness and Healing through Meeting the "Other"   153

Healing the Wounds of History through Drama and the Arts	154
Understanding Epistemologies of Ignorance	161
Assimilation Into "Turkishness" through Control of Language and the Education System	171
Language	171
Village Institutes	178
Boarding Schools	180
Mainstream Education	181
The Intertwined Nature of the Evolution of Turkishness and the Ignorance around Armenian Suffering	183
Hrant Dink's Assassination	187
Armenians in Turkey	188
Turkish Identity Struggles	190

Conclusion	201
Notes	205
References	210
Index	236

Foreword by Fatma Müge Göçek

The analysis of collective violence is especially exacting because violence simultaneously contains structural *and* emotional elements, the first based on reason and the latter on sentiment. At our particular juncture of world history, we as critical scholars have realized that these elements are not studied equitably: Western European modernity dominating the globe today has produced a tunnel vision whereby social scientists privilege the rational, behavioral, and publicly observable social structural processes at the expense of beliefs, of the emotional, the private, and the publicly silenced or oppressed. I think the recent emotional turn in the social sciences has attempted to overcome this inequity by focusing on everyday practices of violence from the ground up, capturing the contours of meaning construction around violence throughout, including the perpetrators as well as the victims. In my own work, for instance, I employed hundreds of contemporaneous memoirs to analyze the collective violence committed by the Turkish state and society against Armenians from the Ottoman Empire to contemporary Turkey, ending up mostly with the narratives of officials and officers of first the empire and then the republic (Göçek, 2015). At the time, only a few scholars had had the insight to move beyond formal state documents to focus on feelings and sentiments—which is why I was so wonderfully surprised to meet Nermin Soyalp and learn about her unique approach to the same collective violence.

When Nermin first contacted me, I was immediately struck by the similarities in our positionality: she is an ethnically "White Turk" like me, a woman, and one ready to join the ranks of conscientious Turks who think, like us, that a peaceful democratic Turkey can only be possible if and when the Turkish state and society come to terms with their violent past. Not only did she have to put up with the criticism of nationalist Turks, but she also got into a lot of trouble with her family regarding her liberal views, just as I did. She also privileged studying the repertoire of meanings in Turkish society surrounding collective violence from the bottom up, rather than focusing on structures and political institutions from the top down. What stunned me in particular was her ability to intuit the social significance of emotions embedded in collective violence at such a young age—it had taken me decades to reach the same vantage point.

There are differences between our endeavors, however, in terms of how we have approached collective violence, especially in terms of our specific uses of space and time. My work focused on the formation and transformation of collective violence in Ottoman and later Turkish society with the intent to identify patterns across time and space; Nermin instead highlights historical traumas mainly in terms of their social and psychological consequences in Republican Turkey. While I started my analysis in early Ottoman history and traced patterns into the Republic and then moved, as much as possible, into the present, Nermin instead commences with late Ottoman history, especially focusing on the cycle of initial violence against Armenians from the 1894–1896 Hamidiye Massacres to the 1915 Armenian Genocide until 1922, the last year of the existence of the Ottoman Empire. She then studies the collective traumas after the 1923 establishment of the Republic of Turkey to the present across all minorities, specifically focusing on the systemic violence committed by the Turkish state and society against the Kurds from the early years—such as the 1925 Sheikh Said rebellion and its brutal suppression and the 1938 Dersim Massacres—until today as well as on the pogroms against Greeks in 1955. Given that the 1955 pogroms were secretly planned and executed by the Turkish military, Nermin ends her coverage of historical traumas with the violence committed directly and publicly by the Turkish military: the 1960, 1971, and 1980 military coups; the pogroms against Alevis; and their violence against Kurds in the Diyarbakır Military Prison and against PKK (*Partiya Karkeren Kurdistan*)—the party representing Kurds in Turkey today, a group that is still officially stigmatized, marginalized, and excluded by the Turkish state and society.

While I stopped my analysis of collective violence there and then, Nermin's excellent analysis becomes outstanding because she has taken the additional step of proposing a way from violence into peace. In her final chapter on "the epistemologies of ignorance of Turkishness and healing through meeting the 'other'," Nermin proposes post-traumatic healing for all the peoples of Anatolia by courageously bringing perpetrators and victims into dialogue. She focuses on the arts to survey the representation of violence on the one hand and, on the other, subsequent healing especially through role play of the "other." Nermin then empirically delves into the significance of formal and informal education in constructing and reconstructing meaning in Turkish society; she specifically focuses on language use, village institutes (initially established to educate the [Turkish] citizen from the ground up, only to be abandoned by a state that did not want to include the newly educated with its elite cadres), boarding schools (established for the Kurdish "minority" with the intent to forcefully integrate them to Turkish society at the expense of their own identity, similar to the United States, Canada, and Australia), and mainstream education (where textbooks whitewash the role that hegemonic Turks played in collective violence and stereotype all other ethnic and religious groups in terms of the violence they committed against Turks).

Nermin aptly terms this process of hegemonic nationalist meaning construction "the intertwined evolution of Turkishness and ignorance" that systematically overlooks, marginalizes, and silences the suffering of others. To move beyond this ethnic trap, she employs the transdisciplinary framework afforded by Healing the Wounds of History workshops to heal people in Turkey and in the diaspora. And this is what has impressed me the most: Nermin has held these amazing workshops throughout the world, bringing Turks into the same space as their others, having them trade viewpoints to understand suffering fully. I hope that you will be as enthused in reading this book as I was—and still am—not only with Nermin's brilliant analysis of historical traumas in Turkish history, but also by her ability, unlike the rest of us, to offer solutions to such suffering through her post-traumatic healing practices.

PROFESSOR FATMA MÜGE GÖÇEK
University of Michigan

Preface

I grew up in Turkey having a Turkish identity. My father's side of the family are Balkan Muslim migrants, and my mother's side is rooted in Central and Eastern Anatolia. Writing a book about Turkish, Armenian, and Kurdish historical traumas, a topic that is seen as controversial in Turkey, is a big undertaking. As a person of Turkish origin, during the research and writing of this book, I had to overcome limitations in relation to my historical ignorance—to examine and challenge my own Turkish identity. Through the process of identification, which begins after birth, we form our personal and group values, norms, and taboos. For example, individuality and hard work ethics are valued in the United States, whereas in the Middle East, relationships and the health of the collective come first.

Furthermore, these values feel very close to our hearts as our identifications, values, and norms determine who we are. When we meet someone who does not share our values and norms, the experience can trigger suspicion, mistrust, or even offense. Collective norms, values, and taboos play a significant role in how people with different identifications view each other. In part, conflict or identity crisis arises when two people or groups meet with different norms, values, and narratives about each other.

Because I grew up in a homogeneous culture in Ankara (the capital city of Turkey), I was not aware of my own identifications. Metaphorically, fish are not aware of the water they swim in. Thus, when I left Turkey and went to places where norms, cultures, language, religion, and ways of living were drastically different from my own, and moreover through this writing process, I met with people whose narrative conflicted with mine and challenged my beliefs—a naturally deep questioning of my "self" emerged.

Identity is inherently fluid, malleable, and social. My identity is a combination of what I take myself to be and what society projects, therefore as soon as I stepped outside of my comfort zone and began to meet new, divergent types of people, activists across cultures, Turks, Kurds, and Armenians alike, the question of "Who am I?" at times became central to my inquiry. Subsequently, my relationship with my Turkish identity has been transformed.

I frequently had to take time to digest particular materials regarding the shadow of society. As a Turkish person, reading and learning about the perpetuation of violence by the Turkish state and Turkish people was hard to swallow. I remember having a strong reaction to some of the earlier materials I read. For example, I initially had an issue with the connection Kupelian and colleagues (1998) made between the Armenian Genocide and Jewish Holocaust in the *International Handbook of Multigenerational Legacies of Trauma*, one of the seminal books in the field. Knowing how terrible the Jewish Holocaust was, I could not comprehend something similar taking place in Turkey. I remember closing the book as soon as I read the paragraph with a sense of disappointment, anger, and offense and thought, "How dare they make that connection!" A seemingly common reaction among Turks.

A couple of years into my research, my reactionary position dissolved and shifted. After realizing that injustice and suffering took place in Anatolia at the hands of the Young Turks, the Committee of Union and Progress (CUP), and later assimilation politics and massacres at the hands of the modern Turkish state, I felt betrayed by the state for keeping the truth away from me while attempting to control me and my thoughts. I began to have a sensitivity for anything I read with a Turkish nationalist position. Reading about the glorious formation of the Turkish state became saddening for me. I could not find pride in my national identity when I also knew of its deep shadow.

This work is the culmination of 10 years of active research, facilitation, and production of workshops with Turks, Kurds, and Armenians, multiple journeys to Turkey for several months at a time, including visits to towns across Anatolia, interviewing family members, scholars, villagers, activists, and journalists. By doing so, I felt struck by the depth of history, culture, and how much more there was to explore. Turkish, Kurdish, and Armenian experiences are also diverse within their large-group identifications. Giving voice to all would be a hopeless task to take on for one person in one book. I think of this book as an Anatolian carpet that weaves diverse experiences of Turks, Kurds, and Armenians with an overview of Turkey's generational and historical traumas, pointing out interrelations and complexities along the way with an intention to present the connection between past, present, and future to inspire change for better futures.

Acknowledgments

Healing from any collectively traumatic experience is a shared journey that may take several generations. This book stands on the work of scholars and practitioners who have made substantial contributions to exposing and healing historical and current traumas in Turkey and other parts of the world. I bow to the brave scholars, activists, and practitioners, who paved the way for scholars like me to follow despite the difficulties they face. Their work has been cited and filled many pages of this book.

Foremost, amongst these scholars, I thank Fatma Müge Göçek for serving on my dissertation committee, reading this book before publication, and for her valuable feedback. I thank Alfonso Montuori for chairing my dissertation committee and teaching the transdisciplinary framework. Transdisciplinarity provided the groundwork for studying such complex and interrelated topics. I also thank Alfonso for connecting me to Sussex Academic Press as a potential publisher of the adaptation of my dissertation. And thank you, Sussex Academic Press, for your feedback and your responsiveness. I never worked with any other organization that was so effective and fast in responding!

Thank you, Armand Volkas, for your mentorship and collaboration in co-producing and facilitating Healing the Wounds of History workshops with Turks, Kurds, and Armenians over the years. These workshops were tremendous learning and healing opportunities for me, filled with shared bonds of mourning, tears, and kinship. I brought some examples from these workshops to this book. I feel deep gratitude to the emotional pioneers, Armenians, Kurds, and Turks alike, who courageously came and participated in these Healing the Wounds of History workshops. The pleasure of meeting you and working with you will continue to nourish my soul for the rest of my life.

The California Institute of Integral Studies (CIIS) of San Francisco, where I did my doctorate and wrote my dissertation, deserves a big shout-out. Thank you for the vigorous and exceptional learning environment which made such controversial academic work possible. From idea to actualization, so many scholars helped me along the way. In particular, Burcu Tung, and Flora Keshgegian, I am forever grateful to you. You know the art of providing difficult feedback. Your feedback and hands-on edits carried the work to the next level. Thank you for your vigilance, honesty, friendship, and insights. Thank you, Jennifer McDougall and Marky Kelly, for your feedback for some of the sections of this book, which helped me re-organize some of the concepts for a better reader experience. Thank you to my editor, Anne Kinne, for your critical eye on the manuscript and your immediate support when I needed help to articulate a complicated sentence. Thank you, Nirmala Nataraj and Leslie Peters, for proofreading some of the final chapters on such short notice. Thank you, Gohar Barseghyan and the team, Garegin (Gary) Mosoyan and Anna Fadzeyeva, for designing the book cover that represents its essence that captures Anatolia's historical traumas, its culture, history, and complexity with eloquent symbolism.

Thank you, Jennifer Wells, for helping me launch my journey, and Filiz Çelik for your support early in the process and connecting me with various communities in Turkey. Thank you, B. Kim Barnes, for the opportunity of working in the leadership development field with you, your mentorship, and your friendship. Thank yous also go to Gabrielle Donnelly, Sam Chen, Sylvia Hartowicz, Christine G., Suzanne Lapidus, Asiye Dalga, Devrim Tekinoğlu, and Rob Rayle for your friendship and support at various times of this process. I am grateful that my life is blessed with many outstanding people whose names I cannot possibly fit on one page. I have met many people throughout the years of writing this manuscript during my travels, workshops, classes, conferences, and other social gatherings. My interactions with them have filled the pages of this book. I am immensely grateful for everyone whose paths crossed with mine. Thank you!

Finally, to my mother, sister, father, and childhood friend, Ülkü, thank you all for continuously believing in me. Foremost, sincere thanks go to my husband, Jef Stott, for your love, patience, and continued support. Furthermore, our dog, Sansa, who entered our lives two years ago and brought so much joy and laughter—helped keep my heart open and reminded me of the beauty of life when I felt the toll of engaging with the dark side of humanity.

A deep bow of gratitude to you all!

Cover Design Credits and Symbolism

I take this opportunity to thank Gohar Barseghyan, Garegin (Gary) Mosoyan (graphic design), and Anna Fadzeyeva (illustration), for their vision and the design of the cover, and for Mosoyan additionally illustrating all of the maps and figures.

"In Anatolia, there is no other motif carrying so many different meanings than the bird motif. While birds like owls and ravens imply bad luck, doves, pigeons, and nightingales are used to symbolize good luck. The bird is the symbol of happiness, joy, and love. It is the soul of the dead. It is the longing and expectation of news. It stands for power and strength. It is the imperial symbol of various states founded in Anatolia." – Gohar Barseghyan

Introduction

This book is about the historical, collective, and transgenerational traumas in Anatolia,[1] which are rooted in the collapse of the Ottoman Empire, the establishment of the Republic of Turkey, and nationalist state and military policies conducted in Turkey since its founding. Located between Europe, Africa, the Caucasus, and the Middle East, Anatolia, also known as Asia Minor, literally acts as a bridge between Asia and Europe. Anatolia makes up most of today's modern Turkey. In Anatolia, Turks, Kurds, and Armenians lived side by side for over half a millennium during the Ottoman Empire era, and as a result, their sense of self is intimately tied to the other. The rise of nationalist ideologies concomitant with the fall of the Ottoman Empire resulted in numerous conflicts that created avenues for atrocities such as war, forced displacement, and even genocide, such as the Armenian Genocide in 1915 to occur.

Unfortunately, the deep wounds that exist from a string of long-standing conflicts between Turks, Kurds, and Armenians have not yet been sufficiently addressed, let alone healed. Furthermore, epistemologies of ignorance—promotion, and maintenance of lack of knowledge, misinformation, and unlearning of something previously known for purposes of control and domination in Turkey—have kept the lid on transgenerational experiences and have prevented appropriate healing modalities from being applied. In other words, this book illustrates the multidimensional and transgenerational aspects of present-day conflicts: how collectively and historically shared traumas have become inherently more complicated generation by generation, especially when exacerbated by oppressive state policies. In Turkey, epistemologies of ignorance are consciously produced and maintained by the state with the intent to control and maintain stability. Correspondingly, these epistemologies have created more conflict and turmoil. As a result, Turks, Kurds, and Armenians have been unable to move through their complex emotional and historical stances, creating a political impasse that inhibits mutual recognition and respect, preventing reconciliation.

This book is an adaptation of my doctoral dissertation, completed at the end of 2019 at the California Institute of Integral Studies in San Francisco, California. The original research used transdisciplinary[2] inquiry as an underlying paradigm, in order to explore the complexity of the histories, the psychologies, and the identities of Anatolians with a focus on Turks, Kurds, and Armenians. It is also informed by my experience as both a facilitator and a producer of numerous peacebuilding and conflict transformation workshops called Healing the Wounds of History (HWH)[3] with Kurds, Armenians, and Turks. Using drama therapy, psychodrama,[4] and playback theatre techniques (Volkas, 2009), HWH workshops forefront psychological approaches to conflict, providing a map to help individuals, groups, and communities traverse the emotional terrain toward reconciliation. In these workshops, I witnessed numerous individuals' stories, ranging from how their ethnic and religious identities made them feel within society to how a family story or a personal experience of trauma influenced them for the rest of their lives. These workshops were very influential and played a crucial role in my ability to empathize with Kurdish and Armenian experiences, and then, in turn, more deeply explore my own Turkish identity.

During one of the workshops, a Kurdish participant's drama exemplified the Kurdish people's collective and intergenerational trauma. In her story, Cevher[5] was only five years old and at home with her parents in a Kurdish mountain village in Eastern Turkey. Her story took place in the 1990s when the war between the Kurdistan Workers' Party (PKK)[6] and the Turkish military was at its peak. It was a heavy snowy winter when Turkish soldiers forced her family out of their home. The soldiers said that they were going to occupy their home until guerrilla fighters returned to the town. Because of the village's location deep in the mountains, the guerrillas often demanded support, food, and shelter from the villagers. Knowing this, Turkish soldiers came to the village to try to trap the guerrillas. Cevher said her family felt that they had no choice. When PKK asked for food and shelter, the villagers had to comply because they were on their own with no protection. When Turkish soldiers found out that someone was helping the guerrillas, it was a grave crime, and villagers were punished: tortured or sent to prison for supporting PKK. This created even more suffering as it put the villagers in a double bind.

When the Turkish soldiers came to stay in their home, Cevher's grandfather resisted leaving. He did not know where else the family—his wife, children, and grandchildren—could stay during the winter. In her sharing, Cevher described how the Turkish soldiers started beating her grandfather in front of the family. This is where the enactment of the incident began in the workshop: In defiance, 5-year-old Cevher defended her grandfather when the Turkish soldier beat him. She cried, "Stop!" One of the significant Kurdish traumas is represented in that scene—outright abuse and oppression, and the impossible situations people are pushed to withstand. In essence, her drama is representative of most Kurdish dramas. In the end, her family was forced out, and they spent the next two weeks with their neighbors while Turkish soldiers trashed their home. Cevher remembered coming back to a home littered with empty cans, leftovers, and garbage. Not long after, her entire village was forced to migrate to Istanbul as part of a wide-ranging government order.

Cevher's psychodrama was profound and moving. However, another workshop participant, Berna, who came from a small Turkish town by the Mediterranean coast, responded to Cevher's share. Berna carried a strong Turkish cultural identity as a *Yörük* Turk.[7] She is an outspoken woman and has great will power, exemplifying the strong women *Yörüks* are famous for in Anatolia. Berna said, "I had similar experiences when I was a child. Kurds are not the only ones who have been mistreated. Turkish soldiers would come to our homes and our village looking for guerrilla fighters too." She added that "Kurds were business owners in Marmaris" (a tourist town on the coast of the Mediterranean Sea in Turkey). Kurdish businesses in the tourism sector peaked, especially after the war between PKK and the Turkish military began the forced migration of Kurdish towns from Eastern to Western Anatolia. She said: "I have been mistreated and assaulted by Kurdish men when I worked in these facilities. The Kurdish men I worked with were patriarchal, and they took their anger out on Turkish women workers." Berna acknowledged Cevher's story. However, she felt that there was more to the story of Kurds and Turks in Anatolia. Berna's previous experiences with Kurdish men and her memory of victimization of her own community, even though they were Turkish, brought up a sense of defensiveness in her. The rest of the Turkish participants in the workshop (coincidently, they were all men and 1980s leftists who were tortured by the Turkish military during the military coup), because of their deep empathy for the Kurds at that point, did not respond to Berna. Berna felt alone in her experience. This exchange was a striking example of the complexity and interrelation between Turkey's Kurdish and Turkish experiences. Furthermore, Cevher's share, within the historical and political context, revealed the uniqueness of the Kurdish experience. The distinction in the responses and shares exemplifies the vast differences in experiences based on gender, political views, personal experiences, and cultural background.

Berna and Cevher's experiences were examples of the recent collective trauma due to Turkey's current political environment. To give an example of historical trauma, one American-Armenian participant in the workshop, George, referring to his great-grandparent's story of genocide and escape from Harput and their continued resilience as immigrants in the U.S. said, "I carry the story of perseverance in the midst of great adversity and challenge." He added, "I would be curious about the translation in Turkish, it is called "Grit" in America, so you keep going even though it is difficult." "It is '*Azim*,' we call it *Azım*," a Turkish participant replied. "Yes, I carry *Azim*," George responded. As a diaspora Armenian, he grew up knowing what happened to his ancestors, how brutally they were cut out from their ancestral lands and forced to migrate, how many people died and were massacred during these deportations. He also witnessed how his family persevered and stayed strong despite the odds.

Taking these experiences further, I want to demonstrate how deeply rooted some of these traumas are and how life-altering the fall of the Ottoman Empire and the foundation of the Republic of Turkey was for individuals through the story of a distant uncle, Hüseyin. While we are not tied with blood, Hüseyin comes from the same town as my mother's family—in Eastern Anatolia by the Euphrates River. The historical context represents a summary of events I further discuss in the book. I did not share the characters' real names to protect their confidentially.

An Inter-Generational Story at the Fall of the Ottoman Empire

The year is 2012; I am in my home in Oakland, CA, and talking to a relative in Turkey whom I will name Hüseyin. He is in his mid-80s. We are on a Skype call, and he begins to tell me his father's story. Even though there are thousands of miles between us, we are connected through the Internet and a computer screen. Part of me wishes that I were physically there with him, enjoying some morning tea with him. But I realize I actually have his undivided attention through the computer. With the knowledge of the physical distance between us, the moment has gravity and a sense of preciousness. His grandson (who is my second cousin) sets up Hüseyin's computer and leaves the room. Hüseyin smiles when he sees my face on the screen. Looking at the twinkle in his eyes, I thought to myself, what a miracle it is to see each other, even though there is an ocean between us—so much has changed within his lifetime.

He tells me that about 200 years ago in the early 1800s, during the Ottoman Empire, his great-great-grandfather, Osman, and his two brothers decide to migrate to Constantinople (today's Istanbul) from Bukhara, Uzbekistan. They get onto their horses and ride west, following the old Silk Road. They stop by a town at the edge of the Armenian Plateau for a break. The town, Eğin (Agn), is built on rocky mountain formations along the Euphrates River. The populace is about half Christian Armenians and half Muslims. The town has grown because of its strategic location on the Silk Road and is advanced in producing and trading goods. Needing manpower, an Armenian business owner convinces these young men to stay—promising them a job and marriage to an appropriate Armenian or Muslim girl. While Osman settles and raises a family, the Ottoman Empire is crumbling. In the following decades, Muslim refugees arrive from Eastern Europe, the Balkans, and Russia as the Ottoman Empire loses its grip. The social fabric of Anatolia is beginning to change. Balances in the interdependent relationships of different ethnic and religious groups are breaking.

By 1891, Osman is long gone, but his great-grandchildren are still in the same town. The Armenians in town are weighed down by double taxation policies, demanding Kurdish militias and bandits on the trade routes. Not feeling secure, they ask for protection from the Ottoman governance. The Ottomans increasingly fail to provide security for those living in rural areas and at the edges of the empire. In the guise of addressing this, Abdulhamid forms the Hamidiye Regiment in the East, arming primarily Sunni Kurdish tribes to protect the region (see Chapter 2). This only makes matters worse. Local disturbances increase. The Armenians in town, mostly upper-class residents,[8] bribe the Hamidiye regiment with gold to survive. However, in 1896 following a dispute between the local Ottoman governance and Armenians, the Kurdish militias attack their village and massacre approximately 6,000 Armenians (Dadrian, 1995). Some of the local Muslims enable the attacks (Hayreni, 2015). Hasan, Osman's great-great-grandson, is born only a few years after this incident in 1900. Hasan is Hüseyin's (the relative I am speaking with) father. What made this town appealing to their family has been destroyed. During Hasan's lifetime, the Ottoman Empire continues to crumble.

In 1914, Hasan is a 14-year-old boy when World War I breaks out. The Committee of Union and Progress (CUP; see Chapter 2), better known as the Young Turks, conducts a coup d'état in Constantinople and takes over the government in 1913. The CUP had originally formed in 1886 with the support from non-Muslim minorities to reform the Ottoman Empire. However, the nationalist and pan-Turkish factions of the CUP take control of the party's governance. The CUP leadership sees war as an opportunity to accomplish its political agenda and decides to join World War I on Germany's side. One of the first battles is against Russia in 1914. The Russian army brutally defeats the Ottoman military, causing the Russian army to occupy the Eastern Anatolia/Armenian Plateau, almost all the way to Hasan's village. Hasan's uncle, Ahmed, goes to fight for the Ottoman Army who loses a foot in the war and never comes back to his town.

Hüseyin tells me that his father, Hasan, decides to move to Istanbul to start over and perhaps also to complete his ancestor's, Osman, original dream. The year is 1914; a 14-year-old Hasan leaves his village and opens a café in Constantinople/Istanbul to begin a new life. In the meantime, war and internal affairs are becoming more intense each passing day. Largely in reaction to the loss of wars, CUP's increasing interest in forming a Turkish state, fearing that Armenians will form their own that would shrink the boundaries envisioned by the Turkish state, and due to further monetary interests (see Chapter 2), CUP organizes a gruesome and violent Armenian displacement process across Anatolia that claims 800,000 to 1.5 million

Armenian lives—mostly civilians including women, children, and the elderly. Taking place between 1915 and 1917, the Armenian Genocide, wipes out the remaining Armenians in Hasan's town. Even though town residents claim that they had no involvement in Armenian deportations and massacres, there are other resources that claim otherwise (Hayreni, 2015); portraying a dispute of the narratives. In the end, the town is not the same place anymore—Armenians, who were the town's backbone of economic production are gone.

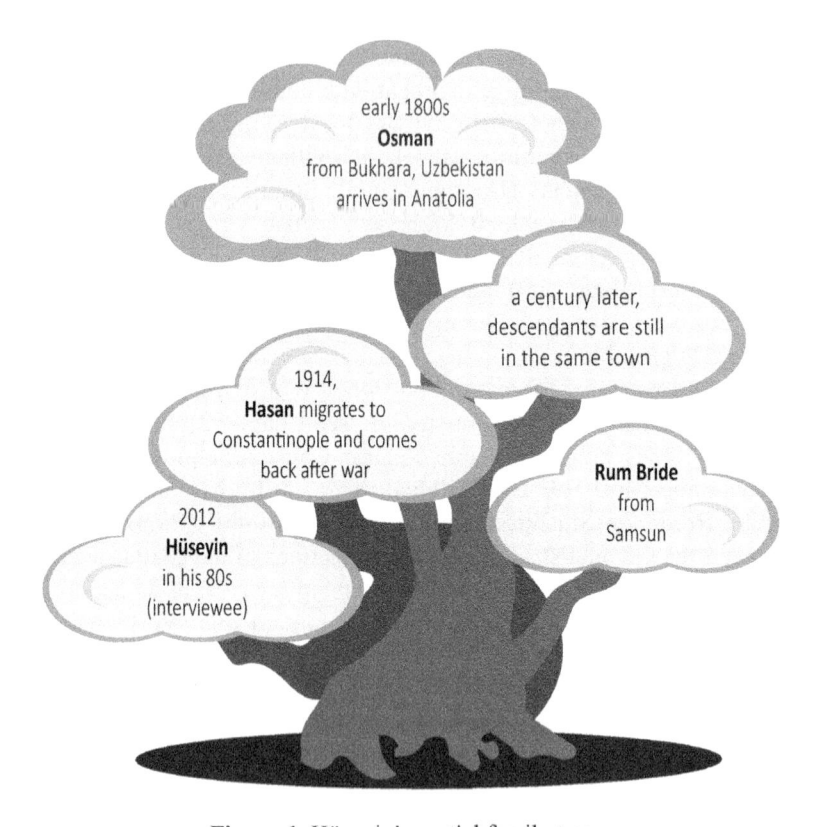

Figure 1 Hüseyin's partial family tree

Back in Istanbul, in Hasan's café, Rum (Ottoman Christian Greek) women dancers would perform Kanto for entertainment. A few years pass in relative peace for Hasan; however, in 1919, a confrontation that takes place at his café changes his life for the second time. Istanbul is invaded by British, French, and Italian military forces after the Ottoman Empire loses World War I. A lieutenant searching for weapons visits Hasan's café and finds a gun in his possession. The lieutenant insults him in front of his friends and customers by spitting in his face. Hasan is not able to do anything at that moment but is outraged. Feeling deeply offended, he is out for revenge. Knowing where the lieutenant would be at night, Hasan approaches him from his back and hits him with a heavy object, killing him. Hasan, knowing that he would be a suspect due to the earlier dispute, escapes Istanbul to the Aegean coast. He is not aware of the war that has broken out between Greeks and Turks.

Before he reaches Izmir, the Greek army stops him. These soldiers, seeing him well-dressed on a horse cart, think Hasan is a CUP member (Unionist). After beating him, they put a string of barbed wire around his neck and suffocate him. Thinking he is dead, the army officers throw him into a creek. However, Hasan is not going to die just yet. Several hours later, he wakes up with his legs and half of his torso in the stream. While having a hard time speaking due to gashes and bleeding around his neck, Hasan climbs out of the creek and finds a nearby village to rest and heal. Once there he hears that the Turkish War of Independence has been declared. Outraged by what happened to him in the hands of Greeks, he decides to go to Ankara, the headquarters of the Independence movement which would become the capital city of the Republic of Turkey, to join the revolutionary army. Because he does not have any military experience, the army sends him to Samsun to fight with the Turkish bandits. According to his story, the Turkish military is providing arms to Turkish bandits to fight against the Rum bandits and also to raid their villages. He fights for this band until the end of the Turkish War of Independence (1919–1923).

A few years before this, during World War I, a Turkish imam (a male prayer leader in a mosque) had rescued a 3-year-old Rum girl in Samsun. Her entire family had been murdered. This young child was the only living member of her family and having seen her mother's dead body in the forest covered by ants, she is traumatized. The imam hides her until she is seven. Soon after, the head of the Turkish band in Samsun (*Hafiz* Mehmed) takes her from the imam and decides to raise her as his own. She grows up in their household with *Hafiz* Mehmed and his wife from the age of 7 to 14. After the war ends, now that she is 14, the age for marriage, *Hafiz* Mehmed is looking for a suitable match. The fierce young Turkish man, Hasan—who happens to be fighting Rum bandits—is a candidate. They get married, and shortly after, their first son (my relative) is born in Samsun. Later, they move to Hasan's original village, Eğin, in Eastern Anatolia by the Euphrates River. Shortly after their arrival, they have two more children. Villagers call this young woman *Samsun'lu yenge*, which means "Aunt from Samsun." According to Hüseyin, her first son, she is well adapted to Turkish culture; at times, her neighbors even consult her about Turkish customs.

Hüseyin's vivid memory and the details in his story struck me. He knew about his lineage much more than anyone else in my immediate family. His timeline was consistent with the historical literature and indeed intimately exemplified the stories of many in the early 1900s Anatolia. Hüseyin, the son of a Turkish man, Hasan, and the young Rum bride, were from the first generation of citizens of the newly formed Republic of Turkey. Hüseyin grew up calling *Hafiz* Mehmed, the leader of the Turkish band in Samsun "grandfather." He grew up with strong Turkish nationalist views, and so do his own children and grandchildren.

War and Trauma

This story is a typical example of the dynamics at the time. Many wars and conflicts that broke out in Anatolia were inter-related. This fierce young man's murder of the lieutenant exemplifies the effects of European invasion and the thin societal sanctions in the crumbling empire. The level of rage that was ready to explode due to an insult was intense. People running for safety were stumbling upon other wars and conflicts. People did not know who was who. Hasan was mistaken for a Unionist, the enemy of the Greek army. Without clarifying, the Greek military thought it was safer to kill him than wait to find out. After almost losing his life, this young man was then ready to do whatever it took for revenge. He decided to fight and joined the Turkish army. Amongst other outraged Turks, his band was in Samsun. Away from home, without a personal connection to the conflict there, this young Turkish man attacked Rum villages and fought against Rum bands. After all was settled and done, he married a young Rum girl from Samsun whose entire family was murdered earlier, possibly by an earlier generation of Muslim bandits. He took this young woman to his village, where she assimilated into the new customs and ways of living.

Imagining New Identities in a New Republic

In the early 20th century, during the Ottoman Empire's fall, a homogeneous Turkish national identity replaced the multi-religious and multi-ethnic Ottoman identity. The new Turkish state launched reforms, policies, and regulations to align with the Western World, which were welcomed and praised by many Turkish communities and Muslim migrants. Hence, during the Republic of Turkey's formation, to create a homogeneous Turkish identity that people could feel an emotional connection with, the state erased both perpetration and victimhood narratives and used the reforms in education, language, and control of the public narrative as a state practice to maintain control and dominance in Anatolia. The newly emerging Turkish state not only eliminated the historical narrative depicting Turks as perpetrators, but also erased the moments when they were victims. The century-old victimization of Muslims in Eastern Europe, followed by the catastrophic losses during the Balkan Wars of 1912–1913, was dismissed and forgotten in favor of looking toward the future. To blend in, most immigrants adapted a homogeneous Turkish identity in public and eventually they either hid their family/community origins or hid their history altogether.

Hüseyin remembers that when he was a young man and read about Greeks killing Turks, he would cry out loud with outrage: "Greeks massacred Turks, burned down villages." His father Hasan who personally went through the war, when hearing his son's remarks, would respond and say, "Son, if Greeks burned down a village, we would raid a Rum village and execute '*yediden yetmişe*' (meaning everyone regardless of age). What they did to us, we did more to them." While Hasan, from his personal experience, knew and acknowledged the raids made to Rum villages, at a collective level, the Turkish state largely denied such historical facts and the violence non-Muslims experienced during the fall of the Ottoman Empire, also claiming people from both sides died. Of course, such narratives within Turkey have been diverse and variable based on location, family history, and other external influences. And most people, unlike Hüseyin, do not know their family's war stories.

Hüseyin's parents must have made meaning and created narratives and family dynamics that were influenced by war conditions. They tried to cope with pain and the after-effects of war. As parents, they taught the skills they used to survive the war to their children, who in turn taught them to their children and so on. War conditions find a place in family dynamics and can be transmitted to subsequent generations. At the same time, for many families like Hüseyin's, there was a rupture from past traumatic events and a new beginning with the founding of the new Republic. Hüseyin was born into a new Turkish nation with new rules and regulations. He was influenced by Turkish nationalist propaganda through education, media, and military. Thus, his narrative and identity began to diverge from his parents.

Hidden and Oppressed Histories

Forced marriages to Muslims and assimilation, for survival, of non-Muslim women are familiar stories throughout Anatolia. The victims of war, whether they were non-Muslim women or refugees, appear to have employed the strategy of trying to adapt to Turkish culture. Their adaptation was often transmitted to their children and grandchildren in the form of strong Turkish nationalism values, as in the case of Hüseyin's strong nationalist sentiments despite the knowledge of his Ottoman Rum heritage. Despite the hardships present in the story, Hüseyin's mother shared her story with her children. They knew that she was initially Rum, from Samsun. I did not name the young Rum woman when conveying her story, because, like her, many young women lost their families, names, and cultures. In respect to her legacy, I did not believe a Turkish name would have been appropriate. She is the "Rum bride" in this story. Yet, her lineage was not a secret in her family, or the community. Recent oral history research in Anatolia also confirms while many non-Muslim women who married Muslim men hid their ethnoreligious identities, a substantial portion of non-Muslim women, in addition to their adaptation to Turkishness, also shared their stories with their children and later generations (see Chapter 5). These young women maintained their survivor strategy of adaptation despite their trauma of losing their families, villages, and customs. They courageously shared who they were, leaving gifts for subsequent generations to receive, to help future generations remember. Furthermore, the village reminded them of who they were. In this story, the Rum bride was called "aunt from Samsun" amongst villagers.

Transgenerational Trauma

History, collective experience, and individual trauma intersect. Men who came back from a decade-long war were most likely struggling with their demons. International research overwhelmingly validates that PTSD and other stress-related symptoms of combat trauma have consequences throughout the family (see Chapter 1). Hüseyin's father, Hasan, was known in the village as "crazy Hasan" due to his unpredictable behaviors, outbursts, and rage. From what we know today, they might have been post-traumatic stress symptoms. Hasan died in his 50s due to complications in his lower torso. He had ongoing health issues from the wounds he received from Greek soldiers that almost killed him. According to Hüseyin, Hasan carried scars around his neck, and his voice was always hoarse. Thus, the next generation, even though they did not experience war at a collective level, may have suffered a micro version of war in their own homes. This version of conflict could be hidden in their family's silence or outrage. Children pick up clues of their parents' wounding—they internalize it—and from it, make meaning.

In Hüseyin's case, one of the ways historical trauma in his lineage may have manifested is a need to tell his story. Villagers and family around him have heard his various stories countless times. At the end of our call, I thanked him and said, "It was great to see you. And thank you so much, Uncle Hüseyin. Thank you for sharing your story with me." He responded, "No, it is good. So, I have been listened to. I fed the animals already; it took me only 15 minutes. Now it is time to rest; my newspapers have just arrived, too." He signaled that now he was ready to end the call.

Hüseyin died of old age four years after this conversation. I was in Upstate New York at a psychodrama retreat when I got the news. I was shaken and grieving his loss. I wished that I was in Turkey and had a chance to say goodbye. I shared what was going on for me in the morning with the class. Some of the instructors suggested that I do an "empty chair conversation"[9] with Uncle Hüseyin and say goodbye that way. When I started my conversation with the empty chair and invited imaginary Hüseyin to sit across from me, I realized that I felt a bond with him through knowing parts of his story. Through that exercise, I came to believe that as we live in the present, we are connected to the past, the future, and each other.

Revealing the Transgenerational Traumas of Anatolians

Transgenerational, collective, and historical traumas are interlinked processes that influence individuals' and groups' identities and sense of wellbeing. I view collective trauma as the complex, lasting, and devastating physical, social, and psychological impacts upon a massive number of people at the same time and in similar ways. Collective traumas can affect society at multiple levels: from micro (individual), to mezzo (local community), and to macro (culture and the society at large). These multilevel traumas can be passed on to subsequent generations and thus become transgenerational and historical. One way of defining transgenerational trauma is the transmission of trauma from one body to another through violence, neglect, or other forms of abuse, resulting in psychological, somatic, and other stress-related symptoms. Historical trauma is the nature of trauma that manifests in the identity formations (personal or large group identifications), belief systems, values, taboos, and norms. Historical trauma may manifest in forms of strong nationalism, in the sense of collective enemy, sense of pride or humiliation concerning a large group identity, and there is often a strong sense of us-versus-them.

Armenian, Kurdish, and Turkish historical traumas of Anatolia are connected. Observing the ways in which they are connected and addressing the lasting consequences can lead us to avenues for peace and reconciliation. For instance, even 100 years after the Armenian Genocide, the Republic of Turkey still does not acknowledge the atrocities that happened as genocide; to an extent, speaking of historical atrocities has become taboo. The mention of the word "genocide" is a source of great discomfort for many Turks today.

The Christian population is now about 1% of Turkey's general population, as opposed to 40%, the estimated projected percentage of Ottoman Christians if they had remained in Anatolia (Ayata & Hakyemez, 2013, p. 6). The remaining Armenians in Turkey still live in fear. Highly populated Kurdish areas in Eastern Anatolia have been in war zones since the 1980s. The level of instability based on government policies and procedures in Eastern Anatolia/Kurdistan has crippled many Kurdish communities from excelling economically and politically. Kurds who resist assimilation to Turkishness face discrimination and oppression in every theatre of life. Psycho-social, political, and socio-economic implications of generations-long trauma unfortunately inform new political disputes and introduce new traumas to society. The conflict between Armenians, Kurds, and Turks reached a point of deadlock. One method of exploring ways of overcoming political impasse is to understand the psychological obstacles that have created and maintained the historical traumas; in other words, an exploration of what makes people invested in the conflict.

Therefore, for my research, I asked the following questions: What kind of psychosocial obstacles may be preventing Armenians, Kurds, and Turks of Anatolia from reconciliation and peace? Drawing from historical and transgenerational trauma theories and extensive historical literature review of Anatolia, what are the most significant factors that might help to support the reconciliation and healing of the historical traumas amongst Armenian, Kurdish, and Turkish ethnicities in Anatolia?

In order to answer the inquiry question, I reviewed historical, sociological, and anthropological accounts of collectively traumatic experiences that took place within Anatolia in the last two centuries while highlighting their interrelationship and effects. Sociologist and theorist Piotr Sztompka (2000) calls such chains of traumatic events a "traumatic sequence." He argues that a traumatic sequence can be explored in six stages: (a) the structural and cultural background (environment) conducive for emergence of traumatic events; (b) the individual traumatizing situations or events; (c) how people make meaning; (d) people's collective behavioral or belief patterns, identity formations as a result of the trauma; (e) what kind of post-traumatic adaptations are present; and (f) how overcoming trauma or avoiding the beginning of a new traumatic sequences has occurred. Therefore, while reviewing these six stages, I asked:

- ☐ What was the nature of the collectively traumatic event? What was its historical context?
- ☐ How were the individuals and the collective affected?
- ☐ How did people cope, make meaning, respond, change? What kind of further consequences did these events cause for the culture, communities, and individuals?

Because of the concern about the psychological consequences of historical traumas, I additionally asked:

- ☐ Are there psychological and transgenerational consequences to these particular collectively traumatic experiences?

Additionally, this research is limited to only three large group identities: Armenians, Kurds, and Turks of Anatolia, or descendants with religions and ethnic connections to the modern era Turkey. The research's findings should not be generalized for all Armenian, Kurdish, and Turkish cultures outside of Anatolia. Likewise, it should not be assumed that the same findings apply to other Anatolian cultures and ethnicities not specifically included in this research.

Epistemologies of Ignorance, Privilege, Suppression, and Oppression

Traditional research methods have aimed to build knowledge based on previous knowledge. Additionally, most researchers focus on reviewing existing literature on their topic and look for ways to augment their discipline's body of knowledge. If the knowledge that was created previously was wrong, intentionally neglected, biased, or partial, the researcher faces particular challenges. This erasure, whether intentional or otherwise, forms the crux of the ignorance dilemma. Thus, shortly after beginning the literature review for my doctorate dissertation, I faced three main challenges. First, I noticed the extreme lack of academic knowledge in some areas of the inquiry question. Secondly, I found strong opposition and controversies within aspects of the literature. Thirdly, even though a transdisciplinary inquiry allowed me, as researcher, to move beyond disciplinary boundaries to explore all relevant literature to answer my inquiry question, I was perplexed by how to synthesize and organize this body of research from different epistemological frameworks with literature from opposing perspectives, and how to create a cohesive survey of the discipline when—in some important areas—there was no scholarly literature. More importantly, I began to realize that this lack of knowledge and the surrounding controversies were actually saying something fundamental about society. These "unknowledges" were becoming my data points, and when the existence of ignorance in Turkey was encountered, I knew it was a place to look deeper. Subsequently, I explored the concept of epistemologies of ignorance and its relevance to my topic.

When the new Republic was born, Turkishness (Turkish national identity, with an emphasis on being "secular" rather than being "Muslim") replaced Ottoman (multi-ethnic multi-religious) identity. This replacement, along with the government's Turkification process to unite the new Republic together under one large group identity (see Chapter 5), elevated those who accepted Turkishness to higher social status. Secular Turks became privileged. This sense of privilege—overtime—prevented many Turks from empathizing with the marginalized in society. In the process, the new government promoted Armenians and Greeks as the enemy, pushed Christian communities out of Anatolia, enabled Christian assets to change hands with the Turks, and created the new Turkish bourgeoisie (see Chapters 2 & 3). The new elite saw Kurds, Muslims, or villagers in small towns as underdeveloped, backward people who needed modernization (see Chapter 5). On the one hand, the newly emerging Turkish elite was against Western imperialism. On the other hand, they embraced its modernization policies, which were paradoxical in their implementation, causing an identity crisis for most Turks (see Chapter 5). The new state projected the "enemy" as the West, while the "modern" West was also an idealized vision for society's future.

Therefore, while I review Turkish traumas, it is also essential to acknowledge Turks, Kurds, and Armenians' multiple identity formations and Turks' privileged status in society compared with Kurds and Armenians. Turkish, Kurdish, and Armenian pain and its consequences are inter-related, yet the experiences are different. More importantly, Turkish pain and any earlier traumas cannot be used as a defense—or an excuse—for the violence against Kurds and Armenians.

Overview of the Book

Chapter 1 explores how collective traumas affect people psychologically and transgenerationally. Several definitions of psychological, collective, and transgenerational trauma are introduced. In later chapters, these definitions are specifically used to explore the transgenerational aspect of trauma in Turkey.

Chapter 2, 3, and 4 provide a historical review of relevant collectively traumatic events that took place in Anatolia. The modernization and social change process of the Ottoman Empire is reviewed, including what led up to its fall and the subsequent birth of the Republic of Turkey. Numerous unresolved conflicts and issues are explored insofar as how they turned into unresolved traumas and continue to cause ruptures in the fabric of society today, creating collectively shared traumas. More specifically, collective traumas that occurred in Anatolia in the 20th century amongst Armenian, Kurdish, and Turkish ethnicities are considered, and, because they are not addressed and recognized, how these traumas have been transmitted to subsequent generations. These traumas continue to perpetuate violence, thus preventing peace and reconciliation at the societal level.

During the fall of the Ottoman Empire and the formation of the Republic of Turkey, state-enforced processes created and maintained the Turkish national identity. Drawing from feminist philosophers Shannon Sullivan and Nancy Tuana's (2007) theory of the epistemology of ignorance (what we know, what we do not know, and what we know to be false), Chapter 5 illustrates how epistemologies of ignorance can demonstrate and perpetuate a particular evolution of Turkishness and societal ignorance that denies Armenian and Kurdish suffering in Anatolia. This level of ignorance continues to perpetuate ethnic tensions, conflicts, and violence.

In the Conclusion and throughout the book, drawing from these arguments, emphasis on how the people of Turkey are caught in a feedback loop, causing the perpetuation of violence was noted. Additionally, discussion concerning how the society needs systemic healing modalities that include and incorporate all affected functions and dynamics are presented. The change needs to come from all levels of society in order to transform the complex nature of historical traumas.

The overarching cultural institutions and society at large are part of the maintenance and perpetuation of the trauma narrative. This narrative is passed down to future generations, ensuring its persistence. I argue that one possible way of healing from this systemic trauma lies in consciously facing our history with all its faults and gifts. In addition to the unresolved issues, tools and healing practices are also passed down. Through understanding contemporary arguments, identifying trauma symptoms and their roots, and reconnecting with our personal and cultural resilience that has been passed down through earlier rituals, teachings, traditions, and stories, we can start building healing communities.

Personal Background

As a Turkish person, I have my fair share of ethnic diversity. My paternal grandfather was a Bulgarian Muslim who migrated to Turkey from Shumen in 1945 when Bulgarian Muslims were under pressure to assimilate. The Republic of Turkey served as a refuge for many Muslims who had been under assimilation policies or persecution in nearby countries. Turkey opened its arms to Balkan Muslim migrants with free education and job opportunities. According to one of my grandfather's stories, his older brother came first. Then, when my grandfather was 14, he escaped to Turkey and found his older brother. He registered in a free boarding school and later became a doctor in bacteriology. He met my paternal grandmother in Western Turkey, whose family were immigrants from Kavala, Greece.

My paternal grandmother's grandfather was an Ottoman Uçbay (Ottoman border official). He and his family were sent to Kavala (now in Greece) by the Ottoman administration. As a family, they owned 9 million square meters of land with thousands of sheep and horses. During the Balkan Wars of 1912–1914, the word was out that Greeks were killing Ottoman officials. The family ran away on foot. My great grandmother remembers leaving a pot on the stove and not being able to take anything with her. They arrived in Anatolia as refugees. Their family went from being a well-provided Ottoman family to poverty. This loss, and later my grandmother's tragic death in an elevator accident, imprinted the family story of loss and grief on my father's side of the family and me. Her father later moved to Eskişehir (a significantly populated migrant (*muhacir*[10]) city) and bought an apartment building where each family would have one of the floors.

Due to a dispute over the building's use between the siblings, my grandfather and mother moved out and rented an apartment in a newly built building nearby. My father was 15 years old at the time and had recently begun attending the Turkish Navy school in Istanbul. Due to the elevator system failure and the door closing on my grandmother, she died tragically in their new home. She was dearly loved, and the grief her death caused was very overwhelming for the extended family that further estranged family ties. I grew up with minimal contact with the extended family on my father's side. I am named after my grandmother, Nermin Soyalp, I also carry her story and legacy.

On graduation day for my doctorate, my father said something very touching. He said, "My mother died in a tragic elevator accident. I also have trauma. Nermin's study of transgenerational trauma has been healing for me, too." A statement that made the years long, arduous process of doing this research worth it. Even though it was not a conscious effort on my end, not to mention my book's content (in reference to Kurds and Armenians) to have this be distressing for my family, both my mother and father mentioned at different times that my engagement in healing historical traumas and inquiries to gather family stories has been personally moving and healing for them.

My maternal grandfather is from an old Armenian town called Eğin in Eastern Turkey. The town was located near the old Silk Road and was one of the trade centers of Eastern Anatolia during Ottoman Empire. My maternal grandmother's estranged father is from Isparta (a Mediterranean city in Southwest Turkey), and her mother is from Istanbul. My mother's family have been rooted in Anatolia for several generations, so they have a particular connection to their village and land which my father's side of family did not have. I grew up with cultural tension between the two sides where both identified as "Turks" but were also culturally different.

Additional complexity to my identity comes from being born in the United States. I was born in Monterey, CA, when, as a member of the Turkish Navy, my father was attending the Naval Postgraduate School. My parents, both Turkish, went back after my father's graduation. I was almost one year old. I grew up knowing I had a U.S. passport, and I was encouraged to move back to California one day, which I eventually did when I was 23.

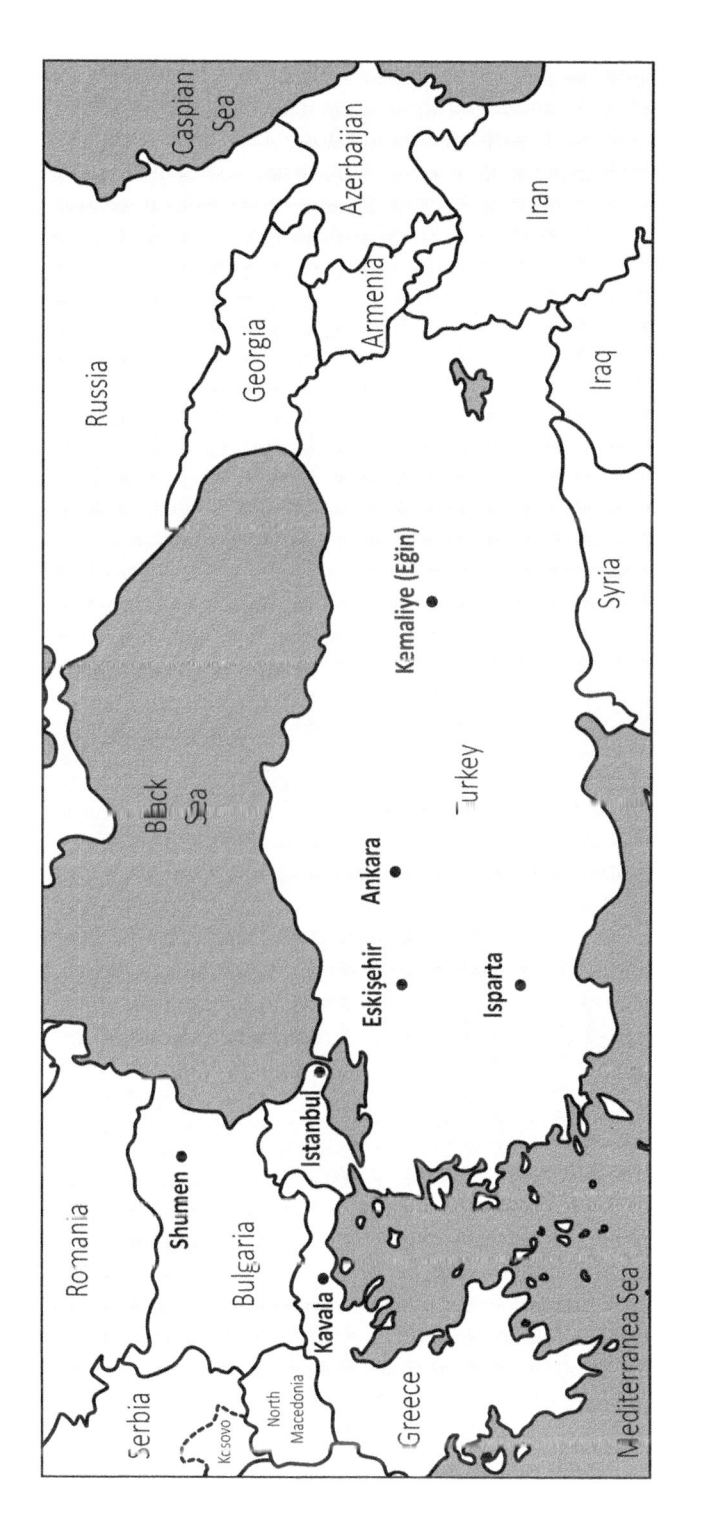

Figure 2 Map of Turkey and Balkans

When I think back on my 22 years of life growing up and living for the first few years in Istanbul and the rest in Ankara in Turkey, my life was mostly homogeneous with my own family and their Turkish friends. Because Sunni Muslim secular Turks established power in the state and my family were members of this group, I had a privileged stance and did not have to be directly concerned about rights of Armenians, Kurds, or any other ethnicity's compromised position in the country. For these reasons, I recall only a few, mostly faded memories about Armenians, Kurds, or any other minorities from the time I was in Turkey.

As mentioned, my maternal grandfather is from an old Armenian town called Eğin (Kemaliye as it is called today). When the word *Armenian* was mentioned around the dinner table when I was very young, I remember hearing that *Eğin* was an Armenian word. My family would sometimes use different vocabulary for some specific things; they said it was the language of Eğin. Later I realized these words were actually Armenian. And yet there was nothing descriptive enough for me to have some form of an understanding about what might have happened in Eğin or to Armenians. It was probably not my family's intention, but the way this information was received, the word *Armenian* floating in the air—not attached to any one particular I knew—caused confusion and questions to arise, such as "Are they ghosts?" "Where are they now?" "Who are you talking about?" I was too young to even be able to articulate this confusion, so I think I dismissed most information I heard then for that reason. However, I remember the word *Armenian* was used in a warm tone and manner in my family. I would learn the negative connotations surrounding the word later from other people.

Another memory comes from an interaction I had with a Turkish woman who was more discriminative and insulting of Armenians. When I was a teenager, I played competitive tennis. I was in Istanbul for a nationwide competition. I remember sitting next to the mother of one of my friends watching a game. Two young boys were vigorously competing on the court. She said the name of one of the players out loud but quiet enough so only I could hear her, and then said, "dirty Armenian." I remember feeling shocked by two things about this statement: (a) the word "dirty" and (b) the tone of hatred in her voice. Hearing the words *Armenian* and *dirty* together was a first for me, the young boy looked perfectly clean to me with his white tennis clothes and not looking particularly different from many of the others. He was a fine boy as far as I knew. Secondly, I was surprised by the hatred in her voice. What might this boy have possibly done to deserve so much hatred from a grown woman who I also liked as a person? I could not help but ask, in naiveté, why she said that. She responded by saying, "They betrayed us. Never trust an Armenian." This statement was so outside of my daily narrative, and it did not fully make sense to me, but the moment was significant enough to stay in my memory. From what I saw from the outside, he was not any different from anyone else I knew, but I realized at that moment he was actually different in a way that was not observable. What was that? I did not have the answer then.

Almost a decade later, in my early 20s, I boldly decided to move to California with a one-way ticket and a suitcase. This was when I started meeting Armenians in the diaspora for the first time. The initial mention of them was when I attended a protest of Armenians at the annual Monterey Turkish Festival. It was about my first month in the United States, my friends took me to the festival; people were talking about Armenians protesting at the festival a year before, and how disturbing it was for Turks who were trying to celebrate their culture. My curiosity was evoked; what were they protesting about? That year the protest was small. I saw only two people with pan-cards quietly sitting on the stairs away from the crowd.

This incident was at the back of my head—I had a few other interactions with people in which I was starting to get some sense of the heat between Turks and Armenians in the diaspora. A few years passed, and my boyfriend at the time and I were at a random dive bar in West Berkeley, CA. We did not know anyone at the bar, so he decided to make new friends. In no time at all, I was introduced to 6 or 7 lesbians who were playing pool at the end of the bar. We ended up playing pool together, drinking, and singing songs. At some point, they found out that I was Turkish. A few minutes later, under the influence of alcohol, one woman walked toward me, looked me in the eye, and with certainty and determination in her voice said, "I am Armenian! I am gay!" and she repeated, "I am a gay Armenian! Do you hear me?" A few other of her friends quickly surrounded us, still there was joy and fun in the air, but clearly something serious was also going on. They wanted to be available for any immediate intervention. I looked back into her eyes and said with softness and hesitation in my voice, "Okay." I did not know what else to say. On the one hand, she could have said, "I am a brunette woman," and I probably would have said the same thing. If I doubled her—a psychodrama technique/term, referring to potential underlying reasoning of an action—her inner voice at that moment might have been: "Are you sure you want to hang out with us because you know, I am an Armenian and I am gay. Your ancestors massacred mine. If you are a nationalist Turk who hates Armenians, I have nothing to do with you. If you are racist or homophobic, you should probably leave now. I am not ashamed to tell you who I am." She expressed the intersectionality of her Armenian and gender identities quite succinctly. I was neither racist nor homophobic and being ignorant of the genocide of her people, her comment did not create a reaction in me. I was feeling neutral, standing, trying to grasp why she might have had told me that, and what the appropriate answer would be. But all I could have said was: "Okay." And silence . . . we were looking at each other. A few women held her, a few others held me, gently we came back to the pool table. The weight of the moment dissipated into the air—still there but not as concrete. We continued having fun, playing pool, and singing with occasional hugs. As a group, we managed to get through the night with fond memories; however, even though I was not a threat of any kind, playing pool with the rest of the group, I represented something bigger for her. The certainty and determination in her voice and how she stood up for herself made an impact on me and stayed with me.

These personal narratives are some of the brush strokes of how I have become aware of the Armenian history in Anatolia and the heated debate surrounding it. The reason I added Kurdish trauma to my inquiry is the immediacy of the conflict. For decades, the situation between the Turkish state and Kurdish identity has escalated, continues to cripple many people's lives, and prevents Anatolia from properly healing itself. During the 1990s in Turkey, I grew up hearing about the attacks of PKK, the main armed Kurdish group that claimed over 40,000 lives in 15 years since its violent mobilization in 1984, including the Turkish military, PKK members, and civilians. It is important to note of the fact that Turkey, the United States, the European Union, and NATO all consider PKK to be a terrorist organization. It was normal for us to hear about their bombings and see captured and tortured PKK members in the news. Growing up in this environment in Ankara, the capital city, even though I was somewhat distant from the heat of the fight in Eastern Turkey/Kurdistan, I felt fearful of being a casualty in this conflict. Therefore, for all the reasons mentioned here, in the end, the focus is centered on the exploration of Armenian, Kurdish, and Turkish historical wounding and healing.

CHAPTER

1

Trauma and Its Psycho-Social Consequences

Most recently epigenetic research confirmed, albeit on mice, that certain genes can be turned on or off as a response to a trauma trigger. These epigenetic transmissions, also known as tags, provide instructions to the DNA. Epigenomes can be transmitted to subsequent generations, and in the case of mice, resulted the offspring of traumatized mouse respond with fear to specific stimuli, despite not having prior experience of trauma. Epigenetics is a relatively new field of research yet geneticists have found more than four million genetic switches that could be turned on or off depending on lifestyle and environmental factors. There is still so much that researchers do not know in terms of how epigenetic transmission functions, but scholars have argued that these factors could also impact the emotional limbic brain and therefore the social interactions of humans. Regardless of the unknowns surrounding epigenetic transmission, there is now scientific proof that babies are not born with "clean slates" and earlier traumatic experiences may make the next generation more vulnerable to developing stress-related symptoms or other health problems.

The transgenerational nature of trauma emerged as an important inquiry within psychology in the last three decades through research done with the children and grandchildren of Holocaust survivors, well before epigenetic research. Further, in the US, activists and scholars coming from disenfranchised communities such as Native Americans and African Americans have long been voicing their concerns about the trauma in their communities and its intergenerational effects. What Native American psychotherapist Eduardo Duran calls the soul wounding of Native Americans and what clinical psychologist and public speaker Joy DeGruy calls post-traumatic slavery syndrome of Africans Americans are such examples.

This chapter is a transdisciplinary review of trauma with a focus on its transgenerational aspect. Psychologists studied the nature of psychological trauma and its transgenerational nature. Anthropologists, through oral history, looked at the trauma narrative and the meaning-making process and identity formations. Sociologists, in the last few decades, looked at how collective trauma affected the culture of the society. Psychotherapists who work with oppressed populations and social activists also looked at the institutionalized and governmental levels of perpetuation of violence and its traumatic consequences on populations. This chapter introduces various definitions of psychological, collective, and transgenerational trauma from multiple disciplines. In this chapter and later ones, these definitions are used to specifically explore the transgenerational aspect of trauma in Turkey.

Psychological Trauma

Feminist psychiatrist Judith Herman (2015) says, "Psychological trauma is an affliction of the powerless" (p. 33). In cases of threats to life, bodily integrity, or a close personal encounter with violence or death, (torture, rape, displacement), a natural disaster (earthquake, fire, hurricane), or the cumulative effects of repeated atrocities (captivity, child abuse, torture) may overwhelm the individual's sense of control, connection, and meaning. Substantial portions of individuals affected by psychologically traumatic events develop what is clinically referred to as posttraumatic stress disorder (PTSD) or other stress-related symptoms. PTSD is when the human system of self-preservation goes on permanent alert after a traumatic experience as if the danger might return at any moment.

Rachel Yehuda (2002) conceptualizes that, "to be given a diagnosis of PTSD, a person has to have been exposed to an extreme stressor or traumatic event to which he or she responded with fear, helplessness, or horror and to have three distinct types of symptoms consisting of reexperiencing of the event, avoidance of reminders of the event, and hyperarousal for at least one month" (p. 108). PTSD typically manifests as distressing memories or nightmares related to the traumatic event, flashbacks, attempts to avoid reminders of the trauma and a heightened state of physiological arousal. Furthermore, the exposure to collectively traumatic environments may result in experiencing secondary or vicarious trauma (Figley, 1995, 2002; Zara & İçöz, 2015). Meaning, health care professionals, first responders, or anyone in day-to-day contact with the shadow of society, are at risk of developing stress-related symptoms.

Traumatic experiences may impact people of any age, including children, adolescents, and adults. If the experiences of trauma were in childhood or were prolonged in conditions where the person could not flee (e.g., childhood abuse, prisons, concentration camps, or labor camps), even more complex symptoms could develop. When the trauma is prolonged and repeated, the diagnostic formulation extends the PTSD. These new observations introduced the understanding of complex trauma and its multifaceted symptoms (Cook et al., 2005; Herman, 2015), such as characteristic personality changes, and the survivor may be vulnerable to repeated harm both self-inflicted or caused by others (Herman, 1992, p. 379). In addition to PTSD symptoms, survivors experience somatization, dissociation, disruption of secure belief systems, and pathological changes in their relationships and their identities. Additionally, traumatized children could develop issues with reading social cues accurately and responding to social demands appropriately. In some cases, in a captivity situation, an unexpected bond could develop between captive and captor, including having positive feelings for the captor and learned helplessness, which is also called Stockholm syndrome (De Fabrique, Romano, Vecchi, & van Hasselt, 2007).

Biologically, traumatic experiences can cause alterations in brain regions, such as in the amygdala and hippocampus, which are associated with the experience of fear and memory. Bessel van der Kolk (2003, 2014) explained that from birth, the amygdala is fully functional in a baby's brain, which means they are able to experience fear and assess danger as soon as they are born. However, the first five years of a child's life are vital for the maturation of their hippocampus, which is the part of the brain that identifies and organizes the nature of a threat. Early abuse and neglect may affect the maturation of the hippocampus, which could make a child vulnerable to misinterpret sensory input in the direction of danger and threat. Severely traumatized children, due to abuse or neglect, could develop pathophysiology and difficulties with cognition, impulse control, aggression, and emotion regulation. Van der Kolk adds that lack of stimulation in the brain due to neglect could be even more detrimental than abuse. Neglect in human infants is a strong predictor of subsequent aggressive behaviors in the future. Furthermore, children who experience trauma could experience physical illness, such as cancer, heart disease, and diabetes in the future. What is more, due to self-destructive behaviors, especially in adolescence and adulthood, the abused or neglected child is more vulnerable to drug abuse, self-mutilation, and violent and aggressive behavior against others than non-abused children.

If a traumatic event or series of events happen during the development period of a child, it might prevent the child from trusting and feeling a sense of safety with others. If the child–caregiver relationship becomes the source of a child's trauma, the attachment relationship is severely compromised; more than 80% of maltreated children develop insecure attachment patterns (Carlson, Cicchetti, Barnett, & Braunwald, 1989, p. 525; Friedrich, 2002, p. 66). It was through their observations with adolescents and infants in the 1960s and 70s, that British psychologist John Bowlby and American-Canadian developmental psychologist Mary Ainsworth created attachment theory. Attachment theory describes the vital infant–caregiver bond and how this bond's quality determines the health of a child's personality and relationship development into adulthood. When the mother is responsive, the infant often develops a secure attachment and grows up to be an adult with healthy self-esteem. If the caregiver is unresponsive to the child's needs, inconsistent, unable, abusive, or negligent, the child develops insecure attachment styles (avoidant or anxious). Most adults with insecure attachment styles, even though they may find themselves in dysfunctional relationships later in life, are mostly functional adults. However, if the disruption to the bond is severe, which may happen in times of collective atrocities, impacts could be detrimental. On rare occasions, children develop a mix of avoidant and anxious attachment which some researchers call disorganized attachment. According to Cook et al. (2005) the most problematic for children's adaptation is disorganized attachment because it may lead to older children, adolescents, and adults enacting survival-based behaviors that are rigid, extreme, dissociative, or violent.

When children with insecure attachment styles grow up to be parents, their parenting skills may be maladaptive to what they witnessed and learned from their caregivers. Both adaptive and maladaptive behaviors are generationally passed down. Depending on the severity of the disruption in the bond between caregivers and their children, insecure attachment in communities may create relationship dynamics that are reactive, anxious, avoidant, or violent. Several generations later, even though the original wounding might be long gone, families and the communities who were affected by the original trauma continue to suffer from multigenerational traumas consequences—moreover, their behaviors that were built based on insecure attachment are then normalized and find a place in culture, traditions, and relationships.

Studies of Psychological Trauma in Turkey

In Turkey, most current psychological trauma studies cluster around traumatic experiences of natural disasters (mostly earthquakes), domestic violence, violence against women, child maltreatment, accidents, torture, and forced migration. Research in Turkey also aligns with international literature and shows that the experiences of an atrocity or natural disaster can cause psychological trauma and stress-related symptoms in victims, witnesses, health professionals, and first responders.

Marmara Earthquake of 1999. The Marmara earthquake of 1999 is the most researched collectively traumatic experience in Turkey, one that has left a mark on myself as well. On August 17, 1999, incidentally my 18th birthday, at 3:02 a.m., the Marmara earthquake (centered in Izmit near Istanbul) hit with a magnitude of 7.4 (Mw = 7.4), which caused a ~145-km-long (90 miles) surface rupture in the Eastern Marmara region (Dikbaş et al., 2018, p. 738). My childhood friend was visiting from Istanbul for my big birthday party in Ankara, approximately 220 miles away from the center of the earthquake. My sister was in Istanbul for a tennis tournament, approximately 50 miles away from the center of the quake. Our landline phone rang at 3:15 a.m. One of the phones was right next to my bed, so I answered. My mother's friend had just found out about the earthquake, and she was in a panic because she could not reach her son, who was with my sister in Istanbul for the tournament. She said, "Istanbul is gone . . . collapsed . . . gone." Half-awake, I could not comprehend what was happening. My friend, who was also woken up by the phone call, asked who was calling, I said, "My mother's friend, she says there was an earthquake in Istanbul, buildings collapsed." She jumped off her bed and started crying, "Oh my family!" And the seriousness of the situation suddenly hit me. While we were getting up, we realized the electricity was out in the neighborhood. But we were hundreds of miles away from the earthquake itself; we wondered how the quake could affect us this far away. While my mother was on the phone with her friend, my uncle arrived. He was woken up by the quake, on the 12th floor of his apartment building, as it swung like a pendulum. Deeply shaken with fear, he grabbed his car keys and drove straight to our place. Apparently, our home complex was built on solid rock formations, and they were an earthquake-safe design, so we did not feel the shaking as much as others. We dialed in to one of the radio stations in our car and heard the screams of panic from people trying to rescue their family and friends under the wreckage. We were also in a panic, trying to get in contact with my sister. Finally, we received a call from Istanbul. The tennis coach informed us that my sister and all the team members were safe and accounted for. One of the walls at the hotel had cracked, but they were all safe and were going to sleep outside that night in the garden. My friend also got a hold of her family, and they were safe as well. While we were panicking trying to reach family in Istanbul, we did not realize that the earthquake center was actually in Izmit, near where my grandparents live, where most of the damage occurred. Now our attention had shifted trying to reach the family in Yalova near the epicenter. It was a very long night. Fortunately, my family was safe, but reportedly 18,373 people had lost their lives, 27,781 were wounded, and another 505 people were disabled. More than 80,000 domestic and commercial structures collapsed; another 160,000 buildings had medium to light damage (AFAD [Government Crisis Center], 1999, para. 1).

   I remember the next day, as a family we were glued to the television, no one was saying a word, watching the footage of collapsed buildings, dead bodies, with hopeful glimpses of footage of rescued people from concrete ruins. The wide-ranging damage was visible from helicopter footage. I remember my father finding out that an entire neighborhood where his friend lived had collapsed. He spent the day avoiding calling him. He did not want to find out if something tragic had happened.

A friend of mine lost his mother and younger brother in Yalova. They were vacationing at their summer house at a luxury condo complex by the sea, while my friend and his father were back in Ankara. It was a harrowing experience for both of them, losing not only one but two family members at the same time. Our neighborhood in Ankara, their family, and friends made sure that during the next few months, my friend and his father were not alone, and their house always filled with guests. I also went to give my condolences. When I was there, the news reported a construction mistake and how the building contractors in Yalova had used soft earth, which is why three- to four-story buildings had collapsed to the ground. As we heard the news, there was dead silence at first, and then almost everyone rushed to the balcony for a cigarette or to get some fresh air. I remember my eyes teared up and the shock I felt because I realized their passing could have been avoided. Another friend whom I met a few years later in college, said that in Adapazarı (where he was from) apartments were generally family apartments where one large family would purchase a building and every apartment unit was occupied by extended family members, including uncles, aunts, and grandparents. When the building my friend lived in collapsed, their first response was calling each other to get a sense of who was still alive. While they were waiting for a rescue, survivors were talking to each other, trying to give each other support. When they stopped hearing someone's voice they knew one more family member had passed away.

Thousands of buildings collapsed due to unsafe, non-earthquake-resistant construction. Disorganization and failure of immediate aid and rescue operations also contributed to the loss of lives and possessions (Pınar & Sabuncu, 2004). In the aftermath of the Marmara earthquake, the public first blamed the construction contractors because it turned out that the contractors, despite their knowledge of high-risk earthquake zones, especially in Gölcük, Yalova, and Adapazarı, had used soft ground soil from lower elevations for construction. In these areas, most buildings collapsed (Özerdem & Barakat, 2000). In addition to unsafe construction, Özerdem and Barakat (2000) argue that "everyone who had a role in the building process, from contractors and civil engineers to council inspectors and clients, each played their part in making a disaster out of a natural hazard" (p. 426). When the public realized the prevalence of unsupervised construction, the usage of soft soil from lower altitudes, the neglect of national and local planning authorities, and the witnessing of the poor civil defense system that came after, they lost their trust in government and felt unsafe. A similar claim was made when two sequential earthquakes occurred in Van, Turkey, in 2011 (Tabanlı and Edremit) with a magnitude of 7.1 and 5.6 where a total of 28,512 buildings were heavily damaged or had collapsed (Tapan et al., p. 606).

After the Marmara earthquake, there was a significant increase in studies of psychological trauma in relation to the experience of earthquakes in Turkey. The majority of the research consists of the Marmara earthquake. This is followed by studies from the Van earthquake in 2011. Only research on a few earthquakes predates Marmara.

The general finding of research with the Marmara earthquake survivors over the years found statistics ranging between 34.5% and 76% of earthquake survivors experienced PTSD and depression symptoms (Bulut, 2006, p. 29; Dogan, 2010, p. 1; Livanou et al., 2002, p. 816; Pınar & Sabuncu, 2004, p. 257). Their symptoms persisted for months or even years (Ayas, 2005; Bal, 2008; Ceyhan & Ceyhan, 2006; Oncu & Wise, 2010; Önsüz et al., 2009). PTSD is strongly related to the amount of time spent under the wreckage (Özerdem & Barakat, 2000), experience of an actual threat to life (Eksi & Braun, 2009), and the level of fear people experienced during the earthquake; conversely, depression was related to the loss of family members (Livanou et al., 2002; Salcıoğlu et al., 2007). Because the quake hit at 3:02 a.m. while many were asleep, the majority of the people showed difficulty sleeping and related symptoms, such as either falling asleep or staying asleep, avoidance of going to bed before 3 a.m., and the preference to be outside. The occurrence of several aftershocks amplified fear and the sense that they were still not safe. Survivors had hyper-arousal and helplessness responses (Kasapoğlu & Ecevit, 2003; Livanou et al., 2002; Sumer et al., 2005; Yorbik et al., 2004). Those who were in search and rescue teams or were health professionals also showed an increase in stress-related symptoms (H. Çakmak et al., 2010; Çetin et al., 2005); therefore, the effects extended from survivors to witnesses and first responders.

A year after the earthquake, a study with 500 survivors showed how their "internal fabric of family life, social networks, community ties, work routines, financial income, and the physical health or life of family members" (Kasapolu & Ecevit, 2003, p. 347) were affected. Families lost their homes, appliances, income, and a sense of security. Therefore, not only the safety or mitigation but also the resilience of the urban fabric needed to be addressed (Platt & Drinkwater, 2016). Women appeared to be psychologically impacted more than men (Ak, 2014; Ayas, 2005; Ikizer, Karancı, & Doğulu, 2015; Karancı et al., 1999; Livanou et al., 2002; Sumer et al., 2005; A. Tekin et al., 2016). The majority of women in urban areas in Turkey are housewives. When they were forced out of their homes, their lives were completely interrupted. When their homes, which were a safe haven for most (Sümer et al., 2005, p. 340) collapsed, their entire world crumbled to the ground. This differs from the experience of men who were more externally focused. Moreover, men might also have a tendency not to report their issues.

Not everyone responds to a traumatic event with PTSD or stress-related symptoms. Depending on life experiences before an earthquake, the severity of the experience during the earthquake, the level of loss, post-earthquake support, and aid affect an individual's psychological response. For example, the state's reaction, aid, resources, and the fairness of distribution of those resources were crucial in ways and which survivors were able to cope (Doğulu et al., 2016). Even knowing that resources were available was enough for some to recover from a traumatic experience (Norris et al., 2002).

Moreover, resilience is often part of the experience; however, to what extent is it variable and complex. Resilience is not a universally defined concept. Current definitions vary from the absence of psychopathology in a child of a severely mentally ill parent, to the recovery of a brain-injured patient, to the resumption of healthy functioning in survivors of extreme trauma (Agaibi & Wilson, 2005). One of the common definitions of resilience is one's ability to come back to neutral or balanced state (Papadopoulos, 2007); another common definition is a lack of or lower than expected levels of posttraumatic stress disorder following trauma (S. Z. Levine, Laufer, Stein, Hamama-Raz, & Solomon, 2009). In some rare cases, after the traumatic experience, positive growth may also occur. This is known as posttraumatic growth, in which the individual has significant growth spiritually or personally, such as experience of personal strength, spiritual transformation, and appreciation for life (e.g., Frankl, 2006; Morrill, 2015).

Christine Agaibi and John Wilson (2005), based on their literature review, argue:

> . . . to understand the plasticity of behavior in response to traumatic life events, it is necessary to recognize the multidimensional nature of traumatic experiences. Traumas are not equal in their impact to the psyche and vary greatly in their stressor dimensions. (p. 210)

Resiliency is mainly connected to the person–environment paradigm related to the perception, processing, and adaptation to traumatic stress. For example, based on research with earthquake survivors in Turkey, there was psychological, sociological, and structural resilience within the collective response. From a psychological point of view, crucial factors of resilience were spiritual belief systems, self-esteem, optimism, perceived control (Sumer et al., 2005), physical health, positive personality characteristics (Gözde, 2014), and avoidance (Ikizer et al., 2015). From a social point of view, there were also healthy collective responses, such as community mobilization and coordination where people felt a sense of community, social support, and the ability to prepare for potential future catastrophes

(Doğulu et al., 2016). Finally, from a structural point of view, when people knew that they were living in an earthquake-safe building structure, they were able to better cope with the post psychological effects of the earthquake (Doğulu et al., 2016). Additionally, trauma therapy also lessened traumatic symptoms (Eksi et al., 2008), but only for a small number compared to the thousands who sought treatment. An appropriate state response and fair distribution of aid and support at the time of catastrophes is vital for collective resilience and well-being. For instance, one research study found that when survivors perceived an inefficiency of governance actors and unfairness due to political problems in the provision of aid and services, it negatively impacted their adaptive capacities and resilience (Doğulu et al., 2016, p. 112).

Domestic Violence. After the Marmara earthquake of 1999, there has been a significant increase in studies of psychological trauma with earthquake survivors. Research on domestic violence and child maltreatment correspondingly had a significant increase in the corresponding years. Violence against women is the most common issue.

A systemic meta-analysis of domestic violence research between the years of 2000 and 2015 in Turkey found that violence against women was often verbal followed by physical, emotional, economic, and sexual abuse, and concluded that violence against women, as it is globally, one of a common issues in Turkey (Özcan, Günaydın, Çitil, 2016). In Turkey alone, according to the government office, Woman's Status Head Office *(Kadının Statüsü Genel Müdürlüğü*, KSGM) 42% of women have been victims of both sexual and physical violence (Toktaş & Diner, 2015, p. 611). Similarly, according to an ethnographic, mixed-method, research study, one out of three women have been victims of violence in Turkey. Some 35% of women in general in Turkey and 40% of women in Eastern Turkey have been victims of physical violence at least once; women are the most vulnerable at home as their perpetrators are often their husbands (Altınay & Arat, 2007, p. 79). The majority of women who sought safety in women's shelters were experiencing depression, hopelessness, and difficulty in concentration and making decisions (Kısa, Zeyneloğlu, & Sergek Verim, 2018).

Furthermore, at least 50% of women who shared that they experienced violence also said they had not shared what happened to them with anyone before (Altınay & Arat, 2007, p. 80). Given that not every incident is reported or talked about, these statistics speak to the frightening reality that every day, one out of two women, if not more, have been sexually or physically assaulted in Turkey. In one study, 94.4% of men acknowledged that domestic violence against women is disturbing and a major public health problem (Adıbelli & Yüksel, 2019, p. 149). However, reaching such a high level of domestic violence speaks to men's own sense of hopelessness around their actions. There is a disconnect between what men in this research cognitively believe and the actions they take in a moment of a psychological trigger; furthermore, these belief systems and triggers are shared experiences. Therefore, individually isolated but collectively shared experiences, such as violence against women and child abuse, are also collectively traumatic experiences with transgenerational consequences.

Exemplifying the transgenerational aspect of domestic violence in another study in Turkey asked people about their experience from childhood to adulthood, revealing a vicious cycle of domestic violence. Altınay and Arat's (2007) research, which encompassed 27 cities where they surveyed a total of 1,800 married women, found that girls who grew up witnessing domestic violence will, in the future, more likely to be a victim of domestic violence in adulthood. On the other hand, boys who witnessed domestic violence are more likely to batter their wives as they reach adulthood. Both results speak to the transgenerational aspect of domestic violence in Turkey.

Children who witness or face violence growing up are vulnerable to repeating similar patterns in adulthood or suffering from stress related symptoms. Poor socio-economics, negative family dynamics, displacement, lack of education, weak parent–child relationships, and caregivers' alcohol or substance addictions are determining factors for child abuse or neglect (Erkan, 2018). One research project, based on 2,608 reports, found that the majority of parents in Turkey "consider rebukes, insults and corporal punishment effective ways of disciplining children" (Sofuoğlu et al., 2016, p. 217), and they correspondingly under-report abuse cases. Furthermore, though educators or other professionals have to report child abuse cases by law in Turkey, they are also often under-reported in practice.

Another disturbing yet widely underreported form of abuse in Turkey is the occurrence of sexual abuse within a family. According to Rahşan Siviş-Çetinkaya (2015), school principals and the families of the abused discourage school professionals from reporting incest cases. In fact, there are instances when cases are reported, the next day—enraged at the report—families have raided the school out of reprisal of honor. Those who report incest in Turkey face harsh social consequences. Unfortunately, innocent, non-offending mothers often are blamed for not reporting, because in most cases they are aware of the incest but are too afraid for their own safety to do so. Unfortunately, In Turkey women's socio-economic dependence to their spouses and their fear of not being able to care for their children on their own are major determining factors for their silence and lack of action (Kardam & Bademci, 2013). Zoroğlu and Sar (2001a, 2001b) report that adolescents who experience psychological, physical, or sexual abuse and neglect can lead them toward self-mutilative behaviors, attempted suicide, and high-level disassociation. Furthermore, the majority of these individuals experience depression in adulthood (Aydın, 2018), and as survivors, often abuse or neglect their own children. Most parents in Turkey are simply not aware to what extent maltreatment can impact their children in the future (Sofuoğlu et al., 2016).

Thinking About the Socio-Cultural Context of Trauma in Turkey

Psychological research in Turkey concerning history, ethnicity, and socio-cultural diversity is limited, and there is only a handful of research in Turkish, Armenian, and Kurdish experiences in relation to their historically collective traumas and atrocities. In contrast, there is a significant amount of psychological trauma literature concerning earthquake in Turkey. The research concentration with earthquake survivors may be because Turkey is on a major fault line and has, historically, experienced big earthquakes that devastated communities. The experience of earthquakes as a collective trauma naturally has caused many psychologists to study its psycho-social impacts. However, Turkey has also faced major historical traumas and ethnic conflicts, and not finding much literature reviewing the historical traumas in Turkey begs further inquiry.

In Turkey, there are gaps and inconsistencies in knowledge in terms of what is available in academia, which research is funded, or which types are not supported. What is allowed to be studied and what is prohibited by law, which kind of research is considered so dangerous to study that it could lead to their potential imprisonment, affected people in their choice of what to study. Understandably, most researchers tend to shy away from studying potentially "dangerous" topics that might potentially imprison them or cause them to lack job opportunities.

Aker et al. (2007) reviewed psychological trauma research between the years 1971 and 2003 and argue that there had been a lack of research into the scope of trauma and, more importantly, how symptoms in Turkey may develop differently due to unique socio-cultural differences. Moreover, most research in Turkey has been using a one-time psychological trauma scale that was internationally created and validated, lacking culturally significant aspects in Turkey. They write, "For example, the individual's Islamic or fatalistic stance and the relationship between the society and the state may affect the survivor's perception of the event and his or her coping behavior" (p. 54). Since Aker et al.'s review in 2007, more research explored socio-cultural differences (e.g., Doğulu, Karancı, & Ikizer, 2016; Gözde, 2014; Sümer, Karancı, Berument, & Güneş, 2005, p. 340), and yet the political, historical, and ethnic stances are still limited. Except for research with forced displacement and torture survivors, very few researchers have references to political and historical contexts.

However, even though society in Turkey, at large, experienced current and historical traumatic events, Kurds have been socio-politically victimized, and their collective experience deserves a highlight. For one, most victims of forced displacement due to armed conflicts since the formation of the Republic of Turkey are ethnically Kurdish (see Chapter 4 for a detailed analysis). Additionally, countless Kurdish children in Kurdistan who grew up in war zones due to conflicts between the Turkish state and Kurdistan Workers' Party (PKK) have faced extreme forms of abuse and neglect. Rıfat Bilgin (2014) summarizes possible victimization of children in Kurdistan—due to political violence—as being physically wounded; disabled, or killed; experiencing torture, maltreatment, or loss of family members or caregivers; being raised by wounded or disabled caregivers; psychological, sexual, or physical abuse, being ostracized; being manipulated for political agendas; or being exposed to nationalist extremist ideologies, sickness, illness, and malnutrition. Because the war between PKK and the Turkish state has been active for over 30 years as of this writing, children who were affected are the new generation of parents and grandparents, making the issue multigenerational while deepening the collective wounding for Kurds and everyone in Turkey.

In the following chapters I will be discussing the different historical contexts in which historical, collective, and transgenerational traumas occurred in Turkey. I will provide personal narratives from different drama therapy workshops I conducted, which to me illuminate how some of these events continue to have lasting consequences for individuals. But first, I want to contextualize what I mean by collective, cultural, and transgenerational trauma.

Collective Trauma

Trauma is an interruption to the flow state of an individual (P. A. Levine, 1997). At their flow state, people are like a flock of fish, a swarm of birds, or a colony of termites; there is a sense of flow and order to their experiences. A healthy collective is self-organized and better able to shift between chaos and order simultaneously, is responsive, and resilient to outside and inside factors (Miller, 2010). Collectives can be ruptured however, to the point at which, from a sociological perspective, a collective trauma occurs (Sztompka, 2004). Transgenerational, collective, and historical traumas are interlinked processes that influence individuals' and groups' identities and sense of wellbeing. I view collective trauma as the complex, lasting, and devastating physical, social, and psychological impact on many people simultaneously and in similar ways.

One highlight I would like to make here is that in comparison to natural disasters and accidents, though both potentially traumatic to everyone involved, atrocities are psychologically harder to bear as they involve dehumanization and undignified practices and challenge the structure of morality and the values that define humanity (Danieli, 1985; Herman, 2015; Janoff-Bulman, 1985; Volkan, 2006). Major accidents are unintentional catastrophes such as nuclear explosions. Natural disasters are earthquakes, hurricanes, and floods. Atrocities (or in other words, human-made disasters) are when the cause of the trauma is from other humans; examples are rape, physical abuse, political violence, mass murders, massacre, ethnocide, and genocide. After any form of collective disaster, survivors experience societal grief, anxiety, and change. However, massive environmental destruction, natural, or accidental disasters should generally be differentiated from those in which the catastrophe is due to ethnically based or other large-group conflicts because atrocities cause significantly different results in large group identities and meaning making processes (Volkan, 2000).

Drawing from Lifton and Olson's (1976) work, Vamık Volkan (2000) differentiates the experience of disasters as follows. After natural disasters, victims ultimately tend to accept the event as fate or as God's will; in contrast, when one group victimizes another, those who are traumatized do not typically turn to fate or God. After human-made accidental disasters, even though the "other" did not intentionally hurt them, survivors may blame individuals or governmental organizations for their carelessness. When trauma results from war or other ethnic, national, or religious conflict, there is an identifiable enemy group who deliberately inflicted pain, suffering, and helplessness on its victims. Volkan describes this type of trauma that affects large-group identity (i.e., ethnic, national, or religious) issues, does so in ways entirely different from the effects of natural or accidental disasters.

For example, a 2000 study by Goenjian et al. (2000) that compared the severity and longitude of PTSD, anxiety, and depressive reactions of Armenians who were directly affected by the 1988 Armenian earthquake (with a magnitude of 6.8) and Armenians exposed to violence between Armenian-Azerbaijan ethnicities in the same year. Their research concluded that there were no significant differences in PTSD severity between people exposed to severe earthquake trauma versus those exposed to severe violence. However, Volkan (2000) points out that societal processes may also result from catastrophes and their long-term transgenerational effects. Many injured Armenians refusing to accept blood donated by Azerbaijanis after the earthquake, indicated that the tragedy had enhanced ethnic sentiments, including resistance to "mixing blood" with the enemy.

Another distinction between atrocities and natural disasters is when the effects of natural disasters are enhanced due to conscious human-made decisions, which makes it a form of atrocity. For instance, the massive August 1999 Marmara earthquake in Turkey that killed an estimated 18,373 people is identified as a natural disaster. However, it is also an example of a human-made disaster. Disorganized urban planning with the rise in urban migrations caused unsafe structural developments. Many of the structures that collapsed during the earthquake had not been built according to appropriate safety standards. Furthermore, it became known after the earthquake that builders had bribed certain local authorities in order to construct cheaper, unsafe buildings. Another example of natural disaster and atrocity relation is the increase in natural disasters (such as wildfires, hurricanes) worldwide because of human-caused climate change.

Cultural Trauma

As I already explored earlier in the chapter, the transmission of trauma occurs at several levels, such as through the biology of the person, their psycho-dynamics, family dynamics, and socio-dynamics, which makes the exploration of historical traumas transdisciplinary and complex. Large-scale atrocities can cause extreme personal trauma for the individuals involved, whether victims, witnesses, or perpetrators. Such events are "paralyzing rather than enabling agency" (Sztompka, 2000, p. 450). The traumatic experiences caused by such events could become part of the collective narratives and begin to live and breathe within the culture.

Cultural trauma develops when such trauma narratives find their place in stories, myths, cultural norms, institutions, and political conflicts which then contribute to collective and transgenerational traumas and their long-term effects on communities and societies at large. Events that are collective in nature do not happen in isolation; they often develop over centuries, with consequences impacting subsequent generations. Depending on the severity of the traumatic event, multiple levels of a society could be impacted from the micro-level of families to the macro levels of systems and nations, in orchestration with social change (Sztompka, 1993).

Not every social change causes collective trauma. However, when the social change is through destructive impacts, which are sudden, rapid, wide ranging, and comprehensive, causing radical, deep, and fundamental changes in the core aspects of social life and personal fate, cultural trauma may develop. Below is a list of examples of collective experiences of various magnitude and importance that may cause cultural trauma in society:

- ☐ revolution (whether victorious or failed) coup d'état, racial riots
- ☐ collapse of the stock market

- radical economic reform (e.g., nationalization or privatization)
- forced migration or deportation, ethnic cleansing
- genocide, extermination, mass murder
- acts of terrorism or violence
- assassination of the political leader, the resignation of a high-ranking official
- opening secret archives and revealing the truth about the past
- revisionist interpretation of national heroic tradition
- collapse of an empire, or lost war. (Sztompka, 2000, p. 452)

Except for opening secret archives and revealing the truth (though necessary), all these examples from Piotr Sztompka's (2000) article have taken place in the geographic location of Turkey within the last century. Experiencing all these events in one single century speaks to the severity of traumatic sequences there as well as to the interrelationship of these types of traumatic events. It would be hard for a society to recover from only one of these collectively traumatic events and yet given that generation-by-generation people in Turkey have experienced a range of atrocities, the cause and effect of these events have been completely entangled (see Chapters 2, 3, & 4 for chronological exploration of collective traumas in Anatolia). Effects of collective traumatic events and what their accumulated effects do to the people's psyches and communities need to be carefully studied and understood. This is why, in the following chapters, I explore the collective traumatic experiences leading up to the 20th century concerning the intersectionality amongst Turks, Kurds, and Armenians. In a nutshell, the collectively traumatic experiences explored in this book are as follows:

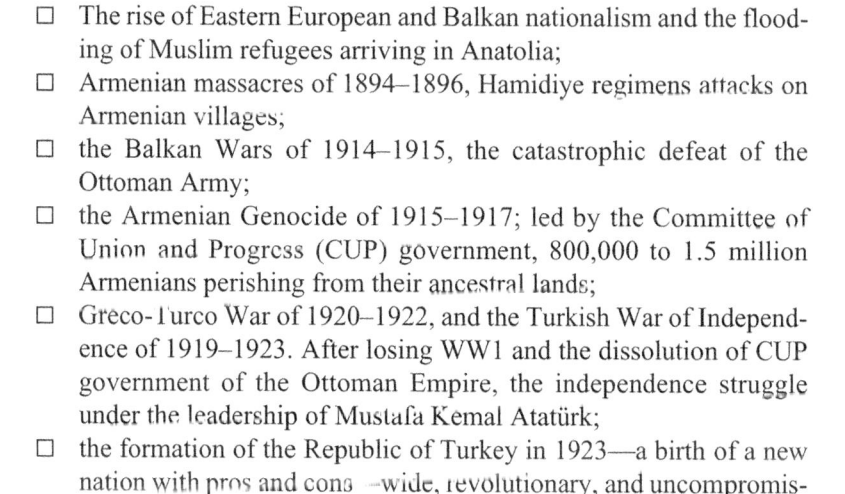

- The rise of Eastern European and Balkan nationalism and the flooding of Muslim refugees arriving in Anatolia;
- Armenian massacres of 1894–1896, Hamidiye regimens attacks on Armenian villages;
- the Balkan Wars of 1914–1915, the catastrophic defeat of the Ottoman Army;
- the Armenian Genocide of 1915–1917; led by the Committee of Union and Progress (CUP) government, 800,000 to 1.5 million Armenians perishing from their ancestral lands;
- Greco-Turco War of 1920–1922, and the Turkish War of Independence of 1919–1923. After losing WW1 and the dissolution of CUP government of the Ottoman Empire, the independence struggle under the leadership of Mustafa Kemal Atatürk;
- the formation of the Republic of Turkey in 1923—a birth of a new nation with pros and cons—wide, revolutionary, and uncompromis-

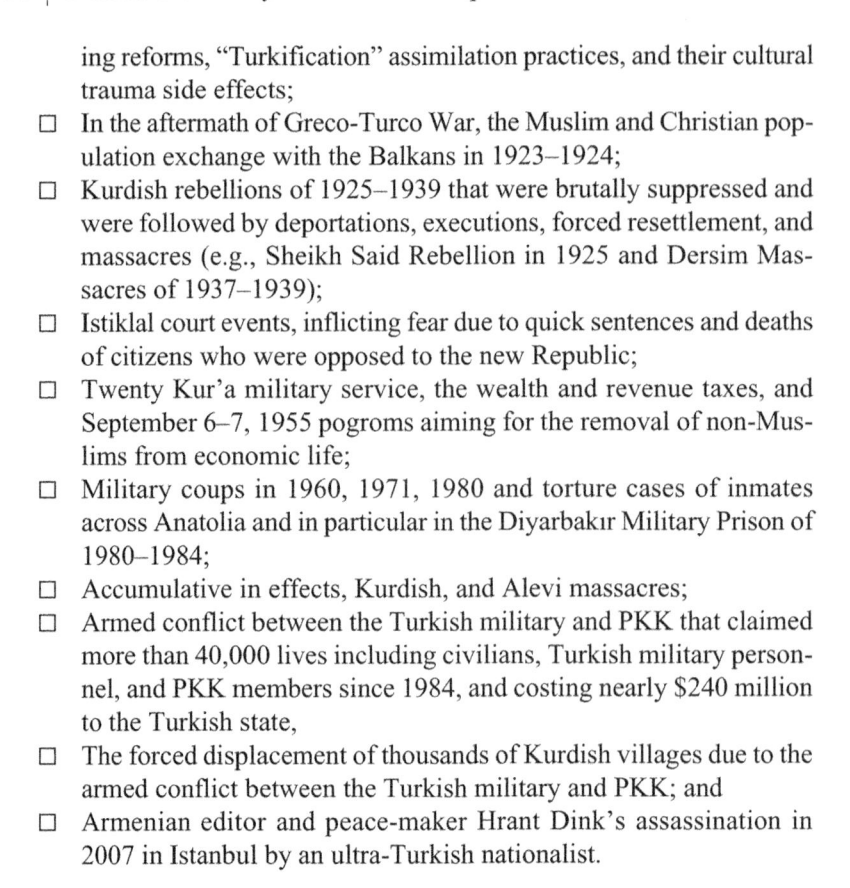

ing reforms, "Turkification" assimilation practices, and their cultural trauma side effects;
- In the aftermath of Greco-Turco War, the Muslim and Christian population exchange with the Balkans in 1923–1924;
- Kurdish rebellions of 1925–1939 that were brutally suppressed and were followed by deportations, executions, forced resettlement, and massacres (e.g., Sheikh Said Rebellion in 1925 and Dersim Massacres of 1937–1939);
- Istiklal court events, inflicting fear due to quick sentences and deaths of citizens who were opposed to the new Republic;
- Twenty Kur'a military service, the wealth and revenue taxes, and September 6–7, 1955 pogroms aiming for the removal of non-Muslims from economic life;
- Military coups in 1960, 1971, 1980 and torture cases of inmates across Anatolia and in particular in the Diyarbakır Military Prison of 1980–1984;
- Accumulative in effects, Kurdish, and Alevi massacres;
- Armed conflict between the Turkish military and PKK that claimed more than 40,000 lives including civilians, Turkish military personnel, and PKK members since 1984, and costing nearly $240 million to the Turkish state,
- The forced displacement of thousands of Kurdish villages due to the armed conflict between the Turkish military and PKK; and
- Armenian editor and peace-maker Hrant Dink's assassination in 2007 in Istanbul by an ultra-Turkish nationalist.

When there is a collective trauma in society, people's shared experiences change the present and the future. If not healed, the effects are normalized and find a place in the culture, myths, family values, and large-group identities, which Vamık Volkan (2004) calls these belief systems *"chosen" traumas,* or as Armand Volkas (2009, 2014) calls them eventual *historical traumas.* According to Armand Volkas (2009),

> the impact[s] of the collective trauma are carried in people's psyches in the form of images, stories, sense memories, spoken and unspoken messages transmitted by parents, teachers and the media. Ultimately, this process evolves into a collective narrative. This narrative is absorbed unconsciously through a process akin to osmosis and has an impact on the cultural and national identity of the individual and the group. (p. 145)

The exposure to collective trauma creates a rupture and victimization in the timeline of the social fabric; Danieli (1998) calls this *fixity* (p. 7), a possible regression which continues to travel in time; a state of being "stuck" in this free flow. The degree of fixity depends on the severity of the event and how individuals and the society coped, made meaning, and adapted over time. Volkan argues if the affected groups from a collectively traumatic experience cannot mourn their losses or reverse its feelings of helplessness and humiliation, the experience obligates subsequent generation(s) to complete these unfinished psychological processes. These transgenerationally-transmitted psychological tasks shape future political/military ideological development and decision-making processes. Under certain conditions, an ideology of entitlement of revenge develops, initiating or contributing to new societal traumas, and from there—the cycle of violence perpetuates. Centuries later, even if the nation might have lived under relative peace, under collective stress, historical traumas could become re-triggered. People may find themselves in the whirlpool of rage, hatred, grief, worry, paranoia, political conflict—depending on the original wound and the type of collective trauma, reactions may emerge.

In review, collective trauma affects ethnic or national identities and political perspectives. Consequently, these identifications and ideologies may play a significant role in political and institutionalized decisions. Over time, these shared traumatic experiences refine the definition of the enemy and intensify us-versus-them mentalities.

Transgenerational Trauma

According to Roman Law, the dead pass down to the living.

> We continue the chain of generations and, knowingly or not, willingly or unwillingly, we pay debts of the past: as long as we have not cleared the slate, and "invisible loyalty" [our conscious or unconscious implantation to our own culture and our own roots] impels us to repeat and repeat a moment of incredible joy or unbearable sorrow, an injustice or a tragic death. Or its echo. (Schützenberger, 1998, p. xii)

Collective trauma is not directly transmitted. There is so much more at play in society; research has also not been consistent in claiming a direct transmission (Dekel & Goldblatt, 2008; Kellerman, 2001). Other family members' influence, social support, or lack thereof, education, and institutions are part of individuals' life experiences, influencing their vulnerability for developing transgenerational trauma symptoms. In other words, not the trauma itself but the impairment of the survivor's adaptation and their parenting style is often what is transmitted to the children (Fossion et al., 2003). Traumatization does not only happen within a family line. Violence can be brought in from outside the family or community. Furthermore, when the experience is collective, the transmission of trauma becomes a systemic issue.

What Volkas (2009) calls historical trauma, in my view, also describes the transgenerational transmission of trauma, as a trauma that is

> transmitted inter-generationally from parent to child where a father's alcoholism or depression, for example, may be directly due to the unresolved PTSD of his experience in the Vietnam War, but the historical and collective aspect of the trauma is never fully addressed. (p. 146)

Volkas further postulates inheritors of this type of trauma can unconsciously carry "unexpressed grief" (p. 146).

The victim's identification with the traumatic event is two-fold. On the one hand, victim identification develops, but on the other, perpetrator identification also develops. When victims internalize murderous rage even though they may never act on it, energetically and emotionally, they are carrying the perpetrator energy. Perpetrator energy can be directed outside in forms such as "blaming others," "hatred toward others," or toward self in forms of "self-hatred." Duran (2006), who researches Native American trauma, which he calls the Soul Wound, uses the vampire bite metaphor to describe historical trauma. A vampire by their very nature will infect other individuals they bite. A vampire's bite can only be healed with the curing of the vampire itself. The nature of the vampire is also relevant here. In folklore, vampires live in the dark; they are part of a secret society, and only special spiritual means can eradicate or heal them. Similar are the symptoms of transgenerational trauma such as domestic abuse, alcoholism, substance abuse, women battering, rage, and uncontrollable outbursts of anger. The inflicted may feel in the dark, alone, in the shadow, and healing requires special attention and intention like the stories in the vampire folklore. The immortality of the vampire or other forms of monsters, devils, or demons also speaks to the transgenerational nature of trauma, that it is immortal and continues to live until eradicated. We see the traces of our projection and our historical trauma's healing journey in pop culture in the archetypes of the monsters and demons and their relationship with society.

Despite such darkness, through their resilience, humans often try to make the best out of their situation. They try to cope, learn, and heal. For example, Danieli, based on her work with Jewish Holocaust survivors and their children, argues that they, in an attempt to do their best, taught their children how to survive and, in the process, transmitted to them the living conditions under which they had survived the war. The main post-trauma adaptation styles of Holocaust survivors were being a victim, becoming numb, being a fighter, and "those who made it." She observed the victim adaptation styles mostly with concentration camp survivors, the fighter with partisan or resistant fighter parents during the war; additionally, a person could have more than one style (Danieli, 1982, 1985; Danieli, Norris, & Engdahl, 2016). Danieli describes the victim-style includes sadness, worry, mistrust, fear of the outside world, and symbiotic clinging within the family; the fighter-style consists of an intense drive to build and achieve, compulsive activity and prohibition of weakness or self-pity; the numb-style is characterized by pervasive silence and depletion of all emotions, minimal tolerance to stimuli, and their children expected to grow up on their own; and those who made it is less homogeneous than the other three. Many of these survivors were motivated by a wartime fantasy and desire to "make it big" if they were liberated in order to defeat the Nazis. Persistently and single-mindedly, they sought higher education, social and political status, fame, and wealth. As with other survivor families, they used their money primarily for the benefit of their children. Danieli (1998) asserts that for healing, "integration of the trauma must take place in all of life's relevant dimensions or systems and cannot be accomplished by the individual alone" (p. 7). In her model, "'getting better' involves a continuous and consistent unraveling and working through of the individual's or the family's particular (unconscious) rigidified and self-perpetuated victim-survivor context or stance" (Danieli, 1985, para. 52).

Healing Transmission of Trauma at a Personal Level

Healing from trauma may be a painful journey; and people often reenact their trauma narratives in dysfunctional relationship patterns or take their pain out on other people like in the vampire metaphor. African American Somatic Experiencing Practitioner, Resmaa Menakem (2017), defines the vampire within the "dirty pain" where the person puts their pain on other people through judgment, criticism, insults, physical attacks, or other forms of verbal or physical abuse. "Dirty pain" transmits pain and suffering on other people—this is how one-way trauma in one body causes trauma in another.

In contrast, what Menakem defines as "clean pain" is the pain one needs to feel in order to heal from their soul wounding. When clean pain is experienced, people do not necessarily act on their impulses, or unconsciously take their suffering out on other people or themselves, but they learn from their pain. Each person can develop a capacity to be able to be with their pain, and as they do so, they heal from it. It is not an easy process. There is not a clean-cut division between dirty or clean pain either; people often find themselves experiencing both. However, with enough intention and the help of mental health professionals, spiritual work, or other community support, healing is possible.

That said, healing avenues should incorporate a person's cultural and historical context to prevent further oppression. Because if the well-intended tools of the oppressor are used on the oppressed, liberal psychology scholars argue, this further colonizes the person, such as pathologizing Native Americans with Western medicine and using only Western modalities for their healing not only proven to be ineffective but also re-traumatizing for Native Americans (Duran, Firehammer, & Gonzalez, 2008). Furthermore, community, family, mental health professionals, and other areas of society involvement are crucial in healing as the origin of the pain did not come from one person alone.

Reflecting on experiences in Turkey, practitioners could explore what I call "context-centric healing" modalities. Meaning, Anatolia has been a host for centuries-old spiritual and mystic developments, which have healing modalities and practices incorporated into society, such as pre-Islam shamanism and divination practices, breathing rituals, esoteric Islam, teachings in Sufism, traditional dance, mystical poetry, music, the rituals in a Cem house, and so on. Historically, in Anatolia, shamanism intermingled with Muslim devotion and rituals, where some of the pre-Islam healing practices were adopted and continue to be performed complementary with religious practices (Zarcone & Hobart, 2017). The prophet Muhammed and his daughter Fatima were also healers. Islam incorporated many healing modalities within its practice, which, in part, allowed the intermingling of various existing healing practices between it and pre-Islam.

Healing avenues depend on the cultural and historical context of the person. Given the complexity and diversity of Anatolia's population, every healing modality should not be assumed to work effectively for each individual. Indigenous and spiritual or mystic practices that originated in Anatolia could provide some of the critical healing avenues. In light of liberation psychology, the thoughtful combination of traditional and contemporary practices could be useful for Turkey's specific populations.

Volkas, Duran, Danieli, and most other psychotherapists work with their clients within therapeutic contracts in their confidential therapy offices. During the deep psychological healing work of collective and historical traumas, most psychotherapists also observed that clients often are drawn to make a healing contribution within their community.

Trauma survivors, often as part of their healing process, find themselves involved in projects that focus on the prevention of further traumas or the healing of others who suffered from similar traumas. In Volkas' (2009) group dialogue, at the last stage workshop, participants began to make commitments and create artistic forms and theater pieces to carry their influences out into the world. In Jungian psychology, this phenomenon could also manifest as a "wounded healer." Those who have been able to heal from their own wounding can be transformed to become healers themselves

(Hartowicz, 2018; Robertson, 2011). In every area of life, from social activism to education to parenting skills, healing could spread. Therefore, healing from historical traumas opens paths for societies to experience "clean pain" as opposed to "dirty pain," helps prevent transmission of trauma from one body to another; and expands healing into communities.

Healing Transmission of Trauma at a Systemic Level

The transgenerational nature of trauma does not only manifest from one individual body to another. Collective atrocities may lead to massive medical, economical, and institutional problems. Furthermore, in the process of healing from historical traumas, present circumstances may be less than ideal. Individuals may be reenacting their trauma and may be in an abusive relationship. From the socio-dynamic perspective, oppression, war, or other collectively traumatic experiences may still be, in fact, intact. Healing, then, is coming face to face with present circumstances of the good and the bad without blindly defaulting to a historical trauma narrative—but being informed by them—and doing what is necessary to break the cycle of perpetuation, and simultaneously working on the societal healing processes.

The living generation's responsibility becomes the tedious process of (re)remembering and sorting through what serves current circumstances versus what should be healed or left behind. In psychotherapy, this process is where the client could recall some of their earlier traumatic experiences, begins to understand their trauma response was perhaps useful, such as disassociation, fight, or flight; however, they are not helpless anymore—they have options.

Psychiatrist Herman argues that the final stage of healing from psychological trauma is when the survivor recognizes their trauma as part of their life story, and not the leading indicator of who they are (Herman, 2015, p. 155). From collective experiences, communities who carry historical trauma, such as it is with a trauma survivor where trauma is central in their experience, communities also get fixated on the collectively traumatic event as if the history did not exist before. For example, a Dersim 38 massacre survivor's third-generation descendant gives 1938 as her birth year even though she was born decades after the atrocity (Neyzi, 1999). When systemic healing is underway, such as apologies, recognition, or other conscious efforts toward healing, over time, communities may not be as invested in the traumatic past. For example, Joy De Gruy describes her visit to South Africa and people's responses to her questions regarding the collective trauma of apartheid, institutionalized racial segregation, and discrimination that existed in South Africa from 1948 until the early 1990s. To De Gruy's (2005) surprise, people were not emotionally invested in the apartheid narrative. They would say, "Yeah. Joy, it was awful, the oppression of the blacks, the behavior of the whites. Glad it's over though. Welcome to the new South Africa" (p. 19). The reasoning may be, De Gruy adds, because the oppression was shorter-lived than 500 years of chattel slavery[1] in the United States, or perhaps the state voluntarily gave up on their unjust system, and the truth and reconciliation process took place after. Whatever the reasoning was, to De Gruy's observation, people seemed as if they were not as invested in the trauma narrative (pp. 18–19). Moreover, not being invested in the trauma narrative did not mean they forgot about it. Because the consequences were finally acknowledged and addressed, and the system that has caused it was changed, there were less emotional investments with the trauma; finally, the tension could begin to release.

From denial to commemoration, the stages of healing from collective traumas could happen in eight stages. As it is in all healing modalities, stages are not necessarily linear for all aspects of the society. Jennifer Dixon (2018) writes that the logical flow could be similar to (a) denial or silence about the collective atrocities; (b) myth–making or relativizing, which can involve justifications and recreation of narrative to claim "it is not what it looks like"; (c) with the acknowledgment of what happened, people realize the catastrophic loss that it has caused; (d) people acknowledge the harm and express genuine regret; and (e) perpetrators as individuals or at the institutional level admit responsibility. After admitting responsibility, there is a sense of transparency about the events and the consequences, and more reparative efforts could begin, following with (f) apology; and (g) offer of compensation for losses; and (h) commemoration (p. 16).

It is a long and painful process to get to commemoration if the society could even move through these stages. For example, Turkey is still between stage two and three—myth-making and relativizing. Even 100 years after the Armenian Genocide, the Turkish state is still claiming that Armenians and Turks were engaged in a civil war and the killings happened in the backdrop of WWI where people died on both sides (Dixon, 2018). This narrative does not reflect the complete truth of what happened (Göçek, 2015). In the recent years, President Erdoğan vaguely acknowledged the Armenian and Dersimi's suffering, but quickly after back paddled.

In the healing process, society acknowledges its history—the bad and good. There needs to be appropriate sanctions to carry out policies and practices that help victims (or descendants) recover from their losses. Perpetrators need to be brought into some form of justice through processes such as court systems or restorative justice. These steps often get very problematic, especially when perpetrators are currently in a position of authority. They would do anything in their power to prevent the healing process, because it would reveal any wrongdoings, demand justice, burden the economy due to potential compensation for victims, and may require the system to change. Therefore, people in power become invested in the status quo, even if it meant maintaining the trauma narrative and the perpetuation of violence. Even if they do not directly support perpetration, a good portion of society may become bystanders (people who consciously or unconsciously ignore wrongdoings, remain silent, or do not take any action). Because, for most people, their day to day lives, work, pension, and home are dependent on the status quo. Change may mean the unknown, a threat to what they have; so often, the majority, even within oppressive systems, if they feel relative stability, may become bystanders, and remain silent to injustice to "protect" what they have.

In summary, despite the variations in transmission, major collective traumas continue to haunt the lives of those even after several generations. Any political dialogue and psycho-social interventions need to consider historically traumatic events and their potential impact today. Otherwise, as Volkan (1998) describes, researchers, politicians, social change agents or activists may be perplexed by collective behaviors.

Individual healing critical for grassroots developments, when supported by institutional developments, change on the societal level may emerge. Volkan developed what he calls the "tree model," which bridges psychology and policy. It is a psycho-political approach to unofficial diplomacy to reduce ethnic tension. In this model, the "roots" of the tree consist of a diagnosis phase, when the facilitating team, as a start, collects background information on the conflict and makes a tentative diagnosis of the problems and issues involved. The "trunk" is a process of facilitated psycho-political dialog amongst influential members of the conflicted groups. The "branches" are the independent organizations and institutions that develop out of the dialog phase. The tree needs water, and the funding provides that so the tree can grow. Volkan noted that "the uniqueness of the Tree Model is its utilization of an interdisciplinary facilitating team that includes psychoanalysts, psychiatrists, (former) diplomats, historians, and other social and behavioral scientists" (Volkan, 1998, p. 343). This model helps integrate psychological insights gained by influential members with the societal level practices. Theoretical sociologist Sztompka (2004) says the impacts of collective atrocities shake society at multiple levels, and when one changes, all else does as well. Volkan's (2006) tree approach is one of the examples where the approach attempts to address all affected functions. Within the last decade, Volkan consulted a project team with *Ekopolitik* in Turkey, applying his tree model. He wrote his reflections in one of his later books (Volkan, 2013). It appears that, despite Volkan's efforts to contain and project members' good intentions, the project grew too fast and dissolved in the end. Nevertheless, an essential effort toward societal healing in Turkey.

Understanding Perpetrator Motives from a Psycho-Social Lens

In 2004 television interview, American writer, filmmaker, and political activist, Susan Sontag said, "10% of any population is cruel, no matter what, and 10% is merciful, no matter what, and the remaining 80% can be moved in either direction." Sontag's quote has been widely used since to describe the dynamics of perpetrator versus bystander versus helper behaviors, as well as those in between. During collective atrocities, perpetrators cannot do their work alone. They are supported by the rest of society, most of whom are not actively or directly involved in the violence. Ervin Staub (1993) argues that the passivity of internal bystanders (members of the society) and external bystanders (other nations) is what encourages perpetrators. Further as the strength of the movement grows, some bystanders could, over time, become perpetrators as well.

One of the essential ways of exploring collective atrocities is also to understand the mind of the perpetrators and the tendencies of the remaining majority who are mostly bystanders. Staub (2011) even writes that during times of atrocities there may be large pockets of society that do not understand to what extent atrocities are taking place. On the other hand, psychotherapist Volkas (2009) believes that "there is a potential perpetrator in all of us and that under certain circumstances, every human being has the capacity for dehumanization and cruelty" (p. 147). I believe it is important to explore the processes that lead communities and individuals to become perpetrators or bystanders of violence.

The image of the perpetrator as an ordinary person, while most perplexing, is quite often the case. In the 1970s, Hannah Arendt (2006) coined the term "banality of evil," which dominated the discussion on perpetrator experience in the last three decades. The banality of evil, not in the sense to excuse common behaviors, but "the sheer mechanical thoughtlessness of the evil-doer . . . looking human but not quite *being* human" (Lang, 1994, p. 47).

For example, in the context of the Holocaust, Volkan (2004) believes that a generation of German children experienced neglect due to Nazi propaganda leading them blindly to be more vulnerable in adulthood, exemplified by their faith to a leader, and show aggressive tendencies. Volkan calls this "blind trust." According to Volkan, Nazi physician Joanna Haarer's child development books for mothers

> counseled parents to feed their children only on a rigorous schedule and not to rush to their children when they cried or encountered trouble with their surrounding; children were left to rely on their own undeveloped coping mechanisms and not on parental care. Further, parents were warned to

reject the parenting advice of older generations and instead to consult the Nazi magazine *Mother and Child*. . . . [and suspects that German mothers] ignored their children's natural dependency needs and ruined their sense of basic trust. (p. 76)

These children, according to Volkan's (2004) review,[2] were additionally exposed to Nazi propaganda in school, media, and motion pictures. Family bonds had to be broken further as Nazi propaganda idealized Nazi figures, inflicting shame into young adolescents' minds about their parents and grandparents. Psychologically, the breaking of family bonds causes difficulty in feeling remorse, and in experiencing mourning or empathy. Therefore, Volkan argues that children who grew up under the Nazi regime grew up to be "exceptionally loyal and closely-bounded followers" (p. 76).

I believe a greater problem in collective atrocities is not the ignorance of perpetrators or bystanders (which very well may be the case in many instances), but the perpetrators' belief that what they are doing *is* the right thing to do. Haslam and Reicher (2007) argue that there are three main dynamics that might be at play in the creation of perpetrators within a society. First, one needs to ask: "Who is drawn to tyrannical groups?" (p. 619) because not everyone would choose to join them. Secondly, one needs to ask: "How does group membership transform people?" (p. 619), because becoming a member of a group also changes people over time as they are exposed to extreme propaganda and their belief systems are impacted accordingly. Thirdly, one needs to ask: "When do authoritarian views gain influence?" (p. 620), because at some point as the movement grows, as a result of social influence, those initially less extreme might go along with extreme views. The combination of social pressure and social prejudice eventually could lead a person to become a perpetrator of violence (Fiske, Harris, & Cuddy, 2004).

In other words, large-group identification is an important factor in both the perpetration of a crime and bystanding. Volkan describes large-group identities as a big tent where people are not so concerned about the tent itself on a day-to-day basis. They go about their life, tending to their families and friends and are often only aware of their subgroups, such as their clan, colleagues, and families. However, If the tent is under threat, communities will do whatever it takes to protect and repair it. During the repair process, individuals may become aware of who they are and who they are not in comparison to other people and groups in the tent. Hostility often emerges if there is an intergroup threat. Threats come in different shapes, as Suny (2004) describes:

Threats to one's family or friends, to one's own life, to the ordinary, the quotidian, the way things normally are, to social status, to personal and group interests—lead to fear, hatred, or resentment, which in turn can motivate people to act. (p. 30)

Furthermore, when groups feel threatened, differences between the conflicted parties are amplified, large groups regress, which is when leaders could either create reparative/adaptive or destructive leadership (Volkan, 2004). Volkan writes,

> Regressed large groups are prone to reactivate . . . their shared chosen traumas and chosen glories. Many leaders know intuitively how to stimulate chosen traumas and glories as well as how to bring the emotions pertaining to these past events to present issues, thus magnifying fears and defenses against them. (p. 71)

Regressed large groups could find themselves in significant conflicts; under leadership that feeds fear, anxiety, and paranoia, atrocities may emerge in the name of protecting group identity. Such was the case in Cambodia where between the years of 1975 and 1979, 1.5 to 3 million died under the leadership of Khmer Rouge.

Difficult life conditions, such as economic problems, political violence, rapid changes in technology, social institutions, and values by themselves do not lead to genocide or mass murders. They carry the potential, though, that specific social and institutional groups can exploit a push for violence (Staub, 1989). Staub (1989) argues that "a society that has long devalued a group and discriminated against its members, has a strong respect for authority, and has an overly superior and/or valuable self-concept is more likely to turn against a subgroup" (p. 5).

In Chapters 2–4, I further explore how such dynamics played out in Anatolia. For example, institutionalized manipulation and propaganda of the masses led to collective brutalities during the fall of the Ottoman Empire, causing 1.5 million Armenians to vanish from their ancestral lands. Later, during the September 6–7 pogroms in 1955, an outraged Turkish Muslim mob demolished non-Muslim homes and businesses in Istanbul. A more recent example is the Sivas Massacre on July 2, 1993, at the Hotel Madımak (*Madımak Otel*), where Sunni Islam religious extremists attempted to lynch participants in an Alevi cultural conference, mainly targeting writer and intellectual Aziz Nesin who supposedly insulted their religion. The events resulted in the arson of the hotel and the killing of 35 people. Historically, we have seen that psychological, social, and environmental factors can cause a particular group to dehumanize another group. Dehumanization, prejudice, and blaming create a psychological distance that allows atrocities to happen. When the "other" is dehumanized, it is easier for ordinary people over time to become a bystander, an enabler, or even a perpetrator.

There is a psychological cost to perpetrators when an ordinary person finds themselves in such an act. For example, in one oral history research study, a participant's grandfather talks about a man, who was involved in the Armenian Genocide and was scarred for life as a result of the crimes he committed. One research participant remembered his grandfather stating:

> We rounded up all the Armenians from the villages around midnight. There is a very deep cliff at Eskar. We took them there and threw them down the cliff one by one. I can no longer sleep. Whenever I close my eyes, the children I threw off that cliff, take hold of my hands, and pull me towards the cliff. (Neyzi & Kharatyan-Araqelyan, 2010, p. 36)

The participant's grandfather is haunted by what he did to the children. Clearly, within the heat of war, fear, and social pressure, he found himself doing things that he could not have imagined himself doing, and is feeling remorse. The remorse, however, does not excuse a past wrongdoing. But it does demonstrate the weight of such actions on some individuals, and perhaps gives us a better understanding of the different dynamics that lead some individuals and communities to engage in such horrific events.

Yet within this dynamic, there are others who become heroic helpers (Staub, 1993). The complexity of the human mind and social dynamics allow them (either wounded psychologically or not) to act a bit differently even in the most violent environments, and they do not become perpetrators. In the midst of great terrors, the most amazing human generosity also presents itself. As the pendulum swings so far to the shadow of a society, it goes equally far to the other side, where heroism presents itself in the most unexpected ways. Several factors affect helpers' behaviors.

Samuel Oliner and Pearl Oliner (1988) found that most of those who chose to help often did not exist in a social vacuum. They had some form of social support, organization, or the resources to help. A majority helped to the extent of their resources, social networks, and circumstances allowed. For example, Dersimis (people from Dersim, Dersimli) tell proud stories about how they protected Armenians in Dersim (Kieser, 2019). Dersimis had the internal dynamics, values, belief systems, and the power to be able to help, and so they did. Oliner and Oliner thought, therefore, that most rescuers did not feel that they had done anything extraordinary and repeatedly said anyone in their position would have done the same thing.

Another heroic example is Haji Halil, a devout Muslim Turk who saved members of an Armenian family from deportation and death by keeping them safely hidden for over half a year, risking his own life (Akçam, 2006). During the Armenian Genocide, while thousands took advantage of orphans by taking them in as servants, there were cases where families genuinely tried to help. In some areas in Eastern Anatolia, groups of Kurds followed the deportation convoys and saved as many people as they could.

However, these efforts were minor experiences in comparison to the brutality that took place during the Armenian Genocide. The majority of the population did not help, and they became either bystanders or witnesses to the crimes. To sum it up, the creation of the perpetrator is a process that includes preexisting psychological conditions, belief systems, and social influence. Propaganda, media, and promotion of ideologies over time can dehumanize the victim group and spread the belief that forced displacement, massacres, torture, or raids are right and just things to do. People who believe the propaganda may also have prior prejudice, an us-versus-them belief system, or perpetrators may be a victim of an earlier atrocity themselves. The key to preventing such atrocities is the education and mobility of the bystanders (the 80%) toward peace and reconciliation. Staub (2011) writes: "If we were all active bystanders, even to a limited degree, both doing what we can and influencing other people—our neighbors, the media, our leaders—so that they take appropriate action, we could prevent most group violence" (p. 5). Prevention, or un-learning of the us-versus-them mentalities, building empathy, education of what is happening in society, and together building tools for action are keys to preventing or recovering from atrocities.

CHAPTER 2

A History of Collective Traumas
The Decline and the Fall of the Ottoman Empire

In the 19th century, the Ottoman Empire began to lose its dominance in places where it had influence for centuries. The increased sense of local autonomy and the rise of nationalistic values made it more difficult for Ottoman Empire to maintain their control. Furthermore, by 1800 the Ottoman Empire opponents—European powers (Britain, France, and Russia)—gained novel resources. As the British colonized India, it needed active involvement in the Mediterranean. France was not able to colonize Egypt but gained access to Algeria in 1830 and Tunisia in 1881. The Habsburg monarch made advances in the Balkans, and most of all, Tsarist Russia presented the most significant threat to Ottoman Empire's livelihood by hovering over the Balkans and the Northeast boundary of the empire, in the Eastern Front where the majority of the Ottoman Armenian populations lived (Faroqhi, 2009, p. 111).

The French revolution in 1789 was a signifying marker for societal shifts from strong empires to nation states. In the 18th century and onward, the time of strong empires came to a halt. Influenced by European nationalism, Turkish, Greek, Arab, and Armenian nationalist movements began to break out within the Ottoman Empire, accelerating the fall. Sociologist Fatma Müge Göçek (2002), reviewing the emergence of Greek, Armenian, Turkish, and Arab nationalism, writes:

> Greek nationalism was the first to become established with ample European support of its independence in the early nineteenth century; [the] Armenian nationalist movement, which developed almost a century later, faced a harsher, polarized, and more nationalistic Ottoman state that totally destroyed it. The Arab nationalist movement, which emerged in [the] early twentieth century and gained momentum during and after the First World War, led, with Western help, to the succession of the Arab provinces from the empire. Escalating military defeats and social polarization enabled

Turkish nationalism to gradually triumph over Ottomanism, culmination in the foundation of a Turkish nation-state on the ruins of the empire. (p. 16)

To stay relevant in the world's changing power dynamics, the Ottomans also tried to modernize their tools and practices (The Tanzimat era—a period of reforms from 1839 to the First Constitutional Era in 1876). Beginning with the military, some Ottoman reforms were adopted after careful study of European practices. The Ottoman's efforts for staying relevant and robust enabled them to delay their demise for about a century; however, eventually, in the early 1900s (1908–1922), the empire collapsed. From the ashes of the Ottoman Empire, the Republic of Turkey arose.

The communities of Anatolia faced major collective traumas during the fall of the empire and the new Republic's emergence. Even if a collective event is perceived in a positive manner, such as how many Turks viewed the Republic of Turkey's emergence as a victory, the process might have caused many side effects and grim consequences for the parts of society. After a decade-long war, the people of Anatolia were exhausted. Epidemics, famine, poverty, and daily threats to livelihood were happening; facing, witnessing, or involvement in violence, were some of the shared experiences at that time.

Concerning the collective hardships experienced then, this chapter and the next two (Chapters 2, 3, & 4) chronologically explore the collectively traumatic experiences of Turks, Kurds, and Armenians. Chronological exploration allows one to see how collective traumas impacted each generation and how, when not healed, the experience of collective trauma may have caused another "traumatic sequence."

The interrelation of all these traumatic events evidenced the perpetuation of violence in Turkey spanning generations and their accumulative effects. In this chapter, I introduce a brief review of the Ottoman Empire, its fall, and the consequential collective traumatic events that followed until the Republic of Turkey's formation: the Hamidiye Massacres, Balkan Wars, World War I, Armenian Genocide, the Turkish War of Independence, the Greco-Turco War, and the population exchange that followed between Ottoman Greeks and Balkan Muslims.

The Ottoman Empire

Turkic tribes, as early as the 6th century, from Central Asia and Mongolia started migrating toward Anatolia. Their reasoning for the move varied from change in the climate to political pressure from neighbors. Among those tribes were the Oguz (also called Oghuz or Ghuzz) people who accepted Islam in the 10th century. They settled around Bukhara in the

Transoxania region under Seljuk Khan. After the Seljuks won the Malazgirt War in 1071 against the Byzantine Empire near Lake Van, the Turkic tribes began advancing into Anatolia. As the Seljuk Empire declined in the 13th century, Anatolia was divided amongst numerous Turkic principalities (*beylik*). One of them, the Ottoman Emirate, was founded by Osman, a Turkic tribe leader from the *Kayı* tribe of *Oguz* Turks. Ottoman (*Osmanlı*) was located in Northwest Anatolia by the Black Sea. Osman died in the mid-1320s. The principality he founded later became the Ottoman Empire. All Ottoman Sultans are descendants of Osman.

The first significant victory for the Ottomans was during Osman's son, Orhan's, time. In 1326, Orhan took over Bursa, a cosmopolitan city near the Marmara Sea. Ottoman's conquering armies promised military protection and favorable trading and tax terms. Another significant milestone for the Ottomans was under the seventh Sultan's leadership, Mehmet II "Fatih the Conqueror." The Ottomans defeated the Byzantine Empire in Constantinople in 1453, marking a significant rise for the empire.

The ninth Sultan, Selim I, born in 1470, also known as the "Grim Selim" due to ruthlessly eliminating his internal and external rivals, was the most influential of all the Ottoman's 36 Sultans and his legacy shaped the empire until its end. Selim I was also the first Sultan who started developing lasting relationships with Eastern Anatolia Kurdish tribes (see Mikhail, 2020 for a detailed analysis of Selim I's rule and the Ottoman Empire). Selim I's life had global implications. The role of Islam (Ottomans, Mamluk Empire based in Cairo, other Muslim states in Northern Africa) shaped global politics from the 15th to the 17th century. To an extent, Alan Mikhail (2020) argues Europe's Crusade mentality, their hatred toward the Ottomans and the Muslims, and the European empires' inability to take control over the land that Ottomans occupied, limiting their access to the rest of the Middle East and Asia, was eventually what led Christoph Columbus on his first voyage to the "new world." Mikhail's argument adds another controversial perspective to Christopher Columbus' voyage. Notably, his inclusion of Muslim powers at the time provides a critical ground in exploring ongoing prejudice against Muslims in the "West."

Selim I was the most influential Sultan; under his rule, the Ottoman Empire made global impacts and expanded its territory three times in size. Sultan Suleiman (Selim I's son), known as "Suleiman the Magnificent" (1520–1566), continued the expansion of the Ottoman Empire's territory over three continents. The empire expanded steadily from 1300 to 1699 and held dominance over the Near East, Middle East, North Africa, Arabia, and much of Southeast Europe until the beginning of the 20th century. In the 18th century, the empire did not expand, and, despite losing wars, they maintained a vital internal balance until the beginning of the 19th century (Faroqhi, 2009).

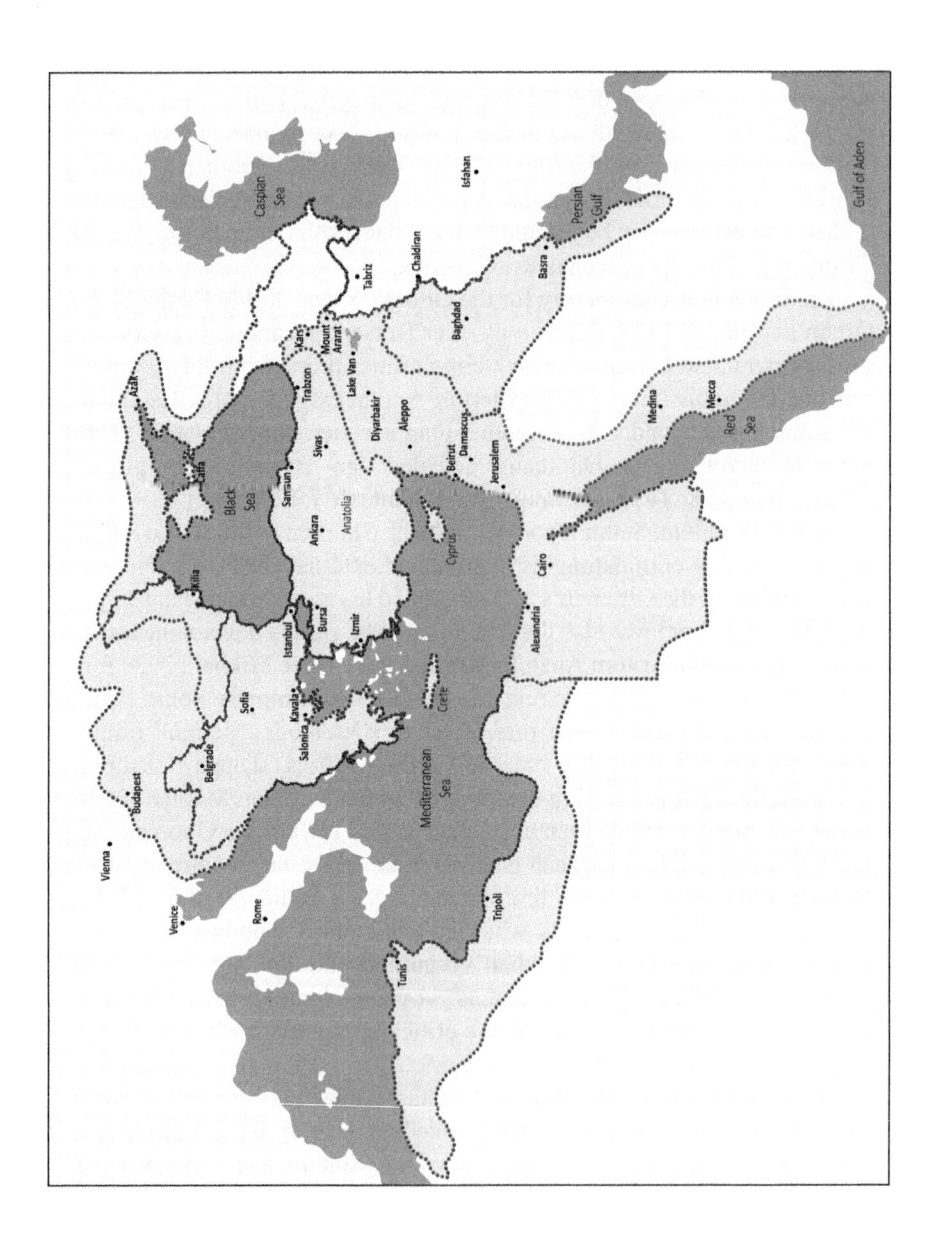

Figure 3 The Ottoman Empire at the height of its power and imperial expansion in the 16th century (adapted from Faroqhi, 2009)

Anatolia

The Anatolia region of the Ottoman Empire was home to 48[1] different ethnicities. Among these ethnoreligious groups were Turks, Armenians, Assyrians, Jews, Kurds, Arabs, Albanians, Circassians, and others (Andrews & Benninghaus, 1989). During the Ottoman years, the religious communities—Muslims, Christians, and Jews—lived separate lives, but came together and formed an economically and culturally productive society. For example, Andrew Mango (2004), in his book *The Turks Today*, describes this multicultural scene as a mosaic: dairymen in Ottoman Istanbul were predominantly Bulgarian; gardeners were Albanian; grocers and fisherman were Greek; glaziers, mostly Jewish; potters and jewelers, Armenian; and other potters, Kurdish. Nationalism in Turkey gradually destroyed this mosaic in the 19th century (Mango, 2004). Recent historical arguments also underline the fluidity and flexibility within labor division claiming ethnic division of labor was not as rigid as many assumed before (Faroqhi, 2009).

Armenians/Armenian Plateau

Armenians formed their culture and identity during thousands of years of residence in one geographical location, so they were closely tied to land and place. A recent genealogy study argues that Armenians and Kurds are indigenous to Anatolia (Hennerbichler, 2012). In other words, their ancestors arrived in Anatolia (and other surrounding regions as Armenian and Kurdish presence expanded Anatolia), and people formed their language and culture (that later became distinctly Armenian and Kurdish) over thousands of years of being in those specific geographic locations.

Between 1877 and 1914, the Armenian population was estimated to be between 1.5 to 2 million, which was approximately 15% of the general population of the Ottoman Empire in Asia Minor (Anatolia). The majority of Armenians (about 40% of the general population) lived on the Armenian plateau, which was north of Lake Van (Kevorkian & Paboudjian, 2012, pp. 57–64; see Figure 4). Armenians were the largest Christian population in Anatolia. They spoke Armenian—a unique, early branch from the Indo-European root, and followed the Armenian Apostolic faith.[2]

Jewish and Christian ethnoreligious communities lived amongst Kurds and Turks in Eastern Anatolia. Based on the patriarchate's census in 1913–14, 80% of Armenians were living in rural areas. They were peasants and farmers (Kevorkian & Paboudjian, 2012, p. 65). Armenian and Jewish communities who lived in nearby cities were skilled artisans, business owners, and builders. For example, Diyarbakır, Sivas, Bitlis, Van, Erbil, Mosul, Sanandaj, and many other minor towns were centers of

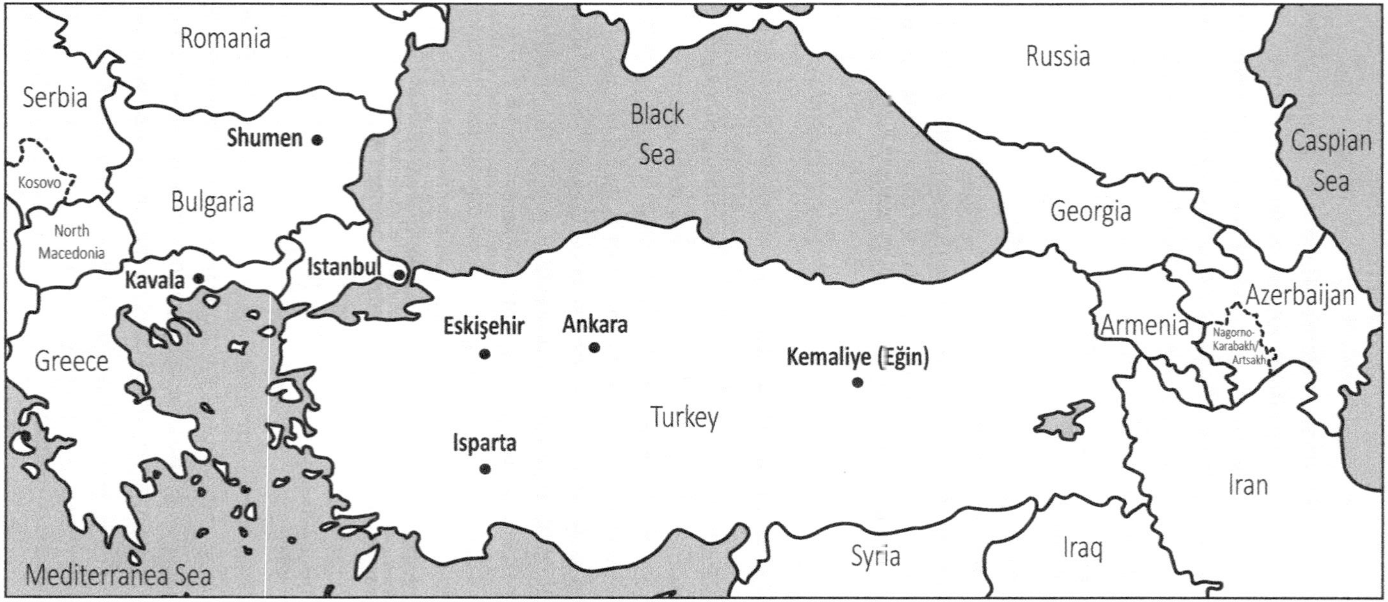
Romania
Russia
Serbia
Black
Sea
Caspian
Sea
Shumen
Kosovo
Bulgaria
Georgia
North
Macedonia
Istanbul
Kavala
Azerbaijan
Eskişehir
Ankara
Armenia
Nagorno-
Karabakh/
Artsakh
Greece
Kemaliye (Eğin)
Turkey
Isparta
Iran
Iraq
Syria
Mediterranea Sea

craftsmanship (e.g., the weaponsmith, jewelers, and tanners). The majority were Armenians, and a certain degree of contact and trade between the Anatolian residents happened as a result. Armenians also had superior horticultural skills. They were able to maintain terraced mountain plots and complicated irrigation systems.

Kurds/Kurdistan

The Armenian plateau in some parts overlaps Kurdish regions in Northwest Kurdistan. Kurdistan (the land of the Kurds) is a paramount location in the Middle East comprising parts of each, and divided amongst Turkey, Iran, Iraq, and Syria. Though there has never been a state of that name, Kurdistan, as a territory name, was used during the Ottoman Empire (referring mainly to the province of Diyarbakır); Iran also called their majority Kurdish region Kordestan. There are Kurds who live outside of these regions as well, but historically the majority of Kurds lived in Kurdistan. The Turkish state calls these regions within Turkey's national-boundary—(South) Eastern Anatolia/Eastern Turkey. I use all these terms interchangeably throughout the book.

Kurdistan served as a buffer zone between Persia and the Ottoman Empire for centuries, deterred invading armies, and provided refuge to the persecuted and bandits. Kurds were involved in both animal husbandry and agriculture. Their presence between two powerful empires imprinted their collective identities. Kurds have been superior mountain warriors and also offered protection to the local Christians in exchange for food and shelter.

Kurds are diverse culturally and linguistically.[3] Additionally, not all Kurds belong to a tribe, as many assume. Kurdish social members consist of both tribal and nontribal people. The landscape of Eastern Anatolia consists of high forbidding mountains and high plateaus with frigid winters in the higher elevations. During winter months, snow isolates many mountain villages. Kurdish populations and tribes have been nomads, semi-nomads, or have settled either voluntarily or under government compulsion (van Bruinessen, 1992).

Figure 4
1. The Armenian Plateau during the Ottoman Empire, around and north of Lake Van (adapted from Kevorkian & Paboudjian, 2012, p. 56).
2. Kurdistan, the area inhabited by a Kurdish majority today (around and south of Lake Van). Kurds have lived in Armenian Plateau only for the last few centuries and have been the majority since the Armenian Genocide of 1915–1917 (adapted from van Bruinessen, 1992, p. 12).

Nomadism/Transhumance

Many different nomadic groups[4] have lived in Anatolia. This lifestyle is often associated with communities continuously changing their location without establishing a specific connection to the land or environment wherever they go. However, nomadism in Anatolia is different and is called transhumance. In Anatolia, nomad populations were an essential part of the human populace and were connected to the Ottoman administration, finances, and regulations. In summers, due to hot weather, villagers move to the higher elevations with more agreeable climates to treat their animals and to take advantage of the fresh air. This lifestyle was one of the crucial aspects of Anatolian life. For example, recent research with Mediterranean nomads found the following:

> Transhumance has helped shape a complex mosaic of habitats in one of Mediterranean's most interesting Ecosystems. . . . The mobile pastoralist with conservation and natural resource management skills over a long period has reduced erosion control, improved soil quality and deterred the likelihood of forest fires, whilst weaving a resilient social web. (Ocak, 2016, p. 439)

However, beginning in the 16th century, the Ottoman Empire started to lose their security in the Eastern Anatolia mountains, which put trade routes and travel in danger. The Ottoman administration decided to settle nomad populations in areas where they could function as guards and provide security. Mainly Turkmen nomad groups and also a few Kurdish tribes were forced to settle. Turkic tribes who continued nomadic lifestyle remained in Central and Western Anatolia.

Millet System

As the Ottoman Empire conquered and widened its geography across the Middle East, North Africa, Arabia, and much of Southeast Europe, the millet system allowed for a multi-ethnic and multi-cultural system that maintained ethnic and religious autonomy and internal balance across the land. Under the relatively stable conditions of the Ottoman Empire, different ethnoreligious communities established tolerable and interdependent relationships. Within this interdependency, Anatolia as a region was self-sufficient and sustainable. Also, the historic Silk Road passed through its mountains and plateau, making some of the central cities global trade centers.

The Ottoman administration divided communities into two main administrative categories: *ummets* and *millets*. All Muslim communities, regardless of their ethnicity, were considered *ummet,* and all non-Muslim communities were *millet.* In return for higher taxes, *cizye,* millets could practice their religion, speak their language, and set up their schools. Millet principles also affirmed the protection of the communities and the organizational and cultural autonomy of each community. The millet system was functional, which enabled the Ottoman administration to categorize its religious groups into culturally autonomous and self-regulating communities with religious leaders acting as the intermediaries between the Ottoman governance and the community (K. Barkey & Gavrilis, 2015). However, for the Ottoman government administration, the co-existence of Muslims (*ümmet*) and non-Muslim (*millet*) was not based on equal citizenship. With the Muslims having a privileged status, the non-Muslims felt they were second-class citizens. Armenian American historian Ronald Grigor Suny (1993), in one of his earlier works in Armenian history, argues:

> The sheer power and confidence of the ruling Muslim worked for centuries to maintain in the Armenians a pattern of personal and social behavior manifested in submissiveness, passivity, deference to authority, and the need to act in calculated devious and disguised ways. It was this deferential behavior that earned the Armenians the title "loyal millet." (p. 101)

The dynamics and the perception of Armenians as a "loyal millet" in the eyes of the Ottoman administration began to change in the mid-19th century. The rise of nationalist ideologies, Western influence, already existing resentment, and us-versus-them mentalities—and what is more, thousands of Caucasian, Circassian, and Bosniak Muslim refugees—at different times entering Anatolia—began to change the social fabric of the society.

The Ottoman Empire's centuries-old millet system—a division based on religion—heavily influenced and strengthened religion-based group identifications. In Anatolia, economic competition, war conditions, and struggles over the limited amount of land among Turks, Kurds, and Armenians intensified interethnic tension. Stereotypes and the us-versus-them mentality between Muslims and Christians had existed for a long time (Göçek, 2015; Suny, 2004). The centralization reforms during the 19th century by the Sultan created egalitarian Muslim and Christian citizenship rights, whereby previously in the citizenship hierarchy, Muslims were first, and Christians were second-class citizens. Muslims were offended and resented the change in the institutional hierarchy. War conditions, fear, and anxiety about the future, and past resentments of Christians created a climate that political entrepreneurs could exploit. Ultimately in 1915–1917, orchestrated by the state CUP government/Young Turks and mobilized by Anatolian Muslims' resentment (Turks, Kurds, other Muslim communities), anxiety, and accompanying stereotypes led to genocidal violence against Armenians. By 1920, the Armenian populations of Anatolia nearly disappeared. The Hamidiye Massacres of 1894–1896 marked the beginning of collective decline of Armenians in Anatolia signaling their lack of safety.

The Hamidiye Massacres of 1894–1896

Connected with the Ottoman Empire, Kurdish autonomous emirates were typical regimes in Eastern and Southeastern Anatolia. Controlled by Kurdish sheikhs/mirs, Kurds co-existed with Armenians and continued to be a crucial buffer zone between the Safavids of Iran and the Ottomans. Martin van Bruinessen (1992) writes, "In the first half of the sixteenth century Ottoman military success and diplomatic wisdom secured the incorporation of the greater part of Kurdistan by winning the loyalty of local Kurdish rules (*mir*)" (pp. 136–137).

In the meantime, Kurds and Armenians had a tolerable—but not terribly strong—co-existence (van Bruinessen, 1992, p. 107; C. J. Walker, 1990). Kurdish overlords provided protection of Armenians in exchange for an unofficial "protection tax" called the *hafir* (Deringil, 2009). Kurdish nomads also found warmth in Armenian homes during harsh winters in exchange for animal products or other types of transactions, depending on the tribe's surplus (J. Klein, 2007; van Bruinessen, 1992).

By 1869, Ottoman law recognized all non-Muslims as citizens of the empire, which created a contradiction with the earlier system. Each community complained about the changes to the millet system; Muslims did not like being put on the same social and legal plans as non-Muslims, while Christians and Jews were not convinced that citizenship benefits were worth the new obligations, such as military service (Davison, 1973). The first Tanzimat centralization and modernization reforms terminated the Emirates (Kurdish lords, *mirs*), who had been functioning as mediators between Kurdish tribes since the 16th century. Emirates were established to protect and establish safety in the eastern frontier of the Ottoman Empire (McDowall, 2004). Major Kurdish lords, who previously controlled large territories, lost most of their power by 1880.[5] With these internal dynamics and shifts, the power balance in the region changed significantly. The absence of mirs left a power vacuum which was filled by Kurdish tribes, which were previously kept in check by them. Sheikhs who were generally from Naqshbandi or Qadiri Sufi orders, through their piety, charisma, connections, and wealth emerged as the new kind of political leader, were the only remaining moral force (Olson, 1989).

Armenians were having to deal with double taxation and the depredation of the Kurdish tribes' demanding further payment (Dadrian, 1995).

Additionally, throughout the 19th century, Muslims in Europe were not welcome as the Ottoman Empire was losing its grip and thousands of Caucasians, Circassians, Tatar, Abaza, and Bosniak refugees, at different times, were entering Anatolia. American historian Justin J. McCarthy (infamous amongst international academia for his denial of the Armenian Genocide) argues that Muslim communities faced massacres and forced deportations from the Russian Empire (1721–1917) and later from the Balkans. McCarthy (1995) claims approximately 10.3 million Ottoman Muslims were the victims of atrocities between 1821 and 1922; 5 million driven from their lands and another 5.5 million died (p. 1).

After the loss of the Russo-Turkish wars of 1828–1829, thousands of Muslim refugees arriving in Anatolia were struggling to make a home and find stability in the crumbling empire. The Ottomans continued to lose land. Later in the century, the catastrophic loss of the Russian War of 1877–1878 and losing the valuable remaining Ottoman lands in the Balkans amplified the Sultan's and his entourage's fear of Christians, as well as that of Armenians' presence and the fear that Anatolia would go the same way. According to the Prime Ministry Ottoman Archive (1893), the Sultan referred to the issue at hand to be addressed differently than the Balkan situation because "it has arisen in Anatolia which is the crucible of the Ottoman power" (as quoted in Deringil, 2009, p. 345).

Caucasian and Circassian refugees in Eastern Anatolia were vulnerable and desperate. Some found solutions in thieving and robbing Armenian residents (Adanır, 2015). Armenians, bothered by double taxation, demanding Kurdish tribes, and Caucasian thieves were not feeling secure, and they were asking for protection from the Ottoman government. The Ottoman government increasingly failed to provide security for rural Armenians, and local disturbances increased.

The Sultan came up with a local solution and, in 1891, organized local Kurdish tribes and Caucasian refugees to bring order to the region. Named after Sultan Abdulhamit, the Ottoman administration created the Hamidiye regiments. Hamidiye "regimens failed to bring peace instead aggravated the existing unrest by aggressing upon rural Armenians and poor Muslim peasants" (Göçek, 2015, p. 126). In part, the Sultan wanted to protect the Russian border and prevent their occupation, yet an inordinate increase in the power of the Hamidiye regiments led to extreme abuses (van Bruinessen, 1992, p. 185)

Some Armenians indeed aided the Russian invaders in 1877 and 1878. Not only that, the Armenian question was a topic in the Berlin Congress in 1878. Kurdish loyalty was also in question. After the Berlin treaty, Russia withdrew their troops from Eastern Anatolia, and the Ottoman governance agreed on reforms. However, as soon as Russian troops left the region, Kurds started plundering Armenian villages. Armenian bands (armed gangs and bandits) became active (Suny, 2015). Van Bruinessen (1992) points out that the formation of the Hamidiye regiments was also the Sultan's attempt to make it more rewarding for Kurds to be loyal to the Sultan (p. 185). The unrest and the fighting between the revolting Armenians and the Hamidiye regiments got out of hand.[6]

Based on oral history, there are stories in which local Turks and Kurds tried to help some of the Armenians during the massacres. For example, according to one survivor account, "Turkish neighbors [in Misis] hid Armenians during the 1894–96 massacres. In Keghi, the neighboring Turks actually armed themselves and blocked the roads in order to protect the local Armenians from attack" (D. E. Miller & Miller, 1993, p. 63).

Despite resistance, and because the Ottoman security forces' delayed intervention, the "Muslim populace exercised popular justice by attacking Armenian neighborhoods" (Göçek, 2015, p. 125), and between 1893 and 1896, approximately 100,000 to 300,000 Armenians lost their lives. The Armenian casualties were much higher than those of the Muslim populace because, per the rules of the millet system, Muslims were able to carry arms, unlike non-Muslims. A few Kurdish leaders were able to save some Armenians from violence. Göçek adds that it was no surprise that the first Armenian parties were founded during this period. The Armenian Party was established in 1885, the Hunchakian in 1887, and the Armenian Revolutionary Federation in 1891.

The Hamidiye regiment attacks and mass murders of Armenians caused these villages to request mass conversions to Islam so they could escape massacres (Deringil, 2009, 2012). Conversion to Islam was not a simple process and given that forced conversion was banned by Islamic law, there were also administrative steps in place to ensure its genuineness. Many Armenians converted or became caught in administrative loopholes. Some Armenians who converted to Islam returned to their Christianity again, but others remained Muslims. In particular, young women who were dispersed, kidnapped, or married Muslims during the massacres did not come back to their Christian communities, which Selim Deringil argues was because of shame and stigmatization regarding loss of virginity and rape.

It was a very dark time in Anatolia. In summary, these acts of mass violence toward Christians in the mid-1890s caused a lot of Armenians to convert to Islam out of fear; approximately 100,000 to 300,000 Armenians lost their lives; thousands of children were orphaned; young Armenian women were kidnapped or forced to marry Muslims; tens of thousands fled the empire for safety, all of which was beginning to change the fabric of religious diversity in Anatolia even more dramatically.

Yervant Alexanian (2018), in his memoir, writes how the Hamidiye massacres of 1894–1896 and the subsequent Armenian Genocide of 1915–1917 changed the trajectory of his family. Alexanian was born during the

Hamidiye Massacres in 1895, which his mother referred to having been born under an evil star. He writes, "As soon as I came into this world, I was thrown into violence" (p. 3). These massacres claimed his father's life in 1896 at the age of 42. His widowed mother raised him and his seven older siblings. His memoir describes the hardships his mother had to endure after losing her husband, and then what he called "being at the mercy of their other family members." Alexanian grew up witnessing some of his family members dispersing and migrating to the United States, while he was drafted into the Ottoman Army. During the Armenian Genocide (1915–1917), his ability to play the bugle miraculously saved his life, yet the atrocities claimed the life of 51 members of his family, including his mother and sisters, whom Alexanian claimed were innocent. All 51 members of his family were neither associated with a political party nor activity. Alexanian's story exemplifies how two significant waves of atrocities impacted innocent Anatolian Armenians and utterly changed their lives.

Unlike what happened two decades later, the Hamidiye regiments did not inflict a systemic expulsion and extermination of Armenians. The Sultan even attempted to heal some of the wrongdoings. When the Young Turks came in power in 1908, they disbanded those regiments. However, because Kurdish tribal units proved to be useful and even necessary to complement the army, "the Hamidiye were soon revived as militias, more closely integrated into [the] army ... fought in [the] Balkan War of 1912–13 (where they suffered heavy losses), and in the Eastern Front in the First World War and the Turkish War of Independence" (van Bruinessen, 1992, p. 189).

The Young Turk Revolution 1908

Göçek (2008), in her review of the 1908 Young Turk Revolution, argues that when the revolution began in its early years, it was clear and more inclusive—mainly influenced by European modernity that they observed in exile—when leaders wanted to bring modernity and equality to all. However, over time its meaning and legacy became historically ambiguous and increasingly nationalistic, which at the time, internally caused harsh opposition from some of the Young Turks. Over time, military and political individuals that were associated with modernity emerged, and the violence was normalized in the name of patriotism. Young Turks developed their organization in exile, mainly in cities such as Paris, Geneva, and Cairo, and only after they recruited military officers in Macedonia did they begin to attain success there. In 1908, the Young Turk Revolution forced the Ottoman Sultan, Abdulhamid II, to permit the Ottoman Chamber of Deputies to re-convene on July 24, 1908, and re-establish the Constitution (after a brief one during 1876–1878), which was the end of Ottoman era and the beginning of the second Constitution rule.

The Balkan Wars of 1912–1913

The two Balkan Wars of 1912–1913 were sharp conflicts that brought about the onset of the First World War (Adanır, 2011). In the First Balkan War, loosely aligned Balkan states eliminated the Ottoman Empire from most of Europe. In the second, the recent Balkan allies fought against each other to acquire land from the Ottoman. Again, these wars emerged through the tension and conflict between the status quo and nationalist sentiment. The wars were a catastrophic loss for the Ottomans and "erased a generation for Bulgarians, Greeks, Montenegrins, and Serbs" (Hall, 2000, p. 135). Richard Hall (2000) argues that casualty estimates are hard to discern due to confusion on the battlefield, poor record management, preservation, epidemic diseases, and civilian deaths. He estimated that during the first and the second Balkan Wars, in total, the Ottoman army lost almost 100,000 people; Bulgarians lost approximately 75,000, the Greeks 7,500, the Montenegrins 3,000, and the Serbs almost 91,000 (pp. 135–136).

Around 800,000 people fled in different directions. Erik-Jan Zürcher (2003) writes that half of them were fleeing the battle zones, and the other half were solely Muslims who were fleeing toward Anatolia out of fear from Greek, Serbian, or Bulgarian atrocities. My paternal great-grandparents and their immediate family were two of the countless families who left everything behind and fled their land. According to my family story, my great grandfather was caught by Balkan soldiers when he was escaping from Kavala in the Balkans. Amongst other Muslim men, they were lined up for mass murder. He thought to say that he was married to the priest's daughter, which saved his life.

Along the way, tens of thousands of civilians died from cholera, as well as other diseases and causes (Hall, 2000; Zürcher, 2003). The catastrophic loss of the Balkan Wars constituted a traumatic experience for the late Ottoman society at large (Adanır, 2011), and an even greater loss because the Ottomans lost an area that had been within their empire for over 500 years with approximately 42 million inhabitants, and included the most developed and richest provinces (Zürcher, 2003). Its effects could still be seen in Balkan behaviors in the 1990s (Farrar, 2003) and its psychosocial transmission (Volkan, 1996).

Turkish historian Fikret Adanır (2011), reviewing the Ottoman army's response to the defeat in the Balkan Wars, argues that during them, the Ottoman army blamed non-Muslim recruits for having caused the defeat. Claiming that the mainly Bulgarian and Greek Christian soldiers lacked participation, patriotism, and commitment—changing sides with the enemy during the war—the Ottoman army claimed they had exerted a negative influence on Muslim comrades.

The 1908 Young Turk Revolution and later Balkan Wars were major breakpoints that radically mobilized Anatolian and migrant Muslims. Muslim Ottomans and migrants were uniting together and visibly beginning to exclude non-Muslim Ottomans from previous "us" narratives (Zürcher, 2013). Local Muslims of Anatolia, such as Turks and Kurds, and migrants from the Balkans, such as Bosnians, Albanians, Tartars, and Circassians began to unite under a Muslim identity against Christians (B. Ünlü, 2016). The outcome of the Balkan Wars, the blame leveled at Christians for the failure of those wars, and the ideologies, prejudice, and grim conditions of thousands of Muslim migrants from the Balkans and Eastern Europe arriving in Anatolia created an ideological climate ripe for ethnic homogenization policies with Turkish-Islamic political agenda in Asia Minor (Adanır, 2011).

Zürchen (2003) writes:

> The loss of the Balkan provinces had a tremendous impact on the political and administrative elite of the empire, not only because the history or economic importance of the provinces. A disproportionate part of the elite hailed from the Balkan provinces. Politicians like [the] interior minister and party leader Talât Pasha, administrators like Evranoszade Rahmi, the governor of Smyrna (Izmir), or officers like Mustafa Kemal (Atatürk) all hailed from the Balkans themselves and had lost their own homeland. In most cases, their families were among the refugees. This helps to explain why the political leadership of the empire from 1913 onwards focused strongly on Asia Minor, or Anatolia, as the Turkish heartland. They adopted it consciously as their new homeland, which was to replace the lost provinces. (p. 2)

The Balkan Wars of 1912–1913 marked the end of Ottomanism as a multicultural project. Muslim intellectuals, trying to draw lessons from this catastrophe, saw it as a chance for a "national rebirth," enabling the CUP to return to power through a military coup in early 1913 that established a virtual dictatorship. The Unionists saw the coming war of World War I like as a chance to solve the national question with their "ethnic engineering" inspired by positivism and Social Darwinism (Adanır, 2011).

A critical societal point to note here is that Muslim solidarity was not only distributed from the top down, but it was also a societal movement. Nationalist bourgeois, intellectuals, government officials, institutions, public organizations, and nationalist establishments played a crucial role; over 100,000 people were mobilized (Çetinkaya, 2014). Muslim solidarity was turned against both outside communities and inside local Christian communities and resulted in Christians' near-complete expulsion from Anatolia.

Committee of Union and Progress (CUP or Unionists) Takeover in 1913

The Committee of Union and Progress (CUP or Unionists) did not immediately form a party, but over time invited all those interested to join, opened centers, and created a strong network throughout the Ottoman Empire. Göçek (2008), in her review, adds that on January 23, 1913, also known as the Bab-ı Ali Raid, the CUP, with the help of the special secret fighters (*silahşör*) of the organization, overthrew the Young Turk government and established power. International literature often refers to CUP as Young Turks, which sometimes creates confusion. These two groups have a lot of shared members and leaders; there is no clear difference between them; however, CUP leadership (a political party and military power that emerged through Young Turks) marked the beginning of the violent and dictatorial turn in the Constitution.

Beginning with the Young Turk revolution and later the CUP, the Turkish government was founded as being the defender of the multi-ethnic and multi-religious structure of the empire. In the 19th century, over a million Muslim refugees from Russia and Balkans were arriving in Anatolia. Over time, and running out of strategies to keep the Ottoman governance together, the leaders of the CUP foresaw the potential emergence of Turkishness as a solution to the rising nationalist values and Anatolian disputes. Thus, they changed their discourse. The CUP government consciously promoted Turkishness as opposed to other national identities as an avenue of bringing together Balkan and Anatolian Muslims under one national ideology. From the CUP's point of view, Turks identified more closely with Anatolia as their homeland and had the resources to mobilize the military, education, and other institutions to create and further their ideologies and reforms (Şeker, 2005).

When the CUP came to power, they became fully dictatorial and began to assassinate their opponents. The CUP exploited war conditions and laid the foundation for the emergence of the Turkish national bourgeoisie and a Turkish homeland in Anatolia at the expense of the Ottoman Greeks (also called Rûm, Millet-i Rûm, Rûm Millet) and Armenian minorities. Political scientist, Barış B. Ünlü (2016), argues that "the root of Turkishness can be traced back to unspoken and unwritten agreements amongst Muslims of Anatolia between 1915 and 1925, what [he calls] the Muslimness Contract and the Turkishness Contract, respectively" (p. 399). The Turkishness

Contract, Ünlü argues, used to be the Muslimness Contract. From 1915–1925, the contract was based on Islam. Local Muslims of Anatolia, such as the Turks and Kurds, and migrants from the Balkans, such as Bosnians, Albanians, Tartars, and Circassians, all fought together against Christian powers.

Group identities that form around social relationships, shared interests, and emotions can mobilize people toward a common goal (Jenkins, 2014). Hamza Alavi (1973) coined the term "primordial loyalties" to describe how people mobilize due to loyalty of their kinship and caste, to where they might even take actions that may not align with their personal objectives or interests. Van Bruinessen (1992) exemplifies the primordial loyalties of Kurds

> as firstly those to the family and tribe and then tribal chiefs' man and agha (the land owners). Equally strong are religion loyalties, especially those to sheikhs, the popular mystics or saints who are also leaders of religious brotherhoods (the dervish order). (p. 6)

Religion and tribal loyalties played an important role through which people of Anatolia united and collectively acted during the fall of the Ottoman Empire. Most peasants followed their religious or tribal leaders' direction. A religious-based us-versus-them mentality between Muslims and Christians divided previously interdependent communities into two divergent paths.

The Armenian Genocide of 1915–1917

By 1911, the trust between the Armenian Revolutionary Federation (ARF) and the CUP/Unionists was broken (Adanır, 2011); the fear had grown that Armenian citizens might betray the empire as well, which foreshadowed the course of events leading to the mass persecution and massacre of Armenians in 1915 and thereafter—a catastrophic trauma of Anatolia.

Historian Taner Akçam (2012) argues that the CUP (Unionists) had a simple and strategic agenda. Unionists feared that because Armenians were the majority in Eastern Anatolia (Western Armenia), this could have paved the way for an Armenian nation state. Worried about "national" security and the idea that the Ottoman governance and Muslim Turks would disappear from the face of the earth, mainly in the early years of the century, Unionists wanted to do whatever it took to protect their (Ottoman) government from dissolution. One way to do that was to keep the numbers of Muslims higher in Anatolia compared to Christians. With somewhat mathematical accuracy, Taner Akcam writes that CUP planned a demographic restructuring process where they aimed to keep the Armenian numbers not exceeding 5% to 10% in Western Armenia (p. xviii). Akçam argues that based on what he called crumbs of information found in official records, telegrams, and reports, Unionists foresaw demographic policies with genocidal characteristics against Armenians. In other words, "demographic policy and national security were intertwined in a manner that made genocide a possibility" (p. xix). Subsequently, the CUP government orchestrated a massive relocation and deportation of Armenians in Anatolia between 1915 and 1917.

Ethnic violence is ultimately about conflict and strong emotions (rage, anger, hatred, and resentment) that mobilize into collectively violent action. Not every conflict turns into an atrocity, however. The lines between conflict and collective violence are crossed often when there are institutionalized power structures in place alongside people in leadership who are prone to exploiting preexisting tensions and emotions (Suny, 2004). Along those lines, during the fall of the Ottoman Empire, orchestrated by institutionalized power and charismatic leaders, preexisting ethnic tension, centuries-old resentment between Muslims and non-Muslims imploded. With CUP's leadership, nationalist bourgeois, intellectuals, government officials, institutions, public organizations, nationalist establishments, local officials, and civil leaders, from the micro to macro levels of society, all played a crucial role in the exploitation of Armenians. Hundreds of thousands of people were mobilized, which is what made the executions, massacres, deportations, pogroms, and wealth redistribution able to be carried out so widely. With the combination of CUP's leadership and Muslim solidarity, Armenians were collectively removed from their ancestral lands. This removal included the deportations of people, their physical injuries, death, distribution of their wealth, and the assimilation process that followed.

According to Uğur Ümit Üngör's (2015) summary, three main events paved the way for the Armenian Genocide. First, after the defeat of the Balkan Wars of 1912–13, the Young Turks and the CUP government members were increasingly becoming paranoid that Armenians could side with Russians and revolt. Secondly, CUP members conducted a coup and took over the government, which gave them the power to carry out their plans including Armenian deportations. Finally, the outbreak of World War I provided the necessary conditions for massive deportations, massacres, wealth distribution, and assimilation politics.

After the catastrophic defeat of the Balkan Wars, on January 22, 1913, the CUP, consisting of Talat Bey, Enver Bey, Dr. Bahaeddin Sakir Bey, Dr. Mehmet Nazim Bey, spokesperson Omer Naci Bey, and several other armed members, attacked the government building in Istanbul. They executed most of the officials and forced Grand Vizier Mehmet Kamil Pasha to resign, and they successfully took over the government (Üngör,

2015, pp. 357–358). After, the CUP government became increasingly crueler and uncompromising.

In the summer of 1914, a chain of events followed the assassination of Archduke Francis Ferdinand, who was heir to the Habsburg throne, and provoked significant effects that resulted in Europe at the beginning of World War I. The era of the professional army was over, and everyone became involved in the conflict. Drawing from historians Krzysztof Pomian and Francios Fejtoe's works, Gianluca Bocchi and Mauro Ceruti (1997) write that emerging national ideologies transformed the European imagination of conflict and war. "[War] became ideological. War was not fought to turn the enemy away, to trap the enemy, or obtain concessions. From now on the enemy was to be annihilated" (p. 14).

Drawing from Mustafa Aksakal's 2008 work, *The Ottoman Road to War in 1914*, Üngör argues that the CUP government saw the war as an opportunity to implement their nationalist agenda, and strategically this was one of reasons why they chose to enter. Suny (2015) points out that at the beginning of World War I, there were approximately 100,000 to 200,000 Armenian soldiers fighting alongside the Turkish army. Enver Pasha, during the winter of 1914, declared an invasion of Iran and Russia. The war with Russia took place along their shared northern border. Ottoman troops along the edge of Russia (northern Armenian region) suffered a catastrophic defeat. Forty-five thousand soldiers died during the fighting or due to fatigue, epidemic, or harsh, cold weather (p. 242). Suny argues that the main reason for the Ottoman army's defeat was that it was not prepared to fight in such frigid conditions. The Ottoman army arrived at the Russian border fatigued after walking thousands of miles, whereas elsewhere, the Russian army arrived by train. A few Armenian soldiers changed sides during the war with the Russian military; however, other Armenians remained on the side of the Ottomans, which is also important to acknowledge. Furthermore, the small group of Armenians that changed sides was not the main reason that the Ottomans lost the war with Russia. Stumbled by the defeat, Enver Pasha, rather than looking for the source of the problem in his wrongful strategy, chose to blame Armenians for the loss and claimed that all Armenians were "traitors." The loss of the Russia-Turco war was the last event that paved the way for Armenian deportations and massacres (Suny, 2015).

On April 24, 1915, in Istanbul, the CUP regime arrested leading Armenian merchants, religious figures, politicians, and intellectuals. These men were taken into custody, tortured, and murdered. Arrests and murders continued throughout Anatolia (Üngör, 2015, p. 361). In September 1915, the CUP regime rolled out a new regulation that allowed them to seize Armenian wealth. According to Talat Pasha's documents, the Ottoman government took a total of 41,117 buildings throughout Anatolia (p. 362). The commodities that were confiscated from Armenians were sold to

Muslims for a meager price. The process of selling to Muslims allowed wealth to change hands. On May 23, 1915, Talat Pasha gave the official order for the deportation of all Armenians from Anatolia. Only a small number of Armenians avoided the deportations. The most violent events against Armenians took place in Erzurum, Van, Trabzon, Sivas, Mamuretulaziz, Adana, Diyarbakır, and Halep.

According to hundreds of oral stories from survivors, Turkish gendarmes "supposedly" protected Armenian deportation caravans; however, on many occasions, they enabled Kurdish attacks where they robbed, killed, raped, or kidnapped young women and children and brought them home as servants or wives. People even were stripped of their clothes and had to continue their walk naked. Hundreds of Armenian women committed suicide to escape rape. Mothers had to make unspeakable decisions, such as to leave a child behind, or give the last food they had to their children so they would live (D. E. Miller & Miller, 1993) Scattered, homeless Armenian orphans had to beg for food, trying to survive (Kharatyan-Araqelyan, 2010).

A few cities were able to slow down and hinder the deportations. Celal Bey in Konya, Hasan Mazhar Bey in Ankara, and Rahmi Bey in Izmir made conscious efforts to prevent them (Üngör, 2015). There are oral stories where the Turks and Kurds of Anatolia tried to protect and hide Armenians. Many homes took in children and young women so they could escape deportations. On one rare occasion, thousands of Armenians found refuge in Dersim, where the majority were Alevi Kurdish/Zaza populations (Kieser, 2019, p. 9).

One survivor's story from Donald Miller and Lorna Touryan Miller's (1993) oral history research with Armenians in diaspora exemplifies the unspeakable horror that many Armenians experienced during the genocide and how some survived (pp. 94–97). The survivor's name is Aghavni. She was an infant during the Hamidiye massacres in 1895 when her father was killed. Before the deportations began in 1915, Aghavni recalls many local Armenian politicians were imprisoned and hanged. Her husband, who was in the army, also was killed. Aghavni had only two days to prepare before she had to leave. Deported Armenians, accompanied by gendarmes, walked for seven months, up and down through mountains. Along the way, she lost her two children: one was three years old, the other just a baby. She lost all of her family members one by one—either by being drowned by a Turkish gendarme, being shot, having their throats cut, or other, horrific ways. She remembered women in their caravan being raped by the gendarmes at night. She witnessed hundreds of women committing suicide. She tried committing suicide herself, but one of the good gendarmes saved her. She remembered Kurds attacking their caravan and stealing any remains they had.

When she arrived in Der-Zor, a deportation area in Syria, she was emotionally, physically, and spiritually spent, starved and naked. She laid down on the bank of Euphrates River, ready to die. Two elderly Turks found her. They poked her, and when they realized that she was still alive, they took her home where the family and their servant's wife nursed her back to health. Many survivors like Aghavni survived insurmountable odds. Like Aghavni, many women lost their children, entire family, and meaning to their life. She survived, however, because someone cared for her. Several stories like this exemplify how children and young women lost their entire families and were taken into Muslim homes and lived. In some cases, Muslim homes cared for orphans like their own, but in most cases, they were servants. Some of those Armenians escaped their Muslim homes and went to Armenian orphanages that opened in Anatolia in the hope of finding their families and of not forgetting their heritage. Several others stayed and became Muslims. From these orphanages, many escaped to nearby countries and found further refuge in the diaspora. Unfortunately, in most cases, Armenians were deported, massacred, or died of starvation before they even arrived at their destinations.

The final genocidal events were forcing the remaining Armenians to leave their ethnic and religious identities, assimilate, and become Muslims (Üngör, 2015). Even though Talat Pasha later extended his deportation and massacre activities to those who had converted to Islam as well, some Armenian women and children who remained in Anatolia survived through assimilating. Young women were married to Muslim husbands and later assimilated to Turkishness. Orphan Armenian children who remained in Turkey were sent to orphanages or were taken in by Muslims. These orphanages changed their names, and forced Armenian children to speak Turkish and become Muslims. Over time, these children forgot their Armenian heritage and assimilated to Turkishness. According to Üngör, besides kidnapped women and orphaned Armenians, any who were able to survive did so in five different ways: either they used bribery, hid, ran away, survived out of luck, or they changed religion and became Muslims.

It is also essential to mention that right after 1917, the Ottoman's defeat in World War I, and the signing of the Sèvres agreement, with intentional help several organizations collectively called *vorpahavak* were opened. *Vorpahavak,* an Armenian word meaning "the gathering of orphans," attempted to rescue women and orphaned Armenians from Muslim homes (Ekmekçioğlu, 2013, p. 534). The Sèvres agreement had a clause that stated that the majority of Armenian populated areas could become an independent Armenian state. This clause also intensified *vorpahavak*'s efforts to find as many Armenians as possible to prevent them from being assimilated. Several Armenians left their Muslim homes this way and embraced their Armenian lineages; however, others—either by choice or force—

remained in their Muslim homes and were assimilated (Ekmekçioğlu, 2013).

The violent events between 1915 and 1917 specifically targeted Anatolian Armenians and their Armenian identity. Whether loyal to the Ottoman or not, or political or not, all Armenians became targets, which is why scholars argue whether the events that took place between 1915 and 1917 constituted a genocide.[7] To this day, the Turkish state has not acknowledged the collective violence against Armenians as genocide. Many Turkish scholars and government officials have argued that it was an organized displacement rather than genocide (e.g., Beyoğlu, 2004; Halaçoğlu, 2004; Laçiner, 2008). Internationally, intellectuals and scholars (e.g., Akçam, 2006; Bloxham, 2003, 2005; Dadrian, 1995; Göçek, 2015; Suny et al., 2011) say that throughout Anatolia, in 1915 and 1916, Armenians were forcibly deported from their ancestral land by the CUP/Young Turk government and that the mass killing of Armenians was the result of government and party action, with Armenian resistance being most notably present in Van in 1915 and minimal in the rest of Anatolia.

There is also a dispute among scholars about the number of Armenians that died in the course of the deportations: estimates range from as low as 200,000 to as high as 1.5 million,[8] with most scholars agreeing on at least 800,000 deaths. Approximately 300,000 Armenians were left in Anatolia. Today the Armenian population in Turkey is even less: approximately 50,000—and mostly concentrated in Istanbul (Pattie, 2004, p.133). The Armenian Genocide was a catastrophic loss for the Armenian people, and the ongoing denial by Turkey continues to haunt Armenian identities in Turkey, Armenia, and the diaspora. Turkey's continual denial of the Armenian Genocide and suppression of Armenian suffering in Turkey is, in contrast, strengthening Armenian loyalty to their collective memory of victimization and intensifying the divide between two narratives (Keshgegian, 2006).

During this time, not only Armenians but non-Muslim minorities across Anatolia fell victims. For example, in the old Greek Ottoman town Foçateyn (Eski Foça) near the Aegean coast, there was no apparent conflict between local Muslims and Ottoman Greeks. However, according to historian Emre Erol's (2013) research, in 1914, Ottoman Greeks had to flee their homes due to "organized chaos" orchestrated by CUP and attacks started by armed bands. Local security forces did not intervene, leaving Foçateyn residents to their fate. The homes and businesses of Ottoman Greeks were demolished. Due to the effects of the panic, people also died. Some sources reference local Muslims trying to protect their Greek neighbors' assets. Others argue how local Muslims also collaborated with armed attacks. According to Kerimoğlu's (2008) review of various resources, the number of refugees ranges between 98,552 and 200,000 (p. 316). Approximately

160,000 Ottoman Greeks from Western Anatolia became refugees and were forced to leave their homelands (Erol, 2015, p. 315).

Transgenerational Aspect of Armenian Genocide

Atrocities can cause extreme personal trauma for the individuals involved, whether victims, witnesses, or perpetrators. Ample research with Jewish Holocaust survivors evidenced both survivors' and generational transmission of trauma. Given the similarly devastating effects of the Armenian Genocide, it was surprising for me not to find much research about transgenerational trauma with Armenian Genocide survivors. An Armenian American theologian, the author of *Redeeming Memories: A Theology of Healing and Transformation*, Flora Keshgegian, during a conversation, suggested that the lack of transgenerational trauma research of Armenians might be because Armenians are very pragmatic. She suggested that after the genocide, they focused their energy on surviving and community building. Later on, the focus shifted to genocide recognition. More recently, there has been increased attention directed toward researching and discussing intergenerational trauma among descendants of survivors. Additionally, after Germany's defeat and post-war attention to the Jewish Holocaust, survivors had to submit proof of either physical or psychological injury in order to get compensation from the German government. The need to have a psychological assessment might have encouraged more Jewish people to visit psychiatric clinics, which might have provided a platform for more research as well (F. Keshgegian, personal communication, April 20, 2019). I summarize a few of the transgenerational trauma research studies with Armenian Genocide survivors mostly in diaspora in what follows.

Though the research I share in this section sheds important light on Armenian experiences, more research is required to fully understand the nuanced and complex ways in which trauma is transmitted from generation to generation. For instance, Keshgegian (2002), whose parents were genocide survivors, writes that growing up, she was immersed in a legacy of victimization but later, to her surprise, as she was emerging as a religious leader in the Episcopal Church and diverging from her Armenian religious community, her grandmother began sharing memories of women's leadership with her. She realized that both types of stories were being passed down to her—of victimization and strength. She asks: "What did it mean to remember on [my Armenian community's] behalf: was it victimization I was to remember or agency and leadership?" (p.15). Both perhaps, she concludes. Memories can be both a problem and a resource for people dealing with a history of victimization. Given the tendency to either emphasize victimization or the "overcoming" or denial of it, it is important to honor the suffering and yet remember what, albeit limited, agency people exercised in relation to it. This dynamic is not unique to Armenians, Keshgegian adds. Jews also question whether their remembrance should emphasize the victimization of the Holocaust or be able to name and claim their resistance and agency, even within victimization. Such acts of agency are not heroic, and given the circumstances they cannot be. Rather they are small actions that assert the strength of humanity and find ways to maintain life. This dynamic applies to African Americans as well: should they put an emphasis on remembering the horrors of slavery or claim the myriad ways they asserted their humanity and agency, such as communicating through song and planning escapes on the underground railroad. Or are both types of memory—stories—important to pass on?

For Keshgegian, trauma theory and the dynamics of recovery from it are important resources for understanding these issues. Others, examining the aftereffects of the Armenian Genocide, have also tried to understand Armenian Americans' responses to this traumatic past. Some have observed that, following the Armenian Genocide, Armenian survivors initially focused on rebuilding their lives and community. They spoke little of their experiences. During the Ottoman Empire, Armenians maintained their identity and security through family relationships, work, church, and schools. The importance of community prior to the genocide was also perhaps one reason why the (re)building of communities became vital in survivors' adaptation (L. Boyajian & Grigorian, 1998). Additionally, Armenian clinical psychologist and child psychotherapist Aida Alayarian (2008) writes that the "response of Armenians to the genocide was a traumatized silence, as survivors and spectators alike struggled to comprehend what they had witnessed" (p. 30). The totality of the catastrophe, irreparability, and irreversibility of the loss, and the feeling of being collectively attacked, were beyond the imagination of survivors and witnesses to comprehend and mourn; they were only able to express bits, pieces, and fragments of what happened.

> Indeed, everything can be said with human speech, everything can be understood, pardoned, accepted, even loved. Only one thing remains beyond all speech, beyond every power to integrate, beyond all human apprehension. This thing is not death, it is not murder or burned houses, it is not even extermination. It is the will to extermination . . . because it cannot be integrated into any psychological, rational, psychical explanation whatever. This is also why historical and political interpretations of the event, while they are always necessary, carry so little weight. They are at best contextual. They can never articulate the most profound experience, that of the stricken, of the infinite-undefinable, of the being trampled through several generations. (Nichanian, 2003, pp. 115–116)

After the initial shock, Armenians began to share their stories but rarely outside the context of their trusted community (Alayarian, 2008; Neyzi & Kharatyan-Araqelyan, 2010). This was not too different from Jewish Holocaust survivors' experience which Danieli called "Conspiracy of Silence"; they remained silent because the pain was too overwhelming, and they did not want to revisit their memories. When they could, they only shared their stories with family and community because they felt no one who had not gone through their experience would have understood what happened to them (Danieli, 1985). Armenian researchers argue that many of the psycho-social dynamics in effect in the Jewish experience are similar to Armenians', including anxiety, depression, compulsive associations to trauma-related material, guilt, nightmares, irritability, anhedonia, emptiness, and a fear of loving (K. Boyajian & Grigorian, 1982), additionally phobias, psychosomatic disorders, and severe personality changes occurred (Salerian, 1982). Studies consistently found trauma and stress-related symptoms among Armenian survivors and their descendants (K. Boyajian & Grigorian, 1982; Karenian et al., 2011; Kupelian et al., 1998; Kuzirian, 2012; Manoogian, 2018; Mouhibian, 2016; Salerian, 1982). One recent study found second and third-generation survivors experience difficulty coping with anger in forms of either avoiding, having a temper, projecting, or internalizing it. While some showed increased resilience, a majority carried a pessimistic and distrustful outlook on life.

Additionally, there are psychological consequences from the denial of Armenian suffering by the perpetrators. Unless a tragedy is understood and fully acknowledged, the denial of an atrocity of significant magnitude results in mistrust and holds the potentiality for similar future atrocities to occur (Alayarian, 2008; Manoogian, 2018). Denial reminds descendants of genocide survivors that they are still not safe. Multigenerational studies with Armenians in the diaspora consistently show that Armenians from all three generations (survivors, their children, and grandchildren) experience rage, anger, frustration, and stress due to Turkey's continual denial of the Armenian Genocide. Consequently, denial has interfered with survivors and their descendants' ability to mourn, process, and integrate their deeply painful history (Alayarian, 2008; Kay, 2015; Kupelian et al., 1998).

Furthermore, most Armenian Genocide survivors were children. When trauma is experienced in childhood, in a situation in which someone loses a caregiver, this person might carry historical burdens of rejection, denigration, persecution, and abandonment (Alayarian, 2008). The families, communities, traditions, and ways of life of these children were utterly destroyed. Therefore, Alayarian (2008) argues that widespread feelings of inadequacy, shame, and helpless rage were imprinted on Armenians' psychology, and these experiences were passed on to subsequent generations through silence and other adaptive behaviors.

One oral history book outlines an interview with Diyarbakır Armenian in Turkey. One of the descendants of a survivor described how fear has been passed down a generation and was shared amongst his uncles and father as well. His grandfather was afraid that the same things would happen to his family and would tell his grandchildren never to say, to anyone, that they were Armenians. There is a logical reasoning to this adaptation as well, given Armenians in Turkey are still not safe. Hiding their identity for an Armenian in Turkey is an understandable coping strategy. Raised with these warnings, his father shared similar fears and concerns. His grandfather, who was orphaned when he survived, would say, "It was so bad we forgot everything, including motherly and fatherly love" (Balancar, 2013, p. 59).

Along with the experience of transgenerational trauma symptoms, families exhibited avoidant attachment, anxious attachment, difficulty leaving family, and difficulty being autonomous and independent within the community. Armenians' shared-wounding experience brought communities closer. They lived split lives, though, whether in the diaspora, in Turkey, or in Armenia. Armenian communities navigated between their own intimate ones, where they were able to share their stories, where they were not paralyzed by the state of deep despair and muteness, and were able to weep, counsel one another, and grieve. Elsewhere—in the outside world—they hid their stories and identities. The emotional depth of Armenian wounding was initially unknown by outsiders which eventually changed in the 1960s in Armenia and in diaspora due to public demonstrations and commemorations.

The Turkish War of Independence of 1919–1923

After the loss of World War I (1914–1918), in 1920, the Treaty of Sèvres reduced the Ottoman's geography to the northwest and north-central parts of Anatolia. The Sèvres agreement established an independent Armenia with the promise of access to the Mediterranean Sea. With the European power's particular interest in Anatolia, the new Turkish state faced becoming a colony. Greece showed interest in Izmir and surrounding regions, Italy to the Antalya and Konya regions. France paid attention to the Adana, Antep, Urfa, and Mardin regions. British and France recognized independent states of the Arabia region, and these new Arabic states were subject to mandatory service. The newly emerging Turkish nationalist movement, under Muslimness unity, rejected the Sèvres treaty and declared what is now known as the Turkish War of Independence—which entailed suppressing local disturbances, conflicts, and even war in all four directions. The war on the Eastern Front secured today's north–east borders. The Greco-Turco war on the Western Front, the Franco-Turco war on the

Southern Front, and in Constantinople (now Istanbul), Turks fought British and Italian occupation—there was a lot going on.

Mustafa Kemal (Atatürk), the victor of the Gallipoli war of 1915 (Çanakkale), led an army that was mostly responsible for maintaining Ottoman order through Syria. He was ordered to suppress political and non-political banditry. The date Mustafa Kemal arrived in Samsun, May 19, 1919, is celebrated as his adjourning from the Ottoman army and beginning the Turkish independence struggle.

The new assembly had its first meeting in Sivas in 1919, where Mustafa Kemal had a key role. They believed that CUP was responsible for the loss of World War I, and swore that they would not revive Unionists; moreover, they agreed on the demand for an independent state (Faroqhi, 2009). Mustafa Kemal and his closest collaborators established themselves in Ankara in late 1919, which later became the capital. The first National Assembly was formed in 1920.

Göçek (2015) writes based on published memoirs:

The imperatives [of new nationalist movement] were to resist the Armenian armed bands, defend the Mediterranean and Black Sea shores in the event of an enemy attack, transport all arms and ammunitions out of the regions under Allied control, increase the number of soldiers in the battalions through recruitment, establish guerrilla units for emergencies, and prepare large buildings for destruction if necessary (p. 298)

Armed bands that were loyal to the Sultan and the Ottoman, ones that were loyal to the new nationalist movement, and others that were Armenian, Rum, and Greek all fought one another to establish their vision of Anatolia. This also aligned with my relative's story that I shared in the introduction. After almost dying in the hands of the Greek Army, my relative heard about the recruitment efforts and—filled with revenge—went to Ankara to join the Turkish army. They assigned him to fight for a Turkish band in Samsun by the Black Sea against the Rum bands.

One other important note to mention is that many who previously played a part in the Armenian Genocide or other war crimes, to avoid being tried by the British and their allies, took arms, joined bands, and fought for independence (Göçek, 2015). Most CUP leaders escaped to Europe. However, several members remained in Turkey.

After four years of struggle and success in their effort, the Republic of Turkey was born on October 29, 1923. However, people in Anatolia were living in war conditions from 1911 to 1923. In the end, the military was exhausted, and ordinary people's lives were completely disrupted.

Frederic Shorter (1985), who reviewed the Ottoman censuses before and after independence, writes,

The people of Turkey at the end of the War of Independence could hardly have imagined the long era of peace and national development that would follow. They had just been through more than a decade of struggle to survive against the odds of warfare abroad and at home, epidemics, and serious interferences with the normal material means of livelihood. Loss of life and permanent disability were legacies for many families of the 1911–1922 period. Practically every community was affected in some life-threatening way by the ambitions of outside powers and their local allies or by the last Ottoman campaigns (the Balkans, North Africa, Gallipoli, the Russian front, Mesopotamia, Palestine, and the Hejaz). Only the independence struggle itself finally resolved the issues of territoriality, governance, and the right to reside in peace. (p. 417)

The Lausanne Peace Treaty in 1923 established the boundaries of today's Republic of Turkey with one exception that the city of Hayat on the Syrian border joined Turkey's borders in 1939.

The Greco-Turkish War of 1920–1922

The Greco-Turkish War was one of the significant aftershocks in the wake of the first World War, and was one of the major fronts of the Turkish War of Independence (1919–1923). The Greco-Turkish War, which Greece lost, was a turning point for the new Turkish nationalist movement. The Greek government accepted the demand of the Turkish movement and returned to their pre-war borders (today's Greece), thus leaving Western Anatolia to the Turks. Turkey's victory was sealed with the Lausanne Peace Treaty of 1923. Based on this treaty, Greek and Turkish leaders agreed to engage in a population exchange between Ottoman Greeks who were Christians and Muslim Greeks/Turks.

> The convention for exchange of populations between Greece and Turkey (1923) stipulated reciprocal exchange of the Greek Orthodox population of Anatolia, except those residing in Istanbul, Imbros (Gökçeada), and Tenedos (Bozcaada), and the Muslims living in Greece, except those residing in Western Thrace. As a result, over a million Greeks immigrated to Greece from Anatolia and approximately a half million Muslims moved to Anatolia from Macedonia and Greece. The number of Greeks left in Istanbul is estimated to be about 100,000. (Şeker, 2012, p. 265)

Population exchanges between Ottoman Greeks and Greek Muslims was deeply disruptive and traumatizing for both. "1,250,000 Greek Rum left for Greece and 500,000 Muslims muhacirs 'returned' to Turkey" (Göçek, 2015,

p. 267). Minorities of both countries became refugees. To host and find housing and resources for almost 2 million people, Greece and Turkey both faced incredible challenges. Thousands of people who were ripped from their homelands were now homeless, hungry, and jobless (Selahattin & Abdullatif, 2017)

Following the Greco-Turkish War, both countries entered into their respective nation-building process. Historian Onur Yıldırım (2006) described that both countries, due to their top–down political nation-building ideologies, created different narratives. The Greek nation remembers the war as a catastrophic defeat, and their collective narrative carries wounding over the loss of Asia Minor. However, the Turkish nation, adopting forgetting politics, remembers the war as glorious, a process of unification, and the birth of independence for the Turkish nation—and silences its negative consequences. Vamık Volkan and Norman Itzkowitz (2000) reviewed the psychodynamics of both Turkish and Greek national identity evolution since the establishment of both Greek and Turkish nation states. They argue that the way each nation's identity differently evolved contributed to a lack of empathy for one another. Greek national identity and their historical trauma was first based on the loss of Constantinople in 1453 and then on Asia Minor and the Greco-Turkish War. The Greek collective narrative sees the loss of Constantinople as rape and Turks as lustful savages. The Turkish collective narrative silenced the wounding of almost half a million Muslim refugees. Only later generations in Turkey began to explore their Balkan ancestries, especially since the 1990s, when more academic research and memoirs began to emerge and challenge Turkey's politics of forgetting or epistemologies of ignorance.

In the aftermath of the Greco-Turkish War, the remaining Anatolian Christians either were massacred, deported, or fled to Greece and the Balkans. Ten thousand Greek Rums died on the way from epidemics and malnutrition (Selahattin & Abdullatif, 2017, p. 219). Zürcher (2003) argues because most shared the same religion and language with the existing residents and were skilled artisans or workers, most Christian migrants to Greece and the Balkans easily adopted and integrated into the economic structure. However, ethnographic studies show otherwise. According to anthropologist Renee Hirschon (1989), arriving Ottoman Greeks in Greece suffered from refugee syndrome and identity crisis. For example, Hirschon, in her ethnographic study five decades after the war, looked at the social life of Asia Minor refugees in Piraeus, a port city in the region of Attica, Greece. She argues that refugees fleeing Anatolia looked for ways to cope with the trauma of forced displacement. Memories of their lost homeland of Anatolia played a significant role in the ways in which they established their separate status as a refugee group within the population, even though most shared the same language and religion.

That said, the experiences were not uniform. Greek historian Giannuli Dimitra (1995) points out:

> Settlement in Greece was not a uniform experience for the approximately one million Ottoman Greeks who fled Turkey in the aftermath of the Greco-Turkish war of 1920–1922. Contemporary primary sources ranging from government reports to eyewitness accounts and memoirs of relief workers point to a mixed reality: while some Ottoman Greek refugees enjoyed hospitality and warm support upon arrival in Greece, many others found settlement in the new country a painful experience of material hardship, segregation, and status deprivation. The precarious circumstances of the massive exodus created the refugee drama. The inability of the Greek state to handle a crisis of such magnitude, along with serious incidents of refugee discrimination and exploitation by Greek officials and civilians, exacerbated the refugees' plight. (p. 271)

Dimitra summarizes that Ottoman Greek refugees were fleeing for their lives and had to abandon their homes and wealth in Anatolia. Their hasty and forced departure to Greece impoverished the refugees and seriously undermined their ability to overcome their trauma and hardships.

After the Armenian Genocide, Greco-Turkish War, and population exchange, there were barely any Armenians or Greek Rums left in Anatolia. Their absence left a large void that could never be filled. Anatolia's cultural diversity and economic balance was utterly destroyed. Most historical literature in Turkey does not cover the catastrophic effects of the Greco-Turco War and the population exchange that followed. Only recently have a few memoirs and oral history studies outlined the lives of Muslim refugees who were displaced. Third-generation Muslim migrants interested in their history and the recent emphasis on oral history and memoirs (also known as "memory from below") are beginning to challenge "top–down" created state narratives (Alpan, 2012, p. 199). The Ottoman Empire was diverse and yet differentiated in terms of each community's responsibilities that were separate from one another; nevertheless, they relied on each other. For example, Greek Rums who resided predominantly by the Aegean coast, occupied essential positions in trade and industry services. When they were forced to leave Anatolia, their absence threw off the economic balance of the entire west coast and central Anatolia.

Moreover, based on published memoirs, Göçek (2015) writes that during the Greco-Turkish War and after the Rums left, Greek homes were burned down, and businesses looted. When Muslim migrants arrived, they were sent to previously non-Muslim neighborhoods across Anatolia—some areas were untouched and left behind furnished—but in many cases buildings were demolished, and businesses closed or destroyed. Migrant Muslims, for the most part, had to start from ground zero (p. 268).

Migrants that arrived as part of the population exchange were often from rural areas and assigned to regions based on their skills. For example, tobacco growers were sent to Samsun, where the land was suitable for tobacco plants. Umut Düşgün (2017) analyzes some recent migrant novels and points out the discrimination migrant Muslims faced upon their arrival. Some Muslim migrants did not speak Turkish but shared the same religion as local Muslims. However, local Muslims perceived migrants' religious beliefs as not being strong enough. Migrants, dressed differently, spoke a different language, and their customs were different from local Muslims. Thus, locals saw them as "the other"—as "Greek" or "Rum." Muslim migrants faced discrimination, insults, and psychological violence which forced them to segregate within their neighborhoods and closed communities.

Moreover, local Muslims resented these newcomers. For example, one research study based on oral history points out that local Muslims in Izmir and the surrounding villages felt entitled to the newly empty non-Muslim properties. Local Muslims thought that they were the ones who had gone through the hardship of the war, and they were entitled to a reward. They wondered, "Who are these people coming and settling on their land?" Also, during war conditions, the lack of resources forced some rural people to sell parts of their land to non-Muslims for a low price. Seeing new migrants settle in their land that they not long ago sold for almost nothing caused a sense of additional resentment (Böke, 2006). Local Muslims called Muslim migrants "gavur," a word they used for non-Muslims. Gavur means "infidel" or "non-Muslim." Even though locals and migrants shared the same religion, migrants were discriminated against and seen as the "other," they experienced both resentment and nostalgia.

Despite all these local provincial difficulties, the newly formed Republic of Turkey also launched a large integration project to help migrants assimilate as part of its nation-building practices. In 1923, at the time when the Republic of Turkey was founded, over 20% of the population were *muhacirs* and Muslim migrants (Zürcher, 2003, p. 6). Migrants responded quickly by adapting to the Turkish language and secular ideologies. In the end, the readiness of Muslim immigrant communities to define themselves as Turks by appropriating Turkish culture and language became one of the essential factors that paved the way for the success of the formation of the new Turkish republic (Aydıngün & Aydıngün, 2004). In other words, Muslim refugees that arrived between the 1800s to mid-1900s and their willingness to adopt the new Turkish identity helped determine the success of the Turkish nation, the Republic of Turkey.

According to Volkan and Itzkowitz (2000), the Turkish elite—Atatürk and his followers who laid the foundation for modern Turkish identity—had two main psychological splits. The first split was between Turkish and Greek people. The new Turkish elite and leadership on the one hand, due to the Greco-Turkish war's legacy, saw Greece as an enemy; and on the other, due to Western policies and adaptations, they saw Greek people as the ideal, adapted from their mythology, and translated Greek books in to Turkish for the public to read. The second split was within the Turkish state. The Turkish elite considered Islamic fanaticism the leading cause of the demise of the Ottoman Empire. Due to their alignment with Western secular ideals, the Turkish elite saw themselves as the "enlightened ones," separating from the rest of the Muslim population in Anatolia. The paradoxical belief systems saw Greeks as the enemy *and* the ideal; moreover, self-critique of its Muslim communities added to the complexity of the evolution of modern Turkish identity.

The secular and Westernized Turkish image dominated its early years. Psychologically, Turkish society was in deep shock, and as a result—for decades to come—could not start mourning the loss of wars or other losses they endured during the collapse of the Ottoman Empire. After his death in 1938, Atatürk's body was preserved (embalmed) and not buried for 15 years. The new state immortalized Atatürk (Volkan & Itzkowitz, 1984). The people needed this process to help deal with their immense loss and also to help the transition from the old Ottoman identity to a new national one. Volkan and Itzkowitz (2000) further argue:

> When the Ottomans joined the ranks of the losers in the First World War, there was so much loss and grief among the Turks of the Empire it was said that walking through the streets of Istanbul one could hear nothing but the sorrowful voices of mothers who had lost their sons during this and the preceding Balkan Wars. But after the Turkish war of Independence, the Turks' idealization of Atatürk and his vision of modern Turkey kept them from grieving further over the loss of the Empire. They felt adequately compensated for their losses by having gained something good—a charismatic leader. As long as Atatürk's grand image could be maintained, to have lost an empire was nothing. In fact, Atatürk's image emerged as the sacred symbol of new Turkishness. (p. 241)

In the end, due to the focus on the future and re-building of a new nation, the new Turkish state did not adequately address the wounding of the past. It erased both victimhood and the perpetration of violence and did not consciously work on healing from collective and historical traumas. Seeing the West as the enemy caused Turks' paranoia about outside interference. At the same time, the modern Turkish society idealized the West and projected inferiority within itself (e.g., targeting Ottoman symbolism, royalty, and other traditional and conservative segments of the population). The new Turkish society projected the enemy within itself (and from the outside) entered into new traumatic sequences with self-destructive behaviors and paranoia about manipulation from outside allies on internal affairs.

The Consequences of the New Nation's Turkification agenda

As the CUP government was organizing their movement, individuals and small groups were also mobilizing their own. Their political ideology emphasized Muslim solidarity and turned against both European innovation and the Ottoman Christians inside the Ottoman Empire.

> Between 1924 and 1925, shortly after Muslim solidarity won the Greco-Turkish war and the Republic of Turkey was founded, the Muslimness Contract was modified from above, with [founder and leader of the new state] Mustafa Kemal Atatürk and his followers narrowing it down and Turkifying it. (B. Ünlü, 2016, p. 399)

The new state launched further manipulation projects, which Şeker identified as demographic engineering—a project that aimed to promote and maintain one national identity.

Şeker (2007) defines demographic engineering as "any deliberate state program or policy originating from religious/ethnic discrimination or initiated for political, strategic or ideological reasons which aim to increase the political and economic power of one ethnic group over others by manipulating population through various methods" (p. 461). Nesim Şeker's analysis was based on the four main reasons why the CUP believed that the only way to preserve the Ottoman state was the creation and maintenance of an exclusive Turkish identity. The first was due to the CUP government's failure to prevent the disintegration and territorial losses of the empire. The second was their inability to establish an Ottoman identity. Thirdly, the CUP wanted to eliminate the emerging global nationalist movement that had begun with the French revolution in the late 18th century and its growing influence in Anatolia. Lastly, was the Ottoman's failure to end the great European power interventions in Ottoman internal affairs, mainly targeting considerable numbers of the non-Muslim population in Anatolia. The CUP's Turkification policy of Anatolia was successful in the sense that they were able to execute a full-scale demographic engineering processes that led to the creation and maintenance of the new Turkish nation state.

Eventually, the Ottoman Empire fell, and with Mustafa Kemal (Atatürk)'s leadership, the Republic of Turkey was born in 1923. While the foremost leaders of the CUP fled, many CUP leaders and members helped establish the new nation. Despite the ethnic and cultural diversity in the region, the Republic of Turkey promoted one national language (Turkish) and one sole religion (Sunni Islam) and sought to create a Turkish national identity to unite people under the umbrella of a new homogeneous nation-state.

However, new and re-occurring conflicts also emerged with its implementation due to Turkey's continued multi-ethnic and multi-religious social map. For example, the new state did not recognize the place of the Kurdish ethnopolitical population. Kurds made up the majority of Eastern Anatolia, especially after the near-complete removal of Armenians. Kurdish tribes wished to have an autonomous region to be able to continue the expression of their identities, language, religion, and customs and build a dual-ethnic (Turkish and Kurdish) nation together. The first conflict, the Sheikh Said rebellion, arose when the Kurds, who were Sunni Muslims following the Shari'a rite, conflicted with the secular ideologies of the Turkish nation state. At first, this conflict was assumed to be a religious-based rebellion but was later understood as more than that (van Bruinessen, 1992). The Sheikh Said rebellion was in reaction to the exclusion of the Kurdish ethnopolitical place in the new Turkish state. Despite the Kurds' support and solidarity with Turks during the independence war, Kurdish ethnic identity was dismissed at the state level.

CHAPTER
3
The Collective Traumas After the Formation of the Republic of Turkey

As I reviewed in the previous chapter, after the loss of World War I (1914–1918), the already reduced Ottoman Empire faced becoming a colony. In 1920, the Treaty of Sèvres, signed between the victorious allied powers and representatives of the Ottoman Empire, recognized both Armenian and Kurdish ethnicities as having their autonomous regions (Brown, 1924). However, the Aegean coast surrounding Izmir was occupied by Greece and other territories of Anatolia were also divided between the French, British, and Italian Zones, severely limiting Turkish independence. Though Kurdish nationalism was beginning to emerge in the early 1900s, Kurds at the time more strongly recognized their Muslim identities. With the expectation of gaining an autonomous Kurdish region with a sense of belonging to the empire and the Caliphate (Muslim community), Kurds fought side by side with other fellow Muslims in Anatolia (van Bruinessen, 1992). The emerging Muslim solidarity denied the Treaty of Sèvres and, after declaring and winning what is today now known as the Turkish War of Independence (1919–1923), established its boundaries based on Lausanne Peace Treaty that took place in 1923.

The Lausanne Peace treaty was the final step that declared the closure of World War I. After a seven-month conference in Switzerland, the treaty was signed on one side by a representative of Turkey (a successor of the Ottoman Empire), and by the British Empire, France, Italy, Japan, Greece, Romania, and the Kingdom of Serbs, Croats, and Slovenes on the other. Political scientist and human rights advocate Daskın Oran (2007) writes that in the Lausanne Peace Treaty,

> Turkey has employed a very narrow definition of "minority" [instead of considering race, religion, and language, it recognized only "non-Muslims" as minorities] and used it to limit the applicability of the rights

articulated. . . . Even the rights of non-Muslim minorities that were recognized by the state, have been continuously violated. (p. 36)

Most Armenians were already expunged from Eastern and Central Anatolia by 1920 due to Armenian deportations and the Armenian massacres (also called the Armenian Genocide). The majority of residents in the Eastern Anatolia regions were Kurdish tribes, and their leaders were not pleased with Turkish nationalism and the results of the Sèvres Treaty in terms of their autonomous state. Kurdish tribes who fought side by side with the Turkish army had a prior agreement with Turkish generals that Kurds and Turks were going to create a republic together. The Lausanne Peace Treaty did not include Kurdish input, and the state did not fully honor Sunni Muslim, Kurdish, or Alevi cultural and ethnic rights. Oran (2007) writes,

Kurds' objection to the minority reference [in the Lausanne Peace Treaty] stems from different concerns. (1) Minority classification would be a degradation by the Ottoman millet system which considered the Muslims as the sovereign nation: and the minorities (non-Muslims) as second-class citizens. (2) Kurds are one of the two founding peoples of the Republic of Turkey; the war of Independence was fought together with Turks, but later the Kurdish input was dismissed. And most importantly, (3) Kurdish nationalists consider themselves to be a "people," rather than a minority— this approach, in international legal theory, would place them in a category much closer to external "self-determination" (independence). (p. 44)

Turkey's signature on the Lausanne Peace Treaty and the new state's blatant dismissal of the Kurdish ethno-political place resulted in about 30 local rebellions (Aras, 2014). Kurds resisted the shift from Turks and Kurds building a republic together to a Turkish-only nation state. The Sheikh Said (Muslim-Kurdish) rebellion (1925) and the resistance in Dersim (Alevi) (1937) were the strongest and had the most severe violent reactions from the state. Rebellions were brutally suppressed and were followed by deportation, executions, forced resettlement, and massacres. The new state saw the majority of Muslim or Alevi Kurds as potential "Turks" and launched Turkification and, therefore, assimilation projects. Collective violence continued against Anatolian Christians, which is explored chronologically in this chapter.

During the process of forming the Republic of Turkey, the state erased perpetration and victimhood narratives and rewrote a Turkish nationalist one in hopes of binding the entire nation together. They were successful in a way, as the Republic of Turkey was born. However, the erasure of atrocities and victimhood of Turks during the creation and maintenance of the

Turkish state created epistemologies of ignorance in the society, which continues to inflict collective pain and suffering to this day.

In addition to 30 different Kurdish rebellions that took place in Anatolia following the formation of the Republic of Turkey, at least 150 conflict groups emerged in the 1920s and 1930s who disagreed with the state on political, social, or cultural basis.[1] At the time, Kurdish people did not have one distinct "nationalist" identity that united them. Kurdish people were attached to their families, tribes, and villages, and firmly to Islam or their religious leader. Rebellions across Kurdistan remained limited to their geographic scope and elicited little sympathy from other parts of the region. Furthermore, according to Martin van Bruinessen (1998), the suppression of these rebellions in the 1920s marked the beginning of the Turkish nation-building processes.

Today, Kurdish intellectuals criticize the lack of support between tribes based on sects of religions as the reason why the rebellions were not successful (Aras, 2014). However, Kurdish ethnic identities and their imminent diversity set an excellent example for the complexity of ethnic identifications and the limitations of national identities that deny that complexity. Historically Alevis and Sunni Muslims politically diverged. Sheikh Said and his followers were Sunni Kurds. Dersimis, (people of Dersim, *Dersimli*) as being Alevis, did not associate with the Sheikh Said rebellion, which used religion as their vehicle. Van Bruinessen (1996) writes that some Kurdish Alevi tribes fought against the Sheikh Said rebels. Likewise, other Sunni Muslim Kurdish tribes did not support them, and they remained silent to the Dersim rebellion. Furthermore, the Turkish state secularization process made the gradual emancipation of the Alevis possible. In light of the complexity of the internal dynamics of Anatolian Kurds, the first two major Kurdish rebellions and their extreme suppression by the state were the first two collectively traumatic experiences of the post-Republic of Turkey period.

Sheikh Said Rebellion of 1925

Significant works have been published about the Sheikh Said Rebellion. For example, Martin van Bruinessen's (1992) seminal book *Agha, Shaikh, and State* and Robert Olson's (1989) book *The Emergence of Kurdish Nationalism and the Sheikh Said Rebellion* went into great detail describing the dynamics. According to van Bruinessen, after the definite establishment of Turkish nationalism with Mustafa Kemal (Atatürk)'s leadership, Kurdish nationalist organizations ceased their activities in Istanbul and Syria. In 1923, in Erzurum, Kurdistan/Eastern Turkey, Kurds with military and militia backgrounds founded a Kurdish organization called Azadi

(Freedom). Some of the members of the Hamidiye regiments who fought in the front line with the Turkish army were not pleased with the shift in the direction from the "Muslimness contract" to secular ideologies of the Republic; thus, they also supported this rebellion.

Azadis foresaw sheikhs (religious leaders) as central to the rebellions and co-operated with them. Van Bruinessen (1992) argues the reasoning behind this considered the sheikh's considerable financial means. For example, Sheikh Said and his family were very wealthy from large scale animal trade. Secondly, the sheikh's participation would give the rebellion a religious appearance, which then would attract more support; Sunni Kurds were religiously motivated. Additionally, Azadis wanted to take advantage of the divide within the Turkish government. There was also a divide within the state, where the conservative half were not happy with the divergence from religious values. Thirdly, the sheikh's perceived respect and traditional role in mediation and conflict resolution, which could ensure unity and co-operation among different tribes. In fact, many sheikhs commanded four of the five rebel fronts. The leader of the revolt, Sheikh Said, was a Naqshbandi sheikh with great influence who oversaw the entire operation.

The influence and mobilization of tribes was relatively successful. However, the Turkish government realized that a Kurdish rebellion was underway and arrested some of the critical leaders, which caused a modification in the plan. Sheikh Said emerged as the primary leader and the influencer. On February 8, 1925, a minor event caused a premature start of the rebellion. Quickly getting out of control, sheikhs and leaders had to make the best out of the situation, and the Sheikh Said Rebellion started in February in Northeastern Anatolia Kurdistan region and lasted for about three months. Sheikh Said was caught two months after the revolt started, on April 15. The state declared the law on the reinforcement order (*Takrir-i Sükûn Kanunu*) and the establishment of special independence tribunals (Istiklal Courts), which granted the government extraordinary powers for two years.

At first, the rebellion was successful and secured major cities, such as Diyarbakır and advanced near Malatya (toward central Anatolia). By the end of March, the Turkish army was able to deploy, through the railroad, over 35,000 well-armed men in Syria. Air forces continuously bombed rebels. When realizing the seriousness of the rebellion, Mustafa Kemal (Atatürk) personally became involved and asked several Kurdish tribe leaders to join Turkish military forces, which many did, and sent forces to the Diyarbakır front. Those Kurds that joined managed to avoid real confrontation, and a few others only attacked when it was clear that the rebellion was not going to be successful. The Turkish army created a closed circle around Diyarbakır to stop rebels from escaping. After violent battles, the rebels decided to break large tribal armies into smaller guerrilla warfare groups who could have escaped the military ring—which several did to Iran. Sheikh Said was caught when crossing the Murat River north of Muş on his way to Iran. A dissident chieftain had betrayed them. Guerrilla soldiers who were able to escape continued their activities for a few more years leading up to the Ararat revolt, culminating in 1929–1930.

Van Bruinessen (1992) writes:

> The reprisals [of the Sheikh Said rebellion] were extremely brutal. Hundreds of villages were destroyed, thousands of innocent men, women, and children killed. . . . Thousands of less influential Kurds were slaughtered without a trial. The population of entire district were deported to the west. The role of the sheikhs in the uprising was, moreover, the reason for a law ordering the closure of all tekiyes, tombs and other places of pilgrimage. (pp. 290–291)

After the Sheikh Said rebellion, it was clear to the state that Kurds were resisting the new Turkish national identity and modernity. In response, the Turkish state declared the Orient Reform Plan (*Şark Islahat Planı*) right after the rebellions in 1925. This plan outlined the assimilation projects, which included the importance of education, boarding schools, and the prohibition of the Kurdish language.

Istiklal courts, or "independence courts," were one of the immediate steps of the state's Orient Reform Plan. In the Istiklal courts, citizens who were found guilty under this court and sentenced to death were quickly executed, with no due process. "The intent [was] to "legally" try and punish all those who either criticized or objected to the independence struggle" (Göçek, 2015, p. 326). Göçek (2015) writes, based on oral history, that many judges in the independence courts did not necessarily have legal training. With Sheikh Said, 47 of his followers were executed by "independence courts" in Diyarbakır on September 4, 1925.[2] Executions included several who had no connection to the rebellion whatsoever.

At first, academia referred to the Sheikh Said rebellion as religious, but after a closer look, it became apparent that the revolt was more than religiously motivated. The state's secular agenda conflicted with Kurdish tribal, religious and traditional values, and customs. Abolition of the caliphate in March 1924 made the shift apparent for Kurds, which is why van Bruinessen (1992) argues this was the main signal of the end of the brotherhood between Kurds and Turks (p. 281). He adds that in 1924, not quite yet strategically, but the state did begin to tighten laws and regulations on Turkish nationalism. After the abolishment of the caliphate (religious order), the state took measures to restrict the Kurdish language from being spoken in public places. In the name of the abolishment of feudalism, influencing *aghas* (landowners) and intellectuals were sent to Western Turkey in exile; in some places, landlords' lands were redistributed among Turkish-speaking people and *muhacirs*, migrants from Balkans and Greece. Van Bruinessen (1992) writes that the explicit aim of the Sheikh Said rebellion was for Kurdish leaders and Azadis to establish an independent Kurdish state, where they believed the Islamic principles that were violated in modern Turkey were to be respected; a place where Kurdish people could continue to express their large group identities, and the Kurdish leaders, landlords, and Sheikhs remain in their power.

Ethnic and religious elements motivated both the majority Sunni Muslim Kurmanji and Zazaki-speaking Kurdish *ulema* (class of Islamic scholars) and notables, which mobilized them to stand against the new Republic of Turkey. Because the majority of Kurds were religiously motivated, religion became the focus, while ethnic resistance was also a vital element of the rebellion that operated in the background.

Following the suppression of the rebellion, hundreds of families of rebels were displaced and resettled in the western region of Turkey, where most Turks lived. Several supporters took shelter in neighboring countries, such as Iran, Iraq, and Syria. The displacement of Kurdish tribes and disarming them, in contrast, catalyzed further rebellions in the following years (Orhan, 2012). The remaining members of Sheikh Said's family were separated and sent to live in exile in the western parts of Turkey, where they lived apart from each other in refugee conditions under military control. Abdulmelik Fırat, Sheikh Said's grandson, was raised in exile; his life story describes their family's refugee experience and their sentimental reunion with family members when, finally, they were allowed back in their homes in 1947 when the Compulsory settlement law was declared (Ferzende Kaya, 2003; Fırat, 1996).

Stories of exiled families portray their struggle, and children's trauma of witnessing violence against their parents in the hands of the military, and how the pain and yearning of home imprinted on their life stories (Diken, 2005). Ramazan Aras (2014), in light of memoirs and life stories of exiles writes:

> Their testimonials emerge, on the one hand, as stories of suffering, both subjectively and collectively: they are stories of who they are and their sense of belonging to an oppressed community and history. Their stories tell us how exiled families survived with the burden of "who they are" and the stigma of "traitors of the state" (*vatan hainleri*), which traumatized these families. These kinds of stigmas would later be generalized for all members of the Kurdish community. On the other hand, their memoirs present stories of familial and communal cooperation, a sense of unity and belonging, a shared history and destiny. (pp. 53–54)

Therefore, the authors argue the suppression of the Sheikh Said rebellion, the exile of families, and further assimilation policies marks one of the first turns of Kurdish nationalism and Kurd's collective memory.

The Dersim Massacres of 1937–1939

The collectively traumatic events that took place in Dersim between 1937 and 1939 consist of the Dersim rebellions, the military's brutal suppression, massacres, forced resettlement, detaining and giving orphans and other children to Turkish families as adoptees, and further assimilation policies. The public often refers to these events as "Dersim 38." The army intervened in 1937 to initially "suppress/prevent" Dersim rebellions and yet military interventions were "not merely the brutal suppression of an internal rebellion but part of a wider policy directed against the Kurds" (van Bruinessen, 1994, p. 2). Therefore, van Bruinessen (1994) refers to these events as ethnocides that targeted the destruction of the Kurdish identity. Other scholars and activists have referred to the destructive military intervention and what followed in Dersim between 1937 and 1939 as a genocide because they targeted Kurds as a whole, and aimed to destroy tribes and their distinct culture (İ. Beşikçi, 1990; Dersimi, 1997; Üngör, 2008; Watts, 2000; M. Yıldız, 2014). Nevertheless, military operations that began on May 4th, 1937, and continued until 1939 were the most systematic and destructive massacre of the post-Republican period of Turkey (McDowall, 2004).

According to Turkish official documents, Dersim 38 claimed over 13,160 Dersimis' lives (Aslan, 2010, pp. 398–402; Kieser, 2006). However, numbers are believed to be much higher. Approximately 10% of the entire population of Dersim vanished (van Bruinessen, 1994, p. 6.) Thousands of detained survivors, including women, children, and the elderly, were forcibly exiled from Dersim to populated cities, the majority of which were Turkish, in western and central Anatolia, such as Ankara, Konya, Eskisehir, and Izmir. Detained orphans and other children were given to Turkish families in other parts of Turkey as adoptees. Many of these children assimilated to their new ways of living, while also being aware of their difference—they were from Dersim. If they were young enough and did not have any other living relatives, most of the children completely assimilated and forgot about their lineage. In 1939, the state-appointed government officials who did not have prior knowledge and understanding of the cultural diversity of Dersim. Government officials who were ignorant of Dersim's political and cultural past foresaw assimilation, civilization, and modernization policies in schools and other government institutions.

Until the 1990s in Turkey, the public knew very little about the dark period of Dersim 38. During the 1980s, there was an opening in awareness due to social movements, immigration, technology, and Turkey's interest in joining the European Union. Dersimis, as part of the minority movement in Turkey, also increasingly started to explore and share what took place in Dersim 38; they first spoke out within underground Kurdish communities, and later in the 1990s, publications, music, and other media more widely exposed this information with the public. One of the first studies that looked at the Dersim Massacres was by a Turkish scholar Ismail Beşikçi; his book was titled *Dersim Jenosidi* and was first published in 1990. Beşikçi's book was quickly banned, and he was imprisoned for writing it. Since then, despite the state's silencing efforts, another widely referenced book about Dersim Massacres is from a more Kurdish nationalistic view: Dr. Nuri Dersimi's (1997) book, *Kurdistan Tarihinde Dersim* [Dersim in the History of Kurdistan]. Dersimis published countless books and memoirs, wrote and performed folk songs, made documentaries, conducted research, and through other creative ways, shared their experiences with the world.

Dersim (Tunceli) is a region in Eastern Anatolia/Kurdistan with predominantly Kurdish and Zaza Alevis and some Armenian populations. During the Ottoman Empire, Dersim was a broader region and also consisted of some parts of the cities of Elazığ, Malatya, and Erzincan. After the Republic of Turkey was formed, the administration reduced Dersim's borders to a smaller district. In January 1936, the Law in Administration of the Tunçeli province officially changed the name Dersim to Tunçeli (which was also the name of the military operation) (İ. Beşikçi, 1990).

Dersim means "silver gate" in Zazaki (M. Yıldırım, 2012). There are various arguments about its origin. Some claim Dersim means "the gate of Kurdistan" (Dersimi, 1997), and others claim it was a name of a tribe that lived in the region (Zelyut, 2010). Contemporary Dersimi intellectuals argue otherwise. They say the region's historical name was Dêsim, which means "inside the castle" or "an island"; originated due to the region's geographic location surrounded by mountains (M. Yıldırım, 2012). Because of this geographic isolation, Dersimis have had a distinct culture from neighboring regions.

In Turkish, Tunçeli is "land of (*eli*) bronze (*tunc*)" or it could also be translated as an "iron fist." Most of the Tunceli residents and the descendants I met or whose academic articles I read overwhelmingly still use the older name "Dersim" while referring to the current geographic borders of Tunçeli.

Dersimis are the majority of the Alevi faith. Alevi is the second largest religion in Turkey, believed to be approximately 15% of the overall population today (Alemdar & Çorbacıoğlu, 2012, p. 118). Alevi is a blanket term for a large number of heterodox communities, including Azerbaijani Turkish-speaking Alevis in Kars province, people who follow "orthodox"

Twelver Shi'ism of modern Iran, and Arabic-speaking Alevis, especially in Hatay and Adana.

> The [majority of] Alevi groups [in Turkey] are the Turkish and Kurdish speakers (the latter still to be divided into speakers of Kurdish proper and of related Zaza); both appear to be the descendants of rebellious tribal groups that were religiously affiliated with the Safavids. (van Bruinessen, 1996, pp. 9–10)

Alevis settlements are found throughout Anatolia, including the Aegean and Mediterranean coasts. The majority of Alevis live in central Anatolia, concentrated in the northwestern part of the Kurdish settlement zone. Dersim has been a cultural center and settlement of mostly Zazaki-speaking Alevis (Kırmanç). Dersimis have a distinct culture from the rest of the Kurds in Kurdistan because they speak Zaza, are Alevis, and live away from the rest of the Kurdish populations, who are mostly Sunni Muslims.

Dersim was an autonomous region during the Ottoman Empire. After the formation of the Republic of Turkey, with additional laws and regulations, such as the Resettlement (*Iskan Kanunu* Law No. 2510) on June 13, 1934, and the declaration of the 1935 Tunceli (Dersim) law, the state intensified Turkification and modernization processes that further bothered tribes that had historically been autonomous and only followed their own tribal laws. Van Bruinessen (1994) writes, "Tribal chieftains and religious leaders wielded great authority over the commoners, whom they often exploited. They were not opposed to the government as such, as long as it did not interfere too much in their affairs" (p. 2). Dersimis strengthened their autonomous position by establishing close relationships with military and police officers.

Disputes between tribes were common. The men carried firearms, and when there was an armed dispute between tribes, at times local military officials would be drawn into tribal conflicts. During the first years of the republic, like the rest of Anatolia, the district was desperately poor, but they kept their relationship with the state. The young men carried out their military obligations to the state; in fact, van Bruinessen (1994) argues that by 1935, a considerable number of men had already served in the Turkish army.

One of the Dersimi tribes' Koçgiri resistance (*halk hareketi*) and its suppression in 1925 was the first sign of armed intervention in the region. By the mid-1930s, Dersim was still not under central government control—the last region the new Turkish state did not have control over. In 1935, to bring centralization and modernization, the Turkish military moved in. Explicitly, the declaration of the 1935 Tunceli (Dersim) law authorized military rule in Dersim.

It is important to understand that not long before, Dersim tribes and the Turkish army were a coalition. Tribes fought side by side with the Turkish army during the independence war. Dersimi tribes, being mostly Alevi, had suffered from Sunni Muslim's oppression during the Ottoman Empire. Specifically, Dersimis were looking advantageous to the new state's secular ideologies and they aligned themselves with the state hoping to build a secular nation together. However, the Turkish state's modernization agenda had an assimilative attitude, even for Alevi Dersimis. Therefore, noticing the state's current agenda, tribes' response to the modernization, consisting of roads, bridges, and police posts, were equivocal. Some tribes aligned themselves with the state's modernization projects, others were ambiguous, and still others resisted because the new laws and regulations conflicted with their traditional tribal laws and belief systems. They did not want to change the culture, dynamics, and ways of living in Dersim, and therefore resisted.

Atatürk, in 1936, announced:

If there is one important internal matter, that is the Dersim matter. In order to cleanse this wound, remove this terrifying abscess from its roots, we shall do whatever it takes, and give full authority to the government to make the most urgent decisions. (Dersimi, 1997, pp. 255–256; author's translation)

The book titled *Tunçeli Medeniyete Açılıyor* [Tunceli is Opening for Civilization] (Uluğ, 2007) also exemplifies Atatürk's and Turkish nationalist ignorant perspective of how the administration saw the military intervention as necessary to modernize and civilize a region that was perceived backward, sickly, and rebellious. From the perspective of the state, the conflict was between feudal control seeking bandits in Dersim and the modern ideologies of the republic.

The Turkish state had a biased perception of Kurdish people as backward, tribal, and traditional. In reality, there appear to be core value differences between Kurdish tribal law and the new state law in execution. Hence, the state chose to eliminate anything that was opposed to their future vision. The state has used these false perceptions as a justification to launch military operations to take control of a region that was historically autonomous and would not easily comply. Calling Dersimis bandits also dehumanized them in a way that illustrated Dersimi as people not being worthy of negotiation.

In March 1937, in reaction to the state's increasing pressure, pacification, assimilation, and modernization policies, the Demanan, Haydaran, Abbasan, and Koçan tribes actively and Kalan tribe (partially) resisted. Seyit Rıza, the most influential leader of the Abbasan tribe, a 72-year-old cleric, led this last major Kurdish rebellion. Van Bruinessen (1996) highlights that only five tribes out of 100 were actively engaged in the resistance. Aras (2014) writes there were approximately 60 tribes in Dersim at the time, and does not specify how many tribes were involved. Nevertheless, the authors agree on the disproportional reaction of the state's extensive brutal suppression.

At the time, the state feared that a more significant rebellion could be underway and disproportionately intervened in an otherwise minor incident in March 1937. During the Dersim Massacres, more than 13,000 men, women, and children lost their lives and thousands were displaced. Displaced people were sent away via trains in less than ideal conditions. The documentary and book *Kara Vagon* [Dark Train Compartment] by Özgür Fındık, describes the inhumane conditions during transportation with no food, no blankets, no toilets, or breaks; people traveled in unsterile conditions.

In the process, even the tribes that were known for their support of the current state were massacred, and their villages were utterly destroyed. Van Bruinessen (1994) argues, based on official reports, that the Ankara administration—and the public through media—were aware of the massive military operation in Dersim; however, it appears they were not fully aware of its great extent.

The irony is that the leader of the rebellion, Seyit Rıza, fought side by side with the Ottoman army against Russia. Before the republic was formed, the government had granted Seyit Rıza a military title and a medal honoring his service (Cengiz, 2010, p. 305). However, the coin flipped after the formation of the Republic of Turkey, and in order to retain power and control of the region and due to ideological and national conflicts in the eye of the Turkish state, Seyit Rıza became an "enemy" to be eliminated.

The violence was unprecedented. Military attacks were from both land and air. What is more, Atatürk's adopted daughter Sabiha Gökçen was one of the pilots that attacked Dersim in 1938, and her participation was proudly announced in newspapers portraying a model of a progressive, modern woman inspiring Turkish nationalism amongst all women in Turkey (Olson, 2000). Van Bruinessen (1994) summarizes,

> The army had its warrant for intervention. The first troops, sent in to arrest the suspects, were stopped by armed tribesmen. The confrontations soon escalated. When the tribes kept refusing to surrender their leaders, a large campaign was mounted. Military operations to subdue the region lasted throughout the summer of 1937. (p. 143)

At the time, Seyit Rıza was receiving pressure within his tribe too. They thought if he had surrendered, then perhaps the government would stop their military operations. By then, Seyit Rıza had already lost most of his family members. The date of Seyit Rıza's capture and how he was captured have conflicting narratives. Oral history has it that through the Erzincan governor, Seyit Rıza was trying to communicate their terms and negotiate a cease-fire. With a promise of a constructive conversation, Seyit Rıza arrived in Erzincan, but instead of a meeting, he was captured (Dersimi, 1997). Van Bruinessen (1994) writes that Seyit Rıza and his closest associates surrendered in September. Only a couple months after their capture, in November 1937, Seyit Rıza with his son and five other rebels were hanged. Despite rebel capture or surrender the next spring, the operations resumed with even greater force to thoroughly cleanse Tunceli of tribes (Watts, 2000). Military personal, such as the Erzurum army corps commander Tevfik Pasha, who wanted to follow a more humane approach and was against the brutal military intervention, were quietly removed from their positions and sent back to Ankara (Dersimi, 1997).

The second phase of attacks began in February 1938. The army searched and checked every corner of Dersim during these operations. Women and children who were hiding in caves were not exempt. Based on oral history, eyewitnesses, retired state official Ihsan Sabri Çağlayangil's account, and the way maps and caves were marked up—there is a strong argument that the military used poisonous gas to suffocate women and children hiding inside the caves. Soldiers killed the ones who ran outside. The military massacred thousands of people and burned down villages, food stocks, fields, and other property. Oral accounts describe that when civilians were trying to hide, they passed over piles of dead bodies, and remember the smell of blood.

Detained women and children were forcibly resettled to western and central Turkish regions (Aras, 2014). One of the widely shared book projects by Nezahat Gündoğan and Kazım Gündoğan (2012), called *Dersim'in Kayıp Kızları* [Lost Girls of Dersim], portrays 150 stories of lost young girls who were detained from their families and given away to Turkish officials, armed forces members, and other Turkish families as adoptees. Oral accounts from Gündoğan and Gündoğan's interviews revealed that most children were given as servants/helpers to either middle- or upper-class families who had strong Turkish nationalist views. The aim was for these children to forget or never learn about their Alevi Kurdish upbringing, and assimilate to Turkishness. A substantial number of girls and boys were sent to orphanages where nationalist propaganda and education was instilled to all the children. In her memoir, Sıdıka Avar, the principal at the Elazig vocational school for girls, describes the Turkification process. She called young girls "my mountain flowers." She followed a more humane approach than many of the other personnel in the school. Her sense of protection and care comes across in her words. For example, she was against the detainment of young women without their will, so she went from home to home, trying to influence Dersim families to send their children to the school. However, in her words, it is also clear that she had a genuine belief that modernization and education were for the good of the children. Avar (1986) was influenced by the school system and belief in the new nation; therefore, she was ignorant of the damage of assimilation on these young people and their communities.

Based on Gündoğan and Gündoğan's (2012) work, in most homes that detained young girls, children were well nourished and taken care of. However, again, they were far from "being saved." Young women worked as servants or as potential future wives to the man in the family. Families did not send them to school; in some cases, girls were able to get a Quranic education. The stories from some of the homes portray the abuse and sexual assault these young women endured. One story exemplifies the Stockholm syndrome, an unexpected bond between captive and captor, including having positive feelings for the captor and learned helplessness. In the story, the interviewee feels grateful to her adoptee father (a captain who killed her family in front of her and then adopted her) and says that she would not have been alive if it was not for this man, that she was saved.

The overarching feelings of these girls was utter loneliness and rootlessness. When some of these women finally united with their relatives later in life, in addition to the experience of joy of homecoming, they also realized how they were different from one another. They had difficulty relating because most lost women completely assimilated to Turkishness to the extent that some were extremely religious (Sunni Muslim) or had joined nationalist groups—while the rest of their family identified as Alevi Kurds. Even though they come from the same family genetically, their culture, language, and religion had diverged significantly, which made it difficult for united families to relate. This finding of Gündoğan and Gündoğan's (2012) project illustrates the utter loss of these lost young women and their communities. While many orphans were assimilated, and families who were displaced stayed, some families were reunited and chose to go back to their villages. After amnesty was declared a decade after Dersim 1938, in the late 1940s some of the displaced families went back to their villages and re-started their lives.

Historically, the Turkish nationalist/official government narrative solely focused on the "necessity" to suppress this uprising for the security of the state. Rıza Zelyut (2010) even goes so far to argue that Dersimis had initially been from Turkic tribes. The Kurdish nationalist perspective also focused on the suppression of the rebellions, with an emphasis on the importance of rebellion in Kurdish history, which often portrayed stories of martyrdom, heroism, and bravery as part of the creation of a Kurdish nationalism narrative. For example, Nuri Dersimi (1997) wrote one of the most referenced books, wherein he describes Dersim 38 as the violent suppression of rebellions. His publication, influenced by his Kurdish nationalistic sentiment, might have caused him to highlight and exaggerate the rebellions aspect of Dersim 38. Despite how his writings are interpreted today, he brought further light to the brutal suppressions that took place and stimulated many Dersimis to ask questions and research their history.

Other resources highlight the victimhood and the disproportion of the state's intervention. Gündoğan and Gündoğan's (2012) argue that, based on their interviews, there was no rebellion at all. Villagers felt the state's attack was solely ethnicity-based. Furthermore, the victim narrative speaks to how collective violence at such a high magnitude could never be justified, not even if earlier rebellions had taken place in some parts of Dersim. Resistance stories speak to the resilience and strength of the Dersimi people and culture despite suppression and assimilation. In sum, military interventions were beyond mere suppression of rebellions—they were comprehensive policies that targeted Kurdish identity.

Transgenerational Aspect of Dersim 38

For Dersimis, Dersim 38 is a major cultural loss and imprint that has changed their culture, memory, identity, and narrative completely. Filiz Çelik (2017) writes:

> Experiences in relation to the massacre are unfortunately not well-documented and a veil of silence at [an] individual, collective and national level continues and the effects of the Massacre transcends generations. Today, there is an unbridgeable gap between the pre-Massacre and post-Massacre generations that [are] identified through the loss of a way of life. The way of life described as particular to Dersim is detailed through the socio-cultural order of the Alevi faith as experienced in the region. (p. 51)

The collectively traumatic events that took place between 1937 and 1939 created a deep cultural and personal loss for Dersimis. Van Bruinessen (1994) goes on to say that after the massacre, forced displacements, and other traumatic events that followed later in the 20th century that "the majority of the people of Dersim now live in the diaspora, either in Western Turkey or abroad. Not much is left of Dersim's distinctive culture" (p. 170). In the last decade more research and literature explored individual experiences and the transmission aspect of narrative and trauma in an attempt to understand the cultural loss and consequences of Dersim 38. Research systemically looked at several individual stories of people from Dersim and in particular, they wanted to understand the nature of the transmission of trauma from the Dersim Massacre from earlier generations.

Bilmez et al. (2011) interviewed 146 Dersimis. One of their main findings is the emphasis on *remembering*. Dersimis, as collective, remembers the events that took place in 1937–1938 as a form of resistance and resilience. In response to the process of modernization, the state's systemic violence toward Dersimi culture, identity and belief systems, assimilation policies and displacements, they have collectively faced forgetting their culture. Women, men, children, youth, and elders lost their lives during Dersim Massacres. Dersimis transgenerationally "resist through remembering" (p. 48).

F. Çelik (2015) joined this effort and interviewed the second and third generations of the Dersim 38 survivors. Based on her doctoral study, she found that even though the second and third generation had not personally experienced the Dersim 38 events, they talk about it as if those events had happened to them personally—as if they were there. Çelik concludes that even after two generations being removed from the event, participants still defined their life through its impacts. Identification with the Dersim Massacre was present in Leyla Neyzi's work as well. Neyzi (1999) asked Gülümser her birthdate. Even though her actual birth year was almost 30 years after the Massacre, Gülümser answered the question in reference to 1938 as a starting point of her life story. Her strong identification with the Dersim Massacre and considering the 1938 date as her birth year indicate the strong impact of historical trauma and their transgenerational effects. She was defining her life even generations later through the experience of Dersim 38.

Karatay et al. (2017) conducted in-depth interviews with a total of 27 second- and third-generation survivors to explore the psycho-traumatic effects of Dersim 38. They found that trauma was transmitted to the subsequent generations through experiences of sadness, pain, loss, and intrusive dreams. Because the Turkish government has not taken any concrete step toward acknowledgment and repair of the Dersim 38 collective traumas, subsequent generations still feel the fear of re-occurrence of similar events. For Dersimis, memories of 1938 are still vivid and fresh. In Karatay et al.'s research, participants referred to how they still find actual bones of victims from 1938 in the fields and how they still hear the screams of victims from the field and caves. Other participants remember the children who were detained and sent away by trains. Some others reported intrusive vivid dreams of the Massacres as if it happened to them.

The findings of oral history and psychosocial research demonstrate transmission of the Dersim 38 collective traumas to the second and third generations, and how they continue to do so through daily narratives. Moreover, they also show how trauma is re-generated through ongoing injustice, continued military attacks in the region (see Chapter 4), and physical reminders in the environment (e.g., victims' bones in the field, marks at the gates of caves). Despite all the odds, Dersimis have been resilient. Neyzi argues that the first surviving generation of the Dersim 38 mostly did not speak Turkish and did not have the tools and cultural fluency of the other "Turkishness" in order to excel in the new Turkish state. Survivors made it a priority to send their children to schools, did their best to support them to have a higher education and learn Turkish (Neyzi, 1999). As a result, there are a considerable number of second and third generation Dersimis that have excelled in higher education, research, and the arts. This adaptation may be one of the ways Dersimi parents taught their children how to survive.

Due to the political turmoil in the 1970s and 1980s in Turkey, strong motivation for success had a shift. When the third generation of survivors who were at university campuses became involved with political activism and leftist movements and were arrested, parents wanted to protect them from further traumatization. Even though activism could be a collectively constructive approach to healing from collective trauma (J. C. Alexander, 2004; 2012), in the light of oppressive politics in Turkey, parents suspected that perhaps the schools were not the best for them after all which caused many parents to remove their children (Neyzi, 1999). Yet, in most parts—both in Turkey and in the diaspora—Dersimis appear very active in business and social platforms.

I have facilitated two Healing the Wounds of History workshops with participants from Dersim. One in Istanbul with a group of Turks, Kurds, Armenians, and Zazas, and the second one I flew to Dersim with an invitation from Dersimi colleagues for a workshop with them. The Desimis' respect for nature, their distinct culture, language, belief system as Alevies, and their connection with their ancestors struck me in both workshops. For example, in one exercise, I ask participants to have an "empty chair" conversation (psychodrama technique) with an ancestor. Participants choose whom they want to have a conversation with. In both workshops, Dersimis quickly identified the person and had moving conversations with their ancestors that had threads of grief, resilience, pride, and strength running through. Turkish participants appeared to have a more challenging time deciding whom to invite as an ancestor. One Turkish participant, not able to think of anyone, asked if she could speak with Atatürk, the founder of the Republic of Turkey (the last name literally translates as the ancestor of all Turks). Despite the effort to assimilate and destroy Dersimis, many Dersimis continue to feel a deep connection with their ancestors, culture, and people. For many Turks, ancestral roots were cut out in a way that Atatürk replaced their ancestors as kin. The education system taught children from early on about Atatürk's life, his vision of Turkey, and how he is the "ancestor '*Ata*" of all Turks and created a nation of shared ancestry. To an extent, they succeeded.

After the Dersim Massacre and continued oppression, the distinct Dersim culture that existed during the Ottoman Empire was, in most parts, destroyed (van Bruinessen, 1994). Yet, people of Dersim continue to hold on to their distinct identity and culture as much as the collective remembers, and they continue to differentiate themselves from the rest of the Turkish and Kurdish population in Turkey.

Twenty Kur'a Military Service and the Wealth and Revenue Taxes of the 1940s

The effects of Twenty Kur'a military service and the wealth and revenue taxes were collectively traumatic to specific populations, which for non-Muslims validated that the new Turkish nation recognized them as the "other." Moreover, these events re-triggered and added more to the already existing wounds of the Armenians as a result of the Armenian Genocide and reminded all non-Muslims that they were still not safe. A decade after the Armenian Genocide (1915–17), in 1927 the "Citizen, speak Turkish!" campaign aimed to eliminate any non-Turkish language from the public sphere. Shortly after, Twenty Kur'a (mandatory) military service in 1939 and the wealth and revenue taxes of 1942 both became the next major collective traumas for the surviving and new generations of Armenians.

Twenty Kur'a (Mandatory) Military Service

On September 1, 1939, World War II started. Turkey was still attending to the wounds of World War I, and as long as its borders were not threatened, tried to stay away from World War II. The German army was becoming stronger and moving closer to Turkey's borders. The Turkish state, afraid of a possible German invasion and influence, mobilized a Turkish army of one million conscripts (İbrahim, 2012, p. 273). Additionally, even though non-Muslims did not serve in the military, in November 1939, the state formed non-Muslim military service *Yirmi Kur'a (tertip) Nafia Askerliği* (Twenty Kur'a military service).

According to the summary of Turkish-Armenian scholar Nayan Muratyan (2011), there were multiple reasons for the Twenty Kur'a military service. The state mainly wanted to stop non-Muslims from organizing against the Turkish state, because if the state ended up at war, internal matters would have been harder to handle. Moreover, they wanted to weaken non-Muslims' financial presence by keeping them away from their business and trade practices. With very short notice, 12,000 non-Muslim men were taken into forced military service. "Twenty" comes from the required age range. The state called all non-Muslim men between the ages of 24 and 44 to military service. However, since many people either registered early or late, men between the ages of 15 and 65 ended up going into the military. These men, unlike their separate Muslim comrades, were neither given military uniforms nor arms and used as forced labor for public works. On July 27, 1942, three and a half months before the wealth and revenue taxes were declared, these men were mysteriously released and sent back home.

The Wealth and Revenue Taxes of the 1940s

The state was having difficulty keeping up financially with the extraordinary conditions of World War II. Over one million men were kept ready for a potential war, which prevented them from working in the fields or other places. Merchants, fearing an approaching war, kept their stock away, which raised market prices. Profiteering, thefts, and black markets formed and continued to compromise the state's financial stability (İbrahim, 2012). The concepts of wealth and revenue taxes were not unique to Turkey; in essence, they are designed to tax those who might have made extraordinary income due to speculations and black markets during war conditions (Bali, 2001). The state mainly targeted Istanbul, where most non-Muslims lived after deportations and forced migrations. The state aimed to collect 465 million Turkish lira (TL) from 114,368 people to vitalize the Turkish economy (Aktar, 2000, p. 140). As an outcome, the state wanted to decrease the prices of goods and reduce the amount of money in the market (Furkan Kaya, 2014).

On November 11, 1942, the Turkish National Assembly ratified Law no. 4305, the wealth and revenue tax law. Its implementation had multiple agendas. At the time, non-Muslims still owned the majority of businesses and capital. As part of the Turkification process that was launched with the formation of the new Turkish state, they were also looking for ways to have more Muslims in business, trade, and public works. The tax mainly targeted non-Muslims and converts, *dönme*, who were previously non-Muslim but converted to Islam. Cursory calculations of the tax debt of non-Muslim and converts were considerably higher than Muslims, which brought on the debate that wealth and revenue taxes in practice aimed to eradicate the pioneering role that non-Muslims, Armenians, Greek, Orthodox Christians, and Jews had in the economy. Many non-Muslim taxes were so excessive that even if they sold their entire possessions, they still could not pay their debt.

Those who could not pay their taxes were taken into labor camps in places like Aşkale in Eastern Anatolia, which demanded major physical labor under harsh climate conditions (Akar, 1999). Labor camps only consisted of non-Muslim men, reaching 1,229 people over time. More than half of this number were Jewish, the rest were Armenian and Rum. They were forced to work for one lira a day until they were able to pay their debt of thousands of lira. Twenty-one men died in these labor camps. Some friendly relationships between Turkish soldiers and non-Muslim workers also happened. After approximately working for 16 months, on March 15, 1944, Law 4530 released non-Muslims from the labor camps and shortly after forgave their remaining tax debt.[3]

By 1944, approximately 67.7% previously non-Muslim owned businesses changed hands with Muslims (Aktar, 2000, p. 231). The wealth and revenue tax project aimed to provide the financial backbone of Turkish capitalism. It succeeded in its objective, which was to remove access to shared capital from the minority ethnicities and religions; however, it failed in its attempt to vitalize the Turkish economy. The state collected less tax than what they anticipated, and it did not have positive effects on the Turkish economy. Financial circumstances showed some relief—however quickly after it became worse.

One of the first publications about wealth and revenue taxes was in 1951. The head of the financial director in Istanbul, Faik Ökte (1951), wrote a book that documented how the government played a role in the wealth and revenue taxes and how the law targeted Armenian, Greek, and Jewish citizens in Turkey. His work created huge turmoil and reactions. Ökte states that his department, the Istanbul Treasury and Examiners, did not originally come up with the excessive tax amounts for non-Muslims. Ökte writes, "Politicians multiplied the numbers we prepared and turned taxes into numbers that would be impossible to overcome" (p. 91; author's translation).[4]

In 1990 Yılmaz Karakoyunlu wrote a novel entitled *Salkım Hanım'ın Taneleri*, inspired by the events that took place during wealth and revenue taxes. Its adaptation as a film came out in 1999, which again created turmoil both politically and publicly. The book and the movie portray an Armenian woman who was raped by a Turkish military officer in Eastern Anatolia. She gets pregnant and loses her baby during birth. This experience is too traumatic for her, and she loses touch with reality. She is married to a "convert" (*dönme*), a wealthy man, when they move to Istanbul, the wealth and revenue taxes bring an end to their wealth and lives. The movie, though fiction, not only gives a glimpse of the non-Muslim experience at the time, but also portrays the shadow side of how some Turkish families took advantage of the situation and became wealthy. There is an insidious Turkish character in the movie who takes advantage of the situation. It is common knowledge in Turkey that some of today's wealthiest families acquired their wealth around this time. Thus, acknowledging some of the state officials' and public's insidious practices would have brought shame to their families as well—therefore, the truth about wealth and revenue taxes is also tangled in these families' and government's willingness to face their own significant shadow.

Historically, the government has been justifying what happened as "necessary." For example, in February 2011, a retired finance inspector, Cahit Kayra, published a book titled *Savaş Türkiye varlık vergisi* (Turkey's war wealth taxes) describing the necessity of wealth and revenue taxes. Kayra claims that there was no unjust treatment of non-Muslims. His book had a good public response. Murat Bardakçı, a Haber Turk news channel anchorman, invited Kayra to speak during his show, which also allowed his book to reach a wider audience. In response, researcher and author, Rıfat Bali, wanted to counter-present the truth of wealth and revenue taxes and how non-Muslims were directly affected. Further presenting the non-Muslim experience, Bali (2012) interviewed 161 people and published an extensive collection of non-Muslim memories and stories from the time, along with letters they sent to each other and newspaper extracts. All of which pointed to the severe consequences the majority of non-Muslims suffered from these taxes.

Thus, despite the Turkish government's justification efforts, multiple authors have clearly demonstrated how the government deliberately designed and executed wealth and revenue taxes to eliminate non-Muslims from economic life. Already fatigued from ongoing violence and trauma, non-Muslims once again were psychologically devastated. Ferda Balancar (2012) cites an Armenian research informant who describes this policy's devastating impact on their family and the psychological trauma it caused to their grandfather:

> When my grandfather came to Istanbul in 1921, he began manufacturing pickaxes, shovels, ploughs, buckets and sacks in the Perşembe pazarı district. So, he starts off in life for the third time. There's Tokat [the city] before the Deportation [of 1915], Tokat after the Deportation and finally [moving to Istanbul because of the rough time they were giving Armenians in Tokat]. (p. 5)
>
> But then the Wealth and Revenue Tax really embittered him. After the Wealth and Revenue Tax my grandfather did not speak a word for 8 years, until the day he died. He did not say a word, he didn't leave the house, he spoke only with gestures as if he was mute. I remember very well, they had moved from Harbiye to Osmaniye, he had an armchair there in front of the window, that's where he used to sit. He would have me sit on his lap, he would stroke and caress me for hours, he was so affectionate but he wouldn't say a word. Because that's a very severe trauma, how many times are you going to start off in life again? . . . In the newspapers of those days his name was clearly mentioned in "Convoy 1," "Number 1." All their assets were reduced to nothing, and then my father started all over again.

But my grandfather turned his back on life. For example, I never saw my grandfather in the street. He was a sturdy man; he wasn't ill or anything. He never went out and never spoke. (p. 7)

This example shows the accumulation of deep psychological wounding and its severe effects on non-Muslims. Selective Mutism (SM) is a rare psychological condition that may develop in reaction to a traumatic event. Even if a person is able to speak, they choose not to. This condition is often associated with social anxiety. Based on recent studies, British researchers also found that SM is "characterized by a profound sense of loss, of one's identity, of one's past and future, and of one's social interactions" (A. S. Walker & Tobbell, 2015, p. 468). Severe and continuous collective traumas could psychologically overwhelm even the most sturdy and otherwise healthy person. The wealth and revenue taxes not only undermined non-Muslim economic resilience but also, for some, it was the final straw that broke their psychological resilience as well.

Collective trauma also caused collective adaptation styles and changes in ways which individuals made meaning, related to, and engaged with one another. Muratyan interviewed 15 Armenians in Turkey to understand how they made meaning in relation to the Armenian collective traumas in the last century. One interviewee says,

I was a child during wealth and revenue taxes. But I remember the fear at home. In 1915 my father suffered a lot. He would not talk about it, but we knew. I guess it was the beginning of the 1940s, he had just come back from military. They would talk about the declared tax law. So, it was the wealth and revenue tax. My father did not have any money. How would he pay? I remember he and my mother would talk about it many nights. I would try to understand them with my child mind. They were both very afraid. . . . In 1915, as a child my father suffered a lot, I guess he thought it was repeating again. . . . Thankfully tax was not assigned to us. Can I tell you something? What a damn feeling that was, it transmitted to me too . . . my whole work life I did not want to make money with a fear that something could happen to me (Manuk, age 75).[5] (Muratyan, 2011, p. 57; author's translation)

This example not only illustrates the psychological impact and fear Armenians felt but also one way this fear could have been transmitted to the next generation. Most non-Muslims had to pay excessive tax amounts, and those who had no money, or no possessions, were excused. There were countless other families who had more wealth, and many lost everything. It appears that in response to a real external danger that was out of his family's control, as a child, Manuk was also frightened; thus, this experience informed his future belief and relationship with money. This experience led Manuk to believe that having money as a non-Muslim could make one a target in Turkey, therefore it was safer not to have any. This adaptation for safety reasons and the government's continual discrimination of non-Muslims combined might have prevented people like Manuk from advancing in certain fields, they could have otherwise accumulated more wealth. Muratyan additionally argues that Armenians once again realized that they were the "other" and not safe under the new Turkish nation, thus they continued to adapt by changing their names to Turkish ones, hiding their identities, and not speaking Armenian in public. Many left Turkey, and the remaining Armenians stayed within their smaller communities.

The Pogroms of September 6–7, 1955

After the population exchange in 1923 between Greece and Turkey, the number of Greeks who stayed in Istanbul was estimated to be about 100,000 (Şeker, 2012). The September 6–7 pogroms, violent riots, targeted the last remaining Greek (Rum) populations in Istanbul and resulted in their decline to only a few thousand.

The events of September 6–7, 1955 were a continuum from the 1930s and 1940s and happened in the context of nationalization and homogenization of the economic life of the Republic of Turkey and succeeded in creating a new Turkish "national bourgeoisie" (Güven, 2005, 2011). In 1950, the Turkish republic shifted from a one-party rule to a multiple-party democracy. The general public viewed the Democratic Party's (DP) election in the spring of 1950 as a victory. Non-Muslim minorities hoped that the liberal policies of the new government would also bring in a democratic approach for the minorities of the country. Historian Dilek Güven, who analyzed the events leading up to September 6–7, argues that a couple of precautions taken by the DP gave the impression that they approached the minority groups with a considerable degree of tolerance. However, the happy atmosphere created by the seemingly recovered relationships between non-Muslim minorities and the government was replaced by the fact that the DP's view of minorities was not very different from the previous one-party government, the Republican People's Party (RPP).

Since Ottoman times, non-Muslim minorities had been treated as secondary citizens, which continued throughout the difficulties created by the Turkish authorities. Nevertheless, the DP's liberal minority policy proved to be an impression formed out of foreign policy and party tactics. The intensification of disputes over Cyprus in 1954 brought a complete end to the goodwill that the DP government displayed for non-Muslim minorities. These disputes eventually lead to September 6–7 pogroms.

Cyprus is an island in the Mediterranean Sea. Geographically close to both Turkey and Greece, Cyprus has both populations. Drawing from military archives, Evanthis Hatzivassiliou (2009) argues that Britain acquired the administration of Cyprus from the Ottoman Empire in 1878 at the culmination of the Great Eastern Crisis. They considered the idea of ceding the island to Greece, and made a formal offer in 1915; however, after Greece was defeated by Turkey in 1922, Britain decided to keep Cyprus. For Britain, especially in the early period of World War II (1939–1945), Cyprus became a useful location in the Middle East and against the Soviet Union itself. Thus, strategic and military needs were important reasons why Britain retained the island.

An armed Greek nationalist movement broke out in the early 1950s with two agendas: to push out British colonialism and to integrate the island with Greece, which created a dispute between Turkey and Greece over the island. The eruption of the Greek Cypriot armed revolt in April 1955 further aggravated the already politically intensified situation between Turkey, Greece, and Britain. Britain organized the London Tripartite Conference of August–September 1955 to discuss these situations, which is when the violent riots took place in Turkey.

In 1955, Turkish authorities had already engaged in systematic provocation and manipulation of public opinion against the Greek minority, partly in connection with the ongoing dispute over Cyprus. In opposition, a student movement called "Cyprus Is Turkish" was particularly outspoken in creating anti-Greek propaganda. On September 6, 1955, a nongovernment newspaper reported that Atatürk's house in Selaniko, Greece was bombed by Greeks which resulted in violent riots in Istanbul mainly targeting Greek minorities (also called Rum) and non-Muslims.

Historians argue that the socio-economic, ideological, and political transformations of the current government, allowed the DP led by Adnan Menderes, to make it possible for ethnic entrepreneurs and state provocateurs to mobilize the masses against all non-Muslims (Güven, 2011; Kuyucu, 2005). These events had a particular governmental goal, which was to remove non-Muslims from economic life.

Güven (2011) summarizes that the events of September 6–7 were planned by the DP government, and were accomplished with the participation of the Secret Service, the DP's local administration, and organizations guided by the state, such as student unions, youth associations, syndicates, and the Association of Turkish Cyprus *Kıbrıs Türk Cemiyeti* (KTC). After the Turkish state radio announced that a bomb had exploded at the house in Thessalonica where Atatürk was born, and news spread out with two different afternoon copies of the newspaper *Istanbul Express*, late in the afternoon on the same day, a public demonstration was organized in Taksim Square by various student associations, unions, and the KTC. An estimated 100,000 people took part. Twenty to 30 group leaders were holding flags which were indications of their organizations. Some leaders had a list of non-Muslim homes and businesses. In other cases, these locations were marked with an X for identification. The newspapers were published and distributed immediately. Trains, trucks, taxis, and even military vehicles were readily available to take the masses to non-Muslim neighborhoods. Prior to the attacks, pre-determined destruction objects, such as "stones, cranks, wooden boards, shovels, handsaws, and welding machines" (p. 205) necessary for destruction, were kept ready at central points in the city or at bus stops. Furthermore, police and firefighters did not intervene in time to prevent or distinguish fires. Fire brigades claimed that their equipment was not adequate so they did not become involved. Moreover, historians later argued that the bomb was planted by the Turkish secret service with orders from the government to provide a pretext for an explosion of public sentiment. All of this information presents the pre-planned governmental and institutional orchestration and enabling that occurred. Later, Turkish courts admitted to government involvement in the planning of these events, and concluded that the riots got out of control, turning into mass hysteria.

> In a few hours in the evening of September 6 and early September 7, 1955, according to [a] Turkish official, 4,214 houses, 1,004 workplaces, 73 churches, 1 synagogue, 2 monasteries, 26 schools and 5,317 other establishments such as factories, hotels, pubs, etc., were attacked.
>
> According to an [American] source, 59% of the attacked workplaces, and 80% of damaged houses belonged to Greek-Orthodox people. The 17% of all assaulted workplaces and 9% of all damaged houses were of Armenians. In addition to these, 3 out of 33 Armenian churches and 4 out of 22 Armenian schools were subject to the attacks. 12% of all attacked workplaces and 3% of all destroyed houses were the possession of Jewish residents with respect to the information provided by this source. (Güven, 2005, p. 205)

Additionally, 11–15 people died, and 60 rape cases were reported, which is suspected to be higher given that not all rape cases were reported.

The masses were able to mobilize very quickly against non-Muslim fellow citizens. Many arguments focused on either governmental or Communist involvement as the main contributor of the pogroms (e.g., Demirer, 2006; Dosdoğru, 1993); hence they remain limited in articulating how people, from various strata in the society, could become involved, because, as Ali Tuna Kuyucu (2005) argues, these arguments drew a sharp line between state and society. Kuyucu writes,

In order to understand why and how this sort of collective violence could take place, one needs to situate these riots in the broader historical context of the emergence, development and crystallization of Turkish nationalism and national identity that marked the non-Muslim citizens of the republic as the "others" and potential enemies of the real Turkish nation. (p. 363)

Two recently published books with their collection of photographs show demolished businesses, churches, cemeteries, Rum individuals who were targeted, and narrates some of the stories. Even though the military restricted people from taking pictures, photographer Dimitris Kalumenos was able to photograph some of the destruction. His archive includes 1,500 photographs. For example, his pictures show a wounded man lying on a hospital bed, doors with knife stabs, and empty wardrobes, broken furniture in the street that was thrown out of apartments. In another, people are gathered around, simply staring at the destruction, perhaps in shock (Kaloumenos & Korucu, 2015). One of the editors, Serdar Korucu (2016), revealed in an interview that they published these volumes to correct the shared collective narratives of Turks that these pogroms were village riots or only limited to the Beyoğlu, Istiklal region in Istanbul where most wealthy Rum and Jewish businesses were located. The editors wanted to correct this narrative among Turks and show—with pictures and narrations—that the September pogroms were not simply village riots. They were comprehensive and extended attacks that demolished businesses as well as homes, churches, and cemeteries, and targeted individuals.

The financial cost was estimated at 150 million Turkish liras (TL), equal to the value of 54 million American dollars of that period. Twenty-eight million TL of this financial damage belonged to Greek citizens, 68 million TL was from Greek-Orthodox citizens of the Republic of Turkey, 35 million TL was from churches, and 18 million TL was from foreigners and other minorities (Armenians and Jews) respectively. A proclamation that Prime Minister Menderes would do his best to compensate the losses by any means, proved in the end to be simply a gesture to please international public opinion and foreign countries; most reimbursements were late, bureaucratic, or insufficient. The DP government, twisting their responsibility, blamed communists for the pogroms. On September 7, police arrested 48 reported communists. Through the first interrogations, a total of 5,104 people were arrested, however, many were released due to a lack of evidence. A report also claimed that many who were arrested were absolutely not involved in the pogroms (Güven, 2015).

In some places, Turkish residents tried to protect their non-Muslim neighbors, and some remote establishments were spared. And yet, these massive pogroms caused enough destruction and concerns for safety for most non-Muslims, thus following the September 6–7 events, a large number of Greek-Orthodox, Armenians, and Jews sold what they had left, for a very small price, and emigrated from the country. The events of September made it apparent for non-Muslims that they were not recognized as Turkish citizens, and they were no longer welcome. The belief that they would be subject to discrimination in the future regardless of the political party in power strengthened their motive to emigrate. The developments after 1955 thus also signaled the end of religious pluralism in Istanbul.

From a legal perspective, Alfred de Zayas (2007) argues that the September 6–7 pogroms satisfy the criteria of Article 2 of the 1948 Convention on the Prevention and Punishment of Genocide (UNCG). First of all, the intent was to destroy in whole or in part the Greek minorities in Istanbul. Secondly, evidence shows the pogroms were government orchestrated, and thirdly, in the end, it was successful and led to major population loss in the region, from some 100,000 Rums to only a few thousand.

Güven (2011) argues that the attacks in 1955 should be considered part of the political and financial hardship that the Menderes government had been experiencing. In order to prevent negative circumstances from the opposition and press, they adopted mistrustful methods. Immediately after the attacks, on the 7th of September 1955, martial law was established in Istanbul, Ankara, and Izmir for six months, and the National Assembly was temporarily closed down. These events became an excuse for the government to set a limit on the press, suppress the opposition and student movement, and keep the domestic political developments under control.

Five years later, in response to the DP's controlling practices and compromises to Atatürk era rules, the DP government reopened thousands of mosques, legalized the call to prayer in Arabic instead of Turkish, opened new schools with religious personnel, and shortened the period of mandatory military service among other measures. The Turkish military, who had considered itself the protector of the nation and secular views, intervened on May 27, 1960. One of the major, heated debates was against the DP's involvement in the September 6–7 riots. President Bayar, Prime Minister Menderes, Minister of Foreign Affairs Zorlu, and Minister Köprülü were quickly arrested and tried at the military court due to the events of September 6 along with other accusations. During the case of September 6–7, the aforesaid politicians were firstly accused of violating the constitutionally ensured Turkish citizenship rights of the Greek-Orthodox, and secondly inciting Turkish citizens into demonstration and violence.

Though Menderes' conviction was due to many counts, his death sentence was primarily because of other offenses, such as "abuse of discretionary funds." Despite the gravity of the crimes that took place in September, later generations in Turkey know very little or nothing about the events. de Zayas

(2007) points out that in contrast, responsible parties, such as Menderes, Zorlu, and Polat, are honored in the collective memory—one example is that there are high schools and a university named after Menderes.

The violence of September 6–7, 1955 intensified multiple traumatic sequences that were already in place. One of them was in Cyprus, where the Greek nationalist movement continued to evolve, and the political conflict between Greece, Turkey, and Britain further intensified. British rule left the island in 1960. The dispute continued until the Greek military coup and Turkish army invasion in 1974. Now the island is divided into two parts: Greek and Turkish Cyprus, with buffer zones between and ghost cities, such as Maras, that only the Turkish military has access to. Another traumatic sequence of the pogroms included what began with the end of religious pluralism in Turkey. The developments after 1955, causing thousands of non-Muslims to leave Istanbul, continued to change both the social and economic fabric of the society, which is what Guven argues signaled the end of religious pluralism in Istanbul and intensified nationalist (one religion, one language) sentiment in Turkey.

For example, one participant named Selin, in Leyla Neyzi and Hranush Kharatyan-Araqelyan's (2010) oral history study, summarize an Armenian experience in Turkey related to the ongoing collectively traumatic events targeted at Armenians and their identity. Selin points out the psychological difficulties her family suffered, and the transgenerational impact on her. She says:

> My maternal great-great-grandfather wasn't mentally stable because he was witness to terrible events. He found his own father's corpse in a sack in the church. After that, he lost his ability to speak. All family members have some kind of problem. All these things that have to do with their being Armenian affect me. My mother's way of denying her own existence is passed on to me. (p. 52)

Neyzi (2010) writes the stories of three generations leading up to Selin, which exemplifies changing context and continued the suffering of Armenians in Turkey, and how each generation coped with changing and accumulating collective pain. From Selin's experience, Neyzi summarizes:

> Selin's grandfather's life was bound up with the events of 1915. His family lost their home, farm and flour mills in Bursa. This is how Selin recounts the experience of her grandfather's mother: "When she goes to the mills, she sees that the workers have appropriated them. She becomes very upset and has a stroke. She has a misshapen lip for the rest of her life. . . . Having lost everything, Selin's grandfather grows up selling trinkets on the streets. His eventual success as a trader is repeatedly thwarted by actions against

non-Muslims. During World War II, he is drafted into units made up exclusively of non-Muslims. Subjected to the notorious wealth tax, he goes heavily into debt. During 6–7 September 1955, he is forced to defend his home against marauders. Struggling to make up their losses and living in fear, the family turns their hopes to America. Selin's maternal aunt is made to marry a man she does not care for so that she can move to the U.S. Selin's mother is also sent to the U.S. as an adolescent; an experience which cuts her off from family and friends and which she regrets bitterly. Ultimately, Selin's grandfather is unable to make the move abroad, and her aunt's unhappy marriage is the only reminder of this unfulfilled dream. (p. 53)

According to Selin, her grandfather was very attached to his Armenian identity:

My grandfather was a conservative Armenian. He was going to go to the States, he was going to leave this disgusting country. That made sense for him, he'd been through so much." Though Selin is very close to her grandfather, her own life was shaped by the experiences, choices and feelings of her parents. Her parents chose not to send their children to Armenian schools or to teach them the Armenian language. They also replaced their Armenian surname with a Turkish one: "They spoke Armenian when my brother was a child but his friends in kindergarten made fun of his accent. Then they stopped speaking Armenian. They spoke Armenian when my grandfather came and when he left, they went back to Turkish. (as quoted in Neyzi, 2010, p. 53)

Selin's story is a striking example of how the Armenian Genocide, wealth and revenue taxes, and the September 6–7 pogroms in 1955 affected one family and their transgenerational adaptation. Other factors that added to the already existing fears and collective traumas of Armenians include Twenty Kur'a military service, "Citizen, speak Turkish!" campaigns, and later Hrant Dink's assassination. These traumatic events physically, psychologically, and economically affected Armenian families and reminded them they were still not safe in Turkey. Some families retreated to their Armenian communities, and others chose assimilation or emigration for protection.

The collapse of the Ottoman Empire and the trauma of war was coupled by targeting the economic place of non-Muslims in society caused major social traumas. *Social trauma*, a sociological term, and refers to trauma in social institutions and identities, such as economic, legal, medical, educational, and family institutions. For example, the Great Depression in the United States during the 1930s could be considered a social trauma because it crippled the financial institution within society and led to significant strains and breakdowns in legal and political systems (Smelser, 2004). The September pogrom was the last straw that caused many remaining non-Muslims to close their businesses and flee the country. Within 50 years, a significant part of society (non-Muslims, Ottoman Greeks, and Armenians) was no longer present. They were the backbone of the financial balance in society. The gradual non-Muslim absence continued to cripple societal functions, further compromising economic stability.

CHAPTER

4

The Inheritance of Military Ideologies and Its Consequences

Soldiers played vital roles in late Ottoman politics, especially in the second constitutional period (1908–1918). The military was also at the forefront in both the war of independence (1918–1922) and during the establishment of the modern Republic of Turkey in 1923. The Turkish military had adopted ideologies from Ottoman governance and established a military-reliant system for the Turkish republic. The founder of the Republic of Turkey, Atatürk, gave close attention to the military's organization as the protector of the nation. The Turkish military considered themselves guardians and protectors of the nation and secular views since the republic's formation, and intervened with state politics by staging three military coups in 1960, 1971, and 1980. Turkey's military coups and interventions have had psycho-social side effects for society, introducing more collective traumas. The coup of 1980 and the abuse of power and violent oppression of Kurds caused a violent turn in the mission of one of the Kurdish youth organizations, PKK. The establishment of PKK and their attack on Turkish military facilities in 1984 marks the beginning of the war between the two groups in Anatolia, which has since claimed more than 40,000 lives, displaced more than one million Kurds from their villages in Eastern Anatolia, and cost nearly $240 million to the Turkish state. The conflict has become more tangled generation by generation, which I discuss further in this chapter.

Military Coup (May 27, 1960)

The 1960 coup was staged five years after the September 6–7, 1955 pogroms to overpower the Democratic Party. In the eyes of the Turkish military, the DP and their controlling and compromising of Atatürk-era policies was alarming. DP leaders were tried in military court and faced many charges, including their involvement in the 1955 pogroms. The trials concluded with the execution of three members, including the head of the

DP, Adnan Menderes. General Cemal Gursel assumed power, and thus began the era of military-dominated politics until 1965.

Military Coup (March 12, 1971)

The Turkish economy was stagnant leading up to the late 1960s, and society moved toward widespread unrest. The recession, workers' group demonstrations, and right-wing and left-wing groups carrying out attacks of their own were beginning to concern the Turkish military that the political climate was compromised once again. The state was at the edge of chaos. The military intervened in 1971 to "restore order." The 1971 coup was an organized military intervention to end "anarchy" and carry out reforms "in a Kemalist spirit" (Aras, 2014, p. 69).

In some cases, the military intervention meant arrests without cause, torture, disappearance, and even death. Left-wing movement members were ethnically both Turkish and Kurdish. One of the most influential leftist student leaders and political activists, Deniz Gezmiş, along with the co-leader of the People's Liberation Army of Turkey (THKO), Hüseyin İnan, and Yusuf Aslan were hanged on May 6, 1972.

Still compromised due to their ethnic and political silencing, Kurds were looking for ways to influence government institutions; left-wing politics provided that outlet. Due to the military's uncompromised suppression of left-wing groups during the post-1971 coup era, other radical political groups began to re-emerge, and the Kurdish question became one of the most important topics for the leftist movements (Aras, 2014).

Military Coup (September 12, 1980)

On September 12, 1980, the Turkish Armed Forces declared a coup d'état headed by General Kenan Evren—the third military coup since the formation of the Republic of Turkey. Prof. Dr. Tanel Demirel (2003) argues that in the mid-1970s the Turkish military had been somewhat reluctant to take over the reins of the government. The high military command was aware of the destructive consequences of previous military interventions. However, the rising violence and the danger of civil strife in the country was becoming a concern. Because the army perceived itself as the ultimate guardian of the state, the unrest and escalated violence between opposing groups led them to conclude it was their right to intervene to maintain stability and to protect the nation. T. Demirel adds:

Believing that the democratic system was unable to fight against it [the military], presumed that if they did not intervene, a bloody civil war and the disintegration of the state were inevitable. Perceived threats to the integrity of the Republican state . . . was the key element driving the military towards intervention. (p. 274)

The 1980 Coup: Before and After

Contextually, in the wake of the mid-1970s demographic and economic changes, the democratic regime in Turkey was heading toward a crisis. In his analysis, Demirel (2003) concludes that the rapid social change from the peasant migration to cities changed the social fabric of urban areas. After the 1960 coup, new institutional regulations and state affairs further disturbed that order, which made it difficult to provide effective governance. Labor unions intensified their activities and appeared to be ever-more demanding. The economic crisis—which manifested itself in economic stagnation, rising inflation, and shortages of goods due to a recurrent foreign exchange problem—was a source of resentment. Confrontations between left- and right-wing student groups were escalating and turning more violent. Several left- and right-wing clandestine groups, which precipitated the military intervention in 1971, re-emerged and began to commit acts of violence, including sabotage, armed assaults, bank robberies, and killings. The death toll resulting from these conflicts increased daily.

The military high command received reports that expressed the urgency of taking action, and feedback from at least three ministers said, "Thank god the military has finally taken over" (T. Demirel, 2003, p. 271). The necessity of army action appeared justified from their viewpoint. Knowing the brutal events that took place during the military takeover between 1980 and 1984, the military's justified reasonings and the measure of stability it brought are harder to metabolize.

Unspeakable brutalities took place in the Diyarbakir Military prison between 1980 and 1984 (detailed in the following section). The 2012 Diyarbakir Military Prison 1980–1984 Truth Research and Justice Commission (DMP-TRJC)[1] report indicated that during the coup, the leftists across ethnicities were targeted, with Kurdish leftists the primary targets (Paker & Buğu, 2016).

The 1971 coup and its violent aftermath further mobilized Kurdish nationalism (Aras, 2014); van Bruinessen (1992) argues that the 1980 military coup's main intention was "to wipe out Kurdish nationalism" (p. 33). Ismet Imset (1996), who published various articles and a book portraying and exploring the roots of the emergence of PKK, writes:

In summary ... throughout the coup era ... a total of 650,000 people were detained and most suspects were either beaten or tortured; over 500 people died while under detention as result of torture; 85,000 people were placed on trial mainly in relation to thought crimes or guilt by association; 1,683,000 people were officially listed in police files as suspects; 348,000 Turks and Kurds were banned from traveling abroad; 15,509 people were fired from their jobs for political reasons; 114,000 books were seized and burned; 937 films were banned; 2,729 writers, translators, journalists and actors were put on trial for expressing their opinions. One can hardly argue, as we enter the 21st century, that such a regime had any legitimacy other than to conform with the financial and political expectations of its foreign supporters. (pp. 73–74)

In Eastern Anatolia/Kurdistan, an extensive Turkish army force, stationed to oversee assimilation and Turkification projects led to

the closure of [local] political parties, newspapers, publishing houses and charitable organization. Article 89 of the new constitution prohibited the right of Kurds to political representation stating that "no political party may concern itself with the defense, development, or diffusion of any non-Turkish language and culture." The constitution also legally enshrined the ban on the Kurdish language. (Zeydanlıoğlu, 2009, p. 7)

This was a dark phase for Kurds and leftist youth across ethnicities where their efforts were brutally crashed. Torture, arrests, and other suppressions marked both Turkish and Kurdish identities. Kurdish nationalism took another stronger turn, and the leftist movement died away, leaving crumbs of smaller initiatives behind.

Coup Reflections: Past and Present

In an HWH workshop in 2018 with Kurds, Turks, and Armenians, we asked participants to pair up with someone outside of their culture to debrief after an identity exploration exercise. It was meant to be a short debrief. A young Kurdish man (Zoran) in his early 30s paired up with an older leftist Turkish man (Ahmed). Ahmed participated in the youth movement in the 1970s and was arrested and tortured during the 1980 military coup. As a Turkish man, Ahmed had been part of the Kurdish movement during his youth and adult life. He had been in strong opposition to the Turkish state's oppressive politics. The young Kurdish man, Zoran, not aware of Ahmed's history and said in jest, "I do not want to pair up with a Turk."

Ahmed felt that Zoran put all Turks in the same oppressive category. Feeling hurt, Ahmed approached the door, attempting to leave the workshop. We stopped the exercise at that moment and facilitated a dialogue between Ahmed and Zoran. Zoran's impulse, as a Kurdish man, was understandable. The Turkish state forced his entire family to migrate from their village to an urban location. During the armed conflict between PKK and the Turkish military, Zoran was born and witnessed how the Turkish military abused his family during his youth. He had a natural impulse suspicion and feeling a lack of safety when paired up with an older Turkish man. Zoran later shared that in addition to making a joke, at that moment he also was testing the Turkish man's tolerance to a Kurdish experience because, he added, even leftist Turks (consciously or unconsciously) could be paternalistic toward Kurds. He observed this dynamic in many relationships with Turks and found it degenerative. Zoran argued that Turkish paternalism is an issue, particularly in the context of peace-building. Ahmed, on the other hand, had also fallen victim to state violence during the 1980 coup d'état. Ahmed strongly rejected being put in the same category as "all Turks," and was especially insulted as being thought of as an oppressive Turk. Although they may not have agreed with one another, when both Zoran and Ahmed expressed what was happening for them—and because they were able to express their feelings, were heard without judgment, and were witnessed by the rest of the workshop participants—there was enough trust built for them to continue with the workshop.

The Diyarbakır Military Prison of 1980–1984

"Military nation" and militarism as a culture have been the core of the national ideology in Turkey (Altınay, 2004). General Kenan Evren, in an interview, said that during the 1980–1983 military rule, throughout Turkey more people were arrested than prisons could contain (M. Ünlü & Birand, 1998, 36:29); the military had to use their quarters to detain prisoners. Turkey's Kurdish region witnessed concentrated effects of the 1980 military coup: 4,000 Kurdish inmates were sent to the infamous Diyarbakir Military prison between 1980 and 1984, which witnessed the worst brutalities of all (Hakyemez, 2017).

From nearby prisons, the word was out that this one, newly built, had everything an inmate could have asked for: better conditions, movie theaters, and showers. Some inmates even signed paperwork to be transferred. Later truth revealed that the "movie theaters" were where victims were tortured by electricity, and "showers" were where people were bathed in human waste (Ç. Demirel, 2009).

Despite torture being illegal on paper, in practice this was not the case. One prisoner, Ruşen Arslan, describes her experience after the military took over the management of the prison. Led by the infamous Captain Esat Oktay

Yıldıran, soldiers made an announcement. According to Arslan, they said, "This place is no longer a prison. It is a military school. And this military school has only one purpose. It is to Turkify you" (Ç. Demirel, 2009, 10:29; author's translation).

According to DMP-TRJC's 2012 report, the military's main strategies in the prison were military discipline and education, physical and psychological pressure, brutality, torture, and crippling/killings (over 30 people died due to brutalities, and over 30 people committed suicide in various ways in the form of protest/resistance), insulting the Kurdish language or Kurdishness, forced confessions, and punishment-based assimilation (Paker & Buğu, 2016, p. 88). The extreme brutalities that took place in this prison between 1980 and 1984 only recently came to light, albeit still in a limited manner. The torture that took place in this military prison between 1980 and 1984 has now been documented and presented in the form of personal testimonies, memoirs, documentaries, and in 2009–2010 was even portrayed in a popular TV show, *Bu Kalp Seni Unutur mu?* (Çağatay, 2009).

A former Kurdish politician, Mehdi Zana, describes his experience at the Diyarbakir prison at his statement for the International Day in Support of Victims of Torture. He writes:

> I am a Kurd from Turkey. I was the mayor of Diyarbakir, the most important city in the region where the Kurds live, in Turkish Kurdistan. Starting in 1980, I was imprisoned under conditions some of you might find hard to imagine. I was imprisoned with other Kurds, some of whom are dead today. I was tortured to such an extent that I continue to suffer from the aftereffects. My imprisonment was due to my having repeatedly taken positions in favor of something that seems elementary to me: the rights of Kurds....
>
> For two days they left me alone. On the third day, they came to get me ... [and] ... they blindfolded me and tied up my hands and legs. The session started. First, the falaka, an old [Ottoman] torture that has proved itself. They administer it with a stick or a bat on the soles of the feet. Every time I fainted, they splashed water on me and resumed the torture. After beating me hard on the soles of my feet, they threw me on the ground and stomped on my back one by one—there were a good forty of them. Finally, they took me up to another room where they hung me up by my arms, nude and attached electric wires to my genitals and anus. When they turned on the current my whole body would tremble; they call this "doing the plane." When I fainted, they would wake me up by kicking me with their boots.
>
> This treatment lasted fifteen days. Every night at around one o'clock in the morning, a Kurdish guard came to take off the blindfold that I wore continuously and to give me something to drink. His presence was good for me. Then it started again, especially the electric torture.... Most

prisoners were subjected to the same treatment and worse. After arresting a fourteen-year-old boy, they threatened to rape him if he did not talk. So, the boy let loose a string of names, all of them false, because he did not know anything. Later he came to see me and asked how he could warn those whose names he had "given." ... I saw men beat to death in front of me. Multiple inmates, Kurdish political prisoners, Neci Demir, Rezi Aytur to name only a few, hung themselves in protest. Others, protesting their treatment, starved themselves to death in hunger strikes going on two months. ... Those of us who lived, were frayed from lack of sleep and continuous torture. The pressure was permanent. After a month of this regime, I was separated from my friends and placed in solitary confinement. I stayed there for ten days, handcuffed, waiting. Then I was bought to the prosecutor. Looking at the file, the judge found no reason for my incarceration. "Sorry," he admitted to me, "but the military authorities have given the order to keep you in prison. It's not my fault." And I was imprisoned again, for the next 11 years. (Zana, 1998, para. 1–3)

Elected minister and co-president of the Peace and Democracy Party (BDP), the mayor of Diyarbakir between 2014 and 2016, Gültan Kısanak describes her experience:

Prison manager Captain Esat Oktay Yıldıran was there. ... He came to our women's ward one day. ... Everybody stood up, I didn't. ... Just because I didn't stand up when he came in, only because of this reasoning he had me shoved inside his dog Jo's doghouse. ... A place even a dog didn't want to stay in, full of filth, a very small doghouse this was. ... Not one day, not two days, not a month, not two months, exactly for six months I stayed there. In this doghouse where it was even hard to breathe, they beat me on a daily basis, they tortured me, on a daily basis.[2] (Hakan, 2012, para. 4; author's translation)

Captain Esat Oktay Yıldıran was the mastermind behind tortures and brutalities. Despite complaints against him, he was never brought to justice. On October 22, 1988, one Kurdish militant assassinated him in broad daylight at a public bus stop in front of his wife and two children. The executioner, right before pulling the trigger, said, "Laz Kemal [Kemal Pir] says hi" (author's translation).[3] Kemal Pir was one of the torture victims who had died during one of the death fast protests. A total of 32 people died in Diyarbakir prison between 1980 and 1984 from the brutalities inflicted upon them (Ç. Demirel, 2009, 06:18).

The 2012 DMP-TRJC research identified the main perpetrators of the Diyarbakir military prison atrocities: Esat Oktay Yıldıran, General Kenan Evren, among others, were named. The committee revealed the list of all responsible parties with a detailed analysis urging necessary legal actions to be taken (Paker & Buğu, 2016). In 2012, General Kenan Evren faced legal charges for the 1980 coup and following events. On June 18, 2014, a Turkish court sentenced him to life imprisonment. The sentence was on appeal when he died in 2014 from natural causes.

The Turkish state, in their official statements, denied the brutalities that took place in Diyarbakir prison or has justified them as necessary evils to protect the Turkish state and nation (Zeydanlıoğlu, 2009). Cases filed by torture survivors have been denied due to the statute of limitations expiring (Kamer, 2015). Hasan Dağtekin, one of the people who filed a complaint, was informed that his case was dropped due to statute of limitations.[4] He said, "There cannot be a statute of limitations for a crime against humanity" (Kamer, 2015, para. 6; author's translation).[5]

Psychological research shows that survivors develop a strong emotional response to those whom they held responsible for their torture. The cognitive effects of torture generate intense hatred, rage, and desire for vengeance against their perpetrators and radicalize even ordinary people with no strong political views (Başoğlu, 2009; Başoğlu et al., 2005). Diyarbakir Prison was the main site of resistance and Kurdish political activism (Günçş, 2013). It is therefore not surprising to see that the majority of the survivors who left the prison joined PKK. Sakine Cansız, one of the Diyarbakır torture survivors, when released, became one of the co-founders of PKK. She organized women fighter units and was one of its most influential leaders.

Welat Zeydanlıoğlu (2009) writes:

> ... the practices in Diyarbakır, the unofficial capital of the Kurdish region, played a crucial role in the crystallization of nationalist secessionist ideas and the radicalization of a generation of Kurds, large numbers of which went to join the ranks of the militant Kurdistan Worker's Party (PKK) which launched an armed struggle in 1984 with the aim to establish an independent Kurdish state. (p. 8)

Others chose a different path. Many survivors and their relatives mobilized political platforms; Mehdi Zana, Gültan Kısanak, and Layla Zana, to name a few, strove to find roles in the government and the parliament.

The 1971 and 1980 coups were thus fundamental turns in the evolution of Kurdish nationalism in Turkey. The oppression and high measures of violence against Kurds helped create a siege mentality among them (Aras, 2014).

Zeydanlıoğlu (2009) quotes from Neşe Düzel's 2003 interview in the *Radikal* newspaper:

I am not a political person. I am not well-informed in such issues. But 12 September made everyone aware of the Kurdish question and brought it to the world's attention. Had it not been for the barbarity in the prison, the Kurdish question would not have emerged so soon. They made militants out of people in the Diyarbakir prison. Almost 80 percent of these people went to the mountains [took up arms]. It was very difficult for someone to pursue a normal life after having experienced such brutality. You know, it is said that "the PKK movement exploded in 1984," this date is when many people were released from the Diyarbakir prison. (p. 8)

Despite being illegal, torture in Turkey has systemically been used as a vehicle of Turkification efforts. The brutal events that took place in the Diyarbakir prison between 1980 and 1984 show how, under the right circumstances, the pendulum could swing too far. The torture in Diyarbakir prison is an example of extreme crimes that moved beyond the Turkification process, becoming extremely sadistic; it was a place that tried not to assimilate Kurdish people, but rather to destroy them.

Torture

A form of atrocity, torture is one of the systemically implemented vehicles of political violence in Turkey. Torture can be physical as well as psychological. Battering, electric shock, rape, and other physical practices are widely known identifiers of torture. Deprivation of food and other basic needs are other types. Psychological torture is important to mention because it is often ignored, since it leaves no physical scars, but is nevertheless devastating to the individual (Paker & Buğu, 2016).

Various research has found that, depending on the stress factors, torture survivors could develop symptoms, such as PTSD, anxiety, depression (Başoğlu et al., 2005; Başoğlu, Paker, Özmen, et al., 1994; Başoğlu, Paker, Paker, et al., 1994), attention deficit, and behavioral disorders (Daud, Skoglund, & Rydelius, 2005). In the case of physical torture, depending on the targeted areas and the stressor, a person could experience organic brain damage, facial or dental injuries, burns, wounds, scars, unilateral brachial plexopathy (a complication from electrical injury to the upper limbs), and chronic pain that may last for the rest of their lives (Bradley & Tawfiq, 2006).

A torture survivor would not be able to prevent physical consequences, but some factors could decrease or even eliminate psychological ones. Research with torture survivors has found that social support, political involvement, and mental preparation before torture lessened PTSD and other stress-related symptoms compared with those who did not have as much social support or were not part of a political cause (Başoğlu, Paker, Paker, et al., 1994; Paker, 1999). Murat Paker and Burcu Buğu (2016) argue that this might be one of the reasons why political prisoners in Turkey appear to suffer less from psychological trauma symptoms compared to nonpolitical survivors. Political survivors were informed about torture practices from other survivors; they were mentally prepared and had solidarity both inside and outside the prison. Political prisoners' causes helped them make meaning in some ways, amplified their belief in their cause, and somewhat helped reverse psychological wounding.

Torture is an atrocity that has been used not only to acquire information, but as a practice to humiliate and annihilate (Paker, 1999). A state may use torture to deliberately spread fear and maintain control. There are profound consequences in the social fabric of society, however, when torture becomes a practice. In a *Huffington Post* article regarding torture practices, Sean Meshorer (2013) illustrates this point:

> Torturing other human beings for the sake of our "security" not only corrupts the souls of those who sanction it, [but] it also unleashes negative karmic consequences for our society that not only fails in making us safer, but actively destabilize our foundation. (para. 4)

It is hard to find pride in a society that could torture a human being for the sake of its own security. On the contrary, these practices result in consequences that create threats to the security of a state that it is so desperately trying to stabilize. Victims often give wrong information to prevent pain. Political survivors join rebel groups or continue their activism even more intensely after being released. Survivors develop strong emotional responses to those whom they held responsible for their torture. As mentioned earlier, the majority of Kurdish torture survivors who were released from Diyarbakir military prison after the military rule of 1980–1983 joined PKK's highest ranks; PKK organized their first armed attack against the Turkish military in 1984. It is thus hard to argue the usefulness of torture for national stability. Even though torture is illegal in Turkey, and despite its lack of usefulness for societal safety and order, it is still practiced in Turkey (and around the world). Some police officers, prison guards, or military personnel gravitate toward torture. From a psychological perspective, they may be unleashing their own frustration, hatred, and anger toward the "other," to the de-humanized for self-satisfying purposes. Such a scenario can be seen as an abuse of power used for personal satisfaction. A dark side of human nature reveals itself in a circumstance that gives permission and no real consequences to the perpetrator.

For example, the infamous Stanford prison experiment showed that even a well-behaved person could torture another human being under the "right" circumstances (Haney, Banks, & Zimbardo, 1973). Certain people might be inclined toward professions that they could exploit; this is not to say that every prison guard or police officer would choose brutality. However, I argue that when there is a systemic void that allows brutality, individuals who lean toward violence end up in these professions, making it dreadful for those in the profession for the right reasons—to protect and maintain peace in society. This dynamic pushes out or silences those who are trying to do the right thing.

A balance of opposing viewpoints and diversity of cultures is needed for people to hold one another accountable. If one group with extreme views ends up running an institution, no one is left to stop them from carrying out their extremist plans, creating avenues for exploitation and violence. In Turkey, Martin van Bruinessen (1996) notes that during the 1980s coup, the leftist police force was laid off, and more right-wing (ultra-nationalist) supporters found their place in it. The new employees with prejudice toward Alevis (a religious minority in Anatolia who have historically supported leftist and secular governments) and not enough left-wing personnel created an imbalance within the police force, making way for brutalities against Alevis—as well as other groups.

Partiya Karkerên Kurdistanê (PKK)

Partiya Karkerên Kurdistanê (PKK) has been a dominant armed Kurdish independence group in Turkey since the 1980s. Abdullah Öcalan, the leader of PKK, with five others formed an independent Kurdish political group in 1973 that was based on Marxist ideologies and was initially against the regional Kurdish Aghas and feudal regime. PKK was founded in 1978 in a small village near Diyarbakır (Öcalan, 2014). They organized their first attacks against regional landowners and tried to dominate other Kurdish organizations in the region (Imset, 1996; Marcus, 2007; van Bruinessen, 2000). PKK's earlier violent attacks attracted resentment and led to apathy among Kurds (M. C. Ünal, 2016). However, the Turkish government's violent practices during the 1980–1983 period of military rule resulted in massive sympathy for PKK, which also influenced their mission, which changed to securing an independent Kurdistan in Southeast Turkey through the use of violence (Aras, 2014; van Bruinessen, 1998, 2000; Yavuz, 2001). PKK's attack on military facilities in Eruh and Semdili in 1984 marked the beginning of the armed struggle.

Most violent since 1984, PKK is considered a terrorist organization by Turkey, the United States, the European Union, and NATO. In the 1980s and 1990s, in Turkish television and daily news media, citizens of Turkey were accustomed to seeing "terrorists" being captured and killed. Their dead bodies would be shown on television with a black line through their eyes, which was part of the daily news in the 1980s and 1990s and became a normal part of life. Violence and trauma were normalized in the state's claiming that the executions were for the good of the country.

The military often displayed bloody and sometimes mutilated bodies of guerrillas and other political subjects in towns and city squares. Ramazan Aras (2014) argues that the display of dead tortured bodies in the public sphere was the state's way of promoting and maintaining a culture of fear among all Kurds as well as a "strategy of threatening, terrorizing and humiliating the families of the dead guerrillas and the local population" (p. 81). Similarly, when PKK attacked and killed Kurdish civilians who had aligned themselves with the Turkish government, they also wanted to acquire support through spreading fear and to show Kurds that this also may be their end if they support the Turkish military (Imset, 1996).

Effect on Families

At an HWH workshop in Emeryville, California, in 2017, a Kurdish man, Cem, shared a formative moment in the development of his Kurdish identity in front of a group of empathetic Americans, Turks, and Armenians. This memory was important for him to share in front of Americans because he wanted people outside of Turkey to understand what was happening in the country, and he wanted to educate everyone about Kurdish suffering. He created a sculpture of this moment using other participants as figures and characters. In this sculpture, he picked someone to be his mother, one person to be his sister, and one another to play himself; they are all staged in their kitchen. Cem is holding a newspaper at the kitchen table; his mother and sister are standing behind him. A transparent scarf is a newspaper being held by two other people; behind the scarf is a picture he sees in the newspaper. Three other participants include two soldiers and one person on the ground playing Cem's brother. The legs of his brother's dead body are tied with a rope to the back of a car. Two soldiers, with pride on their faces, are smiling for the camera. This was how Cem found out his brother died: from a newspaper article displaying his brother's tortured body.

The family never recovered the body, so they could not have a proper funeral, which in turn prevented them from having closure about his brother's death. Through this re-enactment, Cem expressed the shock, the pain, the sense of helplessness, the insult of his brother's dead body being dragged on the ground, the sense of indignity, and the deep grief of losing a brother—all experienced in that one moment. In his re-enactment, he is speechless, frozen, looking at the newspaper. He hears his mother screaming in the background and his sister crying. This pain marked his identity as a Kurdish person. This unhealed wounding continues to haunt Cem's and many other Kurdish families—a story of empty graves.

Later Cem shared how he become a political activist overnight. He was not involved with the Kurdish movement earlier in his life. He was one of five siblings; one of his siblings had joined PKK, but everyone else in the family had been apolitical. They had no interest in politics or Kurdish sovereignty; they were mainly trying to get through life. Nevertheless, one sibling's decision to join PKK affected everyone. A few years after he joined PKK, Cem's brother had become a high-level general and was on the Turkish state's wanted list. One night, Cem's house was raided by Turkish military without notice, and the entire family was taken into custody. All family members—siblings and parents—were taken into different rooms as the military was trying to find Cem's brother. Cem and his family members swore that they did not know. His brother would only call to say hello occasionally and never stated where he was or shared anything about what he was doing. At one point during the ordeal, Cem was taken into a room where he saw, through one-way glass, his sister naked and tied to a chair; soldiers threatened to rape her in front of Cem if he did not say where his brother was. He described the terror of that moment and how helpless he felt because he did not know where his brother was. The entire family was eventually sent back home with more threats. Cem explained that this was the night he, and everyone else in his family, became political. Every family member became activists following their arrest, and he emphasized, "Turkish state created us. We were simple citizens turned into political activists over one night."

Civilians have been caught between PKK and the Turkish military since the war began in the 1980s. When a family member joined PKK, no matter how against it the rest of the family may have been, they found themselves in conflict with the state. As the war between PKK and the Turkish military became heated, the propaganda from both the Turkish state and PKK and the pressure to pick a side put many Kurds in a double bind. This dilemma was even more complicated for family members when some members were serving in the Turkish military and others were fighting for PKK, a situation that was not uncommon in Turkey.

Ongoing Strife Under Civilian Rule

In 1987, the Turkish government declared a state of emergency across Kurdistan that continues today. The 1990s marked the most violent phase of the war between PKK and the Turkish state, reaching its peak in 1994. During this peak,

32 people were killed by police during controversial house raids; 1,128 people were tortured while under detention; 32 others were tortured to death while in police custody; 49 disappeared while under the custody of security officials; 97 were killed only for failing to stop when ordered to do so and 432 were killed in mystery murders generally attributed to security forces. (Imset, 1996, p. 86)

In total over the decades, the war between PKK and the Turkish military has claimed more than 40,000 lives, including civilians, Turkish military personnel, and PKK members. In response, feelings of rage, grief, and fear have grown on both sides. Whether directly impacted by this conflict or not, media coverage of suicide bombings, images of battered and tortured rebels, and photos of dead civilians from both sides have created generalized feelings of anxiety, insecurity, and dread for citizens of Turkey living inside and outside the country. A deep mistrust between many Kurds and Turks has emerged.

In addition to lost lives and the economic cost of the war in Eastern Anatolia/Kurdistan, the conflict between the Turkish state and Kurds introduced other problems. Drug and alcohol abuse have significantly increased while the violence in society is rising, which van Bruinessen (1998) observed is similar to the Vietnam War. Some of the police and civilian authorities in Vietnam during the war became deeply involved in the profitable illegal drugs and arms trade.

After Abdullah Öcalan was captured in 1999, PKK abandoned its mission of an independent Kurdistan (H. J. Barkey & Fuller, 1998; van Bruinessen, 2000) and shifted its demands toward democratic reforms and federalism in a Kurdish region of Turkey (see Öcalan, 2014). Moreover, four years after his capture, in 2013, Öcalan and Turkey's president Recep Tayyip Erdoğan called for the end of armed struggle. A fragile cease-fire and peace talks took place, giving both sides of the conflict a spark of hope; however, both abruptly ended in 2015.

There had been peace talks before 2013, which also failed. President Turgut Özal, at the peak time of the war in 1993, attempted a dialogue and Öcalan ordered the first cease-fire on March 20, 1993. However, President Özal's early death on April 16, 1993, diminished these first efforts. Even though, after 1994, PKK repeatedly approached Western leaders and the Turkish government calling for a cease-fire—assuring all weapons would be dropped in case of a dialogue for peace and reconciliation—the war continued. Because the Turkish government believed that they were militarily wiser and stronger and could end the struggle with more force and arms, they did not see the need for a dialogue. Another window for peace occurred in 1999 when Öcalan was captured; he sent a letter to PKK leadership suggesting a "democratic, non-violent, means as of September 1,

1999" (M. C. Ünal, 2016, p. 101). Both sides were pragmatic, and instead of taking advantage of the dialogue opportunity, the state again perceived PKK as weak, and during the time of withdrawal, between 300 and 500 PKK militants were killed; from then on, violence continued to spiral.

Mustafa Coşar Ünal (2016) noted that this conflict has been ripe for a resolution. Both parties are aware of the loss and the violent deadlock the conflict has reached. When the Justice and Development Party (JDP; or *Adalet ve Kalkınma Partisi*, AKP, in Turkish) came into power, they shifted the designation of PKK from counterterrorism to counterinsurgency and wanted to solve the violence between PKK and the Turkish state. Their first effort began in 2009 (Kurdish Opening or Democratic Opening) and failed by 2011 due to poor management and strong reactions from the public, military, and nongovernmental institutions, including Turkish nationalists blaming JDP for betraying the martyrs who lost their lives to the conflict. The second peace talk initiative began in 2012, but, as of 2015 when JDP could not secure the majority vote for the parliament, their political agenda shifted, and violence escalated.

A few scholars point out that the public did not think that the peace talks were ever genuine (Alemdar & Çorbacıoğlu, 2012; Tas, 2016). Furthermore, even if they were genuine, the conflict was identity-based. Thus, the solution was cumbersome and structural in governance (M. C. Ünal, 2016). Furthermore, peace talks were not comprehensive enough to include all affected parties. For example, one critic of the talks mentioned that both efforts did not take any policy measures to address the three-decades-long internal displacement of Kurdish communities from their ancestral lands, which was a pitfall (B. Ayata, 2011). In addition to lifting the restriction on the Kurdish language and allowing public education and broadcasting in Kurdish, PKK has structural demands that make the conflict unwieldy to resolve. The Turkish government continues to resist any structural changes. M. C. Ünal (2016) writes,

> There exists certain other demands in different scales, some of which include: Öcalan's release from prison into a form of house arrest; abolishment of the Provisional Village Guard System; abolishment of the Turkish Counterterrorism Law and related amendments to recognize/legitimize non-violent Kurdish dissent, namely the KCK as a political entity [that emerged from PKK] (release of all incarcerated KCK members); and lowering the 10% threshold in Turkey's electoral system for parties to make it to the Turkish Grand National Assembly. (p. 115)

In addition to practical and structural requests, society has not been psychologically ready for resolution, and the public has reacted strongly to the peace talk process. The prejudice and division are not only happening at the national level, but have also been publicly reinforced at community levels, which heighten the us-versus-them dynamics—making any peace or reconciliation not only concerning top–down, state-level practices but also bottom–up and across community-level initiatives.

Both parties' doubts about each other have accumulated resentment. Due to personal losses in the war, and after decades-long damage in Kurdistan, armed violence between PKK and the Turkish military, people are experiencing tremendous grief and feeling anger and hatred toward the "other." According to the South East Expert Committee Report, *Akil Insanlar Güney Doğu Raporu* by Yılmaz Ensaroğlu (2013):

> The Kurdish question entailed major costs not only to the Kurds but the entire society and country over the years. Without a doubt, the Kurds had to bear the worst circumstances as they were denied and ignored while their language was outlawed and their names had to be changed. The state-imposed forced migration led Kurds to be forcibly removed from their homelands and to live among an unfamiliar people whose language they did not speak. Furthermore, exile inevitably doomed them to unemployment and poverty. All these policies devastated the Kurds in social, economic, cultural, and psychological ways. The trauma became even deeper as violence and oppression grew and the rising number of dead, injured, and arrested Kurds accompanied the increasing population of Kurdish fighters. Particularly the younger generations who believed that they had lost everything experienced the greatest trauma of all. (p. 9)

Younger generations were born into war. Even though researchers have observed adaptation to peace talks in 2013 within Kurdish politics, these generations have not appeared ready. Ensaroğlu et al. (2013) argue that they believe they lost everything and experienced the most significant trauma of all. This resistance might have increased even more since the peace efforts failed in 2015, and violence escalated in the region—where the divide and mistrust between Turks and Kurds is deepening.

After the general elections of June 7, 2015, led by the provisional government under the AKP/JDP (which has been in power since 2002), the politics of violence has escalated, which also brought an end to peace talks. Since 2015, Turkey has increasingly drifted into genocidal politics toward Kurds and anyone who is in opposition to the state's power. Based on compiled reports, Latif Tas (2016) writes,

> In the nine months following the June 2015 Turkish general election and significant political losses for the AKP, six thousand Kurds (including civilians and PKK militants) and 400 Turkish soldiers and police officers have been killed. (p. 26)

Tas (2016) argues that peace talks were never real where AKP/JDP and PKK both were more interested in monopolizing power and violence. As a result, despite JDP's earlier promises of better relations between Turks and Kurds, under the JDP government, the Turkish–Kurdish conflict has worsened, thus leaving the new generation with even more cumbersome problems to tackle.

Combat Trauma

Despite ongoing armed conflicts in Turkey between PKK and the Turkish military since the 1980s, not to mention the catastrophic experience of World War I and all the other collectively traumatic experiences that followed in the last century, it is surprising not to find substantial research examining the psychological impacts of war or combat trauma in Turkey. International research overwhelmingly confirms that armed violence can cause PTSD and other stress-related symptoms and has looked for innovative healing modalities, such as neurofeedback (Zotev et al., 2018), art therapy (Lobban, 2014), and somatic experiencing (P. A. Levine, 1997). When left untreated, these symptoms may lead to attention and concentration issues (Uddo, Vasterling, Brailey, & Sutker, 1993), depression, substance abuse, socialization issues, and homelessness (Bremner, Southwick, Darnell, & Charney, 1996; P. A. Levine, 1997; van der Kolk, 2014).

I could only find limited research that looked at the risk of PTSD and stress-related symptoms in Turkey. Based on the research available to the public in Turkey, economic, psychological, or adjustment difficulties, physical injuries—such as losing limbs or organs—and a sense of loss of self-value are the most common complaints from veterans (Güloğlu & Karaırmak, 2013). One study examining 92 health commission reports of disabled veterans that were prepared by Ankara Atatürk Training and Research Hospital Health Care Commission between 2007 and 2011 found that in veterans from 24 to 36 years of age, 63% of their disability reports were due to mine explosions; 12% lost one or both eyes; and 58% had one or more amputations (Keten et al., 2013, p. 33). Those who were severely wounded and disabled are the most vulnerable to persistent depression and are in great need of support (Güloğlu, 2016; van der Kolk, 2014).

Military service is mandatory in Turkey. Every able young man who is 18 years old or older must do their mandatory military training, also called nonprofessional military service. It can take six months to two years to complete. If the person is still in school or due to some other special conditions, the service can be postponed. In some situations, paid military service—in which individuals pay a fee to have their military requirement reduced or waived—is available, but obviously only for families with the resources to pay. In most cases, men are at the mercy of a random selection process to find out if they are going to a conflict-free or conflict-center zone for their service. That said, if they know officials or people in higher ranks within the military, they may be able to influence location assignments. Since the armed conflict between PKK and the Turkish state began in 1984, most men in Turkey who did their mandatory military service in Eastern Anatolia have been at risk for combat-related traumatic experiences.

In 2013, a controversial report revealed that between 2002 and 2012, more soldiers died of suicide (965) than became martyrs (601), and the number of suicides increased year by year (Karabağlı, 2013, para.1). Shortly after this report was published, the Turkish military established psychological treatment programs. It could be that they may have been embarrassed by these reports because as these numbers were released, the Minister of Defense, İsmet Yılmaz, went on to say that "there is no epidemiological data difference between the Turkish Military Council and civilians in regards to their suicide behavior" (En Son Haber 2013, para. 14; author's translation).[6] This means that their research did not find any empirical difference between soldier and civilian suicide behaviors, which is to imply that a soldier's suicide may not be related to their military experience.

Despite the lack of acknowledgment by Turkish leadership, public awareness of psychological trauma has been increasing. In 2014, Turkish news reported that nearly 140,000 soldiers per year are seeking psychological treatment. Psychological help for soldiers is available at the military hospitals (Özdemir et al., 2014) and in the private sector as well. When I did a simple online search for psychological treatment for soldiers in Turkey, several private institutions came up. They are concentrated in urban cities and require fees, but it is promising to see that there is a sense of public awareness and effort to break the stigma of men's need for psychological help.

The overarching findings of PTSD research in Turkey with veterans is if they come from mandatory military service and experienced combat-related injuries in conflict zones, they might develop PTSD and other stress-related symptoms. For instance, when the conflict between PKK and Turkish military was still at its peak, Berna Güloğlu (2016) writes that after PTSD, the most common psychiatric disorders were conversion disorders (16.6%), anxiety disorders (13.2%), schizophrenia (8.8%), major depression disorders (6.3%), and adjustment disorders (5.9%) (p. 2). Moreover, 46.7% (171 of 366) of combat-injured nonprofessional veterans experienced probable PTSD symptoms, while 16.4% experienced severe depression, and 18% experienced severe anxiety (p. 1). Symptoms of re-experiencing the traumatic event (65.8%) were the most common PTSD symptom (p. 1); anger management issues and loss of pleasure in life were also common experiences.

In 1999, Nadire Mater published a book entitled *Mehmed's Book* (*Mehmedin Kitabı*; Mehmed is a name reference to men who go to their mandatory military training) with a collection of interviews with 41 veterans who fought in Eastern Anatolia. Deniz Yılmaz (2009) analyzed the stories shared in *Mehmedin Kitabı* and his analysis indicated that sleep disturbances, recurrent dreams of traumatic events, hypervigilance, and exaggerated startle responses are the most common symptoms among veterans.

Perhaps not their intention, however, but media also plays a role in the persistence of veteran's symptoms. Research found that ongoing media coverage of martyrs and injured veterans re-trigger their trauma (Güloğlu, 2016; Güloğlu & Karaırmak, 2013). The media, through showing coverage of martyrs, aims to publicize the narratives of heroes as well as raise civilian reaction against the PKK and Kurds. However, this news coverage is re-traumatizing for veterans and could be diminishing, and even preventing, psychological healing.

A veteran's compromised psychological state also makes readjustment back into their home environment problematic. If they are disabled, their readjustment becomes even more difficult. The disability is seen as a loss of status and sign of inability. There are stories in which young soldiers' fiancés left them, or some even faced discrimination in their neighborhood (Mater, 1999). Some physical symptoms experienced by veterans continued even after 13 to 15 years, depending on the severity of their injury (Güloğlu, 2016; Güloğlu & Karaırmak, 2013)

One disabled soldier who lost both legs, says,

> After I came home, they did not allow me to get married [to my fiancée]. I did not do anything wrong. I did not rob the government; I did not seize any place; I did not rape anyone. It was not my choice. A man loses a foot, their fiancée leaves them. In some places, we are treated like second-class citizens. . . .
>
> I did not like fighting before my military service; I was calmer than now. Now I am hot-tempered. What they say about the Vietnam Syndrome . . . I am having a hard time controlling myself. . . . I even think I can shoot someone. I experience things more intensely; I can be aggressive.[7] (Mater, 1999, p. 111)

Psychological trauma related to combat is also called Vietnam Syndrome, referring to stress-related symptoms with U.S. Vietnam veterans (Friedman, 1981). Men who did their mandatory military service in Eastern Anatolia were nonprofessional soldiers, with ages ranging from 24 to 49

(Güloğlu & Karaırmak, 2013; Keten et al., 2013), and were often from lower- to middle-class families (D. Yılmaz, 2009). D. Yılmaz (2009) noted that stronger and younger men were chosen as "commandos" (*komando*) and received more intensive training. Completing military service is a cultural rite of passage into manhood in Turkey. The media's glorified references to soldiers could make it appealing for some to go to war zones willingly to "defend" their country. However, the overwhelming traumatic experience of combat and military experience, being physically wounded with the realization that those who serve in war zones often are the ones from economically unprivileged backgrounds, soldiers often experience deep disappointment. D. Yılmaz (2009) writes:

> There are three different discourses about [the] war in the narratives of the soldiers fighting in the Southeast. . . . First, "this war never ends"; second, "I do not feel [like] a hero", third, "we, poor people, not rich people, protect the borders of [the] motherland." In the making of all these three discourses, soldiers' feeling of disappointment is crucial in the new setting of civilian life where they realize the indifference and insensitivity of the people around them and the society at large with regard to the war in the Southeast. (pp. 108–109)

When veterans came back to their homes where they lived prior to their military service, they often felt that their community was not sensitive to their experience, and they were not welcomed as heroes despite having risked their lives. Furthermore, knowing firsthand the severity of the conflict in Eastern Anatolia/Kurdistan, it was hard to come back to a community ignorant of the dynamics and severity of the situation, which added to their confusion and disappointment.

Due to random selection and the mandatory nature of military service, someone from a Kurdish origin could end up in Eastern Anatolia fighting against the PKK, which complicates their experience and their relationship with their Kurdish and Turkish identities. One soldier, who identifies as Kurdish, referring to his community, states:

> How could they see me as a hero? I fought against my people. I don't think it is necessary to tell people where I did my military service. I know it is not a good thing. If they ask, I say, "I did it in Kayseri" [a city in central Anatolia].[8] (Mater, 1999, p. 31)

There are even Kurdish homes where one relative willingly joined the military and was suddenly fighting against the PKK, and another relative joined PKK, each on opposite sides. One interviewee in Aras' (2014) research shares her deep anxiety because her son joined the PKK, and her grandson was doing his mandatory Turkish military service at the same time. She was haunted by the idea that her son and grandson might accidentally kill each other on the battlefield. Combat trauma can be an inter-ethnically complicated matter.

More research needs to be done—and publicly shared—on the psychological impact of combat trauma, not only for injured veterans and those in mandatory service, but for the entire range of military experience: both professional and nonprofessional soldiers and those injured and not injured, coupled with demographic, cultural, and ethnic differences. Additionally, communities and societal functions need to organize in order to increase awareness of the war in Eastern Anatolia/Kurdistan so they can help to build empathy for veterans. Empathic responses from both family members and their communities could help integrate veterans back into their home environments and could help lessen their PTSD and stress-related symptoms. Furthermore, according to Vedat Şar's (2017) review, the response to these extraordinary events should not ostracize the victim, but rather should view them as survivors. And because the impact of combat trauma is an adverse experience affecting large numbers of people, all aspects of society—from the government to the media, from medical systems to legal institutions—should participate in the management of the crisis.

Regarding the transgenerational aspects of PTSD in veterans, international research has had conflicting results. Based on Rachel Dekel and Hadass Goldblatt's (2008) meta-analysis, while some research found a correlation between a father's and son's PTSD symptoms, others did not (pp. 282–283). Thus, there is no direct link showing that a veteran who has PTSD will have children who also suffer from it. Although a father's PTSD and stress-related symptoms could negatively affect his children's psychological health, the environment, relatives, other caregivers, and the community play a crucial role in the ways that children respond to their father's symptoms (Dekel & Goldblatt, 2008). Community and societal functions appear to be crucial in either permitting/increasing or preventing/lessening PTSD and stress-related symptoms for the survivors and future generations.

Civilians Caught Between PKK and the Turkish Military

Ramazan Aras in his 2014 book *The Formation of Kurdishness in Turkey* shared a personal story that happened when he was 10 years old, a few years after the PKK's armed struggle began. In 1987, in Kebola, Kurdistan, while sleeping on the roof on a warm summer night (a common practice in Eastern Anatolia), Aras was woken from his sleep by the sounds of bullets and women screaming. Frightened by them, his family rushed back inside the house and waited through the night. In the morning, they found out that it was guerrillas attempting to execute a man who was *xayin, xwefiros*, meaning traitor, who was working for the state. However, when the guerrillas came inside, they found the man was not home and instead killed his two wives and four children. Aras says that this was when the troubles in his town began; the culture of fear has spread across Kurdistan more intensely since then.

The culture of fear for Kurds dates back to the formation of the Republic of Turkey and the violent suppression of Kurdish rebellions and resistance (1925–1938). Since then, generation by generation, the region has experienced ongoing assimilation projects and violent practices. Fear has become a way of life; what is more, armed conflict since 1984 has added further fear and trauma to the Kurdish experience. In the 1990s, villagers in Eastern Anatolia/Kurdistan suffered most because they were right at the front line of the war between the PKK and the state (Aras, 2014, pp. 84–85). The state pressured civilians to join government forces, and the PKK demanded support, shelter, and food. No matter what they did, civilians faced the consequences—they were trapped between the two.

If civilians aligned themselves with the state, it put them in conflict with the PKK. The PKK executed spies, village guards (*korucu*), and teachers working for the Turkish government. Being fearful of the state and being against PKK's use of violence and force, many Kurds tried to avoid the conflict and did not want to be associated with the PKK. However, civilians did not always have the choice or the ability to stay away. When armed PKK members turned up at their door demanding food and shelter, those in remote places did not have much choice and did so. Alternately, if the person at their door was a relative, the choice was inevitable despite differences in political views. Civilians found themselves helping a PKK member, either by choice or armed force; a spy or a village guard (armed civilians paid by the state, discussed further in the following section) from their community could report them to the state leading to recriminations for assisting a PKK member.

Assisting a PKK member was a grave crime (Yurtlu, 2016). According to the Turkish Penal Code Item 220 (TCK, 2004, p. 9017), even if a person was not a member of an armed organization, but they consciously helped the organization or praised, supported, or followed their propaganda, they were considered a member of the organization. The punishment came at a high cost that was not only from the judicial system, but also took the form of detainment, torture, or being labeled as PKK sympathizers or separatists—which meant continuous harassment of all family members. If someone was an actual member of the PKK, consequences were even more violent to the extent of being killed or disappearing into thin air.[9] Personal lived experiences and "rumors of tortures, disappearances, murders by unknown assailants, deaths, killings, massacres, denunciations, and accusations" (Aras, 2014, p. 103) became a routine part of Kurdish civilians' daily lives, which Aras (2014) argues had caused a deep culture of fear that imprinted on Kurdish identities:

> Turkish state reproduced its hegemony not only through brutal rule and the administration of corporeal, psychological and symbolic punishments, but also through the use of certain discourses, propaganda machines and influential institutions. . . . Ghostly and elusive methods of the state in perpetuating fear (dragging of people from their beds in the middle of the nights, large networks of spies in the community, and the constant threat of sudden killings, assassinations and arrests by civil, secret and official state agents) were corroborated by the dispersion of stories and rumors about diverse forms of violence, torture, terror, representing the capability of the state apparatuses. Along with the visual material displayed in the media, these stories and narratives were incorporated into a process of forming the state apparatuses in the public consciousness as objects of fear. (p. 82)

Aras (2014) further argues that because the state employed a wide range of spies to report PKK members or supporters, it created a culture of mistrust and suspicion amongst Kurds. The state, from within Kurdish communities, hired or forced some people to become village guards or to spy on political insurgents, which "aggravated fear, distrust, and anxiety within the community" (p. 103). Kurdish people were terrorized by fear of both the state and the PKK, which is why Aras calls the war between the PKK and the state "the dirty war" (p. 112).

Kurdish civilians found themselves in incredibly complicated situations where they felt sandwiched between the PKK and the Turkish state. Therefore, many Kurds, if they were not forced to migrate already, voluntarily chose to leave their ancestral lands to move closer to urban areas or other conflict-free zones in Turkey where they then faced discrimination and social marginalization.

Village Guards

In 1985, Village Law, item 74, launched the village guard system in Eastern Anatolia/Kurdistan. The state did not publicly disclose this law. When they launched the village guard project, they appointed, trained, and oversaw these guards in complete secrecy. Their reasoning behind the secrecy was to protect the guards and their families. Only after 2005, with the efforts of Congressman Mesut Değer, this project caught the awareness of the public, and its abolishment is still in question and appears complex. Due to secrecy, it has been hard for researchers to obtain actual numbers of these village guards. However, according to the migration association *GöçDer*'s (2013) report based on newspapers, books, and congressman general statements, it appears that between 1985 and 2009, a total of 123,000 village guards worked for the government. Their numbers increased in the 1990s and decreased after the cease-fire in 2005 (p. 2).

On paper, state-armed Kurdish civilians, the village guards, helped protect villagers from harm, identified and tracked down people who committed crimes, let officials know of natural disasters, and other activities intended to help maintain safety and order in the villages (GöçDer, 2013). The system's main purpose, however, was to fight against the PKK, and beginning in the 1990s, when the war between the PKK and the state was at its peak, the village guard system—while some scholars argue had been effective against them (e.g., Gurcan, 2015)—also created significant consequences for the civilians who did not want to be guards.

The state tried to use tribalism and the feudal system to influence Kurds. If a tribe leader became a village guard, that meant the entire tribe would also support this decision (GöçDer, 2013). In order to create systemic loyalties for the state, the military pressured families in the Kurdish villages to become guards. Most Kurdish people and tribes did not accept the offer. When there was strong resistance to the idea, the state perceived the lack of enthusiasm as support of PKK and criminalized those opposed (Arap & Erat, 2015). People were given an ultimatum: "Either you are one of us or one of them." Civilians who tried to stay away from the war were under great pressure. If they did not accept becoming village guards, they faced forced displacement from their ancestral lands.

Other parts of the world have faced similar tactics: *rondas campesinas* village patrols in Peru and United Self-Defense Forces in Colombia are some examples where the state created civilian forces to help suppress armed violence in their region. The Hamidiye forces from the Ottoman Empire is another example where the state armed and trained civilians to help bring order to the region, but where they ultimately brought more horror than security, unleashing their power over Armenian villagers. In the end, arming civilians has proven to be counterproductive, causing abuse of power and massive displacements (Arap & Erat, 2015; Forero, 2016; GöçDer, 2013; Tüysüz, 2011).

Nur Tüysüz (2011), in her research, investigated why Kurds accepted becoming village guards. She found that the reasons were not homogeneous and included financial incentives, needing security, or pressure from the state. After most villages were emptied, the only jobs left were being a teacher or becoming a guard. Even then, the income in most cases was not enough to feed a household of, in some cases, 14 or more.

Arming civilians—especially in 1990 when the war between PKK and the state was at its peak—giving exceptional power and privileges, enabling violence in the name of fighting "terrorists," has also created a power to be exploited. Exceptional power has caused abuse of power, harassment of civilians for personal benefit, and crimes ranging from rape to kidnapping to armed assault (GöçDer, 2013). The gap in power also created an alternative economy, such as drug trafficking (mostly heroin) and the emergence of new power centers in the political system (Beriker-Atıyas, 1997).

There was also an assimilation aspect of all this. In the Ademli village, where Tüysüz (2011) did her research, villagers, when they accepted becoming village guards, were then armed and aligned themselves with the government. Because their economic survival was based on their relationship with the state, Tüysüz observed that village guards also went through an identity transformation from being Kurdish to identifying more with Turkishness.

After three decades of the village guard system, the state has been facing a cumbersome problem. As long as PKK is active, abolishing and disarming this system puts guards and their families in a vulnerable position with the PKK. Also, if village guards lose their income from the state after almost three decades of employment, they and their families who have relied on it would be left destitute. Thus, the village guards themselves are resisting ending their duty until peace is established between the state and the PKK, until the state can assure both their financial and physical security. As mentioned above, many village guards became involved in illegal activities and have abused their power; abolishing their service might also make them vulnerable to law enforcement or to people with whom they have been in conflict. Civilians violated by the village guards have asked for justice and do not want to go back to their homes before the perpetrators are rightfully persecuted. Justice may provide a sense of safety and assurance for families to be back in their homes.

Over the last 30 years, 300 village guards have lost their jobs because of abusing their position to kidnap women, engaging in a blood feud (*kan davası*), or because of land-related personal matters. There have been approximately 5,000 criminal cases opened against village guards, and 853 temporary guards have been arrested. However, the numbers of those who are still abusing their power are relatively high and they are bold enough to frighten villagers from going back to their homes (GöçDer, 2013, p. 9).

In the 2000s, when the war between PKK and the state gave a promise of slowing down, some families were allowed to go back to their homes. However, the social and economic fabric of the region had been completely destroyed and posed serious financial issues; returnees had to rely on the income of their migrant relatives, who would send them money. More importantly, village guards posed a serious danger to some of these families: after they had fled, the guards who had moved into emptied homes and fields were not willing to leave without a fight. Therefore, many Kurdish families were not able to go back to their homes because of fear of harassment by village guards; or if they did go back, they have been brutally harassed.

Forced Displacement of Kurds

Forced internal displacement has been a recurring theme in human history, from Biblical times to the present. A governing power's strategic control over certain religious or ethnic groups at specific locations has been used to control the economic and political power structure; these government-imposed conflict regulation practices are quite different from large population movements due to natural disasters (Şeker, 2016). Şeker (2016) summarizes that "to homogenize territories within their jurisdiction by employing the methods of demographic engineering . . . manipulation of population figures by statistical records, deportation, assimilation, massacres, and ethnic cleansing were the most frequently used methods" (p. 3). Manipulation of the demographic population with analytic calculations was a common practice in Anatolia during the Ottoman Empire as well, including *sürgün* practices—displacement of Muslim communities to majority non-Muslim regions in an effort to control religious diversity.

In modern states, nation-building practices, demographic engineering, and forced displacement have been primarily implemented as tools against those who resist the state's nationalist agenda. The early Republic of Turkey also adopted this process as a crucial aspect of its demographic engineering and to help spread the ideologies of Turkishness. After the Republic of Turkey was formed, there have been four distinct layers of collective migrations/displacements. The first two were location-specific after (a) the 1925 Sheikh Said rebellion and (b) the 1938 Dersim resistance and massacre, known as Dersim 38 (see Chapter 3). The latter two, which impacted most of the region, were (c) voluntary labor migrations from 1940 to 1980 and (d) forced displacements due to war between PKK and the state.

Right after the suppression of the Sheikh Said rebellion in 1925, the tribes that supported this rebellion were forced to migrate and live in refugee camps in Western Turkey. The state's goal was to disable resistance to the Turkish national identity. Most of these people went back to their villages after the 1947 compulsory settlement law permitted them to do so. The second forced displacement took place after Dersim 38 to assimilate Alevi Kurds and Zazas of Dersim, in which thousands of people were forced to move to mostly Turkish-populated regions. There was no support to help integrate new arrivals. Internally displaced people (IDPs) lived in poverty and were only able to get lower-paying labor jobs. A decade later, when amnesty was declared that allowed their return, some families went back to their villages. It is important to note that people who did go back to their villages had to start from ground zero to rebuild their homes, farms, and businesses.

The next two collective migrations/displacement impacted most of Turkey. As described by A. B. Çelik (2005), one was due to the industrialization era and the other was due to the war between PKK and the Turkish state. The industrialization era between the 1940s and mid-1980s, when people moved to urban areas to have greater opportunities, was based on an economic foundation; its impact on the collective, therefore, is distinctly different from displacements. When migrations are forced, they are more traumatic for people and their communities; when people voluntarily leave for the workforce, they have better social support both from their village and in their new location.

The fourth wave included both forced and voluntary displacement due to the conflict between the Turkish military and PKK, which started in the mid-1980s and accelerated in the 1990s. Most of these displaced Kurdish people faced poverty, severe discrimination, social exclusion, and marginalization where their new cities had largely Turkish populations.

Women who were displaced had different experiences than their male counterparts. After arriving in crowded urban cities, women were cramped into apartment buildings; those who did not speak Turkish and were economically marginalized had even more difficulty integrating and often suffered from depression. In one study, a migrant woman in Istanbul says (with her daughter's help in translation from Kurdish to Turkish):

> Back in my village, I had more freedom. When men worked, I used to take care of animals and children. Here, I only have to stay at home. When I was in my village, and I needed something, I could go outside and buy it. Here, I do not even have the chance to sit outside in the garden. There, I used to share a lot of things with people. Here, I sit at home with my hands tied up. (Interview, February 5, 2000, in A. B. Çelik, 2005, p. 146)

Kurdish families with greater economic power prior to migration had an easier time adjusting. However, most men and women came from remote villages or places where they relied on social and environmental resources. They had gardens, crops, animals, and a social system that maintained their livelihood. Leaving their home towns, migrants had to find ways to adapt and survive in an environment that was foreign to them. Most women stayed home and those who did work had lower-paying jobs, such as house cleaners. One research study found that some families made it in the big cities, despite the odds, due to women's determination (Erman, 1998).

These were primarily Alevi families that did not have as strict gender and hierarchy rules as Sunni Islam. Men mostly found work in construction or other hard labor. Lack of opportunities and feeling stuck with a lower-paying, and lower-prestige job or staying at home took psychological tolls on both men and women.

Despite the social consequences and struggles of the majority, the state never acknowledged the displacement as an issue, which, as a result, produced societal ignorance. An average Turkish person from a city in Western Turkey did not know or understand the dynamics in which people were displaced (A. B. Çelik, 2015). The Turkish neighbors of IDPs labeled them as terrorists, backward, uneducated peasants, and discriminated against them in every area of life.

In the 1990s, the state emptied many villages to prevent PKK support or influence. Via both voluntarily or involuntary movement, IDPs emptied large portions of rural Eastern Anatolia/Kurdistan. By 1998, 3,428 villages were emptied and 3 million Kurds were displaced (Aras, 2014, p. 91; V. Çetin, 2005; Muller & Linzey, 2007). F. Çelik (2015) points out there is a large discrepancy in the count of people displaced between NGOs—who have claimed up to 4 million—and the state—who has claimed as low as 378,335. This discrepancy problematizes the conceptualization of the issue and also shows the state's willful ignorance toward the seriousness of Kurdish displacement (pp. 204–205).

Van Bruinessen (1999) writes:

> In some cases, villagers were given the choice between joining pro-government militias [village guards] and actually fighting the PKK or leaving their villages. In other cases, the military just came and ordered people to leave the village, which then was burned. There were also cases where PKK guerrilla fighters forced the evacuation of pro-government villages. . . . Many more villages were "voluntarily" evacuated because the inhabitants could no longer survive under the conditions of guerrilla war, in which both sides put pressure on them. . . . Apart from those who joined the pro-government militias (named "village guards"), no other civilians remain. (para. 15)

Facing displacement and seeing their homes and fields burned were traumatic experiences. Aras (2014) writes that in his interviews, when people recalled the moments of watching their homes burning down in the 1990s, they used phrases such as "My heart was burning" or the literal translation "My lung was burning" to describe their experience (p. 90). In 2012, the Kurdish population in Istanbul reached almost one-third of the overall population (Kirişçi, 1998). According to a research report on internal displacement in Turkey:

Children typically make up around 60% of displaced populations or around 600,000 children in this case. Around 36% of the IDPs are believed to live in the south-east, around 30% in central-eastern regions, and 10% in Istanbul. The displacement affects primarily people of Kurdish origin. (Norwegian Refugee Council, Internal Displacement Monitoring Centre, 2010, p. 5)

Undeniably, voluntary or forced displacements have caused sociocultural trauma for everyone involved (F. Tekin, 2011). The consequences of internal displacements have been poverty, difficulty adjusting, discrimination, lack of legal rights, lack of job opportunities, language and cultural barriers, and psychological overwhelm, to name just a few (Aras, 2014; B. Ayata & Yükseker, 2005, p. 37; A. B. Çelik, 2005; Erman, 1998; A. Z. Ünal, 2013). In the last two decades, due to the poverty and discrimination Kurdish communities faced, additional issues have manifested, such as "increasing use of drugs, resort[ing] to prostitution and illegal activities" (A. B. Çelik, 2005, p. 161). Thus, the various side-effects of forced internal displacement and the previous mentioned ethnopolitical issues of the Kurds still need addressing.

The second and third generations of these IDPs, for the most part, have integrated and adjusted fairly well in their new environments. Furthermore, after a decades-long adjustment and integration to Western Turkey, violence and potential conflicts continue in Eastern Anatolia/Kurdistan. With the lack of infrastructure and opportunities in their homelands, it has become less likely that IDPs would want to return to their villages (A. B. Çelik, 2015; Stefanovic et al., 2014).

Arriving in a different climate, language, and culture have caused many psychological issues. Research with IDPs in Turkey show that the consequences of forced migration have causes psychiatric symptoms and disorders such as depression, PTSD, anxiety, and even conditions leading up to suicide (Aker et al., 2002; Akkaya-Kalaycı et al., 2015; Ergun et al., 2008; Gülşen et al., 2010; Knipscheer et al., 2009; Tuzcu & Bademli, 2014). Recent research with 210 children and adolescents aged 6–18 years in Istanbul concludes that "internal migration can be considered a serious risk factor for suicidal behavior. Furthermore, the degree of cultural differences between the area of origin and the new environment can be of vital importance" (Akkaya-Kalaycı et al., 2015, p. 32). Displaced men, women, and children experience economic, societal, and political difficulties, which significantly disrupt family dynamics and create difficulty adjusting to the new environment. A group of psychotherapists in Turkey found that these difficulties may lead to PTSD, depression, and other stress-related and somatic symptoms. Furthermore, forced displacement produces similar psychological consequences as seen in torture survivors, with significantly heightened symptoms when both were experienced. The authors argue that because the internal displacement problem in Turkey is psycho-social, one amplifying the other, the solution also needs to incorporate political, legal, and economic support and additionally address the physical and psychological health of the individuals (Aker et al., 2002).

The voluntary return of the IDPs and their sustainability once back in their homes is integral to the collective healing from displacements (Stefanovic et al., 2014). It would be hard to return when the conflict persists in Kurdistan; however, even if the conditions are resolved, many will choose not to return. Three decades after the war between PKK and the state began, most IDPs have established lives in their new areas. Thus, even if the war ended, most people who integrated into their new homes, learned a new language, established jobs, and attained stability are less likely to return. But for some, the longing for their land is greater than the risks. Two research studies found that elderly people still want to go back to their villages (A. B. Çelik, 2015; Stefanovic et al., 2014). Strong and positive memories about their homes, poverty conditions in displacement, not being fluent in Turkish, seeing most of their community's return, or receiving compensation were additional components that increased the likelihood of IDPs returning to their home villages (Stefanovic et al., 2014). However, continuing war conditions, fear of village guards, and the lack of acknowledgment and accountability from the state prevent millions from fully reclaiming their homes and rebuilding sustainable lives.

Since the 1990s, IDPs organized and opened several nongovernmental organizations (NGOs) to aid the internal displacement crisis. These efforts played a significant role in mobilizing and supporting IDPs (A. B. Çelik, 2005). However, governmental support for IDPs did not exist, and only after international pressure did the government allow some to go back to their villages and agree to pay them compensation. The government enacted the Law of Compensation for Losses Resulting from Terrorism and the Fight Against Terrorism (Compensation Law) in October 2004. However, because the villages and their social fabric were already destroyed, and rehabilitation and monetary support were only enough to fix roads and a few structures, villagers were not able to re-establish socio-economic balance (B. Ayata & Yükseker, 2005, p. 37). Çelik (2005) argues the Compensation Law was not an attempt to resolve the issue from the ground–up—there were too many issues with the distribution and application of the funding—but rather a display for Europe.

The root cause of the forced displacement issue has been the conflict between the Turkish state and Kurdish identity, and part of a large-scale demographic engineering processes. B. Ayata and Yükseker (2005) further argue that because the government has not acknowledged the root causes or the psycho-social and economic damages of forced displacements, has not taken full responsibility for the atrocities that the state caused in the region, and continues to deny the ethnopolitical place of Kurds, they fail to address critical issues and find solutions even two decades after the major waves of displacements. Furthermore, despite international pressure, the state's continual denial of the consequences of the displacement and the military's counterproductive practices continue to hinder not only attending to the wounds of IDPs but also "post-conflict peace-building, such as reconciliation, justice, and accountability" (p. 37). Civil society organizations were recently able to influence and amend a few changes to the Compensation Laws; however, A. B. Çelik (2015) argues that for more sustainable reconciliation, the vision of these organizations needs to expand from being mere "issues of justice, truth-finding, and historical responsibility" (p. 215). She argues that it is essential for any reconciliation effort to also consider the decades-long accumulated mistrust between multiple layers of the society and state.

Thus, forced displacement issues have become transnational. Displacement and diaspora experiences, when viewed in relation to both the country of origin and of exile, can give a deeper understanding of the social reality in which refugees live (Wahlbeck, 1998, p. 2). The large-scale population movements of the 1980s and 1990s were not limited to those within Turkey. Many Kurds migrated to Europe or other parts of the world as asylum-seekers or immigrants. Peasants from the Turkish part of Kurdistan today are more likely to live in places like Van, Istanbul, or Berlin than in their old mountain villages. Quite possibly, their village, like thousands of others, was burned by security forces or guerrillas of the PKK (van Bruinessen, 1999).

These voluntary and involuntary migrations entirely changed the Kurdish collective experience, making their movement not only limited to Kurdistan but also deeply tied to the diaspora experience. B. Ayata (2011) in her dissertation argues:

> ... the Turkish state, by deliberately displacing Kurds from their traditional region in the 1990s, not only caused them to migrate either to the peripheries of Turkish cities or to other parts of Europe, but also inadvertently enabled deterritorialized forms and transnational spaces for Kurdish mobilization. Particularly the recreation of Kurdish identity in and through Europe allowed for a mobilization of ideas and resources of the Kurdish diaspora that produced a "boomerang effect," contesting and resisting the politics of displacement and its denial of the Turkish state. (p. ii)

The state adopted forced displacement projects of assimilation, silencing, and control purposes; however, in the end it created what Ayata (2011) calls a "boomerang effect," which encouraged strong Kurdish mobilization. The contact that IDPs had with each other, either within Turkey or in the diaspora, has been the catalyst of Kurdish nationalism.

Kurdish nationalist organizations and movements exist across Kurdistan, which includes regions in Iraq, Syria, Iran, and Turkey. Their political movements have become powerful in the 1980s and 1990s in the Middle East and later in the diaspora. One of the reasons that the movements were successful was due to political instability in the Arab regions (Bozarslan, 2004). Kurdish nationalism emerged in relation to Turkish, Arab, and Persian nationalist regimes within these countries (van Bruinessen, 2000). Also, the rise of transportation, immigration, and technology brought many together in the diaspora and provided a fertile ground for organizing and mobilizing. Aras (2014, p. 77) points out that Turkish, Arab, and Persian nationalist movements not only marginalized Kurds but also aimed to assimilate their own populations with secularization, Westernization, and modernization projects. Therefore, Kurdish nationalism in recent years is raising awareness against Western influence, becoming more inclusive, and transforming into more of a transnational movement

Violence Against Alevis

In 1991, minority rights gained particular importance given the Turkish government's priority of joining the European Union (EU). In that same year, the state repealed a law that previously banned publication and broadcasting in any language other than Turkish. This relaxation at the state level provided a platform for ethnic identities to explore their narratives. Kurds, Alevis, Laz, and Circassians began publishing and organizing.

Circassians who were refugees from Eastern Europe became interested in their homelands and began taking trips to ancestral lands—some even moving back. Between 1990 and 1995 alone, more books were published in Turkey about the Alevis than about any other ethnic group. They began seeing themselves as another ethnic group that further fueled the identity-based conflict between Sunni Muslims and Alevis, which was somewhat dormant earlier in the century (van Bruinessen, 1996).

Alevis, since the rise of the Republic of Turkey, supported the Turkish state because of its secular outlook. Because Alevis suffered at the hands of Sunni Muslims during the Ottoman Empire, a secular state provided some level of security and relief. They often identify as Alevi first, and Kurdish or Turkish second. In the 1980s and 1990s, an upsurge in violence against them triggered their already existing historical traumas of fear and lack of safety and renewed the alienation between them and the state. Kurdish Alevis, in particular, became more involved with the Kurdish nationalist movement, where they were previously aloof due to religious differences.

According to van Bruinessen (1996), at the time, the counter-reaction—the roots of state violence toward Alevis—came from the public first. The level of cultural visibility for Alevis helped their identity and culture to be expressed, experienced, broadcasted, and communicated; however, in the public eye this visibility caused discomfort amongst extremist Sunni Turkish nationalist communities and evoked pre-existing emotions, such as hatred, resentments, and anger toward Alevis. Taking "justice" into their own hands, with provocations from newspapers and institutions, nationalist extremist groups attacked Alevi villages and conferences where police failed to intervene and protect Alevi citizens. The most violent events included the Maraş massacre in 1978, the Sivas massacre in 1993, and the Gazi neighborhood massacre in 1995. There were also military operations in Alevi-populated villages in Eastern Anatolia between 1994 and 1995.

Maraş Massacre

In 1978, ultra-right-wing groups in Maraş attacked Alevi residents with slogans such as "Maraş is going to be Alevi's grave," and brutally killed over 100 people (Alemdar & Çorbacıoğlu, 2012, p.119). The state defended itself by claiming it did not hear about the events until after the fact, which is why they were not able to intervene. Similar events also occurred in Malatya (1978), in Çorum (1980) right before the military coup, and in Sivas (1993).

Sivas Massacre

During the Alevis cultural festival in 1993, a number of Alevi intellectuals, scholars, and musicians gathered in Sivas. Aziz Nesin, an intellectual, offended Sunni Muslim groups during his speech on July 1. Thousands of angry civilians surrounded the Madımak hotel on July 2, where conference participants were staying, and had slogans against Alevis and Aziz Nesin. People at the hotel had no place to go for fear of being lynched if they stepped outside. The tension grew, and a group firebombed the hotel, causing it to burn while people were trapped inside. A small number of police officers tried to help and were able to save a few people (including Aziz Nesin), but government support was very limited, and in the end, the attack claimed 37 Alevi lives.

Gazi Neighborhood Massacre

In March 1995, in the mostly Alevi- and Kurdish-populated Gazi neighborhood of Istanbul, an unidentified group opened fire on an Alevi tea house killing one, Alevi Dede (a religious leader), and injuring several others. People in the neighborhood were already fed up with police restrictions and brutality. The Gazi neighborhood, because of its demographics, had been under strict police control since the war between PKK and the Turkish military started. Furthermore, the media was featuring the Gazi neighborhood as the "other," amplifying their difference in the public's eye (Yonucu, 2014). Fed up with the unsystematic identification controls, house controls, and finally the death of an Alevi young man under police custody a week before, this attack on the tea house triggered residents already living in pain and anger. In protest, people in the neighborhood began to march to the police station. Police responded with extreme brutality turning the streets into a war zone, which claimed the lives of 15-18 Alevis, injuring several others (Dural, 1995; Tüleylioğlu, 2011; van Bruinessen, 1996; Yonucu, 2014).

Large-Scale Military Intervention in Tunceli (Dersim)

From the autumn of 1994 to the end of 1995, the war between PKK and the Turkish state spilled over into Alevi villages. The Turkish military carried out large-scale operations in the mountainous province of Tunceli, which is mostly Alevi Kurds/Zazas. Military operations resulted in the partial or full evacuation of almost a third of the villages in Dersim/Tunceli. Similar operations were implemented in Turkish Alevi villages in Dersim and Sivas as well (van Bruinessen, 1996).

Furthermore, the events that took place in 1990s Dersim (burning villages and intense forced migrations due to war between PKK and the Turkish state) re-triggered Dersimis' already-existing historical trauma of Dersim 38. The documentary film *bindokuzyüzdoksandört* (*nineteenninetyfour*) describes the 1994 forced evacuation of the villages in Dersim; the state destroyed 183 villages and forced 42,000 to leave their homes (Tekinoğlu, 2017). Several of them lived in shacks under refugee conditions for eight years. One interviewee shared, "Since 1994, it is all pain. . . . Like how a river floods and takes everything on its way with it, 1938 was just like that" (Tekinoğlu, 2017, 50:23). After describing all the villages that were emptied and destroyed, he adds, "What they emptied during 1938, they emptied the same areas during 1994" (50:56). In the eye of similar villages, 1938 repeated itself in 1994, adding to Dersimis' collective wounding.

These events in Dersim and other Alevi-populated cities and neighborhoods, coupled with society's prejudices against them, made it difficult for Alevis to live in Turkey, let alone express their culture and identity. Van Bruinessen (1996) makes the connection from the 1980s onward that police increasingly treated Alevi communities with disproportional violence. He argues that during the 1980–1983 coup and years of military rule, the state mostly purged left-wing elements from government positions. The majority of Alevis, historically left-wing supporters, ended up also purged from the police force. As a result, right-wing Turkish nationalists increasingly dominated the police force. Some of the people who previously rioted in Alevi towns became members of the new generation of police. Thus, the force, mostly populated by people who were prejudiced against Alevis, looked the other way and did not intervene when there was violence against them—and in reality, in many cases, police were the perpetrators of brutality.

The peace talks that began in 2009 also aimed to find a solution for violence against Alevis, an "Alevi opening." Unfortunately, the series of workshops between state officials and the Alevi community, which took place for about a year during the peace talks, did not find any effective solutions. Zeynep Alemdar and Rana Birden Çorbacıoğlu (2012) argue that the meetings had a Sunni government-centric position. Questions such as who came to Anatolia first caused heated debate. Even though no practical solutions arose as a result, one positive aspect of these talks was that Sunni participants came in contact with Alevis in a dialogue format—which in turn changed some of the government views of Alevis. The meetings were therefore able to break some of the dehumanizing perspectives of Alevis and reduce the us-versus-them mentality.

Chaldiran War

The conflict between Alevis and Sunni Muslims goes back to Selim I's rule of the Ottoman Empire in the early 1500s, which, according to historian Fikret Adanır (2015), was the beginning of cultural and violent turmoil in Anatolia. Up until the 15th century, Turkmens, Kurds, and Armenians who shared the same geography—despite wars and conflicts—managed to maintain a culturally and economically vibrant region. However, the Chaldiran War in 1514, a historical trauma of today's Turkish and Kurdish Alevis alike, brought political, cultural, economic, and demographic decline. Caught in the power struggle between the Ottoman Empire and the Safavid dynasty (today's Iran), the region became unstable until the 1639 Kasr-i Sirin Peace Treaty between the Safavid dynasty and the empire.

At the time, the Ottoman Empire and Safavid (Persian) Dynasty were two strong, multi-ethnic empires. The significant confrontations between these two empires took place due to territorial disputes in Eastern Anatolia. The followers of Safavid sheiks were known as *Kızılbaş* ("redhead") because of the red headgear worn by some of the converted Turkmen tribes (Kehl-Bodrogi, 2003, p. 54; van Bruinessen, 1992, p. 139). Safavid sheiks and *Kızılbaş* followed a teaching that grew out of Safi devotional Sufism from Ardabil. The conflict between Ottoman/Kurds and Safavid/*Kızılbaş* (Alevi) was already causing major bloodshed among the Muslim and Christian populace in Anatolia. Selim I, nicknamed "Yavuz the Grim," sworn enemy of Shah Ismael (the head of Safavids), had ascended to the Sultan's throne only two years before. In summer 1514, Selim I marched east to push out the Safavid occupation in Eastern Anatolia. During his march, Selim I led one of the largest domestic massacres in Ottoman history, killing approximately 40,000 Ottoman Alevis for their potential support of Safavids and future unrest. They killed every Alevi that they could find on their way—regardless of their age—in the towns of Tokat, Samsun, Sivas, Amasya, and Yozgat (Mikhail, 2020, pp. 302–303). The Ottomans, led by Selim I, and the Safavids, led by Ismail Shah, battled near Chaldiran (northeast of Lake Van), which ended with the Alevis' crushing defeat (van Bruinessen, 1992, pp 141–143). After the suppression of the Chaldiran War, the Alevis withdrew to remote areas to escape further persecution. In the following centuries, the boundary between the Alevis and Sunni Muslims' socio-religious identities became even more distinct (Kehl-Bodrogi, 2003, p. 55). From 1639 to the late 18th century, Anatolia's dynamics were stable enough, allowing some of the communities to recover from a century-long ongoing dispute. A massacre of great extent is still a vivid part of Alevis' collective memory in Turkey today.

In 2013, President Erdoğan named the newly built third bridge of Istanbul the Yavuz Sultan Selim Bridge. By naming the bridge after one of the Sultans responsible for the massive expansion and success of the Ottoman Empire, he was signaling his embrace of the Ottoman Empire that was cut from secular Turkish experience with the new Republic's formation in 1923 (Mikhail, 2020). His embrace signals his party's wish to reconnect Turkey's roots with the culture and legacy of the Ottoman Empire. However, naming a significant bridge after Selim I "the Grim" was also re-triggering of Alevis' centuries-old historical trauma. Alevi communities were outraged, speaking out about the inappropriateness of naming a large bridge after a Sultan responsible for their people's historical massacres—and the extent to which Erdoğan was willing to embrace Ottoman legacy.

Looking Back From the 21st Century

In the 21st century, most refer to the modern Turkish state as a majority Muslim country. It is true; however, very few understand at what expense. B. Ayata and Hakyemez (2013) write that "the unambiguous reference to modern Turkey as a Muslim country rests on [the] brutal demographic engineering preceding the Republic" (p. 6). If these violent policies had not been carried out, the estimated number of Christians in present-day Turkey would be about 40% of the population, in comparison to less than 1% today (p. 6).

The contemporary issues related to the fall of the Ottoman Empire and the rise of the Republic of Turkey have not been addressed or resolved. Almost 100 years later, the region is going through another identity transformation, this time led by the JDP government that has been in power for over a decade, with a decidedly more Islamic tone. Halil Magnus Karaveli (2018), in his book *Why Turkey Is Authoritarian*, writes:

> [President Erdoğan's] regime has been described as an example of "illiberal democracy." But, clearly, Turkey's political regime has overall been characterized by one form or another of authoritarianism, running from the most unrestrained, with no tolerance for any free expression of the people's will, to more "tempered" versions with a semblance of democracy. . . .
>
> A closer look reveals that secularists and Islamists are, in fact, two sides of the right. And for most of the time, there has been no proper left with a mass following to challenge authoritarian right-wing power. (p. 2)

In 2013, out of environmentalists protecting the small Gezi Park from becoming yet another shopping mall in Taxim, Istanbul, a massive self-organized movement began, called the June Movement. When police attacked protestors with disproportionate violence and destroyed their camp, millions of people from diverse groups who were against Erdoğan's authoritarian regime and police brutality filled the streets for two weeks (Arda, 2015). Police used tear gas and pressurized water to stop protestors. Four protestors were killed, more than 8,000 people were injured, 60 people were severely injured (including losing eyes and long-term disabilities), and millions of people were arrested (Kongar & Küçükkaya, 2013, p. 9). Even though the Gezi Park uprising only lasted for two months with a few smaller-sized protests that followed, it became the backbone of hope for the future of Turkey and democracy for progressive groups.

Erdoğan, the leader of the JDP party, had a much more promising stance in terms of human rights at the beginning of his presidency in 2003. His major focus was Sunni Muslim religious rights—one of the JDP's concerns—and he and the party both lobbied for head scarves being allowed at schools and in government. In the meantime, peace talks with the PKK and the government began, and the meeting between their representatives in February 2015 achieved some level of binding formality. On November 22, 2011, Erdoğan even vaguely "acknowledged" Armenian suffering by offering deep condolences to the descendants of the innocent Ottoman Armenians who lost their lives. Several years before then, Erdoğan also "acknowledged" the suffering of the Dersimis. He said:

If there is [a] need for an apology on behalf of the state, if there is such a practice in the books, I would apologize, and I am apologizing. . . . Dersim is the most tragic event in our recent history. It is a disaster that should now be questioned with courage. (BBC, 2011, para. 6, 14)

To many, Erdoğan's words appeared far from a real acknowledgment. However, his words still had power, and they brought promising signs that there might be an opening for Turkey to face and finally come to terms with its past. It the end, JDP, for the most, succeeded in its religious agenda; however in the process, something visibly shifted and minority and Kurdish rights did not have the same success. Finally, already in fragile peace talks, "Kurdish Opening" (*Kürt Açılımı*), came to a sudden end in 2015, and the tension between political platforms once again intensified.

In January 2016, 1,128 academics signed a petition called "We Will Not Be a Party to This Crime!" protesting the violence against Kurds in Turkey's Kurdistan region. The state's response—instead of engaging in a dialogue—has been to call the academics who signed the petition separatists and PKK sympathizers; many lost their jobs, pensions, and other government opportunities (Abbas & Zalta, 2017).

A few months later, in July 2016, there was an unsuccessful military coup attempt. The JDP government blamed Fethullah Gülen, an Islamic scholar and the leader of the faith-based civil society organization the Gülen movement, and his supporters for orchestrating it. Because Gülen was living in the United States, the JDP government also claimed U.S. involvement in the coup. Gülen and Erdoğan were once allies, both supporting pro-Islamic lines; however, in 2016, Erdoğan declared Gülen and his supporters as the new enemies of the state and launched a massive purge. The media reported the events as "cleansing the Nation" from dirty Gülen supporters. During this purge, academics, journalists, Kurdish politicians, and activists who had previously openly criticized the government became targets. According to Turkey Purge (2019):

The Turkish government has issued a total of 31 decrees since a coup attempt on July 15, 2016. These decrees dismissed a total of 150,348 public servants from their jobs. Additionally, at least 21,000 teachers working at private schools across Turkey had their licenses revoked by Turkey's Education Ministry on July 19, 2016. The Supreme Board of Judges and Prosecutors fired a total of 4,424 prosecutors, judges from their jobs. (para. 1)

When someone is expelled from public service, they are also banned from taking office in public institutions or corporations. The state confiscated the passports of the dismissed public servants—and in some cases also seized their property. Almost 190 signatories of the academic peace petition were removed from their positions and banned from working in the higher education sector. This hopeless purge led one young academic to suicide when he received rejections from all of his job applications. In July 2019, after three years of legal battle, the Constitutional Court finally cleared the peace petition signature academics from spurious "terrorism propaganda" charges. The number of detained may change accordingly, but the damage to the well-being and careers of many is done.

Decades of collective traumatic events caused severe ruptures both in society and individuals. The cultures and ethnicities mentioned have experienced traumatic events similarly or in different ways throughout many generations. Grounded in the 21st century, when one looks back at the last 100 years in Turkey, patterns reveal that even though victims have changed, the regime has been similar. Since the transition to the Republic of Turkey, in most cases perpetrators have not been brought into justice. In contrast, many have been given high-level government positions or other critical duties. Fatma Müge Göçek (2015) argues that historically letting perpetrators get away with their crimes—in fact, in some cases, rewarding them—has created a culture of "I can get away with anything" as long as the perpetration is made in the name of protecting the nation.

Aras (2014) writes that the Kurdish struggle has been against the Turkish state, not the Turkish people per se. Peace and reconciliation efforts are in the hands of the state; however, the Turkish state would need to change its course, meaning stop its violent practices and bring those responsible for torture, humiliation, and murders to justice. It sounds like common sense, but bringing perpetrators to justice and stopping violence in Turkey is a hopelessly tangled mission.

Collective healing is similar to psychological healing in some ways. Through shared ideologies and identities, people merge into one psyche, repeating earlier traumatic narratives. For the healing process to begin, people need to be willing to look at the past and face the good with the bad and learn from these mistakes. Learning from the past and evolving is complicated and is, unfortunately, not the case in Turkey—now or in the past. Remembering, mourning, and forgiving are important aspects of healing from collective historical traumas. Turkish society is much like a person who is in constant denial of who they are, denial of what they did, and repeating familiar patterns. This refusal prevents collective recollection, and since the last century, Turkey has been stalled at the remembering stage of collective healing, which is adding more layers of trauma to each living generation, making the issues ever more complicated.

Victims within this society are struggling to feel safe enough for their own personal healing to occur, causing many to emigrate and apply for asylum elsewhere. A victim of state violence needs a sense of safety to begin their healing process. However, enough safety for psychological healing is not available in Turkey due to government control and totalitarianism. Perpetrators easily get away with crimes. People who speak openly about truth are jailed. Power has an intoxicating nature, and people who rise to power in a patriarchal system literally become different person (Garrard & Robinson, 2015). People in smaller communities are trying to create their sense of safety in the face of the rigid stance of the state. Unfortunately, fear and instability find their way into these communities.

Turkey holds diverse experiences of historical traumas. The last three chapters elaborate on a litany of traumatic events that have happened in the last century. Given the variety of wars, massacres, deportations, forced migrations, torture, and abuse, almost no group of people has been exempt. Historical trauma symptoms are often studied through the behavior of the descendants of victims. However, symptoms may also manifest in the mind and psyche of the state's perpetrators. In other words, the trauma that perpetrators inflict is also imposed on their own physical and social body. Symptoms leading up to the battering of women, child abuse, alcoholism, gambling, drug abuse, silencing and the numbing of emotions, uncontrollable rage, and intolerance of differences are transmitted through the family and the societal functions without a specific cultural and historical reference and are often normalized. Some of these people may end up being in the role of a guard torturing inmates, or a police officer with cruel practices, a teacher exploding with rage at their students. This is not to say that everyone would express these kinds of behaviors; many in this society reject becoming the perpetrator.

Nevertheless, in Turkey's case, abuses are systemically allowed, which makes it difficult for anyone to reject violence as a societal contract. Most Turks who have become today's perpetrators or bystanders are the victims of another, separate personal atrocity, either in their lifetime or from previous generations. A sincere and truthful look at the historical context in Turkey could show how to understand to whom and in which ways these traumas may have infected each person. I present a wide variety of historically collective traumas, and how society has been affected by these experiences. Economic difficulties, wartime struggles, epidemics, and lack of options all could disrupt a family lineage, and the effects of these traumas could be passed down to the generations alive today.

Furthermore, Armenians, Kurds, and Turks have co-existed and shared histories. Their present and future need to be considered in relationship with each other, particularly in their shared victimhood and their relational experiences of collective historical trauma as victims, bystanders, and perpetrators. All intricate groups need to address that each group might have changed roles at different times. Kurds became perpetrators of Armenian violence as part of the Hamidiye Cavalry. Kurds and Turks fought side-by-side against Western imperial invasion, and Kurds played a role in the Armenian Genocide. The Republic of Turkey's formation and Kurds' oppression by the Turkish State are some of the examples mentioned in the last three chapters.

Almost a century ago, over a million Muslim refugees and migrants arrived in Anatolia from Greece, the Balkans, and Eastern Europe. Muslim solidarity resulted in near-complete expulsion of non-Muslim communities. The young Committee of Union and Progress (CUP) reign became fully dictatorial, assassinated opponents, and war conditions were exploited to create a new Turkish national bourgeoisie and a new Turkish homeland in Anatolia. The pogroms of September 6–7, 1955 and other events that targeted non-Muslim communities in Turkey caused capital to change hands and formed the secular Turkish State.

In the 21st century, a different kind of a story with similar uncompromised methods is being repeated. Turkey is experiencing another wave of events that is causing capital to change hands. Once again, society's norms and values are shifting, but this time from secular toward Islamic lines. Moreover, the civil war that broke out in Syria in 2011 created a global refugee crisis. Turkey, as one of its neighbors, has been hosting more than one million refugees from Syria. The increase in refugee numbers has begun to change the social fabric in places where refugees are becoming the majority (Çağaptay, 2014). Traumatized by war and grim conditions of being a refugee, they adapt in any way they can.

Turkish society may be entering a new traumatic sequence with another "destructive" type of leadership with the presidency of Erdoğan. Therefore, it is crucial at transition times like this to understand and learn from our history so as not to replicate traumatic patterns. The learning about and change of a societal pattern does not happen overnight, but there have been various openings in the society, increasing from the 1980s. In light of the last decade's traumatic developments, however, whether Turkish society will continue to open up and begin a reparative period or enter into another traumatic sequence is still to be determined. The direction of the change is in the hands of the living generations today. Each person and community hold tremendous responsibility to determine the future of Anatolia for the rest of the 21st century.

CHAPTER

5

Epistemologies of Ignorance of Turkishness and Healing through Meeting the "Other"

In the context of transgenerational traumas in Turkey, the epistemologies of ignorance, the promotion and maintenance of ignorance for purposes of control and domination (Sullivan & Tuana, 2007), appears as a suppressive and silencing swath covering the entire society, preventing transgenerational trauma from being discussed both at the individual and collective levels. Epistemologies of ignorance have become a societal coping mechanism, a way to learn to forget that, either consciously or unconsciously, people are choosing to ignore specific phenomena or events for the protection of their collective Turkish identity and sense of safety and stability. As a result, transgenerational traumas, coupled with epistemologies of ignorance, have been preventing these and other historical traumas from being appropriately discussed and ultimately healed.

The denial of the Kurds' ethnopolitical place in Turkey and of the Armenian genocide is not based on a mere gap in knowledge. It also results from epistemological ignorance that is produced and maintained by the state and Turkish society. In order to explore avenues of healing and peace, epistemological errors need to be excavated, examined, and addressed. In simple terms: partial information can only find partial solutions. Wrong information can only find the wrong solutions. Unfortunately, both types of information continue to perpetuate violence and suffering. Ignorance does not justify violence or silence. Ironically, there is a saying in Turkey: "*Bilmemek değil öğrenmemek ayıp,*" or, "What is shameful, is not 'not to know,' it is 'not to learn.'" Surfacing truths and implementing solutions is a complex, living, and ever-evolving process where one solution or perspective will always be limiting and ignorant of the complex societal dynamics in place.

Correspondingly, this chapter introduces epistemologies of ignorance, and explores the Turkish state and society's continuous ignorance of Kurds' ethnopolitical place, as well as its ignorance about Armenian suffering.

Furthermore, the chapter reviews how Turkish identity evolved in ignorance of its privilege, and ways in which a regular Turkish person struggles with history and identity due to paradoxical, partial, or lack of information—or downright misinformation.

Based on my research, I found that one can hold four different positions in the narrative: (a) the creators, (b) the complicit, (c) those who do not know any different, and (d) those who question or challenge. The creators deliberately manipulate or change the history and write the history books and other public sources with the truth they desire. The complicit, even though they know truthful narratives, remain silent to protect themselves. Those who do not know any different are utterly ignorant of these dynamics, or has partial knowledge. People who question and challenge, despite the odds, choose to stay steadfast to their truth and show up in opposition to the first three groups. It is possible for someone in a state of ignorance to begin to question and challenge; however, it is an intellectually and emotionally painful process. My journey moved me from complete ignorance to trying to do something about it—now.

Healing the Wounds of History through Drama and the Arts

Healing the Wounds of History (HWH) workshops contributed to my understanding of ignorance and how, epistemologically, Armenians, Kurds, and Turks alike are situated differently amongst each other and also within their own groups. Using drama therapy and psychodrama techniques, HWH takes a psychological approach to conflict, providing a map to help individuals, groups, and communities traverse the emotional terrain toward reconciliation (Leveton & Volkas, 2010; Volkas, 2003, 2009, 2014).

In 2015, Armand Volkas facilitated a Healing the Wounds of History (HWH) training for a group of counseling students in Emeryville, California. In the HWH model, the first few weeks of the class are geared toward skill-building and teaching the fundamentals of this approach. The last day of class is accompanied by a free workshop with external participants who share a common legacy of trauma, so students can witness how Volkas works with his clients. On this particular occasion, he invited me to coordinate the workshop. I posted a call for Turkish, Kurdish, and Armenian workshop participation on various social media sites in the San Francisco Bay Area and recruited participants. I had a phone call with each participant before the workshop, so I could introduce myself and answer any questions they might have about the workshop.

Most of the students who were to assist Volkas during the workshop did not have a direct relationship with and knowledge of the conflict. Therefore, my role was to inform the students about the different perspectives of Turkey's history and frame the variety of experiences that could be present during the day. Cultural competency is one of the most important components of Volkas' HWH approach. Facilitators need to be aware of the historical context and potential differing personal narratives and cultures that participants could bring to the workshop.

I brought materials from different perspectives of the Armenian Genocide, the conflict between the Turkish state and Kurdish identity, the formation of the Republic, and the current news and issues of Turkey. There was another Turkish student in the class. She was deeply offended by some of the materials I brought—mainly the ones about the Armenian Genocide. Just before class ended on the first day, she raised her hand and shared the difficulty she was experiencing throughout the whole session. She appeared frustrated, and her voice was shaky as she spoke. She said she tried not to say anything but did not want to leave without speaking out. She stood up for herself and said, "I don't feel represented. The materials you sent don't represent me. I don't feel seen, and I don't feel safe." Volkas asked if there was anything she needed from us to help her in this process. After a short dialogue, she said she wanted to share historical materials from her perspective with the class. We welcomed this suggestion.

I appreciated her tenacity and willingness to stand up and be heard, because I realized I was educating the class from my scholarly perspective. Her presence and willingness to participate made the experience for the class much fuller—it did not change my perspective, but it expanded my understanding of different narratives of Turks. Moreover, this experience gave the class and me a chance to also understand her perspective, her point of view, how she developed her thinking, and what she believed in.

Since childhood, my reflection of Turks in Turkey has been that children are often given the responsibility of representing their nation in a good light to foreigners. One of the reasons for this adaptation could be in reaction to what cultural critic Edward Said (1978) calls *Orientalism*, a term that describes how the West projected a biased and Orientalist gaze toward the Arab and Muslim world, which was shaped by the cultural attitudes of European imperialism's Occidental paradigm. Secular Turks in particular, who came into power with the rise of the Republic of Turkey in 1923, wanted to align themselves with the Occidental paradigm and prove to the world that they were as modern, forward-looking, and as advanced as the West. The adaptation to Western ideologies caused a form of internalized Orientalism amongst Turks, which Turkish-descent historian Arif Dirlik (1997) calls "self-Orientalism" (p. 13). Hence, the newly formed Turkish nation raised the subsequent generations with the homogeneous Turkish national ideology, which many call "Kemalist ideologies" (based on the founder Mustafa Kemal Atatürk's reforms and regulations).

I also went through a progressive training of becoming a "secular Turk." Additionally, I learned how I should represent my Turkish national identity in the eye of the other. For example, I commonly heard phrases such as, "Do not shame your nation," and, "Be a good representative in the eyes of foreigners." I remember conversations at school or home that posited: "Turks are thought of [or misunderstood] as conservative Muslims by the rest of the world. We have to change that; we have to represent Turks as modern and progressive people." With this thought, people who traveled abroad would be sent off with an unconscious burden to represent Turkey in a positive manner. It occurred to me that perhaps both I and the student who had spoken up had similar historical burdens that were passed on to us. I observed that she, as an international student from Turkey, was focused on the positive aspects of her nation and less receptive to the historical trauma that Anatolia endured, which is understandable when so much beauty and resilience are also present in Turkey. Moreover, feeling proud of one's social and cultural associations is a basic human need and an important pillar of personal self-esteem.

Drawing from psychiatrists William Grier and Price Cobbs' 2000 work on Black rage and identity, and J. W. Klein's 1977 work on Jewish identity and self-esteem, Volkas (2014) writes:

> ... historical trauma can have negative effects on cultural and national identity and self-esteem. Human beings are tribal in nature and have a need to feel good about the tribe to which they belong. When this pride of association is disrupted through a history of war trauma, humiliation, defeat, or subjugation, it negatively affects the collective self-regard in the form of internalized oppression. This can influence the way individuals view or value their own cultures. (p. 46)

In the HWH workshops, personal healing often occurs when participants begin to see the complex layers of their cultural and national identities. As workshop participants claim their ancestral roots, face the good and the bad in their lineage, grieve what needs to be grieved, and process what needs to be processed while being witnessed by their own and opposing cultures, healing from historical trauma occurs.

While personal healing occurs, there is a natural impulse to take constructive action. For example, in Volkas's HWH work, as participants go through the stages of healing, there is an organic development of making commitments to acts of creation or acts of service, which Volkas described as the way an individual bridges their personal and collective experience. Consequently, constructive action in the form of the arts or service allows healing to extend from the individual to the collective.

There may be differing psychological obstacles to healing from historical traumas. For example, different reactions may occur if the person identifies as coming from either a victim or perpetrator culture. They might have a blind spot if they do not know much about their lineage or if they were misinformed. When we are educated about our culture in a certain way, our identity begins to form around those beliefs. With that in mind, when opposing or shadow perspectives from our cultures are presented, we might reject some or all of them. This rejection could either be because of concerns about saving face or fear of betraying our own.

During the class, the Turkish student did not feel seen or represented. Feeling deeply offended, she did not look directly at me or speak to me for days. Perhaps she felt betrayed by me, as a Turk whom she considered one of her own. At the end of the class, she asked me, "As a Turkish person, how come you weren't defending your culture?" In my opinion, defending the Turkish image is a counterproductive concept. Because when the task is healing historical traumas, defense becomes an obstacle. I simply choose not to reject history but to embrace and learn from it. Through my research, I have come to understand that embracing one's lineage and history are the main avenues of collective healing. Through this process of research into multiple disciplines and perspectives, I developed the belief that moving beyond ignorance and facing the reality of our history could be a frightening yet liberating path.

As part of the HWH training, students learn the fundamentals of HWH to facilitate similar workshops; they also learn personal exploration methods, such as psychodrama and other drama-therapy techniques. Later, in the aforementioned HWH training in Emeryville, the same Turkish student conducted a psychodrama for the class, which further unfolded her experience and gave me a chance to understand her underlying reasons for feeling offended in the first place.

Her psychodrama revealed that she felt deep pride in Turkish accomplishments. On the other hand, she also carried the legacy of trauma due to the fall of the Ottoman Empire. In her enactment, the Armenian character showed up bleeding to death, Kurds were hungry and asking for food, and Armenian and Kurdish characters both approached the Turkish character for help. From my interpretation of her performance, she was trying to take care of Armenians and Kurds, but she was short-handed; all of these elements were playing out in her psyche. She did not have enough resources or power to help the Armenians and Kurds; she wanted to but felt unable. It appeared to me that there was a hierarchy in her psyche: Turks were parents, and all the other ethnicities were children under Turkish care. The sense of ethnic hierarchy might arise from the time when the Ottoman Empire ruled many ethnicities and cultures, meaning the Turkish student likely identified with both the Ottoman identity and Turkish elite; as a result, her historical wounding rested in not able to take care of all her children, and the sense of pain she felt. Through the sharing of her psychodrama, it appeared to me that her sense of being offended came from genuine pride for her ancestors, her hierarchical consciousness of class and ethnicity, and her sense of responsibility toward others. After her enactment, she expressed feeling seen in the class and was ready to meet her family, referring to the recruited participants (consisting of Turks, Kurds, and Armenians).

In addition to witnessing her process, her courage to show up in the class despite feelings of offense and anger gave me an opportunity to have a dialogue with someone without agreeing on the "facts." Even though she and I were in disagreement about Turkish history, this was an example whereby I learned that empathy is not about intellectually agreeing with someone else but about understanding their thoughts, feelings, and underlying reasons.

Speaking up in a situation of conflict requires a tremendous amount of courage and confidence from both sides. I know from being on the receiving end of her anger that it was not an easy position to hold. It was emotionally challenging for me to stay in my role as a visiting scholar and also engage with the rest of the class. I felt that I had to be confident about my knowledge, be careful not to get defensive, and, more importantly, remain receptive despite seeming opposition. I have grown personally and professionally through this experience.

Furthermore, we were both educated "modern" Turks who were raised in big cities in Turkey. I could relate to her experience and thinking, because I have been there. Before I started working on my research and making my trips to Turkey, had I been in her situation, I would have probably felt offended, as well. Even though we come from similar cultures, we acquired different perspectives and knowledge over time. We diverged in our thinking due to experience, interest, and relationships. During this process of knowledge formation, what I came to see as truth over time became different from her version of the truth.

Feminist philosopher Linda Martin Alcoff (2007) argues that difference in perception is due to the knowledge and ignorance that are the result of our situatedness as knowers. All knowers are not epistemologically "equals." People are limited and enabled by the specificities of their location, "in time and space, with specific experiences, social locations, modes of perceptual practices and habits, styles of reasoning and sets of interests" (p. 42). These experiences are fluid and open to interpretation but have some objective elements in regard to the conditions of the knower's material reality.

At the time of my encounter with the Turkish student in the story above, I had completed a few years of research and field trips in Turkey, where I was beginning to face the reality of Anatolia in a very personal way. This

Turkish student, on the other hand, was coming from a prestigious Turkish nationalist home; she had just arrived in the United States and her studies were completely different from mine, as she had intellectually immersed herself in different endeavors. Therefore, she believed that the Armenian Genocide did not happen. She called it the "Armenian Issue." In her belief, Armenians in the diaspora were pressuring for genocide recognition in Turkey and internationally for an insidious agenda to disempower Turkish government. The images of dead civilians from 1915 to 1917 were mostly massacred Turks. The genocide lobby is a political pressure meant to hurt Turkey. We must protect the image of Turkey from these lies. In her mind, Armenians in Turkey had no problems. Even her best friend was an Armenian.

Similar to her, I grew up ignorant of certain aspects of history. As an individual, I also grew up with epistemologies of ignorance. I did not know many of the historical arguments I presented in this book before I started working on my research. This is not a personal shortcoming. I grew up hearing one narrative that was continuously reinforced at home, at school, and through media. School narratives during my time did not reference political dynamics among Armenians and Kurds. Turks were the greatest of all. For the most part, in the media, Armenians and Christians did not exist in Turkey. I learned that people in Eastern Anatolia who were mostly Kurds and Northern Anatolians mostly from the Laz ethnic group were considered uneducated and "less than" other populations. Unfounded daily anecdotes made fun of the Laz people. Later, from collective narratives, I heard that the Armenians had betrayed the Turks. The pictures we see of the Armenian Genocide were actually massacred Turks. Kurds want our land. Our ancestors shed their blood to protect this nation. How dare Kurds ask for a piece of it. These are a few examples of the spectrum of narratives one hears and reads.

Depending on one's geographic and cultural location, people's epistemologies of ignorance also differed—but all are dressed in partial truths and misinformation. Whose fault is it if a person believes an untruth from authority and never learned to be able to tell the difference between a truth and a lie? Those who have written historical texts, whom I earlier described as the creators of the narrative, must have known the truth. People who ran the country must have known the truth. A significant number of people must have known.

Since I came to the United States in 2004 and through my research process, I have had experiences that challenged my status quo. I shared some of them in the "Personal Background" section. Eventually, my sense of identity was challenged enough to lead me to conduct a research project about the historical wounding of Anatolia. Eventually, both the Turkish student and I ended up in very different places in terms of our knowledge of Turkish history. Thus, curiosity for truth and active engagement with knowledge could have a transformative effect. On the other hand, not everyone has the time, interest, counter-experiences, or privilege to immerse themselves in such endeavors. Therefore, what has been thought of as truth from the top down through government, family, and media could remain as "truth" for a long time as we busy ourselves with daily routines. Most of these beliefs remain unchallenged until something happens that makes the person wonder. That is where the light of curiosity enters if the person allows it.

Healing the Wounds of History workshops, encompassing drama therapy and psychodrama tools, offer one way participants can learn from one another; through playing roles in each other's stories or simply through witnessing each other's process, participants build empathy and recognition. In these workshops, people who would perhaps otherwise not see the "other" come together for a heartfelt dialogue and intimate story sharing.

At other times, keeping the flame of hope alive becomes a crucial need for both sides of the conflict. For example, for around eight months from 2015 to 2016, Armand Volkas and I co-facilitated ongoing HWH workshops in San Francisco with a group of Kurds and Turks twice a month. That year, in particular, the tension between Kurdish communities and the Turkish state was getting heated. The cease-fire between the Turkish military and PKK, Kurdish opening, and peace talks had recently failed. On December 14, 2015, the Turkish military declared a curfew in Cizre, in the southeastern province of Şırnak, that stayed in place for two long months. Residents were stuck in their homes or basements, unable to go outside for basic needs. If someone was killed on the street, families could not recover dead bodies and were forced to watch them lie on the ground, motionless.

The aftermath of two months of horror was 177 dead bodies, 25 belonging to children. One hundred three deceased bodies were burned and decomposed beyond recognition ("Cizre Basements Will Be Convicted," 2020). When Volkas and I were doing these workshops, participants were receiving this news from Turkey. Many people in the group reported that they were experiencing contradictory feelings: the hope of sharing with a community, and the despair and anger of things they could not control. Some people dropped out because it felt too overwhelming to deal with the stress of the day and work, and then come to these workshops in which heavy topics were being explored. Sometimes, these workshops' purpose was merely to keep hope alive amid great despair, so participants would not feel alone in their grief. At times, the participants thought it was absurd to meet when they could not change anything. "What is the point?" they wondered. "There are more important things to do." The desire for "practical" solutions came up many times. Through this experience, I learned that when the traces of oppression and injustice are present, despite the feelings of despair and profound grief, keeping the flame of hope alive becomes an essential instrument for social activists and scholars.

However, how can we keep the spark of hope alive despite the despair and catastrophes we witness all around us? What do we do when we make close contact with collective pain and injustice, yet there is so little we can do as individuals? Moreover, how do we turn these feelings into constructive action? These are some of the underlying questions I stumbled upon throughout my research.

Critical scholar and educator Paolo Freire (1998) notes, after all, without hope, there is a sense that there is very little we can do, if anything at all. Hope is an ontological need; the attempt to improve the world without hope, and to reduce the struggle of the world with only calculated acts or a purely scientific approach, is a frivolous illusion. Through relevant political analysis, scholars and social activists take the role of unveiling opportunities for hope, despite obstacles. Additionally, in the face of injustice and oppression, it is vital to take action. Even in the face of overwhelming odds, it is vital to hold on to hope and resist oppression, to be in dialogue with the "other" for our psychological well-being and resilience—so that the wells of pain can gradually be transformed into shared grief, reclamation of history, reparations, and hope.

Understanding Epistemologies of Ignorance

The dynamics of knowledge creation, domination, and power have been investigated in the last century with the argument that those who control knowledge control people. Interdisciplinary studies found their way into scholarly works in which political, cultural, and educational practices were combined in unique ways to make critical arguments about society, knowledge, and power dynamics. Critique became a method of investigation. Beginning with critical theory, scholars aimed to expose positions of power between institutions, groups, and individuals, and aimed to uncover the rules, regulations, and norms that prevent people from taking control of their own lives. Feminist research epistemologically investigated how we know what we know, who gets to know, and what theoretical lenses provide a window into the knowledge of women and other oppressed groups, in order to understand the dynamics of knowledge (Hesse-Biber, 2011). A relatively new branch of feminist epistemology from the last two decades illustrates how "ignorance is hardly ever mere 'not-knowing'" (Dotson, 2011, p. 253). Ignorance is a willful adherence to a particular point of view, even if that point of view is proven to be false.

Race and Epistemologies of Ignorance, edited by Shannon Sullivan and Nancy Tuana (2007), references various scholars who have applied the epistemologies of ignorance to the issues of gender and sexuality, the medical industry, and more relevant to this research, to race, racism, and White privilege. Literature in epistemologies of ignorance is widespread. Substantive groups of transdisciplinary areas are converging on the inquiry of ignorance. Exploration of knowledge creation and the lack thereof, as well as the ways in which ignorance has been created and maintained, help reveal dynamics of injustice and who exactly benefits from such dynamics.

For example, Robert Proctor, in his 1995 book *Cancer Wars,* points to controversy and differing arguments among government regulatory agencies, scientists, trade associates, and environmentalists in regard to cancer; he says, "controversy can be engineered: ignorance and uncertainty can be manufactured, maintained, and disseminated" (p. 8). His argument is relevant to Turkey's case because current-day conflicts among Turks, Kurds, and Armenians have deep institutional roots. We must understand the social construction of ignorance to address such societal problems. Furthermore, as I describe later in this chapter, because ignorance is tied to the recurrence of collective traumas and prevents healing from historical wounding, I call for a sense of urgency in understanding epistemologies of ignorance and institutional enforcements for societal healing.

Ignorance can often be seen as a gap in knowledge, "an epistemic oversight that could easily be remedied once noticed . . . an accidental by-product of the limited time and resources that human beings have to investigate and understand their world" (Sullivan & Tuana, 2007, p. 1). Sullivan and Tuana (2007) further argue that while this type of ignorance often exists as the most widely used definition, it is not the only one. In some cases, what we do not know is not a mere gap in knowledge; "sometimes these 'unknowledges' are consciously produced, while other times they are unconsciously generated and supported" (p. 1).

Tuana (2004) additionally writes:

> . . . an important aspect of an epistemology of ignorance is the realization that ignorance should not be theorized as a simple omission of gap but is, in many cases, an active production. Ignorance is frequently constructed and actively preserved, and is linked to issues of cognitive authority, doubt, trust, silencing, and uncertainty. (p. 195)

Thus, what we know, do not know, or know as false also come to reflect societal dynamics. In exploring multiple threads of knowing how and why what is true for one is false for another—and their underlying reasons—researchers can begin to capture a snapshot of a society that is inclusive of differing perspectives, and to identify where gaps and lack of knowledge are exposed.

Epistemologies of ignorance in Turkey have been an important vehicle in the evolution of Turkishness. As such, through wide and uncompromising state-enforced processes, and through institutional sanctions, state and society maintain the denial of the Armenian Genocide and ignorance of the Kurdish ethnopolitical place in Turkey. Consequently, epistemologies of ignorance, generation by generation, continue to fuel traumatization and conflicts.

Political scientist Barış Ünlü (2016) proposes two concepts: Turkishness and the Turkishness Contract, inspired by Whiteness Studies and sociologist Charles Mills' work of *The Racial Contract*. By Turkishness, Ünlü means Turkish individuals and those who accepted the Turkishness Contract; their ethnic position; and their ways of seeing, hearing, feeling, and knowing—as well as not seeing, hearing, feeling, or knowing. He argues that Turkishness was shaped by a set of written/unwritten and spoken/unspoken agreements among the Muslims of Anatolia dating back to 1915. By 1925, through state-enforced practices, the Muslimness Contract was changed to what became known as the Turkishness Contract, which continued to deny the presence and rights of all other ethnicities in the region. As a consequence, those who accepted the Turkishness Contract are unable to understand and reflect on their own privilege and the world they themselves have made.

The experiences of Turkishness also differ based on demographics, such as location (e.g., based on coming from Central versus Western Turkey) or adopted ideologies (based on being Marxist versus Kemalist). However, one thing they all have in common, according to Ünlü, is Turkish ignorance of their own privilege and their inability or difficulty in thinking or reflecting on their privilege in society. These blind spots also create dichotomies, such as between the concepts of *modern* and *backward* (Göle, 1996). Moreover, Turks have seen Kurds as "underdeveloped," "tribal," and "savages" due to ignorance of Kurdish ethnic diversity (Yeğen, 1999a, 1999b). Mills (1997) argues that people from a dominant culture are often blind to the societal dynamics that they created or became signatories to. He writes:

> ... on matters related to race, the Racial Contract prescribes for its signatories an inverted epistemology, an epistemology of ignorance, a particular pattern of localized and global cognitive dysfunctions (which are psychologically and socially functional), producing the ironic outcome that whites will in general be unable to understand the world they themselves have made. (p. 18)

Thus, a person who belongs to a dominant culture (e.g., European Caucasians in the United States, Turks in Turkey) is often blind to most racial dynamics in place, which leads to systemic oppression. It is important to note that this is not a statement about all Caucasian individuals and those who have continuously challenged the status quo; this is about the collective action, oppressive practices, and people who are still invested in their ignorance—people who are acutely the majority. One of the key features of oppressive societies is that they do not identify themselves as oppressive. Dominant cultures as a collective are not only inculcated in harmful epistemic practices, but they often have less motivation to detect their errors or to correct them (Alcoff, 2007). Furthermore, a world shaped by White supremacy has caused oppressors to erroneously see themselves as civilized "superiors" and non-Whites as inferior "savages" (Mills, 2007).

There are transgenerational psychosocial consequences for the oppressed, even centuries later. For example, African American psychologist and public speaker Joy DeGruy has observed particular maladaptive behaviors and belief systems of African Americans in the present, which she refers to as *vacant esteem, ever-present anger, and racist socialization.* She connects them back to centuries-old practices of chattel slavery. De Gruy writes that *vacant esteem,* "believing oneself to have little or no worth" (DeGruy, 2005, p. 125); *ever-present anger,* "where seemingly innocuous incidents become potentially dangerous for no apparent or rational reason" (p. 129); and *racist socialization,* "the belief that white and all things associated with whiteness are superior" (p. 134) are the effects of almost four centuries of legalized abuse, programmed enslavement, and institutionalized oppression. Today's Black Lives Matter movement and Black activists are consciously addressing these maladaptations from several societal functions. Activists and scholars work in platforms from therapy offices to school curriculums, from social media to the entertainment industry.

In addition to societies being ignorant of their own oppressive behaviors, they also can deny their relationality with the oppressed/silenced. Feminist philosopher Sarah Lucia Hoagland (2007) writes that "epistemological and ethical practices of ignorance are strategic and involve a denial of relationality" (p. 96). She additionally argues that cultures evolve in contact with each other and are not autonomous units. As one can see in the example of relationships among jazz musicians, or in *taqsim,* melodic musical improvisation in Middle Eastern music, cultures in contact also affect each other, improvise, respond, and change respectively within particular constraints.

Moreover, Hoagland argued that relationality demands complex communication across, through, and beyond differences. One example of recognizing relationality is the Armenian historian Ronald G. Suny and Turkish sociologist Fatma Müge Göçek's collaborative work with

Workshop for Armenian-Turkish (WATS) in Chicago and Michigan, which later expanded to wider audiences and locations. Suny and Göçek's (2011) co-edited chapter does not deny these relationalities but invites readers to engage with them. They argued that because in Anatolia, Armenians, Kurds, Turks, and many other ethnicities and religious groups had lived side-by-side for more than a thousand years, their histories, identities, and destinies are intertwined and tied to one another. Therefore, one's history cannot exist to the exclusion of the other. Similarly, Ramazan Aras (2014) explained in an anthropological study how Kurdish nationalism in the last century evolved in relation and response to Turkish national identity. Before the Republic of Turkey was formed, Kurdish communities did not consider separatism as strongly. Kurdish separatism evolved in response to the Turkish state's assimilative and oppressive practices against Kurds since the formation of the Republic of Turkey.

In other words, the relatively successful Turkification process, achieved through education, media, urbanization, and other assimilation politics created not only a strong Turkish nationalist identity but also a conscious Kurdish ethnonationalism (Yavuz, 2001). Kurdish anthropologist Ramazan Aras points out the relational and ontological interdependence of the oppressed and the oppressor. Regarding Kurdish nationalism, Aras (2014) writes that Kurds

> subjugated and exposed to integration and assimilation policies. . . , reconstruct their counter-histories. . . . Contrary to the constructed official historiography and social-engineering project of the State, marginalized ethnic groups construct their own worlds through their histories, memories, identities, and culture while struggling with the social, political and military interventions of the State and its apparatuses. (p. 39)

Similar to Kurds in Turkey, Kurds in Iran, Iraq, and Syria have also constructed their identities in relation to the geography, sociopolitical climate, and nations they have been a part of; thus, Kurdish identities, though they have found binding similarities, have also derived differences due to separation by national boundaries over time (van Bruinessen, 1992, 2000). Equivalently, Aras (2014) defines Kurdishness as a "socio-political and cultural domain constructed by religion, cultural history, ideologies, socio-political suffering, and struggle, but not as a homogeneous identity" (pp. 39–40).

I bracket here to explain what I mean by ignorance and denial, as the two may be used interchangeably in some contexts. In this book, I mainly focused on epistemologies of ignorance of Turkishness, as opposed to denial politics. I approached denial and ignorance as two ontologically different terms. Denial could be one of the vehicles or a potential outcome of epistemologies of ignorance. One could deny a fact even if one knows the truth, in which case the denial becomes the vehicle of epistemologies of ignorance. Or, one could be in denial due to lack of knowledge or wrong knowledge, in which case the denial is the outcome of the epistemologies of ignorance.

The Turkish word *yanılma*, which means "error in thinking, opinion, or an idea," comes closer to the meaning of epistemologies of ignorance. For example, Kurdish sociologist Mesut Yeğen (1999a) uses "*yanlış*/error" (p. 22) to describe the Turkish government's wrongful narrative of the "Kurdish problem" as a byproduct or symptom of the Turkish states' wrongful perspective on the current situation. Yeğen argues that the Turkish state's view of the "Kurdish problem" could be summarized in two words: "*Red*/refusal" or "*inkar politikası*/denial politics" (pp. 221, 264).

The Turkish state saw Kurds as "potential Turks" (Yeğen, 2007; Zengin & Demir, 2011). The Turkish state denied the Kurds an ethnopolitical place in society and approached the issues that arose in Kurdistan as a "Kurdish problem" only; as a combination of political reaction, tribalism, banditry; or as based in the underdevelopment of the Kurdish region (Yeğen, 1999a). These assumptions do not include the context of Kurdish culture, ethnic diversity, and history. These false narratives and solutions have been constructed, reinforced, and maintained throughout history.

Aras (2014) writes:

[The] Kurdish question is scrutinized in relation to the dynamics of the nation-state project, underdevelopment, modernization/Westernization and assimilation policies of the state, inter-ethnic relations, nationalism, the surfacing of state violence and the opposing counter-violence, human rights and other socio-political factors that have played a dominant role in the development of this devastating socio-political crisis in modern Turkey. (p. 42)

Some refer to this ethnopolitical issue as the "Kurdish problem," a term that is ignorant in its own framing. When the issue/question is stated as "x problem"—in this case, the "Kurdish problem"—from the beginning, it sounds like the problem is the Kurds', or that being a Kurd is the problem. This framing is highly problematic because it continues to promote Kurds as bad, wrong, and a problem that needs to be solved or dealt with, which maintains ignorance, misinformation, and assimilation. Therefore, throughout this book, I refer to this ethnopolitical problem as the conflict between the Turkish state and Kurdish identity, even though this statement has its own limitations. The problem is not only about identity, or between the state and Kurds, but it was the closest description Dersimi "from Dersim" editor and documentary filmmaker Devrim Tekinoğlu

(D. Tekinoğlu, personal communication, October 20, 2016) and I could come up with at the time.

One may argue that if ignorance is one of the root causes, then resurfacing and communicating truths about historical and current realities should help remedy the situation. Though common sense, this approach is limited, because the sociopolitical context of epistemologies of ignorance and the remedies of conflict between the Turkish state and Kurdish identity is more complicated than simply surfacing and communicating truths about society and history. Over the decades, millions of people have been personally impacted by the conflict: they lost a family member, or they were displaced or wounded. Furthermore, the promotion of truth is a countermovement against existing nationalist narratives and creates a particular reaction from normative Turkish society. From the beginning, national identity in Turkey was built from partial and selected truths to create a state-desired narrative; at its core, the Turkish state sees any opposing argument as a threat to its stability. Therefore, the Turkish state and people with nationalist values react strongly to opposing narratives, as if their livelihood were in danger. Therefore, Kurdish demands to address existing social inequalities, injustices, and their right to be heard are continuously dismissed in the political sphere (Yeğen, 1999a). Moreover, through decades-long oppressive policies and the Turkish government's exploitation of differences and power structures within Kurdish communities, Kurds have also developed conflicting political agendas: from their strong support of the current governments, despite the Turkish government's oppressive politics, to their strong oppositions to them (Yeğen, Tol, & Çalışkan, 2016).[1]

Through the formation of the modern Republic of Turkey and the accompanying radical, widespread, and uncompromising reforms, the Kurdish population in Turkey became severely disadvantaged both culturally and ethnopolitically. They were only able to advance in this new nation-state if they were assimilated into society—in other words, "Turkified." Some Kurds chose Turkishness, but not all. Correspondingly, Kurdish nationalism evolved in reaction to a system that has been willfully ignorant of Kurds' ethnopolitical place in society. Kurdish nationalism has been fueled by radical assimilation policies that have caused violence and oppression.

Kurdish intellectuals argued that violent suppression of the early rebellions and any form of resistance (Sheikh Said in 1925 and resistance in Dersim in 1937) followed by military coups were fundamental turning points in the Kurdish experience (Aras, 2014; Yavuz, 2001). The oppression and large numbers of violent acts against Kurds since the formation of the Republic of Turkey created a siege mentality among Kurds (Yavuz, 2001, p. 12) and resistance as "a way of life" (Aras, 2014, p. 63). Thus, the entanglement of the conflict between the Turkish state and Kurdish identity in Turkey is not because of the mere limitation of knowledge. It is now a combination of century-old collective traumas, epistemologies of ignorance, the ongoing oppression of the Turkish state, and the sometimes-violent resistance of Kurds. That said, over the years and particularly in the last decade, a successful pro-Kurdish political party, PDP (*HDP*), with Kurdish leaders had secured seats within the Turkish parliament, through due democratic progress—which was once again suppressed when the current government, JDP (*AKP*), imprisoned prominent PDP leaders with unfounded claims of their connection with PKK.

Regarding Armenians, the Turkification process and the creation and maintenance of epistemologies of ignorance manifested in forms of forgetting politics. Centuries-old Armenian history, accomplishments, and contributions were erased, and over time were replaced with narratives that only portrayed Armenians as betrayers and enemies. Denial politics as a vehicle for epistemologies of ignorance have caused the majority of today's generation to be in denial because they are ignorant of Armenian history and Armenian suffering in Anatolia.

The first 50 years of the Republic of Turkey can be viewed as the silencing period, which sociologist Şükrü Aslan called a "closed century" (S. Aslan, personal communication, October 2013), during which the state consciously created and maintained epistemologies of ignorance and rolled out uncompromised nation-state building practices. Göçek (2015) summarized that during the fall of the Ottoman Empire and the independence war struggle, non-Muslim elements were the first to be excluded. After the formation of the Republic, secondly, Kurds were excluded from body politics. Kurds who were willing to give up their ethnic identity managed to find a place in the new political system of Turks. Finally, the new secular system excluded its own Muslim Turks. Göçek (2015) writes:

> Non-Muslims were the easiest to exclude from the nation since they had never been fully included in the body politic; the Kurds were also easy to leave out because their inclusion in the body politics had never been fully acknowledged. It was much harder to negotiate the fragmentation and ensuing exclusion within the dominant Muslim Turkish majority since the republican leaders also belonged to this category. The adoption of secularism as a republican principle killed two birds with one stone. (p. 296)

With the adoption of secularism, previously empowered religious communities during the Ottoman Empire, such as religious schools and leaders, foundations, and other institutions no longer had political power. This last exclusion of Muslims allowed secular Turks to be the only ones in power to build the new nation.

The Committee of Union and Progress (CUP) government had already launched the groundwork for the implementation of new reforms. Building on the CUP's earlier activities, the Republic of Turkey's reforms began with the abolition of the Sultanate and Caliphate, introduction of the secular state, Westernization of the judiciary system, establishment of women's rights, replacement of the Arabic alphabet with a Latin one, acceptance of Western social and cultural lifestyles, and adoption of Western economic and business standards. These reforms held a sense of forward-looking pride for many secular Turks.

In his book *Turkey's Modern History,* Hamit Bozarslan (2008) summarizes that on November 1, 1922, under Mustafa Kemal's leadership, the state eliminated the Ottoman Sultanate. Mustafa Kemal made it clear to the Sultan that their titles were purely symbolic. On October 13, 1923, Ankara became the center for government; and on October 29, 1923, Atatürk became the nation's first president. On March 3, 1924, the new government abolished the caliphate (the religious order) and dissolved the religious courts and all judges on April 8, 1924, with a pension. In 1924, a new constitution defined Turkey as a republic, Ankara as the capital, Turkish as the official language, and the Grand National Assembly of Turkey as the sole possessor of sovereignty.

Between October 15 and 20, 1927, Mustafa Kemal Atatürk delivered a six-day speech entitled "Nutuk" to an audience of delegates to the second national congress. The speech was also published in a book format that same year. The end of the speech has a famous calling to the new generation of Turkish youth: "O, Turkish Youth! Your primary duty is forever to preserve and defend Turkish Independence and the Republic of Turkey. This is the very foundation of your existence and your future. This foundation is your most precious treasure." He added that there would be enemies of this treasure, such as Islamic *Shari'a* law, and invited youth to protect this treasure at any cost from any enemy. The constitution was modified in 1928 and removed Islam as the state religion; in 1937, the constitution added Kemalism's six fundamental principles: republicanism, nationalism, populism, reformism, secularism, and statism.

From the start, there were significant core differences between the Republic of Turkey's nationalist views and the Ottoman's multi-ethnic and multi-religious system with pro-Islamic lines. Göçek (2015) writes that the first national assembly in 1920, which guided the country through the independence struggle, was more democratic because it had selected deputies from every region. However, shifts occurred after independence was achieved; and when the second assembly was formed in 1923, when the election was much more tightly controlled, oppositions were carefully eliminated. Newly selected representatives had more loyalty to the state and the nation-building process than to their service to the populace (pp. 309–10).

Reforms were viewed as vehicles that aligned the new Turkish society with the contemporary and modern countries of the world. These reforms had pros and cons. Furthermore, in most cases, these reforms were not instant changes. One example is the establishment of women's rights. The women's movement, even though abruptly presented, appeared as one of the reforms that has its roots in the 19th-century Ottoman Empire. Ottoman women activists, such as Fatma Aliye and other educated urban women, started to write about women's rights and critiqued the patriarchal interpretations of Islam during the late years of the Ottoman Empire.

An earlier seminal work by Nüket Sirman (1989) offers a feminist perspective about women's rights in Turkey; she argues that after the formation of the Republic, new leadership viewed women as "patriotic citizens"—mothers and wives; it turned out that freedom was only for "men." The dynamics changed after the formation of the Republic. Despite the progressive new laws and regulations that gave women the right to elect and vote, women could not establish their organizations, fully participate in politics, and express their voice, which intensified the tension between new republican leaders and women activists. Öztürkmen (2013) writes that

> in this context, women who were opposed to the newly established regime faced difficulties. With her oppositional stance to Atatürk, Halide Edip had to leave Turkey and was not to return until 1939, after his death. Another similar figure Nezihe Muhiddin . . . was prosecuted for corruption as the chair of the Union and was forced to leave her position. . . . In 1935, the Turkish Women's Union dissolved, and like many similar independent organizations, it was invited to join the semi-official People's Houses. (pp. 258–59)

It took more than 40 years before a new grassroots women's movement emerged in Turkey. According to Ayşe Gül Altınay and Yeşim Arat's (2007) research, despite the patriarchal educational system and the continuous oppression of women in Turkey, in the 1980s, Turkish feminists found their voices and started to organize. In the 1990s, several nongovernmental civil women's organizations formed—despite financial struggles—through self-initiatives; since then, the feminist movement has been challenging the status quo. In my early education, the Ottoman women's role in women's rights was mostly excluded or glanced over. I was taught that Atatürk was a "savior" for women in Turkey. Otherwise, if not for him, women would still be sitting at home and not getting an education, and therefore should be grateful. I understand the importance of these reforms and their advantages to women. However, the danger of this simplified statement was that I internalized it as "my rights were given by man, and I should be grateful," which I believe contradicts its intended aim to empower women.

Assimilation Into "Turkishness" through Control of Language and the Education System

As I discussed earlier, the Turkish state and society, consciously and unconsciously, created and maintained the denial of the Armenian Genocide and the Kurdish cultural and ethnopolitical place in Turkey. These multiple layers of ignorance have perpetuated dehumanization, lack of empathy, and violence, and deepened us-versus-them mentalities. Together, the new Turkish national bourgeoisie and the state mobilized education and reforms of the modern Turkish state. They aimed to create a new Turkish identity and national narrative that the people of Turkey could feel proud of. This process of radical change, believed to be implemented for the good of society by the new government, had many side effects. From sociologist Piotr Sztompka's cultural trauma theory, the transition process could be identified as the cultural trauma of social change through destructive impacts. This centralized mandate introduced culturally traumatic sequences to society, resulting in ongoing violence and epistemologies of ignorance. I discussed these sequences in detail in the history chapters. I want to highlight here that within such ignorance, modern Turkish views impacted social and individual memory, erasing both the achievements of minorities and the atrocities of Turks, which resulted in collective amnesia that supported hostility toward the testimony and credibility of traditional Turks who were considered "non-modern" or other minorities.

Furthermore, epistemologies of ignorance within society prevented the "bystander" Turks from having the opportunity to express themselves fully and to think critically. In society's effort to create and maintain a Turkish identity, epistemologies of ignorance developed in many stages. For example, control of language and the education system played integral roles in Turkey's creation and maintenance of epistemologies of ignorance, which I discuss further in the following sections.

Language

In a 2013 Healing the Wounds of History workshop, Rodin, a Kurd in his 40s who was a child in Turkey in the 1970s, shares a memory from his childhood that gives insight into his world. We are in a psychodrama therapy workshop between Turks and Kurds that aims to share, explore, and address historical trauma. Rodin is describing his first day at school at the tender age of 7. Rodin picks people from the group to play himself, the Turkish government, school, media, teacher, and PKK. Rodin, like many of his fellow Kurdish classmates, could not speak Turkish when he started school. In his enactment, he cannot understand what his teacher is telling him.

Moreover, his teacher responds in an angry way that makes him feel stupid for not understanding Turkish. To make matters worse, he is punished every time he speaks Kurdish. In the enactment, the teacher tries to sow distrust among the other Kurdish children. They do this by asking Kurdish students to inform them if and when anyone speaks Kurdish. In this exercise, Rodin is externalizing what he internalized as a Kurdish child growing up in Turkey, through a drama-therapy exercise called "Map of Messages." Rodin directs the actor playing the Turkish Government to say, "We do not want you here." He shares another message from the government: "You are a mountain Turk." The message from his parents is, "We cannot protect you; you are not safe." The message from PKK is, "We have your back." As other workshop participants enact these different roles, Rodin walks around the sculpture of his psyche.

He feels a sense of safety as a political asylee in the U.S. and can finally share his story with a group of people through externalization. It is healing for him to be witnessed as a person in pain as a member of a group oppressed by the Turkish government. Some witnesses are empathetic Turks who hold his story to be true; this shifts something in him and moves him. In the end, he spontaneously sings a Kurdish song as part of his closing statement.

The control of language played a crucial role in the creation of Turkishness, both through the promotion of Turkish as a language (Aydıngün & Aydıngün, 2004) and in prohibition of other languages, such as Kurdish (Cemiloğlu, 2009; Coşkun et al, 2010; Zeydanlıoğlu, 2012). The state policies, laws, and regulations, as well as education, played a crucial role in this process (Derince, 2013).

The 1924 constitution declared Turkish as the nation's official language. One of the first laws put into place was the unification of all education (*Tedridi Tevsirat Kanunu*). This law had roots in the 19th century and the Ottoman's Westernization policies. The language revolution (*Dil Devrimi*) in 1928 abolished the Arabic alphabet and adopted the Roman alphabet. The surname law came into effect in 1934 and required Turkish citizens to obtain a Turkish surname, regardless of their ethnicities and previous status. These first waves of laws and regulations aimed to unite people under one common language and to bring Turkey closer to the West. Welat Zeydanlıoğlu (2012) writes, "It was important for Kemalist ideologies to prove to 'West' that Turks were not backward or members of the 'yellow race' but, in fact, members of the civilized White race" (p. 104).

The new Turkish state launched the "Citizen, speak Turkish!" (*Vatandaş Türkçe konuş!*) campaign in 1927, which covered minority neighborhoods and public areas and transportations with posters to this effect. This campaign not only targeted Kurds but all minorities who did not speak Turkish as their main language. Armenians already traumatized by Armenian deportations and massacres only a decade ago were frightened by this campaign. The campaign peaked in 1937, when Turkish nationalist civilians were harassing anyone who spoke a language other than Turkish. Armenians in Istanbul, beleaguered by harassment and fear of being taken away, stopped speaking Armenian in public.

In 1930, in addition to regulations and campaigns, the state also presented the "science" behind the Turkish language, which dominated academia and the official narrative until the 1970s. These were the Sun-language theory (*Güneş Dili Teorisi*) and Turkish historical thesis (*Türk Tarih Tezi*), which claimed that Turkish was the origin of all languages and Turks were the disseminators of civilization; these were the dominant narratives until the 1970s, when a strengthening leftist movement and Kurdish nationalism began to challenge this official ideology.

During the second half of the century, the state tightened its pressure with more laws and regulations. Article 2, Law No. 7267, passed in 1959, requiring villages to have Turkish names. Article 58, adopted in April 1961, prohibited propaganda in any other language than Turkish. In 1962, the state made the first eight years of education mandatory and opened boarding schools in predominantly Kurdish regions. Kurdish children had to attend school, and the schools were geared toward education, which promoted Turkishness and offered education only in Turkish.

During the 1980–83 military regime, the circumstances were even more gruesome. In 1983, a new law, No. 2932, strictly prohibited speaking, publishing, or promoting in any language other than Turkish, which according to Zeydanlıoğlu (2012), violated several international agreements in regard to the protection of minorities. During this time, anyone who spoke Kurdish or listened to Kurdish music ran the risk of being arrested, tortured, or even killed.

During his presidency in 1985, Turgut Özal attempted to find solutions for the conflict between the state and the Kurdish identity that was intensified by the emergence of PKK and the accompanying violence. His administration managed to repeal Law No. 2932, which allowed speaking, publishing, and the making and listening of music in Kurdish. Education and broadcasting in Kurdish were still illegal. In 1991, when the Turkish state was considering joining the European Union (EU), the government repealed the law that banned publishing in languages other than Turkish. However, on the same day, the Anti-Terror Law No. 3713 (*Terörle Mücadele Kanunu*) passed, which Zeydanlıoğlu (2012) wrote. "defined Terrorism so vaguely that not only were PKK directly targeted by this legislation but also anyone involved in the promotion of Kurdish language and culture" (p. 114). In her ethnographic study, Deniz Yonucu (2018) portrays the ambiguity and unpredictability of how the Anti-Terror Law was used and how the legal system at the time prisoned several people even for up to 26 years (allegedly because of being members of a terrorist group). She wrote, "anti-terror operations . . . targeted pro-Kurdish activists and socialists in the predominantly Alevi-populated working-class neighborhoods of Istanbul and in Turkey's Kurdistan" (p. 717). Anti-terror law aimed to pacify and intimidate certain populations and legalized intensified control and abuse (p. 718).

In the political arena, Kurdish politicians are continuously harassed, murdered, and persecuted due to the expression of their Kurdish identity. For example, a Kurdish woman, Leyla Zana, whose husband, Mehdi Zana, was tortured in Diyarbakir prison during the 1980 coup, became a successful politician and was elected to parliament in 1991. She was sentenced to prison for 14 years due to speaking Kurdish during her swearing-in ceremony. Adding to her oath in Turkish, she exclaimed in Kurdish, "I have sworn this oath for the sake of brotherhood between the Turkish and the Kurdish people."

In the review of the evolution of laws and regulations, the state first tried to promote the speaking of Turkish earlier in the century, and when it did not work and Kurds resisted, the state became more aggressive. According to Zeydanlıoğlu (2012):

> Since the primary marker of differentiation between Turks and Kurds was language, the elimination of the Kurdish language (as well as other autochthonous non-Turkish languages), became the main aim of the Turkish nation-building project. Kurds were to successfully become "Turks," not only by taking on Turkish as their new language and Kemalism as their new ideology but also by rejecting and forgetting their mother tongue, identity, culture, and heritage. (p. 105)

The state's desire to create a strong nation through uniting everyone under one language also aimed to strip people of their ethnic identities. At the beginning of the 2000s, these strict rules began to loosen. Even after the laws changed, the changes, in reality, were blocked by administrative and other aspects of life (Oran, 2004, pp. 124–29). That said, in 21st-century Turkey, the Kurdish language was no longer illegal. Over time, Kurdish and other non-Turkish languages were heard on the radio, and television broadcasts were allowed. Eventually, by 2009, the first Kurdish TV channel, TRT-6, started broadcasting, and private institutions were also allowed to teach non-Turkish languages.

These latest developments created a break in the rigid laws that prevented expression in Kurdish; however, the laws continue to have limitations. First, speaking non-Turkish languages on political platforms is still not allowed. Second, in regard to education platforms, the state only allowed teaching non-Turkish languages and their dialects in private institutions, which is not inclusive for those who cannot afford to attend them. Moreover, it does not allow any class other than a language class to be taught in non-Turkish languages. Historically, international agreements have allowed minorities in Turkey to be educated in their language; however, because the state only recognized Jewish, Rum, Armenian, and Bulgarian non-Muslim communities as minorities, Kurds could not take advantage of this right. Therefore, the right to education in their own language remains unresolved for Kurdish people to this day.

Language is not only communication; it is also a way of experiencing and expressing culture. For a century, and in various ways, when Kurds in Turkey were denied their right to speak their own language, they were also prohibited from practicing their own culture. Survivors of violent state practices adopt ways to survive, to protect, and to heal, which psychotherapists call "adaptive behaviors."

In relation to language, over time, Kurds have also responded with different adaptive behaviors, such as being quiet in the classroom, not participating, or avoiding school altogether. Field research by Vahap Coşkun, Şerif Derince, and Nesrin Uçarlar (2010) done in Diyarbakir (a city in Kurdistan/Eastern Turkey) looked at how Kurdish children responded to education in a language other than their mother tongue. They called the name of their research "the language wound" (*Dil Yarası*); *dil* means both "tongue" and "language" in Turkish. According to their findings, one of the main problems occurred when a teacher did not speak Kurdish and the students did not speak Turkish. The teacher and students had major difficulties communicating. The children were not able to express their intelligence, thoughts, emotions, or even jokes with their teachers and other students, which caused a deep sense of disappointment. Because the children were not allowed to speak Kurdish in the classroom or outside on the playground, or they were punished or ridiculed when they did, Kurdish children adapted by not speaking at all in the classroom; they sat in silence, waiting for the end of the school day. Some research participants in "the language wound" research reported that adopting this not-speaking behavior continued after school, and some children also preferred to remain quiet later in life. Another side effect of not allowing Kurdish children to speak their language and ridiculing or punishing them when they did, was that many students ended up repeating classes or dropping out of school altogether.

According to Coşkun et al.'s (2010) research, teachers often interpreted the children's inability to understand or learn Turkish as a sign there was something wrong with them; either they were not smart enough, or they were not studying or trying hard enough. Teachers were using their students to discourage their parents from speaking Kurdish at home. However, in most homes, parents did not speak Turkish, either. When parents did not speak Turkish or were not literate, then they were unable to help their children with schoolwork or Turkish language skills. Over time, as the child began to learn Turkish, their relationship with their family began to deteriorate.

Coşkun et al. (2010) found that classroom participation experiences were better with Kurdish-speaking teachers who were able to relate to their students with respect to their language and culture. Kurdish-speaking teachers felt that if students identified with them and were able to see how they became teachers, it could also help with children's ability to learn and could increase their self-esteem. Thus, children could begin to understand that nothing was wrong with them. The same research also pointed out that teachers report Kurdish children can spend three to four years just learning how to speak, read, and write in Turkish. Because of this delay, teachers could not begin to include the regular school curriculum until later in their primary education. Consequently, Kurdish children with no prior Turkish language skills felt they started life one step behind Turks. They had to work extra hard to catch up because the Turks did not have to struggle as they did. For example, one Kurdish student thought, "I wished I was born like them" (*Keşke ben de öyle doğsaydım*; Coşkun et al., 2010, p. 47), referring to the children of Turkish government officials with whom the Kurdish student shared the classroom.

Practices in schools could create belief systems that some languages—and therefore, their connected culture—are more important than others. When Kurdish children hear, "Do not speak Kurdish anywhere," they perceive this as, "Kurdish is bad; Kurdish is an obstacle." This perception could also lead to them believing they are bad or inferior. A language that should have been a natural part of a child's life becomes a weight, something to be ashamed of. Coşkun et al. (2010) gave an example of people hearing a child's mother speaking Kurdish; the child had fears of being ostracized, so he claimed that his mother was speaking French.

In addition to how children became estranged from their language, parents were starting to purposefully not teach Kurdish at home. With the support of village military stations, some teachers advised families not to teach their children Kurdish. The teachers claimed that otherwise, the children would not be able to learn how to read and write and would not be successful at school (Coşkun et al., 2010, p. 82). These teachers influenced some Turkish- and Kurdish-speaking parents.

The pattern of parents not teaching their children Kurdish as an adaptive behavior accelerated after the violent experiences that targeted Kurds during the military coups in 1971 and 1980, when Kurdish families increasingly began to refrain from teaching their mother tongue, for their children's safety. By not teaching Kurdish, families hoped that the new generation would assimilate more easily and would not be a target, as they were (Bilmez et al., 2015).

In contrast, the Turkification process and oppressive practices motivated other Kurds to hold on to their language even more tightly. For example, I know a Kurdish colleague in the Bay Area who knows Turkish, English, and Kurdish fluently and only speaks Kurdish (and English). Now that he is part of the diaspora and does not have to speak Turkish on a daily basis, he refuses to speak Turkish. His rejection of speaking Turkish is an act of rebellion and, in a way, shows how deep the language wound is for Kurds.

When the armed conflict between the Turkish state and PKK was at its peak by 1998, 3,428 villages were emptied and more than 3 million people had to move to big cities. Because speaking Kurdish in public could make someone a target, families adapted by only speaking Kurdish inside their homes or in the presence of trusted company. If they did not know Turkish, they simply kept quiet in public.

I remember one story from my childhood that is relevant to this adaptation. When I was about 10 years old, early in the 1990s, I met two sisters in my maternal grandparents' neighborhood in Western Turkey. When I stayed with my grandparents, I would play with them outside. One day, I heard one of the sisters speak with the other in a language I did not understand. I asked her what she'd said. She was surprised and said, "Oh, don't you speak Kurdish?" I said, "No, what is that?" She asked which language we spoke at home, and I said, "Turkish." Again, she was surprised to hear that and did not believe me at first. So, I had to convince her. She told me that in her family, they spoke Turkish outside and Kurdish inside their home. She thought that was what everyone else also did. With the curiosity of a child, I wanted to learn her language. She taught me the Kurdish names of colors and numbers. One evening when I went back home (I do not recall my parents being there, although my older uncle and aunt were), feeling excited by something new I'd learned earlier in the day, I reported all the Kurdish words I had learned, one by one. I did not realize the shock and the anger on my uncle's face. Neither of them said anything right away, but later at the dinner table, my uncle told me not to speak with my friends again. When I asked why, he said they were dirty and that I must forget all of the words I had learned; I was directed to never speak to them again. The next day, I saw my friends outside, and I had to tell them my uncle had forbidden me to be friends with them. I could not reveal my uncle's reasoning, so all I said was that I did not know why; maybe it was something about what they'd taught me—whatever the case, I was sorry. I remember how awkward and sad I felt for having to say something like this to friends. Plus, they were my only friends in the neighborhood. I was not happy with my uncle's rule.

I was aware of some sort of cultural difference between my Kurdish friends and me. I did not realize we had an ethnic difference, though, and I did not know what that meant. So, in my child's mind, the main difference between us was that I was from a city and they were from a village. From my perception, this difference did not give me enough reason for not being friends anymore, because in the playground, it did not matter. Therefore, not long after that, I broke the rule. I was lonely, and I thought the rule was ridiculous, so I decided to continue being friends with these sisters outside of my home. I was glad they took me back as their friend. They even introduced me to more friends. I now knew never to speak about them again to my family. My friends did not mention the language they spoke at home ever again. Over time, it appeared that nobody in my family, except my uncle, had strong issues with these friends; therefore, it was not a difficult rule to break. In recent years, I learned from other family members that my childhood friends were indeed from a Kurdish family. They had migrated to escape the war between PKK and the Turkish state, and their entire family had settled in that neighborhood.

Village Institutes

Village institutes between the 1930s and 1954 provided vocational education for rural people in Turkey. With the aim of promoting both Turkishness and mobilizing economic stability in rural areas, they functioned for over two decades (F. Çakmak, 2007; Karaömeroğlu, 1998; Tonguç, 1970). Mustafa Necati, who was the Minister of Education from 1925 to 1929, contributed to educational reforms and laid the foundation of "teacher institutes" and "village institutes" (*Köy Enstitüleri*). However, he could not complete his vision due to his early death at the age of 35 from appendicitis (Eski, 1999).

In the 1930s, following Necati's death, the Minister of Education, Rasid Galip, led a wave of development in educational institutions (Eski, 1999; F. Çakmak, 2007; Karaömeroğlu, 1998; Tonguç, 1970). After decades of war, the new nation was in an economic crisis. The emerging Kemalist elite thought teaching people in rural areas agricultural skills would also economically mobilize peasants to be "useful and productive members" of the society, thus contributing to the financial success of the new state (Karaömeroğlu, 1998, p. 57). The new nation needed a lot of teachers to promote its educational reforms and unite people from many backgrounds under one national umbrella. However, the administration fell short. In 1936, the new Minister of Education, Saffet Arıkan, calculated that teacher institutes were producing only 300 to 350 working teachers a year. It was determined that they needed at least 35,000 teachers to reach all the rural areas; it would take more than a hundred years to reach that number. The dilemma of having a lack of teachers encouraged more "innovative" solutions, such as village institutes (F. Çakmak, 2007, p. 223).

Ismail Hakkı Tonguç became the Managing Director of Primary Education from 1935 to 1936; he created the vocational primary-school system that was responsive to regional needs (Tonguç, 1970, p. 272). At the time, President Ismet Inönü and the Minister of Education, Hasan Ali Yücel, supported and hastened the process. Managing Director of Primary Education Tonguç believed that people living in rural areas were, in addition to learning regular primary-school curriculum (e.g., how to read and write, history, and geography), also needed to learn vocational skills (e.g., agriculture, husbandry, construction, ironwork, and carpentry). The first village institute opened in 1937 in Eskisehir, and several more followed in Izmir, Edirne, and Kastamonu (Central, Western, and Northern Anatolia cities). On April 17, 1940, after a three-year trial period, the new village institute law legitimized these institutes (Karaömeroğlu, 1998; Tonguç, 1970).

People in urban areas did not know enough about village life or speak the villagers' language. To fill this gap, the institute selected villagers, preferably youth, to achieve the teacher education so they could return to their villages and teach. In the institutes, students were taught strong work ethics and the importance of volunteerism and diligence, all in service of increasing productivity in rural areas. Students "learned through doing," which meant doing chores for the institution, construction of roads or buildings, agricultural work, and other relevant activities (Karaömeroğlu, 1998; Tonguç, 1970).

Even though as an idea, village institutes seemed straightforward, in practice, they were "multifaceted and highly controversial ... and far more than an educational undertaking" (Karaömeroğlu, 1998, p. 55). Fevzi Çakmak (2007) claims there was a silent opposition in the Turkish National Assembly against village institutes from the beginning. Asım Karaömeroğlu (1998) and F. Çakmak (2007), who reviewed the history of village institutes, gave examples of various oppositions. Arguments differ, and some are unfounded. One of the earlier arguments claimed that because village institutes were only offered to rural people, this would increase the divide between rural and urban people. Later, additional issues came up, such as opposition to how students, both boys and girls, were forced to work, which was against the social norms of families that did not want their girls to be in the same classroom with boys. In the 1950s, some arguments claimed schools were "producing communists" and that village institutes were disrespectful to government officials; both were unfounded.

Village institutes emphasized learning through doing, and only rural people were subjugated to this style of education. Thus, some also criticized village institutes for the exploitation of rural labor, overworking children, and discrimination. These arguments had some basis and eyewitnesses. Overall, the main purpose of village institutes was to increase productivity in rural areas. Spreading Turkish nationalism and obtaining control of rural populations were important aspects of village institutes but not aggressive in practice. Students learned through doing and were given more initiative; they had more self-confidence compared to their counterparts in urban mainstream schools (Karaömeroğlu, 1998). For example, there are stories of village institute graduates causing problems with authorities because they would rightfully object to any kind of injustice, and students were able to submit a complaint (Tonguç, 1970). Furthermore, because "students were living, working and learning together, [this] paved the way for developing a sense of collective mentality . . . [which] was seen as a potential threat" (Karaömeroğlu, 1998, p. 70) by the state. Through education and empowerment, the village institutes helped rural people build their own roads and bring electricity to villages, which widened the horizons of rural people and created new class conflicts. Lastly, changing political conditions, shifts from one party to a multi-party system, the Kemalist regime's own ambiguous and uncertain practices, and conflicting oppositions all played a role in the eventual controversial closure of the village institutes in 1950 and subsequent merging with teacher schools by 1954 (Karaömeroğlu, 1998).

Not long after the closure of village institutes, boarding schools opened in a majority of Kurdish regions and other strategic locations. However, they did not provide vocational education. They followed mainstream education with further interest in the promotion of epistemologies of ignorance, assimilation, and more aggressive practices to spread Turkish nationalism (Işık & Arslan, 2012).

Boarding Schools

The first boarding schools opened after 1923 but, because of financial difficulties, closed by 1940. The discussion of boarding schools was revisited closer to 1960 (Arslan, 2015). A decade after the closure of the village institutes in 1962, with the passing of Law No. 222 (primary-education legislation), the state made the first eight years of education mandatory and required all children from 6 to 14 years of age to attend school. From 1962 to 1973, the majority of boarding schools opened in the Eastern Anatolia/Kurdistan area, and 15 years later in Northern Anatolia, where most of the ethnic population of Laz lives. Over time, boarding schools opened across all regions of Turkey. These schools were free, and the ministry of education paid for students' basic expenses, such as books, food, bedding, and clothing. Kurdish villages were spread across Eastern Anatolia, and their access roads were closed due to harsh winters. Therefore, the only school option for these villages was sending their children to boarding schools. Boarding schools opened in strategic locations and recruited children from these remote villages (Işık & Arslan, 2012). If there were no local schools close to a village, Kurdish families had no other choice but sent them to boarding schools if they wanted to send their children to school at all.

Ayhan Serhat Işık and Serhat Arslan (2012), based on their qualitative research with former and current students and boarding-school personnel from cities across Kurdistan, argued that they were a vehicle for education, discipline, modernization, and "Turkifying" the entire nation, and that boarding schools were a part of the widespread demographic engineering project to create a one nation/one language state. The curriculum and the disciplined design of a typical day, which went from 6 a.m. to 9 p.m., were filled with nationalist propaganda (see Arslan, 2015; Işık & Arslan, 2012, for a detailed analysis). Despite how, in its essence, assimilation and promotion of national identity were the main reasons for opening boarding schools, they are often less discussed by scholars and practitioners.

Most research in Turkey around boarding schools does not refer to the ethnicity of the students and mostly highlights the importance of educating underdeveloped populations—or as they thought, modernizing "savages," with the genuine belief that these schools were for the good of the society, so children could have equal opportunities and better futures. This perspective exemplifies the denial of the Kurdish ethnopolitical place in the society and how the Turkish state saw Kurds as "underdeveloped," "tribal," and "savages." This denial creates an erroneous belief that stripping a child from their Kurdishness is good. Therefore, teachers and personnel who followed the state's narrative appeared ignorant to the truth that what they were doing was actually harmful to a Kurdish child's ethnic heritage and identity.

Işık and Arslan (2012) wrote that, in the end, boarding schools did not reach their intended aim to assimilate Kurds. Işık and Arslan connected the degree of failure of boarding schools' assimilation agenda to the Kurdish movement that strengthened in the 1990s, which provided political awareness and a sense of belonging as it mobilized boarding-school students to protect their ethnic identities. Boarding schools are still an integral part of education in Anatolia.

Mainstream Education

The General Secretary and Minister of Interior of the early Republic of Turkey, Recep Peker, referring to a class, "Atatürk's Principles and Reforms," which began in 1934 in early education, said:

> ... every nation should have a belief system. A nation that doesn't have a belief system is nothing but a human stack. The purpose of the "Atatürk's Principles and Reforms" class is to teach the new generations the Turkish

nationalist thought system, which is the "Atatürkist Thought System." [*Atatürkçü Düşünce Sistemi*] (as cited in Özücetin & Nadar, 2010, p. 468; author's translation)

In 1933, Reşit Galip, who served as Minister of Education in the same year, wrote the Student Oath. The Student Oath goes like this:

I am a Turk, honest and hardworking.
My principle is to protect younger, to respect the elder,
To love my homeland and my nation more than myself.
My ideal is to rise, to progress.
My existence shall be dedicated to the Turkish existence.
O Great Atatürk! On the path you have paved, I swear
To walk incessantly toward the aims that you have set.
My existence shall be dedicated to Turkish existence.
How happy is the one who says, "I am a Turk."

I recited this oath every Monday morning and Friday afternoon while screaming my lungs out along with the entire school, from my first grade of elementary school until I graduated from high school. We lined up in the school courtyard like soldiers. Later, I learned from a few Kurds and Armenians that this was one of the painful parts of their school experience as they either lip-synced the words or avoided being at school during those times. One of my Kurdish friends said that he would be punished by his teachers if they realized he was not reciting as enthusiastically as the rest of the class. More than a decade after I graduated from high school, in 2013, the practice of reciting the Student Oath was abolished. At the same time, the law preventing women from wearing headscarves was also abolished in the official registry. However, some schools still choose to continue to practice their nationalistic values and recite the Student Oath.

I admit, as a child, I was deeply impacted by the propaganda. When I was a child, I used to have nightmares, and my mother taught me that praying to Allah before bed would protect me. She told me this was when I could talk to Allah and share my troubles. I could cry, say what I was sad about, and ask for protection. I learned that Allah did not have a gender. My mother assured me that my prayer in the name of Allah (specifically three *kululallah* and one *elham*, referring to the Ihlas and Fatia prayers) would protect me from nightmares, and Allah would listen to anything I said. I began to pray three *kululallah* and one *elham* before going to bed, and when I awoke from a bad dream. I appreciate this advice to this day because what my mother told me allowed me to develop a spiritual practice very early in my life, and I was able to make it my own. I did not end up becoming a Muslim, however. I now identify as spiritual but not religious. However, this process helped me get through some of the most painful times in my childhood and also helped me develop a strong spiritual meaning.

This childhood story also relates to the Student Oath, as there is a second part to it. Later on, in school, I learned about Atatürk, the Turkish national anthem, and the importance of my country. By the fourth grade, teachers made sure children had memorized all 10 verses of the national anthem. We would recite the national anthem in addition to the Student Oath on Mondays and Fridays, at the beginning and end of the school week. I was beginning to get the impression that my national identity was equally important as my spirituality. So, I had an idea. I decided to merge my prayers to Allah with my love for my nation. After my prayers every night, I began to recite all 10 verses of the national anthem, and then, along with asking for the protection of my family, I also asked for the protection of the Turkish nation from Allah. My prayers, recited in bed, would take about 20 minutes, which eventually became a joke in my secular family. I was dedicated to both my spirituality and my country. I did not know what I was doing, but it just made sense to me. I stopped a few years later because, by the time I got to bed, I was too tired to continue my ritual. First, I stopped reciting the national anthem. A few years later, I realized I was rushing through my prayers because I wanted to get to sleep as quickly as possible. Rushing through them did not feel respectful to my practice, so I stopped altogether. When I look back on those years now, I laugh at first, but then I realize how I took everything I was told to heart. I deeply trusted what I was told. This story exemplifies the innocence and impressionability of a child.

Of course, children are different, and so is their response to national propaganda. Also, based on the ethnicity of a child, they might make different meanings and develop different practices, belief systems, and so on—and yet, every child in Turkey went through some form of Turkish nationalist propaganda. As a child, I did not understand what the propaganda was trying to accomplish. I did not know that children, other than Turks, would have such conflicting experiences around the propaganda and what their families had to go through—either to help their children adapt, assimilate, or resist. Looking back, my childhood years at school seem surreal, naive, and ignorant. I grieve the fact that my right to experience the diversity of Anatolia was taken away from me without my consent. I feel violated and lied to.

The Intertwined Nature of the Evolution of Turkishness and the Ignorance around Armenian Suffering

Political scientist Jennifer Dixon (2018), who reviewed the "official narrative" in Turkey about the Armenian Genocide, argued that Turkey's official narrative "has moved from silence and denial to relativizing, myth-making, and a limited degree of acknowledgment" (p. 4). In the 1980s, in response to internal and international pressure, the state had to address the arguments of the Armenian Genocide, calling it the "Armenian Question" and creating an official narrative that justified the removal and killings of Armenians as necessary to war conditions. More recently, President Erdoğan gave his condolences to innocent Armenians who lost their lives, which was a partial acknowledgment but still far from a genuine state apology. Since then, the state has backpedaled to protect the state narrative.

According to Dixon, the "official narrative" is the combination of state narrative, actions, and legislation; education (what is taught at schools and what is allowed to be published in academia); and finally, government-sponsored commemorations, museums, and memorials. When reviewed together, all these aspects of the official narrative tell a story about the ways in which the state officially engages with its history and which narrative the state wants the public to know. When looking at how the "official narrative" changes over time, it is clear that the official Turkish narrative changed in relation to domestic and international pressure, yet despite the international pressure, Turkey continues to deny the Armenian Genocide.

Dixon (2018) highlights that international pressure is only part of the picture. Domestic considerations play a critical role in the process of transforming the state narrative. Domestic concerns, according to Dixon, are as follows:

- ☐ **Material concerns**: Turkish officials have worried that acknowledging the Armenian Genocide would expose the state to demands for territory and compensation.
- ☐ **Legitimacy and identity concerns**: Acknowledging that what happened was genocide, organized and carried out by state officials, could destabilize the founding national narrative and core aspects of Turkish national identity.
- ☐ **Electoral-political concerns**: Since 1980, through the myth-making process about the Armenian Genocide, a large number of the society believed what they had been told. Other thoughts that might offer a counter-narrative could damage the reputation of the political party and cost them their public support.
- ☐ **Domestic contestations**: In order to maintain ignorance and denial, the state has been silencing and putting constraints on academics' and activists' work. In Turkey, anyone who goes against the state narrative risks being prosecuted and possibly jailed. (p. 22)

The fear is that acceptance of the Armenian Genocide could have significant consequences and could destabilize national identity, and if manipulated by institutional power, could even cause unrest. After almost a hundred years of active creation and maintenance of the Turkish nationalist narrative, the society as a whole is invested in the "official narrative" to protect their national identity, national pride, and sense of safety. Now society's personal investments in protecting the state's narrative are in conjunction, creating a cycle that is hard to break.

Much of this ignorance goes back to the last days of the Ottoman Empire and the control of knowledge since then. For instance, from the beginning of the formation of the Republic of Turkey in 1923, the Turkish state controlled which books could be published and which ones were banned. Historian Uğur Üngör (2014) argued that the new Turkish state continued the Committee of Union and Progress (CUP) policy of suppressing all information about the 1915 Armenian massacres and deportations—therein an example of the top-down control of collective memory. A number of books, such as the works of Garabed Kapikian, who offered an account of deportations and massacres; Marie Sarrafian Banker, who wrote *My Beloved Armenia;* Armen Anoosh, an Armenian survivor living in Aleppo; and Franz Werfel, whose novel *The Forty Days of Musa Dagh,* portrayed Armenian suffering during the war, were banned in Turkey due to being "harmful texts." Even generic historical books that acknowledged the Armenian presence were banned. The state instead published "new" history texts that deliberately misrepresented the regions' diverse past: going to great lengths to identify "Turkishness" and erasing all non-Turkish cultures from history.

Dixon (2010) reviewed the official narratives about the "Armenian question" found in Turkish high-school history textbooks over the past half-century. She outlined that what the state has taught its young citizens about the Armenian Genocide has changed over time. She wrote that "in the 1950s, '60s, and '70s, Turkish high school students did not learn anything about Armenians' existence in the Ottoman Empire or about their deportation during World War I (WWI)" (p. 104).

Starting in the 1980s, Armenians began to appear in textbooks. Dixon (2010) writes:

> ... high school history textbooks taught Turkish students that Armenians rose up and violently attacked the Ottoman government and innocent fellow citizens prior to and during WWI, and that the government forcibly relocated Armenians in order to protect and preserve the Turkish nation. A decade later, Turkish high school students were told that Armenians were traitors and propagandists who had tried to take advantage of the weakness of the Ottoman Empire and had "stabbed Turks in the back." And more recently, high school history textbooks in Turkey described the "Turkish-Armenian War" that took place between Turks and Armenians following

the end of World War I, and mentioned that recent research and excavations have documented the fact that Armenians committed genocide against Turks. (p. 104)

According to Dixon, this shift in narrative, from the complete absence of Armenians to justified reasoning of the Armenian Genocide, was in response to both domestic and international factors. The first shift in the narrative was between 1975 and 1983, due to radical Armenian groups[2] targeting Turkish diplomats and other Turkish entities in deadly attacks that were intended to pressure Turkey to acknowledge the Armenian Genocide. In the 1990s, new factors were introduced, both on the domestic front and internationally. The end of the Cold War and the collapse of the Soviet Union introduced a new neighbor in 1991, the Armenian Republic. Domestically, more critical works were being published. The first was Taner Akçam's *Shameful Act* in 1992, which had critical coverage in the media by 1995. In the late 1990s and early 2000s, the pressure of international recognition of the Armenian Genocide increased. Dixon (2010) states: "Moreover, within the past ten years, the taboo on the discussion of the Armenian question in Turkey has gradually been lifted, and the official narrative is now challenged and actively debated within Turkish society" (p. 119).

Üngör (2014) states that "the mass violence of the first decades of the twentieth century was repressed and eliminated from public memory through silence, amnesia, and repression rather than reflection, discussion, [integration,] and memorialization" (p. 153). Consequently, both in relation to Kurdish and Armenian history in Anatolia, there are major disagreements within collective historical narratives and official state documents in Turkey. The Turkish narrative is different from Armenian and Kurdish ones, and from those that actually lived through the catastrophes.

Decades-long control of education and epistemologies of ignorance through education, book publications, academia, media, control of language, public experiences, and international relations eventually created steep differences in the collective narrative regarding Armenian history in Turkey. As mentioned, from Turkish nationalist perspectives, some of the common narratives include: "Armenians betrayed Turks"; "Armenians were used by foreign powers"; "It was a war, and people on both sides died"; and, "The Armenian Genocide is propaganda against the Turkish state." Some scholars define what Armenian scholars have called "death march" as an organized displacement of the Armenian population and that people died due to the difficult conditions of war (e.g., Ayverdi, 2007; Halaçoğlu, 2006; Şimşir, 2005). The authors further emphasize that there was no intention to kill anyone because of their ethnicity or religion; therefore, the events of 1915 to 1917 cannot be considered genocide.

Türkkay Ataöv (1994), responding to the literature on the Armenian Genocide by scholars such as Vahakn Dadrian, claims that the Armenian Genocide issue is a one-sided, biased approach that does not consider the millions of Muslims that were massacred or fled to Anatolia before 1915. In his testimony, Justin McCarthy (1995) compared the Armenian Genocide with the Jewish Holocaust to counter-argue the legitimacy of genocide in the case of Armenians. He argued that the expulsion of Armenians was not as organized and as systematic as Nazi Germany's concentration camps during the Jewish Holocaust. Therefore, what happened during the mass murders and deportations of Armenians from 1915 to 1917 cannot be considered genocide.

Turkish politicians' widely used argument is to leave the Armenian matter to historians to deny any Armenian Genocide–related dialogue. However, even after historians made their claims, politicians said, "But historians did not review all of the resources" (Dixon, 2018). Furthermore, any dialogue for recognition of the Armenian Genocide has created political turmoil. Government officials in Turkey say historians, not politicians, should adjudicate these issues, but at the same time, they undermine or reject scholarly work that is presented if it supports that the Armenian Genocide occurred, as if the historical argument is only valid if it replicates the government agenda. Therefore, asking to leave the matter to historians is more of a political strategy than Turkey's genuine search for knowledge.

Hrant Dink's Assassination

Going against the status quo of ignorance, even to promote peace and reconciliation, is not a simple process. The collective, who carry strong emotions toward "the other" and who also have been exposed to false truths and propaganda for decades, can easily be exploited. Societal institutions and the public develop a reactive muscle that puts those who go against ignorance in real danger. One heartbreaking example is the 2007 assassination of intellectual and editor-in-chief of Turkish newspaper *Agos*, Turkish-Armenian Hrant Dink, by a Turkish nationalist in Istanbul.

Dink was born in Malatya in 1954. After his parents migrated to Istanbul and were divorced, he was raised in an Armenian Protestant Church orphanage. He grew up to be one of the most influential Armenian peacemakers in Turkey. In one of his 2004 articles, a remark was misunderstood as an insult to Turkishness and considered illegal, according to Article 301 of the Turkish Panel Code. After a two-year debate and struggle with the legal system in Turkey, because of the lynching atmosphere that media created at the time and through the deep state's involvement due to Dink's outspoken and influential nature, Dink was assassinated in broad daylight outside of his office at *Agos*, on January 19, 2007. His personal attorney,

Fethiye Çetin (2013), authored a book describing the evidence for how the media and Turkish legal system created a nationalist lynching atmosphere. Ogün Samast, a 17-year-old Turkish ultra-nationalist involved with secret government agencies, was the person charged and convicted for the assassination of Dink. That assassination was a tremendous loss for the community and society. After Dink's assassination, thousands of Armenians, Kurds, and Turks, regardless of their ethnicities, flooded the streets of Istanbul, protesting and chanting, *"Hepimiz Hrant'ız; Hepimiz Ermeniyiz!"* or, "We are all Hrant; we are all Armenians!" These protests by thousands of Turks and attendance at his funeral showed growing attention and understanding of Armenian suffering within Turkish society.

On one hand, the assassination of Hrant Dink was (re)traumatizing for Armenians, reminding them of their accumulative historical traumas in Anatolia. On the other hand, the funeral also brought Turks and Armenians together and emphasized the concept of *we*. Arzum Kopşa (2008), based on her research with Armenian youth at the time, argued that contact during the ceremony helped to heal the increasing tension caused by the assassination. Hence, the funeral led to a positive improvement and helped to change the damaged image of Turks. Kopşa continues by saying "this result points out the power of dialogue in difficult and intractable conflicts" (p. 109).

Kopşa's study illustrates the power of solidarity and dialogue. That being said, however, the people of Turkey, as a collective, embraced a *spectrum* of meanings and interpretations surrounding Dink's assassination. For example, Göçek (2018) argued that a decade after Dink's assassination, people remember Dink from either one or two conflicting narratives. From the ultra-nationalist view, Dink is remembered as a traitor. From the leftist and liberal view, he is a martyr. Dink was a political opponent, and according to Göçek, his assassination was yet another episode in the systemic Turkish state violence that dates back to the Young Turk rule (r. 1908–1918) and previously to Sultan Abdülhamid II (r. 1876–1909), "with the intent to fragment and destroy all potential political opposition and resistance" (p. 162).

Armenians in Turkey

Only a small number of Armenians remained in Turkey, primarily in Istanbul. They continue to live in close contact with Turks. Even though, at the political and day-to-day levels, the struggle and discrimination continue, Dink (2008) argued that this close contact with Turks, being in continuous dialogue with "the other," and remaining in Turkey changed the Armenian experience in that they found methods to adapt, survive, and relate within this new Turkish state.

As feminist philosopher Linda Martin Alcoff (2007) has argued, people from oppressed groups, even though they have less reason to invest in maintaining ignorance, may do so to preserve civil relations with the people with whom they have to work. Doing so enables them to avoid any emotional distress of acknowledging the weight of their own oppression or the humiliation of family members.

At the same time, Armenians in Turkey have had to live in fear for their safety. One of the most recent fear-triggering, traumatic events for Armenians was Dink's assassination. Therefore, in Turkey, Armenians appear to be less concerned about recognizing the Armenian Genocide by the Turkish state but more about their sense of safety and integration within the society. However, because the society they are trying to integrate into has been the source of their fear, it has been a very challenging situation (Muratyan, 2011). Furthermore, the destruction of Armenian churches in Anatolia, the Turkifying of Armenian villages, and the demolition of ancestral graveyards have been offensive to Armenians' sense of belonging to their ancestral lands (Özdoğan et al, 2009). Due to Turkey's ongoing acts against Armenians, fear has been imprinted on their collective identity. Fears manifest in how Armenians choose the schools they send their children to and the neighborhoods they live in, and how they hide their Armenian identity by either not speaking Armenian in public or changing their names to Turkish ones.

Armenians in Armenia and Armenians in the diaspora have had different relationships with Turks and Turkey than those living in Turkey. These differences are shaped by their external and historical circumstances. Armenia is a relatively new nation-state, officially formed in 1991. Geographically a neighbor to the northeast of Turkey, Armenia was under the Soviet Communist regime until 1991, except for a period from 1918 to 1920, when it had a brief independence. The area in Eastern Armenia was not directly affected by forced deportation and massacres, even though Turkey invaded and tried to conquer it. It also served as a refuge throughout 1917–18 for Anatolian Armenians. Later, many Armenian refugees from Anatolia migrated to Armenia at different times. Hranush Kharatyan-Araqelyan (2010) points out that Armenian refugees from Anatolia first had to hide their stories due to the Communist Soviet regime and its oppressive policies, which changed over the years with collective mobilizations, public demonstrations, and commemorations. After the formation of the Republic of Armenia in 1991, the wars in the 1980s to 1994 and 2020 between Azerbaijan and Armenia over the disputed Nagorno-Karabagh/Artsakh region affected Armenia's relations with Turkey. Turkey's closure of its border with Armenia after the first Nagorno-Karabagh war has also occupied Armenia's international relations and politics. Closed borders have caused Armenians in Armenia to have minimal physical contact with

Turkey and Turks, even though they are neighbors. Armenians in Armenia also carry the legacy of the Soviet regime and its ramifications, along with the legacy of the war with Azerbaijan and the complicated political relationships with neighboring Turkey.

Diaspora Armenians have had a very different relationship with Turkey and Turks. Their knowledge of Turkey has been primarily historical and focused on the genocide, which happened over a hundred years ago. The movement into diaspora was precipitated from the Hamidian Massacres period in 1896 up to the September pogroms in 1955 and after. Many Armenians in the Arab worlds migrated to less-hostile environments (before 1915) and integrated well into governance (Chatty, 2010). Armenians in the West, those who migrated to Europe and America, tended to form dual identities (e.g., Armenian Americans; Dink, 2008).

Living in a less-hostile environment, Armenians in the diaspora, and later in Armenia, were able to control their narrative more and were free to be more active in Armenian Genocide recognition campaigns. These different experiences have sometimes caused Armenians in the diaspora, especially in the Western sphere, to critique Armenians in Turkey for not being proactive or not pushing hard enough for genocide recognition.

According to Nayan Muratyan's study with Armenians living in Turkey, research participants showed some distress due to their experience during the diaspora Armenians' genocide campaigns. They either claimed these campaigns did not represent them or feared they might put them in danger. Since 1915, even though Armenians in Turkey have been trying to heal from their historical trauma from the Armenian deportations, new traumatic events (such as "Citizen, speak Turkish!" campaigns in 1927, September pogroms in 1955, and Hrant Dink's assassination in 2007) have triggered new fears for people. Muratyan points out that, as a result, Armenians in Turkey have not been able to move through their stages of healing from historical traumas; these stages include feeling a sense of safety, mourning their losses, and forgiving.

This diversity of experiences and responses in relation to the trauma of genocide make for a complicated landscape when trying to understand Armenian identity and the impact of historical and present-day trauma.

Turkish Identity Struggles

When I think of who identifies as Turkish today, a diverse spectrum of people comes to mind. Common knowledge has it that Turks belong to Turkic tribes and Mongols who migrated to Anatolia from Central Asia or the Near East. Though there is a reality to this argument, the Republic of Turkey citizens, who identify as Turks, are much more diverse. Turkey's Turks are a collection of people from various ethnicities, religions, and geographic origins, including descendants of thousands of Muslim refugees (such as Bosnians, Albanians, Tartars, Circassians, Abkhazians, Chechens, and Georgians) who arrived from Eastern Europe and the Balkans. Many Turks are the descendants of Armenians and Ottoman Greeks, and other non-Muslim communities that might have converted (voluntarily or by force) to Islam generations ago to survive. Additionally, many Kurdish, Laz, or other indigenous Muslim minorities in Anatolia also identify as Turks in addition to their own ethnic origin (e.g., Kurdish and Turkish, Laz and Turkish). In a nutshell, Turkish identity is an umbrella identity for a group of people with different ethnic, religious, and linguistic backgrounds who are either ethnically Turkic or who voluntarily or involuntarily assimilated to Turkishness within the last century.

Kemalist discourse focused on "Turkishness" as being "secular" rather than "being Muslim" as one of its core principles. However, in practice, being Turkish still meant "preferably speaking Turkish" and being from the Hanafi school of Islam, "preferably from the Balkans." This profile dominated the Turkification process of the early years of the Republic (Kirişci, 2000). Furthermore, due to century-old epistemologies of ignorance (assimilation policies, forgetting, denial, dissimulations) and intermarriage, it is not easy today to establish clear boundaries between some of the previously distinct ethnicities. Therefore, anthropologist Leyla Neyzi (2002) wrote that it is essential to understand the counter and hybrid identities that have evolved alongside Turkishness, such as Kurdish-Turkish or Armenian Turkish.

Unpacking Turkishness, B. Ünlü (2016) argued that Turks and those who assimilated to Turkishness went through emotional and intellectual training. Social institutions, such as schools, media, mosques, the military, and families, all worked toward creating Turkishness in Turkey. This progressive education did not include the history of the expulsion and deportation of Armenians from Anatolia or the exploitation and denial of Kurds. Through this education into Turkishness, generation by generation, most Turks—and those who assimilated to Turkishness (including some Kurds, Balkan migrants, and other Muslims)—adapted their identity. They were stripped of their own histories and the wounding that may have resulted from that history.

Dominant Turkish narratives have dismissed any challenge to the power structures and opposing narratives. Drawing from the works of Fatma Müge Göçek and Jennifer Dixon, Ungör (2014) argued that "the new memory of the nation did not permit cracks, nuances, shades, subtleties or any difference for that matter. Much like the new identity, it strived to be unitary" (p. 154). Throughout, Kurds, Armenians, and also the new generation of Turks have been refused their right to learn, process, mourn, and heal.

To ensure the persistence of the new Turkishness Contract, those who accept it are rewarded, and those who reject it are punished. For example, Ismail Beşikçi, who was born in 1939, was a Turkish intellectual and anthropologist. After his field studies in the Eastern Turkey/Kurdistan region, he refused and openly criticized the Turkishness Contract. During the 1971 military coup, he was tried and sentenced to 13 years in prison for his defense of Kurdish rights. He later benefited from amnesty, allowing him to be released in 1974. However, after his release from prison, he was never allowed to teach at any university in Turkey; he was ostracized. Over the years, he was in and out of jail multiple times on charges stemming from his writings about Kurdish populations (van Bruinessen, 2003–04 [2005]).

The rise of the Kurdish movement and Turkish intellectuals, such as Beşikçi, who did not accept Turkishness, challenges the Turkishness Contract and the system it imposed on people. B. Ünlü (2016) writes:

> ... at certain points in history oppressed groups can open up a crack in the power structure of the established order by resisting it and by creating their own power ... once the dominant groups can no longer escape certain facts and knowledge an identity crisis follows. (p. 401)

Kurdish movement both inside Turkey and in the diaspora is continuously challenging the Turkish nationalist narrative. Furthermore, due to domestic and international pressures during the last four decades, Turkish narratives have been continuously challenged. A century after its creation, Turkishness, today, is in crisis (Neyzi, 2018; B. Ünlü, 2016).

Talking about Armenian and Kurdish suffering, making political claims, and writing books about them were all banned in Turkey from the beginning. Furthermore, those who did not talk, write, feel, or empathize with Kurdish or Armenians suffering and causes were able to take advantage of the new Turkish state. Thus, the formation of Turkishness was based on not seeing, hearing, talking about, or empathizing with Kurdish and Armenian suffering—which B. Ünlü (2016) defines as the negative side of Turkishness. These shadow/negative sides are some of the core aspects of the formation of Turkish identity.

Only those who had higher status and power in society would have the privilege of not seeing, learning, being involved, or hearing. For example, B. Ünlü (2016), drawing on Mills' (1997) work in the United States, reminds us that historically, a person who is Black does not have the privilege not to understand Whiteness as they live in it. Their day-to-day survival relies on their understanding of the racial contract. African American drama therapist Arianna Wheat mentioned this contract as "Black Training": the "training that teaches a [Black person] how to navigate implicit and explicit White supremacy in everyday interactions without getting shot, caught, or lynched" (Volkas, Van, & Wheat, in press). On the other hand, a White person has both privilege and power to live with minimal empathic, emotional, or intellectual contact with a person who is Black or Brown. They can easily survive without the need to understand, empathize, or see their worldview. Therefore, many Whites can be ignorant about how and in which ways this racial contract may be putting them in a privileged position, compared with people who are non-White. In comparison, these racial dynamics are present in Turkey in relation to ethnic dynamics. Power and privilege exist in forms of Turkishness and the Turkishness Contract at the expense of non-Turks and non-Muslims.

Given the diversity in Turkey, Turkishness is not a homogeneous experience. B. Ünlü (2016) argued that varying degrees of Turkishness are found based on location and ideologies. For example, someone from central Turkey has a different sense of Turkishness than someone from the Aegean Coast. The Turkishness of a Marxist is different from that of a nationalist or Kemalist. Given there are individual differences of Turkishness, what they all have in common, according to B. Ünlü, is Turkish ignorance of their own privilege and subsequent inability or difficulty to consider their own privilege. Their ignorance is independent of education levels, as highly educated Turks can be ignorant of privilege. There is an interplay between Turkish ignorance and their inability to come to terms with their historical wounding, which prevents healing. An average Turk is ignorant and numb to their own history and suffering.

While Armenian and Kurdish suffering are suppressed due to domination, exploitation, and assimilation by state policies and practices, the Balkan migrants' and remaining Anatolian residents' traumatic experiences were erased due to the state's mandate to start over and look forward. For either, trauma is not appropriately addressed or healed. More research needs to be conducted to fully understand and differentiate Turkish experiences from Kurdish and Armenian ones—because they are different. When Turkey's history is reviewed within the lens of transgenerational trauma, it is unlikely that millions of Muslim migrants survived wars, forced migrations, famine, and epidemics with apparently no psychological trauma or transgenerational (mal)adaptations at all. Today, one-third of Turkey's Turkish population comprises Balkan migrant descendants; thus, their transgenerational experiences are essential to understand.

The denial of violence and ignorance at a state level has caused contradictions in social memory. During the summers of 2002 and 2004/2007, Üngör interviewed 200 children and grandchildren of Armenians in Eastern Turkey who have been impacted by the Armenian Genocide. Through semi-structured interviews, Üngör revealed that despite denial at the state level, silencing, and apparent amnesia concerning Armenians' anguish, the social memory of Turkish society still remembers. Üngör (2014) writes:

... even after nearly a century ... even though most direct eyewitnesses to the crime have passed away, oral history interviews yield important insights. Elderly Turks and Kurds in Eastern Turkey [have held] vivid memories passed on by family members or fellow villagers who witnessed or participated in the genocide. [His] research results suggest there is a clash, not only between Turkish political memory and Armenian cultural memory, but also between Turkish political memory (the official state narrative) and Turkish/Kurdish social memory. In a nutshell: to some extent, the Turkish government is denying a genocide that its own population remembers. (pp. 156–57)

Below is example from one of Üngör's (2014) interviews by a Turkish woman (born 1928) from Erzincan:

Q: You said there were Armenians in your village too. What happened to them?
A: They were all killed in the first year of the war, you didn't know? My mother was standing on the hill in front of our village. She saw how at Kemah they threw *(döktüler)* all the Armenians into the river. Into the Euphrates. Alas, screams and cries *(bağıran çağıran)*. Everyone, children and all *(çoluk çocuk)*, brides, old people, everyone, everyone. They robbed them of their golden bracelets, their shawls and silk belts, and threw them into the river.
Q: Who threw them into the river?
A: The government of course.
Q: What do you mean by "the government"?
A: Gendarmes. (p. 154)

During my visits to Turkey, I also observed a very similar experience to the sentiments uncovered in Üngör's study. Coming from the United States and being exposed to denial arguments, I was surprised by meeting so many people who actually acknowledged the Armenian Genocide. They had personal stories to share as well, either from their grandparents' involvement or family struggles during the war. At the same time, parallel with these stories were others of denial, not-knowing, or obscuration of reality. More qualitative research needs to be done to understand how truth might have changed over time and how the dynamics of ignorance in Turkey are different based on location and family stories.

For example, I mentioned earlier that my maternal grandfather is from Eğin (Kemaliye), a small town in Erzincan, by the Euphrates River. In Eğin, villagers remember a collectively traumatic experience from 1896, but the truth was obstructed. When I visited Eğin and conducted informal conversations with villagers, I asked about their life there. Even though I did not bring Armenians up, several people mentioned a story back when Armenians lived in the town; an Armenian woman forgot a pot on a stove, which caused a large fire that burned down the entire village. It was after this that most Armenians left Eğin. After conducting my interviews, I searched online and found a missionary's diary in which they wrote about a large fire; however, it was stated that it was caused by Kurds attacking the village. Later I found books that mentioned the attacks (Dadrian, 1995; Hayreni, 2015, pp. 168–71). An American newspaper titled the story "Egin Attacked: Six hundred more Armenians slaughtered by Kurds" (1896). According to France's diplomatic archives from the 19th century, a French ambassador in Eğin claimed that troops killed 2,000 Armenians, including women and children, and burned down 980 of 1,500 houses in the quarter of Eğin (Dadrian, 1995, p. 146). These attacks appear to be the significant cause of collective trauma of Eğin, where reportedly, only 150 Armenians were left in the town after the attack. The timeline aligns with the oral stories I was told—"the fire" was the main reason Armenians left Eğin. Moreover, the fire happened before the Armenian Genocide. Remembered to this day, the catastrophe is not viewed as a massacre. It is remembered in the collective narrative in Eğin as an accident caused by a woman forgetting a pot on the stove—a very different narrative. The aggression of the history and the experience of an atrocity was changed to be remembered as an accident. Nevertheless, the end was the same: the absence of Armenians.

The standpoints of many modern nation-states have broken the collective narrative, therefore making the issue not only an Armenian one but also an issue for Turks, Kurds, migrants, Indigenous people, villagers, and those in urban areas (Özdoğan et al, 2009). Neyzi (2018), relying on oral history in her book, argued that, ironically, even Turks have been in an identity crisis. She writes that those who are categorized as "Turks" come from different ethnic, religious, and linguistic origins. In order to present a homogeneous identity in public, they either hid their different family/community origins or hid their history altogether.

Neyzi and Kharatyan-Araqelyan (2010) conducted a joint research project that explored oral history in Armenia and Turkey. Neyzi discussed the results of the interviews with Turks, Kurds, and Armenians who lived in what were previously Armenian regions in Turkey (Eastern Anatolia). In an open interview format, the researchers asked interviewees about their life stories and what they remembered about their family and history. Both Neyzi and Kharatyan-Araqelyan (2010) and Üngör's (2014) research showed how in areas where Armenians previously lived, their histories were actually still very present. Neyzi (2010) added that although it was not asked of them, many people who were interviewed brought up the events of 1915. The common narrative was that Muslims and Christians lived in peace together, but 1915 caused a big break between them.

From another point of view, Neyzi (2010) adds that Armenians in Anatolia mentioned that Muslims protected them during 1915 and acknowledged their shared culture and devotion to the land. Nevertheless, they lost family members. In order to protect new generations, they did not impart the full story. Furthermore, Armenians in Anatolia expressed the hurt of being the "other" on their own ancestral lands.

Due to oppression and assimilation politics against their people, Kurds have begun to relate to the Armenian experience and acknowledge their role in the Armenian Genocide (Aghbashian, 2016). In Neyzi's interviews of people from Eastern Anatolia (2010), Kurds made references to historical violence against Armenians, as well as how women were forced to marry Muslims and how Armenian assets were taken over and distributed to Kurds and Balkan *muhacirs* (migrants). People knew which establishments were previously owned by Armenians. Thus, Neyzi states that violence against Armenians was not a secret in Eastern Anatolia cities where they conducted the interviews, and where Armenians had previously lived.

Research with Armenians in Turkey using oral narratives has been slowly emerging. Meanwhile, there has been growing historical literature about the Armenian Genocide, most widely since the 1990s (see Chapter 2, Armenian Genocide of 1915–1917 section). Armenians, both in the diaspora and in Turkey, have been publishing books and articles, organizing conferences, and making movies and documentaries—all in the service of surfacing and teaching their history in Anatolia.

While the narratives of Armenian communities have held consistency, the narratives within Turkey have been paradoxical. The denial of the Armenian Genocide at a state level caused contradictions in Turkey's societal memory. Paradoxically, while not-knowing, partial knowing, silencing, forgetting, and assimilation have been essential pieces of the collective experience in Turkey, so, too, has the remembering. Oral-history researchers in Turkey found that in places where the genocide occurred, Turkish and Kurdish residents' (great)grandparents who witnessed or experienced the Armenian Genocide transmitted their stories to the following generations. Consequently, the descendants of the perpetrators or witnesses feel the "weight of remembering Armenians." Even though the state denies the genocide, pockets of Turkish society still remember. This contradiction in the social memory manifests as an identity crisis, which Neyzi (2018) described as the schizophrenic aspect of Turkishness.

The rapidly advancing research in historical, oral, and anthropological studies presents both internal and external pressure on Turkish narratives and has posed a strong challenge to the Turkish identity. Kurds and Armenians from various platforms, such as documentaries, books, journals, and so on, have told Turks that Turkey's history is not exactly how official Turkish texts claim it. One can understand why Turks with different backgrounds and life stories may respond to Kurdish and Armenian narratives differently. From B. Ünlü's (2016) observations, Turks appear to respond to the Kurdish narrative in two different ways. Some Turks become even more nationalist and fearful, and move into closed communities for protection. A small number of Turks respond with shame and guilt for themselves and their families.

Similar to B. Ünlü's observation of how Turks respond to the Kurdish narrative, I observed similar Turkish reactions to the Armenian narrative. Most Turks react to the information about Armenian history in three different ways. They feel a sense of insult/offense/defense, remain neutral (due to lack of knowledge), or become apologetic.

Earlier, I demonstrated insult/offense and defense responses in how the Turkish student responded with a sense of offense and desire to defend her nation against Armenian Genocide arguments. The second type of response, a neutral response, is often connected to ignorance or not-knowing. The person has no idea or intellectual reference to what they have been told. Even though the information they are receiving might have had a deep emotional and historical charge, the person simply remains neutral and devoid of opinion. The understanding simply does not seem to make an impact on them. I shared my experience of "being speechless" with an Armenian woman earlier in the Introduction. The event happened before I knew anything about Armenian suffering in Anatolia. In the story, I am at a bar, playing pool with a group of people I just met. As part of the conversation, I share that I am Turkish. Hearing this information, out of the blue, a woman confronts me and says, "I am a gay Armenian, do you hear me?" with great intensity. I simply go blank and say, "OK," with neutrality in my voice. I have no intellectual reference to know what might have happened to her people, so I wonder why anyone would tell me this. I am thinking: *Sure, OK, no problem*. As innocent as it sounds, this response could hurt the receiver. Lack of acknowledgment is the perpetuation of wounding for diaspora Armenians. My neutral response is yet another example of ignorance and lack of acknowledgment of what happened—it is yet more proof of what many social activists are up against.

I share another personal story here regarding the final, apologetic Turkish response. In 2013, when I did my initial research, gathering information in Turkey, I was fortunate enough to meet Hrant Dink's colleague and friend, Sarkis Seropyan, at the *Agos* newspaper office. I made an appointment to meet him on November 24, 2014. I went through two different checkpoints and steel doors surveilled by security cameras to enter his office. Security had been installed after Hrant Dink's assassination. Sarkis was very generous with his time and gave me a detailed review of Armenian history, and he also talked about his personal story. When I told him that my maternal grandfather was from Eğin, Erzincan, he told me the story of how his mother had hidden in the Eğin vineyards to escape being deported during what Armenians call the "death march." His mother spoke both Greek and Armenian. She was with her children, and their walk began in Gümüşhane along the Black Sea, by the Euphrates River; they were on their way to Syria's deserts. Three hundred miles into their walk, she noticed that soldiers were letting go of Ottoman-Greek (Rum) women. In Greek, she told the soldiers that they were making a mistake and that she and her children were not Armenian; they were Rum. They were let go at the next stop in Eğin. Except for her toddler, they survived the season by hiding in the vineyards, eating walnuts and berries.

After listening to his story for almost two hours, I was overwhelmed by grief and sadness. With the guilt of my privilege as a Turk, I felt a natural impulse to apologize. I looked him in the eye and said, "I am sorry." I still remember so vividly that he first paused for a moment and then smiled and said (author's translation), "Your apology is a bucket of water in the sea. . . . We need an apology from the people who are in charge of the sea, the state, so it is official." He added that he already knew what I thought, given my research topic; otherwise, he would not be speaking with me. He died 16 months later, on March 28, 2015, in Istanbul, due to old age. He did not live to see the day he'd wished. I hope his surviving family is able to see his wish come true.

I do not want to underemphasize the power of an apology from regular people. My story with Sarkis Seropyan portrays a different need for an Armenian in Turkey. Perhaps he did not need an apology from a Turk, only from the state. However, this story would have been different for an Armenian in the diaspora. Because most of these Armenians grew up with minimal contact with Turks, an empathic contact with a Turk could make an important, positive impact on Armenians in the diaspora and should not be undermined.

I met an older Armenian gentleman from Fresno, California, at a social engagement in San Francisco in 2014. When our conversation revealed that he was Armenian and a child of a survivor and that I was Turkish, I said to him, "Yes, I know about the genocide. I am so sorry for what your family has gone through." He wept simply because I had recognized his people's suffering. Surprised by his tears himself, he shared that hearing me acknowledge the pain of his people and receiving my apology was a healing moment for him. Finally, age-old tension in his chest had lifted. He thanked me and invited me to Fresno to speak with his community.

In the HWH workshops I have organized and participated in, when the group moves to a level of recognition and apology, there is often a sweet lightness in the air. The burden that the group had carried lifts. On a collective level, recognition and apology from the state's point of view are immensely important; at a personal level, each person also carries the moral responsibility of knowing and acknowledging their history and its present consequences.

In this chapter, I reviewed historical and current realities that are both political/collective and individual. I provided individual-level examples for tools for healing historical traumas and encounters between individuals with different cultural backgrounds or knowledge. Though every individual and their responsibility are important, I highlight that all strata of society's participation and effort are needed for social and political narratives to change. As I have demonstrated throughout this book, the cycle of violence, collective trauma narrative, and epistemologies of ignorance are orchestrated by institutional, economic, and sociopolitical context; therefore, it is a collective burden to overcome that encompasses larger power dynamics—it is not up to one individual to shoulder alone.

Conclusion

The purpose of this book has been to shed light upon and interpret collectively traumatic events that have taken place in Anatolia in the last century, based on the country's historical dynamics and current research. Throughout the work, I presented the existence of transgenerational trauma in Turkey and its lasting effects. The works of seminal scholars and practitioners were extensively explored. Their work covered many aspects of trauma, ranging from the psychological, collective, transgenerational, and historical—and the healing modalities applied. The psychological and transgenerational aspects of atrocity differ in many ways from natural disasters or other tragic incidents. Specifically, when not addressed appropriately, its result may cause future conflicts spanning generations and the perpetuation of violence long into the future. Over time, the resulting symptoms and consequences arising from the inflicted trauma become increasingly more complex. Therefore, any healing effort also needs to be equally systemic and complex, addressing all affected areas from individuals to families, from communities to institutions. This healing needs to be an integrated effort involving practitioners from multiple disciplines.

However, in the case of Turkey's historical trauma, the state and institutional functions do not appropriately acknowledge historical and current atrocities. The state uses various forms, such as forced migration, torture, and the annihilation of villages as a tool for societal control and domination. Thus, talking about societal healing options before the Turkish state is willing to prevent it from continuing becomes an act of wishful thinking.

As discussed in the preceding chapters, the denial of both the Kurds' ethnopolitical place in Turkey and the Armenian Genocide are not based on a mere gap in knowledge or simple ignorance; they result from complex institutional epistemological ignorance, advocated and maintained by the Turkish state and society. As a by-product of the evolution of Turkish identity ("Turkishness"), some of the widely used and uncompromising state-enforced mandates and policies have created effects of willful ignorance throughout society, thereby amplifying ethnic tension and perpetuating conflict. Furthermore, the Turkish state and society at large has consciously and unconsciously created and maintained the denial of the

Armenian Genocide and the ignorance of the Kurdish ethnopolitical place in Turkey since the formation of the Republic. These different layers of ignorance have caused severe dehumanization, a lack of empathy, and the perpetuation of violence within society. In the Armenian Genocide case, the lack of acknowledgment by the Turkish state prevents closure on the incident and continues to perpetuate Armenian suffering. In the Kurdish case, ongoing policies of assimilation and armed conflicts are preventing reconciliation and introduce yet more traumas to citizens everywhere.

The literature, based on collective trauma and identity-based conflicts, reveal that historically preexisting us-versus-them mentalities, conflicting interests, competition, scarcity, peer pressure, socialization, biased belief systems, institutionalized organizations, strong and charismatic leaders, and powerful emotions, such as fear, resentment, hatred, and rage, or even arbitrary divisions—under the right circumstances—have the strong potential to mobilize the masses and result in extreme consequences, such as massacres, displacement, and assimilation. Throughout this monograph, I have explored how these consequences may cause deep psychosocial wounding in all those involved, and how these consequences may also be transgenerational. On an individual level, people may experience PTSD, anxiety, and other stress-related symptoms. When entire communities are displaced, this creates voids in areas that are hard (if not impossible) to fill and severely breaks the balance of the social fabric. Such was the case during the collapse of the Ottoman Empire. Displaced Armenian communities—those who survived—were severely compromised physically, emotionally, economically, and socially. The new Muslim migrants and the remaining Anatolia residents faced collapse of the financial market, famine, epidemics, and other severe hardships.

Corresponding to collective atrocities, emotions such as grief, anger, resentment, and fear could imprint collective identities and deepen the us-versus-them mentalities. Division, conflict, and the resulting collective wounding (maladaptive belief systems and behaviors) can accumulate over generations, becoming more complex and affecting collective identities and memory for years to come.

Collective events do not happen in a vacuum, they often develop over centuries, with consequences impacting subsequent generations. I provided a detailed chronological discussion of collectively traumatic experiences concerning Turks, Kurds, and Armenians from Chapter 2 to 4. The chronological exploration allowed me to understand the interconnections—how one event or circumstance followed the other. For example, from the Armenian Genocide to the September 6-7 pogroms, events that targeted non-Muslims had the same goal: to remove non-Muslims and their presence from the towns, the capital, and the society. Either through violence (such as the pogroms) or state-enforced practices (such as "Citizen, speak

Turkish!"), the state aimed to make life more difficult for non-Muslims to stay in Anatolia; the new state wanted to open more opportunity and space for secular "Turks" to excel in this new nation.

The shift from "Muslimness" to "Turkishness" dominated the first years of the Republic of Turkey—not all Muslims were going to excel in this new construct; Secular Muslim Turks or those who accepted the Turkishness contract were going to create and maintain the new Republic. There were fundamental differences between the Kurdish people's core tribal belief system and the new secular, homogeneous ideology of the Turkish nation. Moreover, since the rise of the Republic, the conflict between the Turkish state and Kurdish identity has been due to the consistency of many of the Kurdish people to resist assimilation to Turkishness, and their wish to have the freedom to express their culture, language, and ways of living.

State violence has been normalized under the umbrella of "revolution" and "protection of the state." As discussed throughout this work, it is through epistemologies of ignorance that historical events were obscured, forgotten, or partially presented— creating a cycle of ignorance which in turn has caused the perpetuation of further violence. I focused on the epistemologies of ignorance of state violence in Chapter 5, and reviewed how today, Turkey's government is trying to keep its people ignorant of historical events, collective traumas, and the actual conditions affecting various ethnicities. While other scholars have discussed the epistemologies of ignorance of Turkishness (e.g., B. Ünlü, 2016; Yeğen, 1999a), this book builds on those arguments and is the first to identify ignorance as a systemic problem, as a hindrance that, in itself, prevents people from healing their transgenerational and historical traumas. This lack of healing, in turn, destabilizes society further by contributing to the violence that only perpetuates transgenerational trauma. "A Transdisciplinary Perspective toward Reconciliation" performs the social-action function of dispelling ignorance by informing people of these conditions and their historical antecedents. A prime intention is to inspire people to make informed social action decisions to encourage healing. Collective healing is not only an individual process but also a societal process that demands systemic change. In that context, it is often not an easy step to face the nature of psychological trauma.

American feminist psychiatrist Judith Herman (2015) writes:

> The knowledge of horrible events periodically intrudes into public awareness but is rarely retained for long. Denial, repression, and disassociation operate on a social as well as individual level. The study of psychological trauma has an "underground" history. Like traumatized people, we have been cut off from the knowledge of our past. Like traumatized people, we need to understand the past in order to reclaim the present and the future.

Therefore, an understanding of psychological trauma begins with re-discovering history. (p. 2)

In Turkey, numerous unresolved conflicts and issues have evolved into unresolved historical traumas and continue to cause tears in the fabric of society, creating collectively shared traumas. These collectively traumatic events have taken place in a continuum from the Ottoman Empire to the Republic of Turkey. Therefore, re-discovering history and understanding transgenerational trauma in Turkey is essential for societal healing. That said, individuals and their communities may carry unique and, at times, conflicting historical legacies. It is essential to explore how the individual, community, society, history, and present-day reality intersect. For example, the historical traumatic experience of a Turkish Alevi from Sivas will be different from a Zaza Alevi from Dersim. They may share a common legacy of historical trauma as an Alevi in Anatolia that goes all the way back to the Chaldiran War in 1514. However, their individual thread, culture, and identity may be different due to an Alevi from Dersim also carrying the Dersim Massacres' legacy. Also, Dersimis have had a distinct culture due to being geographically isolated from the rest of the region. Turkish Alevi from Sivas may have a different family history. Another example could be the child of a Balkan migrant mother and a Kurdish father, whose upbringing would involve the complexity of both legacies; however, it might differ based on how assimilated their father or mother are to "Turkishness." A final example could be the descendant of a Turkish family who became wealthy after the wealth and revenue taxes in 1942 and would have a different investment in the status quo than a Turkish socialist family with no historical connection with the taxes. Chapter 2, 3 & 4 set out examples of these multilayered and complicated histories and legacies.

While re-discovering history and addressing the nature of transgenerational trauma, it is vital to acknowledge and address those of present-day. Examples might include the psychological, physical, and social trauma of wounded veterans and their families, and the families of the martyrs from the war between PKK and the Turkish military. Further examples could include tortured inmates, displaced people, family members who have disappeared, village guards who are financially dependent on their job, people who have been harassed and hurt by those guards, being part of a small and surviving community of Armenians in Istanbul, and Kurdish youth who are now born into conflict. Sadly, the list of examples goes on and on. Furthermore, one needs to take into account present day context. People may have economic struggles, or they may have faced a natural disaster or another form of trauma; when faced with personal survival issues, their ability to open up to historical discussions and political arguments becomes particularly challenging.

This book has provided a comprehensive review of impacted communities and their complex adaptations in the face of collectively traumatic events concerning Armenians, Kurds, and Turks. However, it is essential to highlight that just one book is not able to give justice to everyone who deserves to be mentioned; furthermore, the arguments presented are from one person's vantage point—mine. Therefore, the events and examples provided should be expanded with future research and arguments by people from all backgrounds to provide a fuller, more comprehensive picture of historical and present-day collectively traumatic events.

On a final note: despite tightened oppression and authoritarian practices, a new era is continuing to emerge globally, shining and glimmering with hope. Access to resources, information, and modes of communication are becoming easier. It is more difficult for nation states around the world to hide their wrongdoings and cover their tracks. Technology and media tools may provide an alternative to hierarchical paradigms. New integrative societies (Slater, 2008) may allow pathways and forums for reflection, remembrance, and discussion. In this way, the 21st century still holds a light of hope as the century continues to unfold. Each person, and community respectively, carry a tremendous responsibility. The actions each of us take or do not take will collectively determine the fate of this new crucial century.

Notes

Introduction

1 This book's geographic parameter is within the current Republic of Turkey's national boundary. Because the region's history is included before it became known as the Republic of Turkey in 1923, the intent was to use a more neutral name to prevent confusion about time and place. The region is referred to as Anatolia. Some may argue that Anatolia is still a Turkish-centric way of describing the region, as Kurds and Armenians may call it otherwise during different times in history. To create more balance, parts of the region such as Kurdistan, the Armenian Plateau, and Turkey are referred to when these terminologies may be more relevant. Because I am Turkish and grew up referring to the region as Anatolia (Anadolu), Anatolia was adopted as the central description of the area.

2 My perspective and application of transdisciplinarity are mainly influenced by the works of Edgar Morin, Tanya Augsburg, Patricia Leavy, Alfonso Montuori, and Jennifer Wells. From their perspective, transdisciplinarity is an issue-based or inquiry centered approach and views knowledge building and dissemination as a holistic process that requires innovation and flexibility. Transdisciplinary research can be inquiry-driven, socially conscious, and oriented toward systems thinking and complexity theory and is a mode of inquiry with the potential for transcultural engagement in both theory and practice. Transdisciplinary research draws literature across and beyond disciplines, without assuming disciplinary boundaries (Augsburg, 2014; Leavy, 2011; Montuori, 2010, 2012, 2013; Morin, 2008; Wells, 2012). See Soyalp (2020) for more details on how transdisciplinarity was applied in this research.

3 The healing the Wounds of History (HWH) process was created by psychotherapist Armand Volkas in the early 1980s in Los Angeles, CA. Armand Volkas, MFT, RDT/BCT is a child of Jewish Holocaust survivors and resistance fighters. He formed his approach of healing historical trauma by first facilitating dialogue between children of Holocaust survivors and the Third Reich. HWH is based on the premise that there can be no political solutions to intercultural conflict until we understand and take into consideration the emotional and unconscious drives of the human being. Using drama therapy and psychodrama techniques, HWH takes a psychological approach to conflict, providing a map to help individuals, groups, and communities traverse the emotional terrain toward reconciliation.

4 Psychodrama is a profound action method that was developed by Jacob Moreno (1889–1974), while Sigmund Freud (1856–1939) was developing talk

therapy. Psychodrama is often used as a psychotherapy technique, in which the client (protagonist) uses spontaneous dramatization and role-playing to gain insight and to express what they want.
5   I individually reached out to all HWH workshop participants and asked for permission to utilize their narratives. Nevertheless, I removed all identifiable markers of each participant to protect their identities.
6   *Partiya Karkerên Kurdistanê* (PKK) is a Kurdish armed group in Turkey. See Chapter 4 for the dynamics between the Turkish military and PKK.
7   Yörük Turks are an ethnic subgroup of Oghuz descent.
8   Also called the Amira class within the Ottoman Empire
9   Gestalt therapy, a widely known psychotherapy tool in which one speaks to an empty chair, grew out of Jacob Moreno's work with psychodrama. The protagonist sits on one chair and puts an empty chair across from them for someone with whom they want to speak. With facilitation, the protagonist switches between chairs; they share what they need to share, and also speak from the perspective of the other person. This kind of dialogue helps the protagonist uncover deeper insights into their experience, have an opportunity to say what they wanted to say, and to feel a sense of completion.
10   The migrants that arrived during earlier immigration waves between 1878 and 1913 were called *Muhacirs* and remained a recognizably different group. They created their own neighborhoods and were segregated from the rest of society.

1 Trauma and Its Psycho-Social Consequences

1   This book references various major collective and historical traumas such as chattel slavery and the genocide of Native Americans. These subjects are intentionally not reviewed in detail but given to exemplify cross-cultural trauma.
2   An idea that is similar to one conveyed by Benjamin Spock (1946) in his book *Baby and Child Care*.

2 A History of Collective Traumas: The Decline and the Fall of the Ottoman Empire

1   Andrews and Benninghaus' work, first published in 1989, claimed the number of ethnicities was 47. In their more resent publication in 2002, with light of new research and resources, the number has increased by one, to 48, identifying the Zaza language and their ethnic difference.
2   Armenians were proud to claim they were the first organized group who adopted Christianity as an official religion in 301 AD. Another large population were the Greek Ottomans (Rums), who mostly lived in Northern and Western Anatolia with minimal contact with Kurds in Kurdistan. Other minority Christian populations who had more integration with the Kurds included the Ashuri (Assyrian) and Suryani, who spoke Aramaic dialects. Assyrians belonged to the Nestorian church, and Suryanis belonged to the Syrian Orthodox or Jacobite church (Kevorkian & Paboudjian, 2012).
3   Kurdish language has different dialects. A few distinct ones are the Northwestern dialects, often called Kurmanji; Southern dialects, often called Sorani; and Southeastern dialects, such as Sine'i, Kemanshahi, and Leki. Large

groups of tribes also speak Zaza in Northwestern Kurdistan, mainly in Dersim/Tunceli, Erzincan, and parts of Bingol and Diyarbakır. In many places in Northwest Kurdistan, Zaza and Kurmanji speakers share the same geography. Most Kurds are Sunni Muslims, following Shari'a rite, and distinguish themselves from Turks and Arabs, who are also Sunni Muslims but follow the Hanafi legal school. Also, many Kurds embrace orthodox Twelver Shiism, mainly in Iran, or follow heterodox syncretistic sects, such as Alevis and mystic Sufism. Not all Alevis are Kurds; a considerable number of Alevi Turks also live in Turkey (van Bruinessen, 1992).

4   For example, Laz and Georgian nomads live near the Black Sea in the Northern Anatolia region. The Turkic, Turkomen, and Tahtaci communities live in Western Anatolia and Central Taurus Mountains. Furthermore, the Turkomen, Turkic, and Tatar nomads reside in Central Anatolia. Kurdish nomadic groups predominately transpass (transhumance) in Eastern Anatolia (see Sayılır, 2012).

5   See Chatty, 2010, p 241–260 for the summary of the 19th century Kurdish revolts and uprisings in Kurdistan in their effort to protect status quo: The Baban Revolt of 1806, Mir Mohammed's Uprising in Soran of 1833–1836, Yezdan Sher Revolt of 1855, and Shaykh Obeidullah's Revolt of 1880.

6   According to Ottoman official reports, the collective violence during the 1893 1896 Massacres took 953 Muslim and 3,891 Armenian lives, and left 963 Muslims and 1,545 Armenian wounded (Göçek, 2015, p. 133). Göçek (2015) points out that in these official reports, Armenian losses were almost four times more than Muslims' and that the actual numbers for Armenian loss are also much higher than those in the official statement.

7   *Genocide* is a term that was first used after the Jewish Holocaust by Germans after World War II. After the judgment of the International Military Tribunal at Nuremberg in 1946, the Convention on the Prevention and Punishment of the Crime of Genocide was first adopted in 1948. Only with the establishment of the body of the United Nations (UN) International Criminal Tribunal for the former Yugoslavia (ICTY) in 1993, did international criminal jurisdiction begin to prosecute such crimes (Akhavan, 2012). Although the term genocide is a relatively new word, it does not mean that it did not exist before the Jewish Holocaust nor that the Holocaust was the worst horrific evil the world has seen. Regretfully, human history has witnessed many other collective atrocities of various magnitudes to this day (e.g., Native American Holocaust in America, African slavery, Rwandan genocide, the mass murder of thousands of Bosnia Muslims in 1995).

8   For estimates ranging from 800,000 to 1.5 million see Akçam (2012), Bloxham (2003, pp. 36–37; 2005, p. 10), Dadrian (1995), Mann (2005, p. 140), Naimark (2001), and Üngör (2015). For a lower estimate, see J. McCarthy (1995).

3 The Collective Trauma After the Formation of the Republic of Turkey

1   According to Olson (2000), "The Sheikh Said rebellion of 1925, the Mt. Ararat revolt of 1930 and the Dersim rebellion of 1937–1938 were significant developments in the history of modern Turkish and Kurdish nationalism" (p. 67).

2   Execution date: September 4, 1925 (van Bruinessen, 1992, p. 291); see also another argument for Sheikh Said's execution date—on June 29 (Olson, 1989, p. 127).
3   For detailed chronological developments, see Aktar (2000, pp. 141–161).
4   "bizim hazırladığımız baremi [siyasi adamlar] kat kat ağırlaştırarak vergiyi altından kalkılmaz hale sokmuşlardı."
5   "Varlık Vergisi zamanında ben daha çocuktum. Ama hatırlıyorum evdeki korkuyu. 1915'te çok acı çekmiş, babam. Anlatmazdı ama bilirdik. 40'ların başıydı galiba, askerden yeni gelmişti. Bir vergi çıkmış derlerdi. İşte o Varlık Vergisi'ymiş. Babamın parası yok, nasıl ödeyecek? Gecelerce annemle konuştuklarını hatırlıyorum. Çocuk aklımla anlamaya çalışırdım. İkisi de çok korkmuşlardı. Korkmaz mı güzel kızım? 1915'te çocuk yaşında çok acı çekmiş, tekrarlanıyor sanmış herhal. . . . Neyse ki vergi gelmedi bizim eve. Sana bir şey diyem mi? Nasıl bir hisse bu meret, bana da sirayet etmiş. İş hayatım boyunca hep 'Başımıza bir şey gelir' korkusuyla çok para kazanmak istemedim" (Manuk, 75) (Muratyan, 2011, p. 57).

4   The Inheritance of Military Ideologies and Its Consequences

1   Diyarbakır Askeri Cezaevi 1980-84 Gerçeğini Araştırma ve Adalet Komisyonu (DAC- GAAK).
2   "Cezaevi müdürü binbaşı Esat Oktay Yıldıran vardı. . . . Birgün bizim kadınlar koğuşuna girdi. . . . Herkes ayağa kalktı, ben kalkmadım . . . sırf içeri girdiğinde ayağa kalkmadım diye, sırf bu gerekçeyle beni köpeği Co'nun kulübesine tıktırdı. Köpeğin bile kalmak istemediği, pislik içinde, küçücük bir kulübeydi bu. . . . Bir gün değil, iki gün değil, bir ay değil, iki ay değil, tam altı ay orada kaldım. Nefes almanın bile zor olduğu o kulübede bana her gün dayak attılar, her gün işkence yaptılar" (Hakan, 2012, para. 4).
3   *"Laz Kemal'in sana selamı var!"* (Sağır, 2015, para. 5).
4   The rule of law whereby a person otherwise is entitled to enforce a right in legal proceedings is debarred from doing so because of the length of time that has elapsed since the cause of action.
5   Hasan Dağtekin de suç duyurusunda bulunanlar arasındaydı:
    Eylül ayında takipsizlik kararı verildi. Zaman aşımı dediler. İnsanlık suçlarına karşı zaman aşımı olmamalı. Karara itiraz ettik ama itirazımız da reddedildi. Bireysel başvuru hakkı ile konuyu Anayasa Mahkemesi'ne taşıyacağız. Evren öldü ama keşke Ankara'da açılan mahkeme ondan ve o darbeyi yapan kesimden; yaşatılan o işkencelerin, ölümlerin hesabını sorabilseydi. Fakat ne yazık ki mahkeme çok ağır işliyor. Bu yüzden (Kenan Evren) binlerce insana yaşattıklarının cezasını çekemeden öldü" (Kamer, 2015, para. 6).
6   "İntihar davranışı açısından TSK personelinde benzer yaş ve cinsiyet grupları açısından sivil örneklerden daha farklı bir epidemiyolojik veri olmadığı tespit edilmiştir" (En Son Haber, 2013, para. 14).
7   "Geldikten sonra bana kız bile vermediler. Kötü birşey yapmadım. Devleti soymadım, bir yeri gasp etmedim, kimsenin ırzına namusuna saldırmadım. Benim seçeneğim değildi ki. . . . Adamın ayağı koptu, nişanlısı terk etti. İkinci

sınıf vatandaş muamelesi gördüğümüz yerler oluyor. . . .
Askerden önce kavgadan pek hoşlanmazdım, daha sakin bir tiptim. Şimdi çok asabiyim. Vietnam sendromu dediklei. . . . Kendimi kontrolde zorlanıyorum. . . . Birini vurabileceğime inandığım zamanlar oluyor. Olayları daha yoğun yaşıyorum, saldırganlaşabiliyorum." (Mater, 1999, p. 111)

8 "Beni nasıl kahraman olarak görebilirler? Kendi halkımla savaştım. Askerliğimi nerede yaptığımı söyleme gereği duymuyorum, iyi bir şey olmadığını biliyorum. Soranlara, 'Kayseri'de yaptım,' diyorum" (Mater, 1999, p. 31).

9 In response to disappearance and torture cases, on May 27, 1995, a group primarily mothers, called Saturday Mothers *(Cumartesi Anneleri)*, started gathering at noon for half an hour at Galatasaray, Istanbul. Initially protesting and asking for clarification for their missing relatives. The group attracted more support from 15–25 people and grew to hundreds of people gathering every Saturday. The group sits in silence, holding pictures of their lost loved ones. Saturday mothers are one of the longest-running peaceful protest movements that are still active.

5 Epistemologies of Ignorance of Turkishness and Healing through Meeting the "Other"

1 For example, quantitative data about those who consider themselves Kurds, those who speak Kurdish, where they live in Turkey, their political preferences, how their views change based on gender, age, education, and religion are all underresearched. Yeğen et al's (2016) research is one of the projects that attempts to answer these questions. For example, they found that a high number of Muslim Kurds with less education and higher income support the JDP *(AKP)*—Justice and Development Party *(Adalet ve Kalkınma Partisi)* government, and they are not as involved in political activism as PDP supporters. On the other hand, Kurds with higher education and lower-income support PDP *(HDP)*—Peoples' Democratic Party *(Halkların Demokratik Partisi)*, and they are much more outspoken about the injustice in the region. Yeğen (2011) additionally reflects that even though Kurdish parties in Turkey have always nurtured the idea of an autonomous Kurdistan, the ideal of an independent or federal Kurdistan has always been weak among Turkey's Kurds. However, the violence against Kurds, which has accelerated since the 2015 election, may begin to change this situation for some.

2 Mainly two radical Armenian groups emerged: The Justice Commandos for Armenian Genocide (JCOAG) and Armenian Secret Army for the Liberation of Armenian (ASALA).

References

Abbas, T., & Zalta, A. (2017). "You cannot talk about academic freedom in such an oppressive environment": Perceptions of the We Will Not Be a Party to This Crime! petition signatories. *Turkish Studies, 18*(4), 624–643. https://doi.org/10.1080/14683849.2017.1343148

Adanır, F. (2011). *Non-Muslims in the Ottoman army and the Ottoman defeat in the Balkan War of 1912–1913*. Oxford University Press.

Adanır, F. (2015). "Ermeni meselesi" nin doğuşu [The beginning of "Armenian issue"] In F. Adanır & O. Özel (Eds.), *1915 Siyaset, Tehcir, Soykırım* [1915, Politics, Deportation, Genocide] (pp. 3–43). Tarih Vakfı Yurt Yayınları.

Adıbelli, D., & Yüksel, R. (2019). Views of Turkish men about violence against women: A community mental health issue. *International Journal of Caring Sciences, 12*(1), 149–162.

AFAD [Government of Crisis Center], (August 17, 1999). *Ağustos 1999 Gölcük Depremi*. https://deprem.afad.gov.tr/tarihteBuAy?id=37

Agaibi, C. E., & Wilson, J. P. (2005). Trauma, PTSD, and resilience: A review of the literature. *Trauma Violence Abuse, 6*(3), 195–216. https://doi.org/10.1177/1524838005277438

Aghbashian, H. (2016, April 8). Turkish intellectuals who have recognized the Armenian genocide: Gültan Kışanak. Retrieved from https://massispost.com/2016/04/turkish-intellectuals-who-have-recognized-the-armenian-genocide-gultan-kisanak/

Ainsworth, M. D., Blehar, M. C., Waters, E., & Wall, S. (2000). *Patterns of attachment: A psychological study of the strange situation*. Psychology Press.

Ainsworth, M. S. (1979). Infant–mother attachment. *American Psychologist, 34*(10), 932–937. http://dx.doi.org/10.1037/0003-066X.34.10.932

Ak, B. (2014). Determination and evaluation of effects of earthquake on school age children's (6-12 Years Old) behaviours. *Procedia - Social and Behavioral Sciences, 152*, 845–851. doi:10.1016/j.sbspro.2014.09.332

Akar, R. (1999). *Aşkale yolcuları: Varlık vergisi ve çalışma kampları* [Aşkale passengers: Wealth taxes and labor camps]. Belge Yayınları.

Akçam, T. (2006). *A shameful act: The Armenian genocide and the question of Turkish responsibility*. Metropolitan Books.

Akçam, T. (2012). *The Young Turks' crime against humanity: The Armenian genocide and ethnic cleansing in the Ottoman Empire*. Princeton University Press.

Aker, T., Ayata, B., Özeren, M., Buran, B., & Bay, A. (2002). Zorunlu iç göç: Ruhsal ve toplumsal sonuçları [Forced internal displacement: Psychological and social consequences]. *Anadolu Psikiyatri Dergisi, 3*(2), 97–103.

Aker, T., Önen, P., & Karakiliç, H. (2007). Psychological trauma: Research and practice in Turkey. *International Journal of Mental Health, 36*(3), 38–57. https://doi.org/10.2753/imh0020-7411360306

Akkaya-Kalaycı, T., Popow, C., Winkler, D., Bingöl, R. H., Demir, T., & Özlü, Z. (2015). The impact of migration and culture on suicide attempts of children and adolescents living in Istanbul. *International Journal of Psychiatry in Clinical Practice, 19*(1), 32–39. https://doi.org/10.3109/13651501.2014.961929

Aktar, A. (1996). Varlık Vergisi ve Istanbul [*Wealth Taxes and Istanbul*]. *Toplum ve Bilim, 71*, 94–147.

Aktar, A. (2000). *Varlık vergisi ve "Türkleştirme" politikaları* [Wealth taxes and "Turkification" policies]. (Vol. 4). İletişim Yayınları.

Alavi, H. (1973). Peasant classes and primordial loyalties AU. *The Journal of Peasant Studies, 1*(1), 23–62. https://doi.org/10.1080/03066157308437871

Alayarian, A. (2008). *Consequences of denial: The Armenian genocide*. Karnac Books.

Alcoff, L. M. (2007). Epistemologies of ignorance: Three types. In N. Tuana & S. Sullivan (Eds.), *Race and epistemology of ignorance* (pp. 39–57). State University of New York Press.

Alemdar, Z., & Çorbacoğlu, R. B. (2012). Alevis and the Turkish state. *Turkish Policy Quarterly, 10*(4), 117–124.

Alexander, J. C. (2004). The trauma of social change: A case of postcommunist societies. In J. C. Alexander, R., Eyerman, B. Giesen, N. J. Smelser, & P. Sztompka, *Cultural trauma and collective identity* (pp. 155–195). University of California Press.

Alexander, J. C. (2012). *Trauma: A social theory*. Polity Press.

Alexanian, A. G. (2018). *Forced into genocide: Memoirs of an Armenian soldier in the Ottoman Turkish army*. Routledge.

Alpan, A. S. (2012). But the memory remains: History, memory and the 1923 Greco-Turkish population exchange. *Historical Review / La Revue Historique, 9*, 199–232. http://dx.doi.org/10.12681/hr.295

Altınay, A. G. (2004). *The myth of the military-nation: Militarism, gender, and education in Turkey*. Palgrave Macmillan.

Altınay, A. G., & Arat, Y. (2007). *Türkiye'de kadına yönelik şiddet* [Violence against women in Turkey]. Author.

Andrews, P. A., & Benninghaus, R. (1989). *Ethnic groups in the Republic of Turkey* (Vol. 1). L. Reichert.

Arap, I. & Erat V. (2015). Bir Kamu Politikasının Analizi: Türkiye'de Geçici Köy Koruculuğu [An Analysis of Public Policy: Temporary Village Guard System in Turkey]. *Mülkiye Dergisi*, 39 (4), 73–108.

Aras, R. (2014). *The formation of Kurdishness in Turkey: Political violence, fear and pain* (Vol. 59 of Routledge Studies in Middle Eastern Politics). Routledge.

Arda, B. (2015). Apolitical is political: An ethnographic study on the public sphere in the Gezi uprising in Turkey. *Interface: A Journal on Social Movements, 7*(1), 9–18.

Arendt, H. (2006). *Eichmann in Jerusalem: A report on the banality of evil*. Penguin Books.

Arslan, S. (2015). Asimilasyon ve iskân politikaları bağlamında yatılı ilköğretim bölge okulları [Regional elementary boarding schools in regards to assimilation and settlement politics] Assimilation and (YİBO). *Sosyal Bilimler*, 139-151.

Asbarez Contributor. (2011, November 23). Erdoğan offers half-hearted apology for Dersim massacres. *Asbarez*. http://asbarez.com/99522/erdogan-offers-half-hearted-apology-for-dersim-massacres/

Aslan, Ş. (2010). *Herkesin bildiği sır: Dersim* [The secret that everyone knows: Dersim]. İletişim Yayınları.

Ataöv, T. (1994). The "Armenian question." *The Turkish Yearbook, 24*, 121–156.

Augsburg, T. (2014). Becoming transdisciplinary: The emergence of the transdisciplinary individual. *World Futures, 70*(3–4), 233–247. https://doi.org/10.1080/02604027.2014.934639

Avar, S. (1986). *Dağ çiçeklerim: Anılar* [My mountain flowers: Memories]. Öğretmen Yayınları.

Ayas, T. (2005). Depremden 42 ay sonra deprem bölgesinde yaşayan çocuklarda görülen psikolojik belirtilerin bağzı değişkenlere göre incelenmesi [After 42 months of the earthquake children who live in the earthquake area psychological symptoms which seem to the children are researched according to some variable]. *Eğitim Bilimleri ve Uygulama Dergisi, Journal of Educational Sciences & Practice, 4*(8), 1–15.

Ayata, B. (2011). *The politics of displacement: A transnational analysis of the forced migration of Kurds in Turkey and Europe* (Doctoral dissertation). Retrieved from ProQuest Dissertation and Theses database. (Publication no. AAI3463620).

Ayata, B., & Hakyemez, S. (2013). The AKP's engagement with Turkey's past crimes: An analysis of PM Erdoğan's "Dersim apology." *Dialectical Anthropology, 37*(1), 131–143. https://doi.org/10.1007/s10624-013-9304-3

Ayata, B., & Yükseker, D. (2005). A belated awakening: National and international responses to the internal displacement of Kurds in Turkey. *New Perspectives on Turkey, 32*, 5–42.

Ayata, S. (2014). Buyurganlığa ve yasakçılığa karşı direniş: "Gezi Hareketi" [Resistance against dictatorship and prohibition: "Gezi Movement."] *Gazi Üniversitesi Öğretim Üyeleri Derneği Akademik Bülten, 12*(1), 22–26.

Aydın, E. (2018). *Çocukluk çağı travmatik yaşantılarının psikolojik sağlamlılık ve depresyon belirtileri üzerine etkisi [Impacts of childhood trauma on symptoms of resilience and depression]* (Master's Thesis). Fatih Sultan Mehmet Vakıf Üniversitesi, İstanbul.

Aydıngün, A., & Aydıngün, I. (2004). The role of language in the formation of Turkish national identity and Turkishness. *Nationalism and Ethnic Politics, 10*(3), 415–432.

Ayverdi, S. (2007). *Türkiye'nin Ermeni meselesi.* [Turkey's Armenian issue]. (Vol. 125). Kubealtı Publishing.

Bal, A. (2008). Post-traumatic stress disorder in Turkish child and adolescent survivors three years after the Marmara earthquake. *Child & Adolescent Mental Health, 13*(3), 134–139. https://doi.org/10.1111/j.1475-3588.2007.00469.x

Balancar, F. (2012). *The sounds of silence: Turkey's Armenians speak*. Hrant Dink Foundation.

Balancar, F. (2013). *The sounds of silence II—Diyarbakır's Armenians speak*. Hrant Dink Foundation.
Bali, R. N. (2001). Toplumsal bellek ve varlik vergisi [Social memory and wealth taxes]. In E. Özyürek, (Ed.) *Hatırladıklarıyla ve Unuttuklarıyla Türkiye'nin Toplumsal Hafızası* [Turkey's social memory with what they remember and forget]. (pp. 87-126). Iletişim yayınları
Bali, R. N. (2012). *Varlık vergisi: hatıralar-tanıklıklar* [Weath taxes: memories-testimony]. Libra Yayıncılık.
Barkey, H. J., & Fuller, G. E. (1998). *Turkey's Kurdish question*. Rowman & Littlefield.
Barkey, K., & Gavrilis, G. (2015). The Ottoman millet system: Non-territorial autonomy and its contemporary legacy. *Ethnopolitics, 15*(1), 24–42. https://doi.org/10.1080/17449057.2015.1101845
Başoğlu, M. (2009). A multivariate contextual analysis of torture and cruel, inhuman, and degrading treatments: Implications for an evidence-based definition of torture. *American Journal of Orthopsychiatry, 79*(2), 135–145. https://doi.org/10.1037/a0015681
Başoğlu, M., Livanou, M., Crnobarić, C., Frančišković, T., Suljić, E., Đurić, D., & Vranešić, M. (2005). Psychiatric and cognitive effects of war in former Yugoslavia: Association of lack of redress for trauma and posttraumatic stress reactions. *JAMA, 294*(5), 580–590.
Başoğlu, M., Paker, M., Özmen, E., Taşdemir, Ö., & Şahin, D. (1994). Factors related to long-term traumatic stress responses in survivors of torture in Turkey. *JAMA, 272*(5), 357–363.
Başoğlu, M., Paker, M., Paker, O., Özmen, E., Marks, I., Incesu, C., . . . Sarımurat, N. (1994). Psychological effects of torture: A comparison of tortured with nontortured political activists in Turkey. *American Journal of Psychiatry, 151*(1), 76–81.
BBC. (2011, November 23). Turkey PM Erdogan apologises for 1930s Kurdish killings. *BBC News*. https://www.bbc.com/news/world-europe-15857429
Beriker-Atıyas, N. (1997). The Kurdish conflict in Turkey: Issues, parties and prospects. *Security Dialogue, 28*(4), 439–452.
Beşikçi, İ. (1990). *Tunceli kanunu (1935) ve Dersim Jenosidi* [Tunceli law (1935) and Dersim Genocide]. Belge Yayınları.
Betancourt, T. S., Borisova, I., Williams, T. P., Meyers-Ohki, S. E., Rubin-Smith, J. E., Annan, J., & Kohrt, B. A. (2013). Research review: Psychosocial adjustment and mental health in former child soldiers—A systematic review of the literature and recommendations for future research. *Journal of Child Psychology and Psychiatry, 54*(1), 17–36. https://doi.org/10.1111/j.1469-7610.2012.02620.x
Beyoğlu, S. (2004). Ermeni tehciri ve ihtida [Armenian deportation and conversion]. *Yakın Dönem Türkiye Araştırmaları and* (6). http://search.ebscohost.com/login.aspx?direct=true&db=cdsagr&AN=edsagr.TR2016026709&site=eds-live
Bilgin, R. (2014). The problem with children growing in the environment of confliction and violence. *Fırat University Journal of Social Science, 24*(1), 135–151.

Bilmez, B., Aslan, Ş., & Kayacan, G. (2011). *Toplumsal bellek, kuşaklararası aktarım ve algı: Dersim '38'i hatırlamak* [Social memory, intergerational transmission and perception: remembering Dersim '38']. Tarih Vakfı Yurt Yayınları.

Bilmez, B., Kayacan, G., & Aslan, Ş. (2015). *Belleklerdeki Dersim '38'* [Dersim '38' in memories]. Tarih Vakfı Yurt Yayınları.

Bloxham, D. (2003). The Armenian genocide of 1915–1916: Cumulative radicalization and the development of a destruction policy. *Past & Present, 181*(1), 141–191.

Bloxham, D. (2005). *The great game of genocide: Imperialism, nationalism, and the destruction of the Ottoman Armenians*. Oxford University Press.

Bocchi, G., & Ceruti, M. (1997). *Solidarity or barbarism: A Europe of diversity against ethnic cleansing* (A. Montuori, Trans.). Peter Lang.

Böke, P. (2006). *İzmir 1919–1922: Tanıklıklar* [Izmir 1919–1922: Testimonies]. Tarih Vakfı Yurt Yayınları.

Boyajian, K., & Grigorian, H. (1982, June). *Sequelae of the Armenian genocide on survivors*. Paper presented at the International Conference on the Holocaust and Genocide, Tel Aviv, Israel.

Boyajian, L. Z, & Grigorian, H., M. (1998). Reflections on the denial of the Armenian Genocide. *Psychoanalytic Review, 85*(4), 505–516.

Bozarslan, H. (2004). *Violence in the Middle East: From political struggle to self-sacrifice*. Markus Wiener.

Bozarslan, H. (2008). *Türkiye'nin modern Tarihi* [Turkey's modern history]. Avesta Yayınları.

Bradley, L., & Tawfiq, N. (2006). The physical and psychological effects of torture in Kurds seeking asylum in the United Kingdom. *Clinical Knowledge, 16*(1), 41–47.

Bremner, J. D., Southwick, S. M., Darnell, A., & Charney, D. S. (1996). Chronic PTSD in Vietnam combat veterans: Course of illness and substance abuse. *The American Journal of Psychiatry, 153*(3), 369–375. http://dx.doi.org/10.1176/ajp.153.3.369

Brown, P. M. (1924). From Sèvres to Lausanne. *American Journal of International Law, 18*(1), 113–116. https://doi.org/10.2307/2189228

Buğu, B. (2016). *Working with the cancer of the diseases phenomenology of being a psychotherapist working with torture survivors in Turkey* (Master's Thesis). Istanbul Bilgi University. Available from openaccess.bilgi.edu.tr. (113627006)

Bulut, S. (2006). Comparing the earthquake exposed and non-exposed Turkish children's post traumatic stress reactions. *Anales de Psicología, 22*(1), 29–36.

Çagatay, C. (Executive producer). (2009–). *Bu kalp seni unutur mu?* [Television series]. Istanbul, Turkey: Show TV.

Çağaptay, S. (2014). *The impact of Syria's refugees on Southern Turkey* (Policy Focus 130). Washington Institute for Near East Policy. https://www.washingtoninstitute.org/uploads/Documents/pubs/PolicyFocus130_Cagaptay_Revised3s.pdf

Çakmak, F. (2007). Kuruluşundan kapatılışına kadar Türkiye Büyük Millet Meclis içerisinde köy enstitülerine yönelik muhalefet [The Turkish Grand National

Assembly's opposition to village institutes, from their establishment to their closure]. *ÇTTAD, 1*(15), 221–250.

Çakmak, H., Er, R. A., Öz, Y. C., & Aker, A. T. (2010). Kocaeli ili 112 acil yardım birimlerinde çalışan personelin Marmara depreminden etkilenme ve olası afetlere hazırlık durumlarının saptanması [Determining the Marmara earthquake's impact on Kocaeli province, 112 emergency unit personnel and their preparedness for possible disasters]. *Akademik Acil Tıp Dergisi, 2*, 83–88.

Carlson, V., Cicchetti, D., Barnett, D., & Braunwald, K. (1989). Disorganized/disoriented attachment relationships in maltreated infants. *Developmental Psychology, 25*(4), 525–531.
http://dx.doi.org/10.1037/0012-1649.25.4.525

Çelik, A. B. (2005). "I miss my village!": Forced Kurdish migrants in Istanbul and their representation in associations. *New Perspectives on Turkey, 32*, 137–163.
https://doi.org/10.1017/S0896634600004143

Çelik, A. B. (2015). Resolving internal displacement in Turkey: The need for reconciliation. In M. Bradley (Ed.), *Forced migration, reconciliation, and justice* (pp. 195–222). McGill-Queen's University Press.

Çelik, F. (2015). *Intergenerational effects of the Dersim massacre (1937–38)*. (Doctoral dissertation). Birkbeck College, University of London.

Çelik, F. (2017). The Alevi of Dersim: A psychosocial approach to the effects of the massacre, time and space. In T. Issa (Ed.), *Alevis in Europe* (pp. 46-67). Routledge.

Cemiloğlu, D. (2009). Language policy and national unity: The dilemma of the Kurdish language in Turkey. *CUREJ: College Undergraduate Research Electronic Journal, University of Pennsylvania*.
https://repository.upenn.edu/cgi/viewcontent.cgi?article=1115&context=curej

Cengiz, D. (2010). *Dizeleriyle tarihe tanık Dersim şairi Sey Qaji* [Sey Qaji, the poet of Dersim, who witnessed history with his verses]. Horasan Yayınları.

Çetin, F. (2013). *Utanç duyuyorum!: Hrant Dink cinayetinin yargısı* [I am ashamed!: The court trial of Hrant Dink murder]. Metis Yayınları.

Çetin, M., Köse, S., Ebrinç, S., Yiğit, S., Elhai, J. D., & Başoğlu, C. (2005). Identification and posttraumatic stress disorder symptoms in rescue workers in the Marmara, Turkey, earthquake. *Journal of Traumatic Stress, 18*(5), 485–489.
https://doi.org/10.1002/jts.20056

Çetin, V. (2005). *Yakılan/boşaltılan köyler ve göç* [Burned/evacuated villages and migration]. İ. HD Yayınları.

Çetinkaya, Y. D. (2014). Atrocity propaganda and the nationalization of the masses in the Ottoman Empire during the Balkan Wars (1912–13). *International Journal of Middle East Studies, 46*(4), 759–778.
https://doi.org/10.1017/S0020743814001056

Ceyhan, E., & Ceyhan, A. A. (2006). 1999 Marmara bölgesi depremlerini yaşayan üniversite öğrencileri üzerine Depremin uzun dönemli sonuçları [The long-termed outcomes of the earthquakes on university students exposed to 1999 Marmara Region earthquakes]. *Sosyal Bilimler Dergisi, 2*, 197–212.

Chatty, D. (2010). *Displacement and dispossession in the modern Middle East* (Vol. 5). Cambridge University Press.

'Cizre basements will be convicted before the law' (2020, December 14). *BIA News Desk, Istanbul*. https://bianet.org/english/law/235989-cizre-basements-will-be-convicted-before-the-law

Cook, A., Spinazzola, J., Ford, J., Lanktree, C., Blaustein, M., Cloitre, M., ... van der Kolk, B. A. (2005). Complex trauma in children and adolescents. *Psychiatric Annals, 35*(5), 390–398.

Coşkun, V., Derince, M. S. E., & Uçarlar, N. (2010). *Dil Yarasi: Turkiye'de eğitimde anadilinin kullanılmaması sorunu ve Kürt öğrencilerin deneyimleri* [Language Wound: The problem of not using the mother tongue in education in Turkey and the experiences of Kurdish students]. Disa Yayınları.

Dadrian, V. N. (1995). *The history of the Armenian genocide: Ethnic conflict from the Balkans to Anatolia to the Caucasus*. Berghahn Books.

Danieli, Y. (1982). Families of survivors of the Nazi Holocaust: Some short-and long-term effects. *Series in Clinical & Community Psychology: Stress & Anxiety, 8*, 405–421.

Danieli, Y. (1985). The treatment and prevention of long-term effects and inter generational transmission of victimization: A lesson from Holocaust survivors and their children. In C. R. Figley (Ed.), *Trauma and its wake* (pp. 295–313). Brunner/Mazel.

Danieli, Y. (Ed.). (1998). *International handbook of multigenerational legacies of trauma*. Springer Science + Business Media.

Danieli, Y., Norris, F. H., & Engdahl, B. (2016). Multigenerational legacies of trauma: Modeling the what and how of transmission. *American Journal of Orthopsychiatry, 86*(6), 639–651.

Daud, A., Skoglund, E., & Rydelius, P.-A. (2005). Children in families of torture victims: Transgenerational transmission of parents' traumatic experiences to their children. *International Journal of Social Welfare, 14*, 23–32. https://doi.org/10.1111/j.1468-2397.2005.00336.x

Davison, R. H. (1973). *Reform in the Ottoman Empire*. Gordian Press.

De Fabrique, N., Romano, S. J., Vecchi, G. M., & Van Hasselt, V. B. (2007). Understanding Stockholm syndrome. *FBI Law Enforcement Bulletin, 76*(7), 10–15.

De Gruy-Leary, J. (2005). *Post traumatic slave syndrome: America's legacy of enduring injury and healing*. Joy DeGruy Publications.

de Zayas, A. (2007). The Istanbul pogrom of 6–7 September 1955 in the light of international law. *Genocide Studies and Prevention: An International Journal, 2*(2), 137–154.

Dekel, R., & Goldblatt, H. (2008). Is there intergenerational transmission of trauma? The case of combat veterans' children. *American Journal of Orthopsychiatry, 78*(3), 281–289. https://doi.org/10.1037/a0013955

Demirel, Ç. (Writer). (2009). *5 Nolu Ceza Evi*. [Documentary]. In. Turkey: Belgesel Sinamacılar Birliği (BSB). https://www.youtube.com/watch?v=XELKyBrWc8Y

Demirel, T. (2003). The Turkish military's decision to intervene: 12 September 1980. *Armed Forces & Society, 29*(2), 235–280.

Demirer, M. A. (2006). *6 Eylül 1955 olaylarına 50. yılda yeni bakış: hangi derin devlet?* [A new look at the events of September 6, 1955 on the 50th anniversary: which deep state?] Demokratlar Kulübü Yayınları.

Derince, M. Ş. (2013). A break or continuity? Turkey's politics of Kurdish language in the new millennium. *Dialectical Anthropology, 37*, 145–152. https://doi.org/10.1007/s10624-013-9303-4

Deringil, S. (2009). "The Armenian question is finally closed": Mass conversions of Armenians in Anatolia during the Hamidian Massacres of 1895–1897. *Comparative Studies in Society and History, 51*(2), 344–371. https://doi.org/10.1017/s0010417509000152

Deringil, S. (2012). *Conversion and apostasy in the late Ottoman Empire*. Cambridge University Press.

Dersimi, N. (1997). *Kürdistan tarihinde Dêrsim* [Dêrsim in the history of Kurdistan]. Doz.

DHA. (2018, December 11). PKK'nın 20 yılda Türkiye'ye verdiği zarar 240 milyar dolar. CNNTurk.com. https://www.cnnturk.com/turkiye/pkknin-20-yilda-turkiyeye-verdigi-zarar-240-milyar-dolar

Dikbaş, A., Akyüz, H. S., Meghraoui, M., Ferry, M., Altunel, E., Zabcı, C., . . . Yalçıner, C. Ç. (2018). Paleoseismic history and slip rate along the Sapanca-Akyazı segment of the 1999 İzmit earthquake rupture (Mw = 7.4) of the North Anatolian Fault (Turkey). *Tectonophysics, 738–739*, 92–111. https://doi.org/10.1016/j.tecto.2018.04.019

Diken, Ş. (2005). *İsyan sürgünleri* [Rebellion exiles]. İletişim.

Dimitra, G. (1995). Greeks or "strangers at home": The experiences of Ottoman Greek refugees during their exodus to Greece, 1922–1923. *Journal of Modern Greek Studies, 13*(2), 271–287. https://doi.org/10.1353/mgs.2010.0196

Dink, H. (2008). *Iki yakin halk iki uzak komsu* [Two near peoples, two distant neighbors]. Uluslararasi Hrant Dink vakfı.

Dirlik, A. (1997). *The postcolonial aura: Third World criticism in the age of global capitalism*. Routledge.

Dixon, J. M. (2010). Education and national narratives: Changing representations of the Armenian genocide in history textbooks in Turkey. *The International Journal for Education Law and Policy*, Special Issue on "Legitimation and Stability of Political Systems: The Contribution of National Narratives," 103–126.

Dixon, J. M. (2018). *Dark pasts: Changing the state's story in Turkey and Japan*. Cornell University Press.

Doğan, A. (2010). Adolescents' posttraumatic stress reactions and behavior problems following Marmara earthquake. *European Journal of Psychotraumatology, 2*(1), 1–9. https://doi.org/10.3402/ejpt.v2i0.5825

Doğulu, C., Karancı, A. N., & Ikizer, G. (2016). How do survivors perceive community resilience? The case of the 2011 earthquakes in Van, Turkey. *International Journal of Disaster Risk Reduction, 16*, 108–114. https://doi.org/10.1016/j.ijdrr.2016.02.006

Dosdoğru, M. H. (1993). *6/7 Eylül olayları: 6/7 Eylül 1955'in karası topluma sürülemez*. [Events of September 6/7: The darkness of September 6/7, 1955 cannot be blamed on society] Bağlam.

Dotson, K. (2011). Tracking epistemic violence, tracking practices of silencing. *Hypatia, 26*(2), 236–257. https://doi.org/10.1111/j.1527-2001.2011.01177.x

Dural, T. F. (1995). *Aleviler ve Gazi olayları* [Alevis and Gazi events]. Ant Yayınları.

Duran, E. (2006). *Healing the soul wound: Counseling with American Indians and other native peoples.* Teachers College Press.

Duran, E., Firehammer, J., & Gonzalez, J. (2008). Liberation psychology as the path toward healing cultural soul wounds. *Journal of Counseling & Development, 86*(3), 288–295. https://doi.org/10.1002/j.1556-6678.2008.tb00511.x

Düşgün, U. (2017). Yeni vatanın ötekileri: Mübadele romanlarında öteki algısı [Other of new homeland: Perception of other in population exchange novels], *Uluslararası Sosyal Araştırmalar Dergisi / The Journal of International Social Research, 10*(48), 59–67.

Düzel, N. (2003, June 23). Üç yılını 'cehennem'de geçirdi. Retrieved from http://www.radikal.com.tr/turkiye/uc-yilini-cehennemde-gecirdi-673856/

Egin attacked: Six hundred more Armenians slaughtered by Kurds. (1896, September 23). *Mower County Transcript* p. 6. https://chroniclingamerica.loc.gov/lccn/sn85025431/1896-09-23/ed-1/seq-6/

Ekmekçioğlu, L. (2013). A climate for abduction, a climate for redemption: The politics of inclusion during and after the Armenian genocide. *Comparative Studies in Society and History, 55*(3), 522–553. https://doi.org/10.1017/S0010417513000236

Eksi, A., & Braun, K. L. (2009). Over-time changes in PTSD and depression among children surviving the 1999 Istanbul earthquake. *European Child & Adolescent Psychiatry, 18*(6), 384–391. https://doi.org/10.1007/s00787-009-0745-9

Eksi, A., Peykerli, G., Saydam, R., Toparla, D., & Braun, K. L. (2008). Vivid intrusive memories in PTSD: Responses of child earthquake survivors in Turkey. *Journal of Loss and Trauma, 13*(2–3), 123–155. https://doi.org/10.1080/15325020701443925

Ensaroğlu, Y. (2013). Turkey's Kurdish Question and the Peace Process. *Insight Turkey.* 15 (2), 7–17.

Ensaroğlu, Y., Hatemi, K., Ekmen, M. E., Ünsal, A. F., Mahçupyan, E., Erdem, F. H. S., . . . Çiçek, M. (2013). *Akil insanlar güney doğu raporu.* [Southeast expert report]. https://www.academia.edu/5186884/AKIL_INSANLAR_HEYETI_GUNEY-DOGU_RAPORU

En Son Haber. (2013, April 8). TSK'dan askerlere psikolojik destek eğitimi [TAF psychological support training for soldiers]. https://www.ensonhaber.com/tskdan-askerlere-psikolojik-destek-egitimi-2013-04-08.html

Ergun, D., Çakici, M., & Çakici, E. (2008). Comparing psychological responses of internally displaced and non-displaced Turkish Cypriots. *Torture, 18*(1), 20–28.

Erkan, I. (2018). Türkiye de çocuk istismarı konusunda yayımlanan lisansüstü tezlerinin adli bilimler açısından değerlendirilmesi [Evaluation of postgraduate theses published on child abuse in Turkey in terms of forensic sciences].

Acibadem Universitesi Saglik Bilimleri Dergisi, (9)4, https://doi.org/10.31067/0.2018.49

Erman, T. (1998). The impact of migration on Turkish rural women: Four emergent patterns. *Gender and Society, 12*(2), 146–167. https://doi.org/10.1177/089124398012002003

Erol, E. (2013). Organised chaos as diplomatic ruse and demographic weapon: The expulsion of the Ottoman Greeks (Rum) from Foça, 1914. *Tijdschrift voor sociale en economische geschiedenis / Low Countries Journal of Social and Economic History, 10*(4), 66–96. http://doi.org/10.18352/tseg.239

Erol, E. (2015). Balkan savaşları: Mülteciler, muhacirler ve şiddet [Balkan wars: Refugees, *muhacirs* and violence]. In F. Adanır & O. Özel (Eds.), *1915 Siyaset, Tehcir, Soykırım* [1915 Politics, Deportation, Genocide] (pp. 304–315). Tarih Vakfı Yurt Yayınları.

Eski, M. (1999). *Cumhuriyet döneminde bir devlet adamı: Mustafa Necati*. [A statesman in the Republican era: Mustafa Necati]. Atatürk Kültür Dil ve Tarih Yüksek Kurumu.

Faroqhi, S. (2009). *The Ottoman Empire: A Short History*. Markus Wiener Publishers.

Farrar, L. L. Jr. (2003). Aggression versus apathy: The limits of nationalism during the Balkan Wars, 1912–1913. *East European Quarterly, 37*(3), 257–280.

Figley, C. R. (1995). Compassion fatigue: Toward a new understanding of the costs of caring. In B. H. Stamm (Ed.), *Secondary traumatic stress: Self-care issues for clinicians, researchers, and educators* (pp. 3–28). The Sidran Press.

Figley, C. R. (2002). Compassion fatigue: Psychotherapists' chronic lack of self care. *JCLP/In Session: Psychotherapy in Practice, 58*(11), 1433–1441. https://doi.org/10.1002/jclp.10090

Fındık, Ö. (2012). *Kara Vagon* [Dark Train Compartment]: *Dersim-kırım ve sürgün*. Fam Yayınları.

Fırat, A. (1996). *Fırat mahzun akar* [The Euphrates flows sadly]. Avesta.

Fiske, S. T., Harris, L. T., & Cuddy, A. J. (2004). Why ordinary people torture enemy prisoners. *Science, 306*(5701), 1482–1483. http://dx.doi.org/10.1126/science.1103788

Forero, J. (2016). State, illegality, and territorial control: Colombian armed groups in Ecuador under the Correa government. *Latin American Perspectives, 43*(1), 238–251. https://doi.org/10.1177/0094582X15571274

Fossion, P., Rejas, M. C., Servais, L., Pelc, I., & Hirsch, S. (2003). Family approach with grandchildren of Holocaust Survivors. *American Journal of Psychotherapy, 57*(4), 519–527. https://doi.org/10.1176/appi.psychotherapy.2003.57.4.519

Frankl, V. E. (2006). *Man's search for meaning*. Beacon Press.

Freire, P. (1998). *Pedagogy of freedom: Ethics, democracy, and civic courage* (P. Clarke, Trans.). Rowman & Littlefield.

Friedman, M. J. (1981). Post-Vietnam syndrome: Recognition and management. *Psychosomatics, 22*(11), 931–942.

Friedrich, W. N. (2002). *Psychological assessment of sexually abused children and their families*. SAGE.

Garrard, P., & Robinson, G. (Eds.). (2015). *The intoxication of power: Interdisciplinary insights*. Palgrave Macmillan.

Giritoğlu, T. (Writer), & Özgül, C. (Producer). (1999). *Salkım Hanım'ın taneleri* [Drama, Tarihi Kurgu]. Türkiye: Avşar Film.

GöçDer. (2013). *Turkiye'de koruculuk sistemi: Zorunlu göç ve geri dönüşler* [Village guard system in Turkey: Forced migration and coming back]. https://hakikatadalethafiza.org/kaynak/turkiyede-koruculuk-sistemi-zorunlu-goc-ve-geri-donusler-goc-der/

Göçek, F. M. (2002). The decline of the Ottoman empire and the emergence of Greek, Armenian, Turkish, and Arab nationalisms. In F. M. Göçek (Ed.), *Social constructions of nationalism in the Middle East* (pp. 15-84). University of New York Press.

Göçek, F. M. (2008). What is the meaning of the 1908 Young Turk Revolution? A critical historical assessment in 2008. *Siyasal Bilgiler Fakültesi Dergisi, 38*, 179–214.

Göçek, F. M. (2015). *Denial of violence: Ottoman past, Turkish present and collective violence against the Armenians, 1789–2009*. Oxford University Press.

Göçek, F. M. (2018). The 2007 assassination of Hrant Dink through the lenses of history, memory and emotions. *Zeitschrift für Religions-und Geistesgeschichte, 70*(2), 149–163.

Goenjian, A. K., Steinberg, A. M., Najarian, L. M., Fairbanks, L. A., Tashjian, M., & Pynoos, R. S. (2000). Prospective study of posttraumatic stress, anxiety, and depressive reactions after earthquake and political violence. *American Journal of Psychiatry, 157*(6), 911–916. http://dx.doi.org/10.1176/appi.ajp.157.6.911

Göle, N. (1996). *The forbidden modern: Civilization and veiling*. University of Michigan Press.

Gözde, I. (2014). *Factors related to psychological resilience among survivors of the earthquakes in Van, Turkey* (Doctoral dissertation). Middle East Technical University.

Güloğlu, B. (2016). Psychiatric symptoms of Turkish combat-injured non-professional veterans. *European Journal of Psychotraumatology, 7*, article 29157. https://doi.org/10.3402/ejpt.v7.29157

Güloğlu, B., & Karaırmak, Ö. (2013). Posttraumatic stress disorder among Turkish veterans of the Southeast. *Anatolian Journal of Psychiatry, 14*(3), 237–244. https://doi.org/10.5455/apd.36696

Gülşen, C., Knipscheer, J., & Kleber, R. (2010). The impact of forced migration on mental health: A comparative study on posttraumatic stress among internally displaced and externally migrated Kurdish women. *Traumatology, 16*(4), 109–116. https://doi.org/10.1177/1534765610388306

Gündoğan, N., & Gündoğan, K. (2012). *Dersim'in kayıp kızları: "Tertele çenequ"* [Dersim's lost girls]. İletişim.

Güneş, C. (2013). Explaining the PKK's mobilization of the Kurds in Turkey: Hegemony, myth and violence. *Ethnopolitics, 12*(3), 247–267. https://doi.org/10.1080/17449057.2012.707422

Gurcan, M. (2015). Arming civilians as a counterterror strategy: The case of the village guard system in Turkey. *Dynamics of Asymmetric Conflict, 8*(1), 1–22. https://doi.org/10.1080/17467586.2014.948026

Güven, D. (2005). *Cumhuriyet dönemi azınlık politikaları bağlamında: 6-7 Eylül olayları* [In the context of republican era minority policies: the events of September 6-7]. (Vol. 149). Tarih Vakfı Yurt Yayınları.

Güven, D. (2011). Riots against the Non-Muslims of Turkey: 6/7 September 1955 in the context of demographic engineering. *European Journal of Turkish Studies, 12,* http://journals.openedition.org/ejts/4538

Hakan, A. (2012, December 18). Co'nun kulübesinde 6 ay işkence gördüm, *Hürriyet.*
http://www.hurriyet.com.tr/co-nun-kulubesinde-6-ay-iskence-gordum-22180481

Hakyemez, S. (2017). Margins of the archive: Torture, heroism, and the ordinary in Prison No. 5, Turkey. *Anthropological Quarterly, 90*(1), 107–138.

Halaçoğlu, Y. (2006). *Sürgünden soykırıma Ermeni iddiaları* [From deportation to genocide Armenian allegations]. (Vol. 8): Babıali Kültür Yayıncılığı.

Hall, R. C. (2000). *The Balkan wars 1912–1913: Prelude to the first world war.* Routledge.

Haney, C., Banks, C., & Zimbardo, P. (1973). Interpersonal dynamics in a simulated prison: A study of prisoners and guards in a simulated prison. *International Journal of Criminology and Penology, 1,* 69–97.

Hartowicz, S. Z. (2018). *Bringing intergenerational trauma and resilience to consciousness: The journey of healing and transformation for the wounded healer exploring ancestral legacy* (Publication No. 10929535) [Doctoral dissertation, California Institute of Integral Studies]. ProQuest Dissertations and Theses database.

Haslam, S. A., & Reicher, S. (2007). Beyond the banality of evil: Three dynamics of an interactionist social psychology of tyranny. *Personality and Social Psychology Bulletin, 33*(5), 615–622.

Hatzivassiliou, E. (2009). Cold War pressures, regional strategies, and relative decline: British military and strategic planning for Cyprus, 1950–1960. *The Journal of Military History, 73*(4), 1143–1166.

Hayreni, H. (2015). *Yukarı Fırat ermenileri 1915 ve Dersim* [Upper Euphrates Armenians 1915 and Dersim]. Belge Yayınları.

Hennerbichler, F. (2012). The origin of Kurds. *Advances in Anthropology, 2*(2), 64–79.

Herman, J. L. (1992). Complex PTSD: A syndrome in survivors of prolonged and repeated trauma. *Journal of Traumatic Stress, 5,* 377–391
https://doi.org/10.1002/jts.2490050305

Herman, J. L. (2015). *Trauma and recovery: The aftermath of violence—From domestic abuse to political terror.* Basic Books.

Hesse-Biber, S. N. (2011). *Handbook of feminist research: Theory and praxis.* SAGE.

Hirschon, R. (1989). Heirs of the Greek catastrophe: The social life of Asia Minor refugees in Piraeus. New York, NY: Oxford University Press.

Hoagland, S. L. (2007). Denying relationality. In N. Tuana & S. Sullivan (Eds.),

Race and epistemologies of ignorance (pp. 95–118). State University of New York Press.

Human Rights Watch. (1999). Provincial Administration Law/ _l Idaresi Kanunu (No. 5442, Adopted June 10, 1949) Article 2/d/2 (Amended 1959:7267). https://www.hrw.org/reports/1999/turkey/turkey993-09.htm

İbrahim, İ. (2012). İkinci dünya savaşı yıllarında Türkiye'de varlık vergisi uygulaması [Wealth taxes application in Turkey during the Second World War]. *Celal Bayar Üniversitesi Sosyal Bilimler Dergisi, 10*(2), 270–290.

Ikizer, G., Karancı, A. N., & Doğulu, C. (2015). Exploring factors associated with psychological resilience among earthquake survivors from Turkey. *Journal of Loss and Trauma, 21*(5), 384–398. https://doi.org/10.1080/15325024.2015.1108794

Imset, I. G. (1996). The PKK: Terrorists or freedom fighters? *The International Journal of Kurdish Studies, 10*(1/2), 45–100.

Işık, A. S., & Arslan, S. (2012). Bir asimilasyon projesi: Türkiye'de yatılı ilköğretim bölge okulları [As assimilation project: the regional boarding schools in Turkey]. *Toplum ve Kuram, 6*(7), 107–140.

Janoff-Bulman, R. (1985). The aftermath of victimization: Rebuilding shattered assumptions. In C. R. In Figley (Ed.), *Trauma and its wake: The study and treatment of post-traumatic stress disorder* (Vol. 1, pp. 15–35). Brunner/Mazel.

Jenkins, R. (2014). *Social identity* (3rd ed.). Routledge.

Kaloumenos, D., & Korucu, M. S. (2015). *Patriklik fotoğrafçısı Dimitrios Kalumenos'un objektifinden 6/7 Eylül 1955* [September 6/7, 1955 through the lens of Patriarchate photographer Dimitrios Kalumenos] (Birinci basım. ed.). İstos Yayın.

Kamer, H. (2015, May 11). 5 No'lu Cezaevi mağdurlarının gözünden Kenan Evren. *BBC News*. https://www.bbc.com/turkce/haberler/2015/05/150511_12eylul_diyarbakir

Karabağlı, H. (2013, December 2). Milli Savunma Bakanı: Son 11 yılda 1035 asker intihar etti. *T24 Bağımsız Internet Gazetesi*. https://t24.com.tr/haber/milli-savunma-bakani-son-11-yilda-bin-35-asker-intihar-etti,245201

Karakoyunlu, Y. (1990). *Salkım Hanım'ın taneleri*. Doğan Kitap.

Karancı, N. A., & Acarturk, C. (2005). Post-traumatic growth among Marmara Earthquake survivors involved in disaster preparedness as volunteers. *Traumatology, 11*(4), 307–323. https://doi.org/10.1177/153476560501100409

Karancı, N. A., Alkan, N., Aksit, B., Sucuoglu, H., & Balta, E. (1999). Gender differences in psychological distress, coping, social support and related variables following the 1995 Dinar (Turkey) earthquake. *North American Journal of Psychology, 1*(2), 189–204.

Karaömeroğlu, A. M. (1998). The village institutes experience in Turkey. *British Journal of Middle Eastern, 25*(1), 47–73.

Karatay, G., Günderci, A., Demir, M. C., Gürarslan Baş, N., & Çevik, Y. (2017). The psychotraumatic effects of "Dersim 38" on the second and third generation. *Academic Research International, 8*(2), 78–88.

Karaveli, H. M. (2018). *Why Turkey is authoritarian: From Atatürk to Erdoğan*. Pluto Press.

Kardam, F., & Bademci, E. (2013). Mothers in cases of incest in Turkey: Views and experiences of professionals. *Journal of Family Violence, 28*(3), 253–263. https://doi.org/10.1007/s10896-013-9495-z

Karenian, H., Livaditis, M., Karenian, S., Zafiriadis, K., Bochtsou, V., & Xenitidis, K. (2011). Collective trauma transmission and traumatic reactions among descendants of Armenian refugees. *International Journal of Social Psychiatry, 57*(4), 327–337. https://doi.org/10.1177/0020764009354840

Kasapoğlu, A., & Ecevit, M. (2003). Impact of the 1999 East Marmara earthquake in Turkey. *Population & Environment, 24*(4), 339–358.

Kay, A. (2015). The representation of the psychological ramifications of the Armenian genocide: A voice crying out in the desert? *Journal of Levantine Studies, 5*(2), 113–141.

Kaya, F. (2003). *Mezopotamya sürgünü: Abdülmelik Fırat'ın yaşam öyküsü* [Mesopotamian exile: the life story of Abdülmelik Fırat]. (Vol. 57). Anka Yayınları.

Kaya, F. (2014). *Minority policies of Turkey and Wealth Tax of 1942*. Yeditepe University. Munich Personal RePEc Archive. http://mpra.ub.uni-muenchen.de/53617/

Kayra, C. (2011). *Savaş Türkiye varlık vergisi* [Turkey's war wealth taxes]. Tarihçi Kitabevi.

Kehl-Bodrogi, K. (2003). Atatürk and the Alevis: A holy alliance? In P. J. White & J. Jongerden (Eds.), *Turkey's Alevi Enigma* (pp. 53–71). Brill.

Kellerman, N. P. F. (2001). Transmission of Holocaust trauma—An integrative view. *Psychiatry, 64*(3), 256–267.

Kerimoğlu, H. T. (2008). *İttihat ve Terakki Cemiyeti'nin Rum politikası 1908–1914 [The Committee of Union and Progress's Rum policy 1908-1914].* [Doctoral dissertation, Dokuz Eylül University]. Izmir.

Keshgegian, F. A. (2000). *Redeeming memories: A theology of healing and transformation*. Abingdon Press.

Keshgegian, F. A. (2006). Finding a place past night: Armenian genocidal memory in diaspora. *Religion, Violence, Memory, and Place*, 100-112.

Keten, A., Karagöl, A., Keten, H. S., Avcı, E., & Karanfil, R. (2013). Terörle mücadele gazilerinde travma sonrası stres bozukluğu [Post-traumatic stress disorder in counter-terrorism veterans]. *Adli Tıp Dergisi, 28*(1), 33–40.

Kevorkian, R. H., & Paboudjian, P. B. (2012). *1915 öncesinde Osmanlı imparatorluğu'nda Ermeniler* [Armenians in the Ottoman Empire before 1915]. Aras Yayıncılık.

Kharatyan-Araqelyan, H. (2010). Research in Armenia: Whom to forgive? What to forgive? In L. Neyzi & H. Kharatyan-Araqelyan (Eds.), *Speaking to one another: Personal memories of the past in Armenia and Turkey: Wish they hadn't left* (pp. 75–167). Dvv International.

Kieser, H.-L. (2006). *Turkey beyond nationalism: Towards post-nationalist identities*. Palgrave Macmillan.

Kieser, H.-L. (2019, March 19). Minorities (Ottoman Empire/Middle East). In *1914-1918 online: International encyclopedia of the First World War.*

https://encyclopedia.1914-1918-online.net/article/minorities_ottoman_empiremiddle_east?version=1.1

Kirişçi, K. (1998). Regional profile, Europe: Turkey. In J. Hampton (Ed.), *Internally displaced people: A global survey* (pp. 197–200). Earthscan Publications.

Kirişçi, K. (2000). Disaggregating Turkish citizenship and immigration practices. *Middle Eastern Studies, 36*(3), 1–22. https://doi.org/10.1080/00263200008701316

Kısa, S., Zeyneloğlu, S., & Sergek Verim, E. (2018). The level of hopelessness and psychological distress among abused women in a women's shelter in Turkey. *Archives of Psychiatric Nursing, 33*(1), 30–36. https://doi.org/10.1016/j.apnu.2018.08.009

Klein, J. (2007). Conflict and collaboration: Rethinking Kurdish–Armenian relations in the Hamidian Period, 1876–1909. *International Journal of Turkish Studies, 13*(1&2), 153–166.

Knipscheer, J., Drogendijk, A. N., Gulşen, C. H., & Kleber, R. J. (2009). Differences and similarities in posttraumatic stress between economic migrants and forced migrants: Acculturation and mental health within a Turkish and a Kurdish sample. *International Journal of Clinical and Health Psychology, 9*(3), 373–391. http://www.redalyc.org/articulo.oa?id=33712038002

Kongar, E., & Küçükkaya, A. (2013). *Gezi direnişi: Türkiye'yi sarsan otuz gün [Gezi resistance: Thirty days that shook Turkey]*. Cumhuriyet Kitapları.

Kopşa, A. (2008). *The assassination of Hrant Dink from the perspective of Armenian youth in Turkey: A time of trauma or solidarity?* [Master's thesis, Sabancı University, Istanbul].

Korucu, S. (2016, September 8). 6-7 Eylül gecesi evlerde ne yaşandı? [What happened in the houses on the night of on September 6–7?]—Ceni Palti/Interviewer: C. Palti. Aktüel Röportajlar.

Kupelian, D., Kalayjian, A. S., & Kassabian, A. (1998). The Turkish genocide of the Armenians. In Y. Danieli (Ed.), *International handbook of multigenerational legacies of trauma* (pp. 191–210). Springer Science + Business Media.

Kuyucu, A. T. (2005). Ethno-religious "unmixing" of "Turkey": 6–7 September riots as a case in Turkish nationalism. *Nations & Nationalism, 11*(3), 361–380. https://doi.org/10.1111/j.1354-5078.2005.00209.x

Kuzirian, K. (2012). *Secondary trauma effects of the Armenian genocide on subsequent generations: Perceived impact, ethnic identity, and attachment style* (Publication No. 3552151) [Doctoral dissertation, Alliant International University]. ProQuest Dissertations and Theses database.

Laçiner, S. (2008). *Ermeni sorunu, diaspora ve Türk dış politikası*. [Armenian issue, diaspora and Turkish foreign policy]. (Vol. 21). USAK Yayınları.

Lang (1994). Hannah Arendt and the Politics of Evil. In Hinchman, L. P. & Hinchman. *Hannah Arendt: critical essays*. (pp. 41–56). State University of New York Press.

Leavy, P. (2011). *Essentials of transdisciplinary research*. Left Coast Press.

Leveton, E., & Volkas, A. (2010). Healing the wounds of history: Germans and

Jews facing the legacy of the Holocaust. In E. Leveton (Ed.), *Healing collective trauma using sociodrama and drama therapy* (pp. 127–146). Springer.

Levine, P. A. (1997). *Waking the tiger: Healing trauma.* North Atlantic Books.

Levine, S. Z., Laufer, A., Stein, E., Hamama-Raz, Y., & Solomon, Z. (2009). Examining the relationship between resilience and posttraumatic growth. *Journal of Traumatic Stress, 22*(4), 282–286.

Lifton R, J., & Olson, E. (1976). The human meaning of total disaster: The Buffalo Creek experience. *Psychiatry, 39*(1), 1–18. https://doi.org/10.1080/00332747.1976.11023872

Lindholm, C. (2007). *Culture and identity: The history, theory, and practice of psychological antropology.* Oneworld Publications.

Livanou, M., Başoğlu, M., Salcioglu, E., & Kalender, D. (2002). Traumatic stress responses in treatment-seeking earthquake survivors in Turkey. *The Journal of Nervous and Mental Disease, 190*(12), 816–823.

Lobban, J. (2014). The invisible wound: Veterans' art therapy. *International Journal of Art Therapy, 19*(1), 3–18. https://doi.org/10.1080/17454832.2012.725547

Mango, A. (2004). *The Turks today.* Overlook Press.

Mann, M. (2005). *The dark side of democracy: Explaining ethnic cleansing.* Cambridge University Press.

Manoogian, J. (2018). *Ottoman Turkish genocide of Armenians: The legacy of trauma* (Publication No. 10812707) [Doctoral dissertation, Alliant International University]. ProQuest Dissertations and Theses database.

Marcus, A. (2007) *Blood and belief: The PKK and the Kurdish fight for independence.* NYU Press.

Mater, N. (1999). *Mehmedin kitabı: Güneydoğu'da savaşmış askerler anlatıyor* [Mehmed's book: stories of soldiers who fought at the Southeast]. Metis Yayınları.

McCarthy, J. (1995). *Death and exile: The ethnic cleansing of Ottoman Muslims, 1821–1922.* Darwin Press.

McDowall, D. (2004). *A modern history of the Kurds.* I. B. Tauris.

Menakem, R. (2017). *My grandmother's hands: Racialized trauma and the pathway to mending our hearts and bodies.* Central Recovery Press.

Meshorer, S. (2013, March 13). The spiritual argument against torture. *Huffington Post.* https://www.huffingtonpost.com/sean-meshorer/torture_b_2448786.html

Mikhail, A. (2020). *God's Shadow: Sultan Selim, His Ottoman Empire, and the making of the modern world.* Liveright Publishing.

Miller, D. E., & Miller, L. T. (1993). *Survivors: An oral history of the Armenian genocide.* University of California Press.

Miller, P. (2010). *The smart swarm: How understanding flocks, schools, and colonies can make us better at communicating, decision making, and getting things done.* Penguin Books.

Mills, C. W. (1997). *The racial contract.* Cornell University Press.

Mills, C. W. (2007). White ignorance. In N. Tuana & S. Sullivan (Eds.), *Race and epistemologies of ignorance* (pp. 11–38). State University of New York Press.

Montuori, A. (2010). Transdisciplinarity and creative inquiry in transformative education: Researching the research degree. In M. Maldonato (Ed.), *Research on scientific research: A transdisciplinary study* (pp. 110–135). Sussex Academic Press.

Montuori, A. (2012). Five dimensions of applied transdisciplinarity. *Integral Leadership Review*. https://www.academia.edu/2330489/Five_Dimensions_of_Applied_Transdisciplinarity

Montuori, A. (2013). The complexity of transdisciplinary literature reviews. *Complicity: An International Journal of Complexity and Education, 10*(1/2), 45–55.

Morin, E. (2008). The reform of thought, transdisciplinarity, and the reform of the university. In B. Nicolescu (Ed.), *Transdisciplinarity: Theory and practice* (pp. 23–32). Hampton Press.

Morrill, B. (2015). Unfolding toward being: Etty Hillesum and the evolution of consciousness. *Integral Review, 11*(1), 80–122.

Mouhibian, R. (2016). *The intergenerational transmission of trauma among second, third, fourth generation Armenian genocide survivors* (Publication No. 10124792) [Doctoral dissertation, Alliant International University]. ProQuest Dissertations and Theses database.

Muller, M., & Linzey, S. (2007). *The internally displaced Kurds of Turkey: Ongoing issues of responsibility, redress and resettlement*. Kurdish Human Rights Project.

Muratyan, N. (2011). *Türkiyeli Ermenilerde kolektif korku gündelik hayatta korku altında varolma pratikleri* [Collective fears of Turkish Armenians existence practices underlying the fear in everyday life] (Publication No. 108611038) [Master's thesis, Istanbul Bilgi Üniversitesi] openaccess.bilgi.edu.tr.

Naimark, N. M. (2001). *Fires of hatred: Ethnic cleansing in twentieth-century Europe*. Harvard University Press.

Neyzi, L. (1999). Gülümser's story: Life history narratives, memory and belonging in Turkey. *New Perspectives in Turkey, 20*(Spring), 1–26.

Neyzi, L. (2002). Embodied elders: Space and subjectivity in the music of Metin-Kemal Kahraman. *Middle Eastern Studies, 38*(1), 89–109.

Neyzi, L. (2010). Research in Turkey: "Wish they hadn't left": The burden of Armenian memory in Turkey. In L. Neyzi & H. Kharatyan-Araqelyan (Eds.), *Speaking to one another: Personal memories of the past in Armenia and Turkey—Wish they hadn't left* (pp. 13–74). Dvv International.

Neyzi, L. (2018). *"Ben kimim?": Türkiye'de sözlü tarih, kimlik ve öznellik ["Who am I?": Oral history, identity and subjectivity in Turkey]*. Istanbul, Türkiye: İletişim Yayınları.

Neyzi, L., & Kharatyan-Araqelyan, H. (2010). *Speaking to one another: Personal memories of the past in Armenia and Turkey: Wish they hadn't left*. Dvv International.

Nichanian, M. (2003). Catastrophic Mourning. In Eng, D. L., & Kazanjian, D. (Eds.), *Loss: The politics of mourning* (99-124). University of California Press.

Norris, F. H., Friedman, M. J., Watson, P. J., Byrne, C. M., Diaz, E., & Kaniasty, K. (2002). 60,000 disaster victims speak: Part I. An empirical review of the empirical literature, 1981–2001. *Psychiatry: Interpersonal and Biological Processes, 65*(3), 207–239.

Norwegian Refugee Council, Internal Displacement Monitoring Centre. (2010). *Principle versus practice: Poverty and discrimination as barriers to the enjoyment of the right to education for internally displaced children—Case study on education and displacement in Turkey.* https://www.refworld.org/docid/4c931a4c2.html

Ocak, S. (2016). Transhumance in Central Anatolia: A resilient interdependence between biological and cultural diversity. *Journal of Agricultural & Environmental Ethics, 29*(3), 439–453. https://doi.org/10.1007/s10806-016-9613-z

Öcalan, A. (2014). *War and peace in Kurdistan–International initiative edition.* Transmedia Publishing (n.l.).

Ökte, F. (1951). *Varlık Vergisi Faciası* [Wealth taxes disaster]. Nebioğlu Yayınevi.

Oliner, S. P., & Oliner, P. M. (1988). *The altruistic personality: Rescuers of Jews in Nazi Europe.* Free Press.

Olson, R. (1989). *The emergence of Kurdish nationalism and the Sheikh Said rebellion, 1880–1925.* University of Texas Press.

Olson, R. (2000). The Kurdish rebellions of Sheikh Said (1925), Mt. Ararat (1930), and Dersim (1937–8): Their impact on the development of the Turkish air force and on Kurdish and Turkish nationalism. *Die Welt Des Islams, 40*(1), 67–94.

Oncu, E. C., & Wise, A. M. (2010). The effects of the 1999 Turkish earthquake on young children: Analyzing traumatized children's completion of short stories. *Child Development, 81*(4), 1161–1175.

Önsüz, M. F., Topuzoğlu, A., İkiışık, H., & Karavuş, M. (2009). Marmara depreminden altı yıl sonra Sapanca'da travma sonrası stres ve anksiyete bozukluklarının değerlendirilmesi [Assesment of post-traumatic stress and anxiety disorders after Marmara earthquake in Sapanca]. *New/Yeni Symposium Journal, 47*(4), 164–177.

Oran, B. (2004). *Türkiye'de azınlıklar: kavramlar, teori, Lozan, iç mevzuat, içtihat, uygulama* [Minorities in Turkey: concepts, theory, Lausanne, domestic legislation, case law, practice]. İletişim.

Oran, B. (2007). The minority concept and rights in Turkey: The Lausanne Peace Treaty and current issues. In Z. F. Kabasakal Arat (Ed.), *Human rights in Turkey* (pp. 35–56). University of Pennsylvania Press.

Orhan, M. (2012). Kurdish rebellions and conflict groups in Turkey during the 1920s and 1930s. *Journal of Muslim Minority Affairs, 32*(3), 339–358. https://doi.org/10.1080/13602004.2012.727294

Özcan, N. K., Günaydın, S., & Çitil, E. T. (2016). Domestic violence against women in Turkey: a systematic review and meta analysis. *Archives of psychiatric nursing, 30*(5), 620–629.

Özdemir, B., Öznur, T., Çelik, C., & Özmenler, K. N. (2014). Güneydogu gazileri ve travma sonrası stres bozuklugu [Southeast veterans and post-traumatic stress disorder]. *Anadolu Psikiyatri Dergisi, 15*(1), 91.

Özdoğan, G. G., Üstel, F., Karakaşlı, K., & Kentel, F. (2009). *Türkiye'de*

Ermeniler: cemaat-birey-yurttaş [Armenians in Turkey: community-individual-citizen]. Bilgi Üniversitesi Yayınları.

Özerdem, A., & Barakat, S. (2000). After the Marmara earthquake: Lessons for avoiding short cuts to disasters. *Third World Quarterly, 21*(3), 425–439. https://doi.org/10.1080/713701047

Özkök, B. (1937). *Osmanlılar devrinde Dersim isyanları* [Dersim revolts during Ottoman period]. Askerî matbaa.

Öztürkmen, A. (2013). The women's movement under Ottoman and Republican rule. *Journal of Women's History, 25*(4), 255–264.

Özücetin, Y., & Nadar, S. (2010). Atatürk lkeleri ve Inkılap Tarihi Dersinin Üniversiteler Düzeyinde Okutulmaya Başlanması ve Gelinen Süreç [Initiation of teaching Atatürk's principles and revolution history class at universities and the current process]. *Uluslararası Sosyal Araştırmalar Dergisi, 3*(11), 466-477.

Paker, M. (1999). *Subjective meaning of torture as a predictor in chronic post-torture psychological response* (Publication No. 9980017) [Doctoral dissertation, New School for Social Research]. ProQuest Dissertations and Theses database.

Paker, M., & Buğu, B. (2016). Türkiye'de işkence mağdurlarının psikolojisi üzerine yapılmış araştırmaların gözden geçirilmesi [Review of research on torture victims' psychology in Turkey]. *Türk Psikoloji Yazıları, 19*, 76–92.

Papadopoulos, R. K. (2007). Refugees, trauma and adversity-activated development. *European Journal of Psychotherapy & Counselling, 9*(3), 301–312.

Pattie, S. P. (2004). Armenians in diaspora. In E. Herzig & M. Kurkchiyan (Eds.), *The Armenians: Past and present in the making of national identity* (pp. 138-158). Routledge.

Pınar, R., & Sabuncu, N. (2004). Long-term traumatic stress responses of survivors of the August 1999 earthquake in Turkey. *Journal of Loss & Trauma, 9*(3), 257–268. https://doi.org/10.1080/15325020490458354

Platt, S., & Drinkwater, B. D. (2016). Post-earthquake decision making in Turkey: Studies of Van and İzmir. *International Journal of Disaster Risk Reduction, 17*, 220–237. https://doi.org/10.1016/j.ijdrr.2016.03.010

Proctor, R. (1995). *Cancer wars: How politics shapes what we know and don't know about cancer*. BasicBooks.

Robertson, R. (2011). *The shadow's gift: Find out who you really are*. Nicolas-Hays.

Said, E. (1978). *Orientalism: Western representations of the Orient.* Pantheon.

Salcıoğlu, E., Başoğlu, M., & Livanou, M. (2007). Post-traumatic stress disorder and comorbid depression among survivors of the 1999 earthquake in Turkey. *Disasters, 31*(2), 115–129.

Sağır, A. (May 20, 2015). *Laz Kemal'in sana selamı var!* https://t24.com.tr/yazarlar/aysel-sagir/laz-kemalin-sana-selami-var,11924

Salerian, A. (1982, June). *A psychological report: Armenian genocide survivors—67 years later.* Paper presented at the International Conference on the Holocaust and Genocide, Tel Aviv, Israel.

Şar, V. (2017). Post-traumatic stress in terror and war. *The Medical Journal of Okmeydani Training and Research Hospital, 33*, 114–120. https://doi.org/10.5222/otd.2017.114

Sargut, C. (2017). *Beauty and light: Mystical discourses by a contemporary female Sufi master*. Fons Vitae

Sayılır, S. B. (2012). Göçebelik, konar-göçerlik meselesi ve coğrafî bakımdan konar-göçerlerin farklılaşması [Nomadism, the issue of nomadism and the differentiation of nomads in terms of geography]. *Türk Dünyası İncelemeleri Dergisi, 12*(1), 563–580.

Schützenberger, A. A. (1998). *The ancestor syndrome: Transgenerational psychotherapy and the hidden links in the family tree*. Routledge.

Şeker, N. (2005). Identity formation and the political power in the late Ottoman Empire and early Turkish Republic. *Historia Actual On Line, 8*, 59–67.

Şeker, N. (2007). Demographic engineering in the late Ottoman empire and the Armenians. *Middle Eastern Studies, 43*(3), 461–474. https://doi.org/10.1080/00263200701246157

Şeker, N. (2012). The Greek Orthodox Patriarchate of Constantinople in the midst of politics: The Cold War, the Cyprus question, and the patriarchate, 1949–1959. *Journal of Church and State, 55*(2), 264–285. https://doi.org/10.1093/jcs/css045

Şeker, N. (2016). Forced population movements in the Ottoman Empire and the early Turkish Republic: An attempt at reassessment through demographic engineering. *European Journal of Turkish Studies, 16*. http://ejts.revues.org/4396

Selahattin, Ö., & Abdullatif, A. (2017). The population exchange between Turkey and Greece after the First World War and the subsequent problems. In A. Barker, M. E. Pereira, M. T. Cortez, P. A. Pereira, & O. Martin (Eds.), *Personal narratives, peripheral theatres: Essays on the Great War* (1914–18) (pp. 215–223). Springer International.

Shorter, F. C. (1985). The population of Turkey after the War of Independence. *International Journal of Middle East Studies, 17*(4), 417–441.

Şimşir, B. N. (2005). *Ermeni meselesi* [Armenian issue]. Bilgi Yayınevi.

Sirman, N. (1989). Turkish feminism: A short history. *New Perspectives on Turkey, 3*(1), 1–34.

Siviş-Çetinkaya, R. (2015). Turkish school counselors' experiences of reporting child sexual abuse: A brief report. *Journal of Child Sex Abuse, 24*(8), 908–921. https://doi.org/10.1080/10538712.2015.1084072

Slater, P. (2008). *Chrysalis effect: The metamorphosis of global culture*. Sussex Academic Press.

Smelser, N. J. (2004). Psychological trauma and cultural trauma. In J. C. Alexander, R. Eyerman, B. Giesen, N. J. Smelser, & P. Sztompka, *Cultural trauma and collective identity* (pp. 31–59). University of California Press.

Sofuoğlu, Z., Sariyer, G., & Ataman, M. G. (2016). Child maltreatment in Turkey: Comparison of parent and child reports. *Central European Journal of Public Health, 24*(3), 217–222. https://doi.org/10.21101/cejph.a4155

Soyalp, N. (2020). Applying transdisciplinarity: Exploring transgenerational traumas of Anatolia, Turkey, *World Futures*, https://doi.org/10.1080/02604027.2020.1788358

Staub, E. (1989). *The roots of evil. The origins of genocide and other group violence*. Cambridge University Press.

Staub, E. (1993). The psychology of bystanders, perpetrators, and heroic helpers. *International Journal of Intercultural Relations, 17*(3), 315–341.

Staub, E. (2011). *Overcoming evil: Genocide, violent conflict, and terrorism.* Oxford University Press.

Stayton, D. J., & Ainsworth, M. D. (1973). Individual differences in infant responses to brief, everyday separations as related to other infant and maternal behaviors. *Developmental Psychology, 9*(2), 226–235. http://dx.doi.org/10.1037/h0035089

Stefanovic, D., Loizides, N., & Parsons, S. (2014). Home is where the heart is? Forced migration and voluntary return in Turkey's Kurdish regions. *Journal of Refugee Studies, 28*(2), 276–296.

Sümer, N., Karancı, A. N., Berument, S. K., & Güneş, H. (2005). Personal resources, coping self-efficacy, and quake exposure as predictors of psychological distress following the 1999 earthquake in Turkey. *Journal of Traumatic Stress, 18*(4), 331–342. https://doi.org/10.1002/jts.20032

Suny, R. G. (1993). *Looking toward Ararat: Armenia in modern history.* University Press.

Suny, R. G. (2004). *Why we hate you: The passions of national identity and ethnic violence* (Berkeley Program in Soviet and Post-Soviet Studies Working Paper Series). https://escholarship.org/uc/item/3pv4g8zf

Suny, R. G. (2015). *"They can live in the desert but nowhere else": A history of the Armenian genocide.* Princeton University Press.

Suny, R. G., Göçek, F. M., & Naimark, N. M. (2011). *A question of genocide: Armenians and Turks at the end of the Ottoman Empire.* Oxford University Press.

Sztompka, P. (1993). *The sociology of social change.* Blackwell.

Sztompka, P. (2000). Cultural trauma: The other face of social change. *European Journal of Social Theory, 3*(4), 449–466. https://doi.org/10.1177/136843100003004004

Sztompka, P. (2004). The trauma of social change: a case of postcommunist societies. In J. C. Alexander, R. Eyerman, B. Giesen, N. J. Smelser, & P. Sztompka, *Cultural trauma and collective identity* (pp. 155-195). University of California Press.

Tapan, M., Comert, M., Demir, C., Sayan, Y., Orakcal, K., & Ilki, A. (2013). Failures of structures during the October 23, 2011 Tabanlı (Van) and November 9, 2011 Edremit (Van) earthquakes in Turkey. *Engineering Failure Analysis, 34*, 606–628. https://doi.org/10.1016/j.engfailanal.2013.02.013

Tas, L. (2016). Peace making or state breaking? The Turkish-Kurdish peace processes and the role of diasporas. *Journal of Review of Social Studies, 3*(1), 25–66.

Tekin, A., Karadag, H., Suleymanoglu, M., Tekin, M., Kayran, Y., Alpak, G., & Sar, V. (2016). Prevalence and gender differences in symptomatology of posttraumatic stress disorder and depression among Iraqi Yazidis displaced into Turkey. *European Journal of Psychotraumatology, 7*, article 28556. https://doi.org/10.3402/ejpt.v7.28556

Tekin, F. (2011). Kültürel travma olarak zorunlu göç [Forced displacement as cultural trauma]. *Edebiyat Fakültesi Dergisi* (25), 91–100.

Tekinoğlu, D. (Writer & Producer). (2017). Bindokuzyüzdoksandört [*Nineteenninetyfour*, Documentary]. Independent.

Toktaş, Ş., & Diner, C. (2015). Shelters for women survivors of domestic violence: A view from Turkey. *Women's Studies, 44*(5), 611–634. https://doi.org/10.1080/00497878.2015.1036158

Tonguç, E. (1970). *Devrim açısından köy enstituleri ve Tonguç* [Village institutes and Tonguç in terms of revolution]. Ant Yayınları.

Tuana, N. (2004). Coming to understand: Orgasm and the epistemology of ignorance. *Feminist Science Studies, 19*(1), 194–232.

Tuana, N., & Sullivan, S. (Eds.). (2007). *Race and epistemologies of ignorance*. State University of New York Press.

Tüleylioğlu, O. (2011). *Namlunun ucundaki mahalle: Gazi Mahallesi olayları, 12–13 Mart 1995* [Neighborhood at the end of the barrel: Gazi neighborhood events, March 12-13, 1995]. Uğur Mumcu Araştırmacı Gazetecilik Vakfı.

turkeypurge.com. (2019). Turkey's post-coup crackdown. https://turkeypurge.com/purge-in-numbers-2

Turkish Penal Code Item 220 (TCK), Madde [item] 220, 5 C.F.R. § 25611 (2004).

Tüysüz, N. (2011). *Yerel güvenlik ve kimlik: Güneydoğu Anadolu'da bir köy üzerinden köy koruculuğu sistemi*. [Local security and identity: Village Guard system through a village in Southeast Anatolia]. (Yüksek Lisans Tezi). Yıldız Teknik Universitesi.

Tuzcu, A., & Bademli, K. (2014). Göçün psikososyal boyutu. *Psychosocial Aspects of Migration, 6*(1), 56–66. https://doi.org/10.5455/cap.20130719123555

Uddo, M., Vasterling, J. J., Brailey, K., & Sutker, P. B. (1993). Memory and attention in combat-related post-traumatic stress disorder (PTSD). *Journal of Psychopathology and Behavioral Assessment, 15*(1), 43–52.

Uluğ, N. H. (2007). *Tunceli medeniyete açılıyor* [Tunceli is opening to civilization]. (Vol. 2). Kaynak Yayınları.

Ünal, A. Z. (2013). "Yerinden olmuşlar"ın yoksulluğunu yeniden üreten habitus [The habitus that reproduces the poverty of the "displaced"]. *Sosyal ve Ekonomik Araştırmalar Dergisi, 15*(25), 105–112.

Ünal, M. C. (2016). Is it ripe yet? Resolving Turkey's 30 years of conflict with the PKK. *Turkish Studies, 17*(1), 91–125. https://doi.org/10.1080/14683849.2015.1124020

Üngör, U. Ü. (2008). Recalling the appalling: Mass violence in Eastern Turkey in the twentieth century. In N. Adler, S. Leydesdorff, & L. Neyzi (Eds.), *Memories of mass repression: Narrating life stories in the aftermath of atrocity* (pp. 175–198). Transaction.

Üngör, U. Ü. (2014). Lost in commemoration: The Armenian genocide in memory and identity. *Patterns of Prejudice, 48*(2), 147–166.

Üngör, U. Ü. (2015). Savaş, tehcir, soykırım [War, Relocation, genocide]. In F. Adanır & O. Özel (Eds.), *1915 Siyaset, Tehcir, Soykırım* [Politics, Relocation, Genocide] (pp. 357–376). Tarih Vakfı Yurt Yayınları.

Ünlü, B. (2016). The Kurdish struggle and the crisis of the Turkishness contract. *Philosophy & Social Criticism, 42*(4–5), 397–405. https://doi.org/10.1177/0191453715625715

Ünlü, M. (Writer) & M. A. Birand (Director). (1998). 7. Bölüm Darbe Günlüğü [Bir TV]. In A. Inandım (Producer), *12 Eylul Belgeseli*. 32. Gün Arşivi.

van Bruinessen, M. (1992). *Agha, shaikh, and state: The social and political structures of Kurdistan*. Zed Books.

van Bruinessen, M. (1994). Genocide in Kurdistan? The suppression of the Dersim rebellion in Turkey (1937–38) and the chemical war against the Iraqi Kurds (1988). In G. J. Andreopoulos (Ed.), *Conceptual and historical dimensions of genocide* (pp. 141–170). University of Pennsylvania Press.

van Bruinessen, M. (1996). Kurds, Turks and the Alevi revival. *Middle East Reports, 200* (July–September), 7–10.

van Bruinessen, M. (1998). Shifting national and ethnic identities: The Kurds in Turkey and the European diaspora. *Journal of Muslim Minority Affairs, 18*(1), 39–45.

van Bruinessen, M. (1999). The Kurds in movement: Migrations, mobilisations, communications and the globalisation of the Kurdish question (Islamic Area Studies Project, Working Paper no. 14). https://www.researchgate.net/publication/27703223_The_Kurds_in_movement_migrations_mobilisations_c
ommunications_and_the_globalisation_of_the_Kurdish_question_Working_Paper_no_14

van Bruinessen, M. (2000). *Kurdish ethno-nationalism versus nation-building states: Collected articles*. Analecta Isisiana: Ottoman and Turkish Studies, Vol. 47. The Isis Press.

van Bruinessen, M. (2003-04 [2005]). Ismail Beşikçi: Turkish sociologist, critic of Kemalism, and kurdologist. *The Journal of Kurdish Studies*, V, (pp. 19–34).

van der Kolk, B. A. (2003). The neurobiology of childhood trauma and abuse. *Child and Adolescent Psychiatric Clinics of North America, 12*(2), 293–318.

van der Kolk, B. A. (2014). *The body keeps the score: Brain, mind, and body in the healing of trauma*. Viking.

Volkan, V. D. (1996). Bosnia-Herzegovina: Ancient fuel of a modern inferno. *Mind and Human Interaction, 7*(3), 110–127.

Volkan, V. D. (1998). Ethnicity and nationalism: A psychoanalytic perspective. *Applied Psychology: An International Review, 47*(1), 45–57. https://doi.org/10.1111/j.1464-0597.1998.tb00012.x

Volkan, V. D. (2000). Traumatized societies and psychological care: Expanding the concept of preventive medicine. *Mind and Human Interaction, 11*, 177–194.

Volkan, V. D. (2004). *Blind trust: Large groups and their leaders in times of crisis and terror*. Pitchstone Publishing.

Volkan, V. D. (2006). *Killing in the name of identity: A study of bloody conflicts*. Pitchstone Publishing.

Volkan, V. D. (2013). *Enemies on the couch: A psychopolitical journey through war and peace*. Pitchstone Publishing.

Volkan, V. D., & Itzkowitz, N. (1984). *The immortal Atatürk: A psychobiography*. University of Chicago Press.

Volkan, V. D., & Itzkowitz, N. (2000). Modern Greek and Turkish identities and the psychodynamics of Greek–Turkish relations. In A. Robben, C. G. M. & M. Suárez-Orozco (Eds.), *Cultures under siege: Collective violence and trauma* (pp. 227–247). Cambridge University Press.

Volkas, A. (2003). Armand Volkas keynote address. *Dramascope: The Newsletter of the National Association for Drama Therapy, 23*(1), 6–9.

Volkas, A. (2009). Healing the wounds of history: Drama therapy in collective trauma and intercultural conflict resolution. In D. J. R. Emunah (Ed.), *Current approaches in drama therapy* (pp. 145–171). Charles C. Thomas.

Volkas, A. (2014). Drama therapy in the repair of collective trauma. In N. Sajnani & D. Johnson (Eds.), *Trauma-informed drama therapy: Transforming clinics, classrooms, and communities* (pp. 41–68). Charles C. Thomas.

Volkas, A., Van I., & Wheat, A. (in press). Society as the client: Drama therapy in healing historical trauma In D. J. R. Emunah (Ed.), *Current approaches in drama therapy*. New Edition Charles C. Thomas.

Wahlbeck, Ö. (1998, July-August). *Transnationalism and diasporas: The Kurdish example*. Paper presented at the International Sociological Association XIV World Congress of Sociology, Montreal, Canada.

Walker, A. S., & Tobbell, J. (2015). Lost voices and unlived lives: Exploring adults' experiences of selective mutism using interpretative phenomenological analysis. *Qualitative Research in Psychology, 12*(4), 453–471. https://doi.org/10.1080/14780887.2015.1054533

Walker, C. J. (1990). *Armenia: The survival of a nation*. St. Martin's Press.

Watts, N. (2000). Relocating Dersim: Turkish state-building and Kurdish resistance, 1931–1938. In *New Perspectives on Turkey, 23*, 5–30.

Wells, J. (2012). *Complexity and sustainability*. Routledge.

Werfel, F. (2012). *The forty days of Musa Dagh*. David R. Godine.

Yavuz, M. H. (2001). Five stages of the construction of Kurdish nationalism in Turkey. *Nationalism & Ethnic Politics, 7*(3), 1–24. https://doi.org/10.1080/13537110108428635

Yeğen, M. (1999a). *Devlet söyleminde Kürt sorunu*. İletişim Yayınları.

Yeğen, M. (1999b). The Kurdish question in Turkish state discourse. *Journal of Contemporary History, 34*(4), 555–568.

Yeğen, M. (2007). Turkish nationalism and the Kurdish question. *Ethnic and Racial Studies, 30*(1), 119–151. https://doi.org/10.1080/01419870601006603

Yeğen, M. (2011). The 2011 elections and the Kurdish question. *Insights Turkey, 13*(4), 147–169.

Yeğen, M., Tol, U. U., & Çalışkan, M. A. (2016). *Kürtler ne istiyor? Kürdistan'da etnik kimlik, dindarlık, sınıf ve seçimler* [What do Kurds Want? Ethnic identity, religion, class and election in Kurdistan]. İletişim Yayınları.

Yehuda, R. (2002). Post-traumatic stress disorder. *New England Journal of Medicine, 346*(2), 108–114.

Yehuda, R., Kahana, B., Southwick, S. M., & Giller, E. L. (1994). Depressive features in Holocaust survivors with post-traumatic stress disorder. *Journal of Traumatic Stress, 7*(4), 699–704.

Yıldırım, M. (2012). Dersimlu aşireti'nden Dersim sancağı'na [From Dersimlu clan to Dersim starboard]. *Tunceli Üniversitesi Sosyal Bilimler Dergisi, 1*(Güz), 32–46.

Yıldırım, O. (2006). The 1923 population exchange, refugees and national historiographies in Greece and Turkey. *East European Quarterly, 40*(1), 45–70.

Yıldız, M. (2014). *Dersim'in etno-kültürel kimliği ve 1937–1938 tertelesi* [Dersim's ethno-cultural identity and 1937-1938 massacre]. Chiviyazıları Yayınevi.

Yılmaz, D. (2009). *War trauma and its subjective meaning: An exploration on "Mehmedi'in Kitabı: Güneydoğu'da Savaşmış Askerler Anlatıyor"* (Unpublished Master's thesis, Istanbul, Bilgi University. Sosyal Bilimler Enstitüsü.

Yonucu, D. (2014). Türkiye'de bir yönetim biçimi olarak mekansal ayrıştırma: tehlikeli mahalleler, olağanüstü hal ve militarist sınır çizimi [Spatial segregation as a technology of governance in Turkey: Dangerous neighbourhoods, state of emergency and the drawing of militarized boundaries]. In Ayfer Bartu Candan, A. B., Özbay C (Eds.), *Yeni Istanbul Çalışmaları*. Metis.

Yonucu, D. (2018). The absent present law. An ethnographic study of legal violence in Turkey. *Social & Legal Studies, 27*(6), 716–733.

Yorbik, O., Akbiyik, D. I., Kirmizigul, P., & Söhmen, T. (2004). Post-traumatic stress disorder symptoms in children after the 1999 Marmara earthquake in Turkey. *International Journal of Mental Health, 33*(1), 46–58. https://doi.org/10.1080/00207411.2004.11043360

Yurtlu, F. (2016). Suç örgütünün propagandasını yapma suçu ve Türkiye açısından AIHM kararlarına yansıması [The crime of making propaganda for a criminal organization and its reflection on AIHM decisions in terms Turkey]. *Gazi Üniversitesi Hukuk Fakultesi Dergisi. XX*(3).

Zana, M. (1998, June 26). What I witnessed in Diyarbakir Prison: The statement by Mehdi Zana on the occasion of the International Day in Support of Torture Victims and Survivors, Friday, June 26, 1998. http://kurdistan.org/what-i-witnessed-in-diyarbakir-prison/

Zara, A., & İçöz, F. J. (2015). Türkiye'de ruh sağlığı alanında travma mağdurlarıyla çalışanlarda ikincil travmatik stress [Secondary traumatic stress in mental health professionals working with trauma victims in Turkey]. *Klinik Psikiyatri,* (18), 15–23.

Zarcone, T., & Hobart, A. (Eds.). (2017). *Shamanism and Islam: Sufism, healing rituals and spirits in the Muslim world.* Bloomsbury Publishing.

Zelyut, R. (2010). *Dersim isyanları ve Seyit Rıza gerçeği* [The truth of Seyit Rıza and Dersim rebellions]. Kripto.

Zengin, S., & Demir, I. (2011). Terörle mücadelede paradigma değişimi [Paradigm shift in counter-terrorism]. *EKEV Akademi Dergisi, 15*(48), 1-21.

Zeydanlıoğlu, W. (2009). Torture and Turkification in the Diyarbakır military prison. In W. Zeydanlıoğlu & J. T. Parry (Eds.), *Rights, citizenship & torture: Perspectives on evil, law and the state* (pp. 73–92). Inter-Disciplinary Press.

Zeydanlıoğlu, W. (2012). Turkey's Kurdish language policy. *International Journal of the Sociology of Language, 2012*(217), 99–125. https://doi.org/10.1515/ijsl-2012-0051

Zoroğlu, S. S., & Şar, V. (2001a). Dissociative disorders in childhood and adolescents: Review of the 36 Turkish cases. *Anadolu Psikiyatri Dergisi, 1*(4), 197–206.

Zoroğlu, S. S., & Şar, V. (2001b). Probable consequences of childhood abuse and neglect. *Anadolu Psikiyatri Dergisi, 2*(2), 69–78.

Zotev, V., Phillips, R., Misaki, M., Wong, C. K., Wurfel, B. E., Krueger, F., . . . Bodurka, J. (2018). *Real-time fMRI neurofeedback training of the amygdala activity with simultaneous EEG in veterans with combat-related PTSD. Neuroimage: Clinical, 19*, 106–121. https://doi.org/10.1016/j.nicl.2018.04.010

Zürcher, E.-J. (2003). *Greek and Turkish refugees and deportees 1912–1924*. Department of Turkish Studies, Universiteit Leiden. http://www.transanatolie.com/english/turkey/turks/ottomans/ejz18.pdf

Zürcher, E.-J. (2013). Introduction. The socio-economic history of ethnic violence in the late Ottoman Empire. *Tijdschrift voor Sociale en Economische Geschiedenis / Low Countries Journal of Social and Economic History, 10*(4), 3–19 https://doi.org/10.18352/tseg.236

Index

Note: Workshop participant names have been changed for reasons of privacy in the text and index.

Abbas, T., 149
Abbasan tribe, 92
Abdülhamid II, Sultan of the Ottoman
  Empire, 5, 59, 60, 61, 188
Abdullatif, A., 77
abuse
  Dersimi women, 94–95
  as form of atrocity, 33
  legalized, 164
  oppression of Kurds, 2, 32, 116, 149, 174
  sexual, 29, 30
  transmission of trauma, 11, 38
  in Turkey, 151
  see also child abuse; domestic violence; drug abuse
accidents, 33
Adıbelli, D., 29
Adalet ve Kalkınma Partisi (AKP)
  authoritarianism, 148
  coup attempt (2016) and purge politics, 149–150
  elections (2015), 127
  Islamic tone, 148
  Kurdish opening peace talks, 126, 127–128, 148, 149
  minority and Kurdish rights, 149
  Muslim Kurd support, 209*n*
  PDP leaders imprisonment, 168
  PKK designation, 126
  religious agenda, 149
  Sunni Muslim religious rights, 148
  Turkish military–PKK conflict, 126, 127–128
Adanır, F., 59, 62, 63, 146
Adana, 68, 74, 91
Adapazarı, 26
adaptive behaviors, 24, 73, 175, 176

Ademli village, 136
Adıvar, Halide Edip, 170
African Americans, 21, 72, 164
  see also slavery
Agaibi, C.E., 28
Aghavni (Armenian Genocide survivor), 68–69
Aghbashian, H., 196
Agos newspaper, 187, 197
Ahmed (Hasan's uncle), 5
Ahmed (HWH workshop participant), 115–116
Ainsworth, Mary, 23
Ak, B., 27
Akar, R., 100
Akçam, Taner, 47, 65–66, 70, 186
Aker, T., 31, 140, 141
Akhavan, Payan, 207*n*
Akkaya-Kalaycı, T., 140
AKP *see Adalet ve Kalkınma Partisi* (AKP)
Aksakal, Mustafa, 67
Aktar, A., 100, 101
Alavi, Amza, 65
Alayarian, Aida, 72, 73
Alcoff, Linda Martin, 158, 164, 189
alcoholism, 30, 38, 125, 151
Alemdar, Z., 90, 126, 144
Alevi
  Anatolia settlements, 91
  assimilation, 137
  books published about, 143
  Chaldiran War, 146–147
  collective memory, 147
  cultural visibility, 144
  in Dersim, 68, 85, 90–91, 92, 94, 95, 96, 137, 145–146
  forced displacement, 137, 139

Gazi neighborhood massacre (1995), 144–145
gender and hierarchy rules, 139
gradual emancipation of, 85
historical traumas, 143–147, 203
identity, 143
Kurdish nationalism, 143–144
Kurds, 207*n*
Maraş Massacre, 144
massacres and violence against, 36, 46, 143–147, 174
military intervention in Dersim (1994–1995), 145–146
military operations in Alevi villages, 144
Ottoman Empire, 143, 146–147
police brutality, 122, 145–146
purged from the police force, 146
relations with Sunni Muslims, 85, 92, 143, 144, 146–147
as religious minority, 84, 122, 139, 207*n*
Sheikh Said Rebellion, 85
Sivas Massacre (1993), 46, 144
support for Turkish Republic, 143
see also Zaza Alevis
Alexander, J.C., 98
Alexanian, Yervant, 60–61
Aliye, Fatma, 170
Alpan, A.S., 78
Altınay, A.G., 29, 30, 116, 170
Amasya, 147
amygdala, 23
Anatolia, 53–58
  Alevi settlements, 91
  Allied occupied zones, 83
  Armenian churches destroyed, 189
  Armenian deportations and massacres, 47–48, 65, 84, 191
  Armenians, 11–13, 53–55, 78, 146, 186
  assimilation, 9, 69–70
  boarding schools, 180
  Chaldıran War, 146–147
  Christians, 53, 63–65, 77, 84, 206*n*
  Circassians, 53, 57, 59, 63, 65
  collective traumas, 50
  diversity, 40, 60, 78, 81–82, 165, 183
  ethnicities, 53, 206*n*
  geographic description, 205*n*
  historical trauma, 11–13, 156, 188
  history, 144, 146–147
  Kurdish rebellions, 85

Kurds, 53, 55, 112, 139, 140, 146–147, 180, 186
labor divisions, 53
location, 1
military operations in Alevi villages, 144
Muslims, 35, 53, 57, 59, 63–65, 152, 163, 187, 191
nomadism, 56, 207*n*
Ottoman Empire collapse, 50
population, 11–12, 82
religion and tribal loyalties, 65
religious communities, 53
Rum (Greek Ottoman) communities, 64, 70–71, 78, 206*n*
sürgün practices, 137
Turkic tribes advance, 50–51
Turkification process, 81
as Turkish homeland, 64
see also Armenian Genocide (1915–1917); Hamidiye massacres (1893–1896)
Andrews, P.A., 53, 206*n*
Ankara, 7, 68, 75, 89, 108, 169
Anoosh, Armen, 185
anthropology, 21
anxiety, 33, 73, 103, 120, 129, 140
apartheid, 41–42
Arab nationalism, 49, 143
Arabia, 74
Arap, Ibrahim, 135
Ararat revolt (1930), 87, 207*n*
Aras, R.
  "Dersim 38", 94
  Kurdish displacement, 139, 140
  Kurdish exiles, 88
  Kurdish nationalism, 114, 119, 165
  Kurdish question, 166, 167
  Kurdish rebellions, 84, 85, 93
  Kurdish struggle, 150
  Kurdishness, 165
  military coup (1971), 113, 114
  nationalist movements, 143
  PKK aims and mission, 122
  Turkish military–PKK conflict, 131, 132–133, 134
  Turkish militia display of dead bodies, 123
Arat, Y., 29, 30, 170
Arda, B., 148
Arendt, Hannah, 44
Arıkan, Saffet, 178

Armenia State
  First Republic (1918–1920), 74, 189
  formation (1991), 186, 189–190
  Soviet satellite state, 189, 190
Armenian diaspora, 68, 69, 70, 71, 73, 74, 159, 189, 190, 196, 197, 198
Armenian Genocide (1915–1917), 65–71
  acknowledgment of, 11, 183–184, 186, 189, 190, 194, 196, 197, 198, 200, 201
  brutality of, 1, 5–6, 35, 47–48, 57–58, 84, 99
  CUP role, 5–6, 35, 57–58, 66, 67–68, 70
  deaths, 70, 207*n*
  denial of, 11, 59, 70, 73, 153, 159, 163, 171, 183–187, 194, 196, 198, 200–201
  diaspora genocide campaigns, 190
  heroic helpers, 47–48
  HWH workshop, 155
  impact on families, 60–61
  Kurdish role, 48, 68, 152, 196
  oral history research studies, 47, 68, 193–194, 195–196
  participant's remorse, 47
  perpetrators, 75
  refugee numbers, 70–71
  transgenerational aspect of, 71–74, 109–110
  Turkish high-school history textbooks, 185–186
  Turkish state narrative, 42, 183–187, 196
Armenian identity, 14, 70, 72, 74, 109–110, 188–190
Armenian massacres (1894–1896), 35
Armenian nationalism, 49
The Armenian Party, 60
"Armenian Question", 184, 185, 186
Armenian Revolutionary Federation, 60, 65
Armenian Secret Army for the Liberation of Armenia (ASALA), 209*n*
Armenian–Azerbaijan conflict, 33, 189
Armenians
  in Anatolia, 11–13, 53–55, 78, 146, 186
  assimilation, 66, 69–70
  collective identity, 189
  collective memory, 70
  collective trauma, 109–110, 194–195
  conversions to Islam, 60, 69
  "death march", 186, 198
  historical trauma, 11–13, 188, 190
  importance of community, 72
  indigenous to Anatolia, 53
  Kurdish militia massacre (1896), 5
  labor camps, 101
  as "loyal millet", 57
  orphans, 47–48, 60, 68, 69
  as the "other", 104
  Ottoman Empire, 53–55, 57–61, 72, 148, 185
  pogroms, 106, 107, 108, 110, 111, 190
  relations with Kurds, 58
  Sèvres Treaty ethnic recognition of, 83
  in Turkey, 11, 70, 72, 74, 109–110, 188–190
  Turkification process, 168, 189
  Turkish high-school history textbooks, 185–186
  Turkish recognition as minority, 175
  Twenty Kur'a Military Service, 99–100, 110
  wealth and revenue taxes, 99, 100, 101, 102–104, 110
  see also Hamidiye massacres (1893–1896)
Arslan, Ruşen, 116–117
Arslan, S., 180, 181
art therapy, 128
ASALA (Armenian Secret Army for the Liberation of Armenia), 209*n*
Aşkale labor camps, 100
Asia Minor *see* Anatolia
Aslan, S., 89, 168
Aslan, Yusuf, 113
assimilation policies, 171–187
  Alevis, 137
  Anatolia, 9, 69–70
  Armenians, 66, 69–70
  boarding schools, 87, 173, 180–181
  Bulgarian Muslims, 15
  control of language, 171–178
  Dersimis, 89, 92, 94, 95, 96, 97
  Eastern Anatolia/Kurdistan, 115
  Kurds, 12, 84, 89, 115, 165, 167
  Orient Reform Plan, 87
  Turkish Republic, 79
  village guards, 136
  village institutes, 178–180
  World War I, 66
  Zaza Alevis, 137
  see also control of education; Turkification process; Turkishness

Association of Turkish Cyprus (KTC), 105–106
Assyrians, Anatolia, 206*n*
Ataöv, Türkkay, 187
Atatürk, Mustafa Kemal
   ancestor of all Turks, 98
   "Atatürk's Principles and Reforms", 181–182
   Balkan Wars, 63
   birthplace house bombed, 105
   control of education, 183
   death, 80
   Dersim, 92
   Kemalism, 155, 169, 172, 174
   military forces, 112
   "Nutuk" speech, 169
   reforms and regulations, 108, 155
   Sheikh Said Rebellion, 86
   symbol of new Turkishness, 80
   Turkey's first president, 169
   Turkification process, 81
   Turkish identity evolution, 79–80
   Turkish military, 112
   Turkish nationalism, 85
   Turkish War of Independence, 35, 75
   Turks' idealization of, 80
   women's role, 170
atrocity versus natural disaster, 32–34
attachment theory, 23–24, 74
Augsburg, Tanya, 205*n*
authoritarianism, 148
Avar, Sıdıka, 94–95
Ayas, T., 27
Ayata, B., 11, 126, 140, 141–142, 147–148
Aydın, E., 31
Aydıngün, A., 79, 172
Aydıngün, I., 79, 172
Ayverdi, S., 186
Azadi (Freedom), 85–86, 88
Azerbaijan-Armenian conflict, 33, 189

Bab-ı Ali Raid, 64
Bademci, E., 30
Bademli, K., 140
Bahaeddin Sakir Bey, 66
Bal, A., 27
Balancar, F., 74, 102–103
Balı, R.N., 100, 102
Balkan Muslim migrants, 15, 63, 191, 193, 196
   population exchange, 36, 50, 76–79, 104

Balkan Wars (1912–1913), 9, 15, 35, 50, 61, 62–64, 66, 80
Banker, Marie Sarrafian, 185
Banks, C., 122
Barakat, S., 26, 27
Bardakçı, Murat, 102
Barkey, H.J., 125
Barkey, K., 57
Barnett, D., 23
Başoğlu, C., 119, 120
Başoğlu, M., 119, 120, 121
Bayar, Celâl, 108
BBC, 149
BDP (Peace and Democracy Party), 118
Benninghaus, R., 53, 206*n*
Beriker-Atıyas, N., 136
Berlin Congress (1878), 59
Berna (HWH workshop participant), 3
Berument, S.K., 31
Beşikçi, Ismail, 89, 90, 192
Beyoğlu, S., 70
Bilgin, R., 32
Bilmez, B., 97, 176
Birand, M.A., 116
Black Lives Matter movement, 164
"Black Training", 192–193
Bloxham, Donald, 70
boarding schools, 87, 173, 180–181
Bocchi, Gianluca, 67
Böke, P., 79
Bosnian Muslims, 207*n*
Bowlby, John, 23
Boyajian, K., 73
Boyajian, L.Z., 72
Bozarslan, H., 143, 169
Bradley, L., 120
Brailey, K., 128
brain regions, 23
Braun, K.L., 27
Braunwald, K., 23
Bremner, J.D., 128
Britain
   Anatolia occupied zone, 83
   Arabic states, 74
   control of Cyprus, 105, 109
   threat to Ottoman Empire, 49
   Turkish War of Independence, 75
Brown, P.M., 83
Bu Kalp Seni Unutur mu? (TV show), 117
Buğu, B., 114, 117, 119, 120, 121
Bukhara, 4, 50–51
Bulgaria, Balkan Wars, 62

Bulut, S., 27
Bursa, 51
bystander behaviors, 44, 48, 171
Byzantine Empire, 51

Çağaptay, S., 152
Çağatay, Cengiz, 117
Çağlayangil, Ihsan Sabri, 94
Çakmak, F., 178, 179
Çakmak, H., 27
Çalışkan, M.A., 167
Cambodia, 46
cancer, 162
Cansız, Sakine, 119
captivity situations, 23
Carlson, V., 23
Celal Bey, 68
Çelik, A.B., 138, 139, 140, 141, 142
Çelik, Filiz, 96, 97, 139
Cem (HWH workshop participant), 123–124
Cemiloğlu, D., 172
Cengiz, D., 93
Ceruti, Mauro, 67
Çetin, Fethiye, 188
Çetin, M., 27
Çetin, V., 139
Çetinkaya, Y.D., 63
Cevher (HWH workshop participant), 2–3
Ceyhan, A.A., 27
Ceyhan, E., 27
Chaldiran War, 146–147, 203
Charney, D.S., 128
chattel slavery *see* slavery
Chatty, D., 190
child abuse, 22, 23, 30–31, 32, 95, 151
childhood
  Nazi Germany, 44–45
  parenting skills, 24, 30–31, 37
  trauma, 23–24, 73
children
  attachment theory, 23–24
  Dersim massacres, 94–95
  forced displacement, 94–95, 140
  in Kurdistan, 32
  neglect of, 23, 30–31, 32, 44–45
  see also orphans
"chosen" traumas, 36, 46
Christians
  Anatolia, 53, 63–65, 77, 84, 206*n*
  Balkan Wars, 62–64
  Ottoman Empire, 11, 53, 57, 58, 81

population exchange, 36, 50, 76–79, 104
Turkish Republic, 11, 14, 148
wealth and revenue taxes, 100
see also Rum (Greek Ottoman) communities
Cicchetti, D., 23
Circassians, 53, 57, 59, 63, 65, 143
Çitil, E.T., 29
Citizen, Speak Turkish! campaign, 99, 110, 172–173, 190, 201–202
Cizre, 160
"clean pain", 39, 41
climate change, 34
Cobbs, Price, 156
Cold War, 186
collective identity, 55, 189, 201
collective memory
  Alevi, 147
  Armenians, 70
  Kurds, 89
  Turkish, 109, 185
collective trauma, 10–12, 14, 32–37
  Alevi massacres, 36, 46, 143–147, 174
  Anatolia, 50
  Armenians, 109–110, 194–195
  Citizen, Speak Turkish! campaign, 99, 110, 172–173, 190, 201–202
  cultural factors, 34
  defined, 11, 32
  Dink's assassination, 36, 110, 187–188, 189, 190, 197
  Eğin village, 194–195
  earthquakes, 24–29, 31
  Healing the Wounds of History workshop, 2–3
  and identity, 189, 201
  impact of, 41–43, 150
  interlinked process, 32
  Istiklal Courts, 36, 86, 87
  Kurdish rebellions (1925–1939), 36, 84, 85, 133
  Ottoman Empire, 35, 49–82, 203
  pogroms, 36, 46, 66, 104–111, 112, 152, 190, 201
  population exchange, 36, 50, 76–79, 104
  social change, 34–35
  sociological studies, 21
  Turkish military–PKK conflict, 20, 32, 36, 112, 116, 121, 122–128, 129, 131–137, 138, 141, 145, 155, 177, 203

Turkish Republic, 3, 80, 83–111, 203
Twenty Kur'a Military Service, 36, 99–100, 110
wealth and revenue taxes, 36, 99, 100–104, 110
see also Armenian Genocide (1915–1917); Balkan Wars (1912–1913); "Dersim 38"; displacement, forced; Diyarbakır Military Prison; Greco-Turkish War (1920–1922); Hamidiye massacres (1893–1896); military coups; Sheikh Said Rebellion (1925); Turkish War of Independence (1919–1923)
Colombia, United Self-Defense Forces, 135
Columbus, Christopher, 51
combat trauma, 10, 128–132
commandos, 131
commemoration, 42
Committee of Union and Progress (CUP)
armed attacks on Ottoman Greeks, 70
Armenian Genocide, 5–6, 35, 57–58, 66, 67–68, 70
assassination of opponents, 64, 152
coup d'état (1913), 5, 63, 66–67
demographic policies, 65–66
dictatorial style, 64, 152
formation (1886), 5
reforms, 169
relations with the ARF, 65
relations to Young Turks, 64
suppression of information, 185
takeover (1913), 64–65
Turkification process, 81
Turkishness, 64
World War I, 5, 63, 67, 75
Constitution
Ottoman Empire (First Constitutional Era 1876–1878), 50, 61–62
Ottoman Empire (Second Constitution period 1908–1918), 61–62, 64, 112
Turkish Republic (1924), 169, 172
Turkish Republic (1982), 115
Turkish Republic modified (1928), 169
"context-centric healing", 40
control of education, 171, 172, 174–176, 181–183
control of language, 171–178
conversion disorders, 129
Cook, A., 22, 24
Çorbacıoğlu, R.B., 90, 126, 144

Çorum, 144
Coşkun, V., 172, 175, 176
critical theory, 161
Cuddy, A.J., 45
cultural trauma, 12, 34–37, 140, 171
Cumartesi Anneleri, 209n
Cyprus, 104–105, 109
"Cyprus Is Turkish" student movement, 105

Dadrian, V.N., 5, 58, 70, 187, 195
Dağtekin, Hasan, 119
Danieli, Yael, 33, 36–37, 38–39, 40, 73
Darnell, A., 128
Daud, A., 120
Davison, R.H., 58
De Fabrique, N., 23
de Zayas, A., 108–109
De Dağtekin, Hasan, 119
Değer, Mesut, 134
DeGruy Leary, Joy, 21, 41–42, 164
dehumanization, 33, 44, 46, 48, 92, 171, 201
Dekel, R., 37, 132
Demanan tribe, 92
Demir, İ., 166
Demirel, Ç., 116, 117, 118
Demirel, Tanel, 113–114
Demirer, M.A., 106
Democratic Party (DP), 104, 105, 107, 108, 112
demographic engineering, 81, 137, 141, 147–148, 181
denial, and ignorance, 165–166, 184
depression, 27, 29, 31, 33, 73, 120, 128, 129, 140
Derince, S., 172, 175
Deringil, S., 58, 59, 60
"Dersim 38"
abuse of women, 94–95
acknowledgment of, 89–90, 96–99, 148–149
amnesty (late 1940s), 95
children, 94–95
deaths, 89, 93
denial of, 89–90
emphasis on remembering, 97
historical trauma, 97, 145
massacres, 36, 41, 84, 89–99
rebellion, 84, 85, 89, 92–93, 167, 207n
transgenerational aspect of, 96–99
Turkish state narrative, 42

Dersim
  Alevi settlements, 68, 85, 90–91, 92, 94, 95, 96, 137, 145–146
  historical name, 90
  meaning of name, 90
  military interventions, 89–99, 145–146
  military rule, 91
  Tunceli (Dersim) law (1935), 91
  Zaza Alevis, 68, 90–91, 137
Dersimi diaspora, 96, 98
Dersimi, N., 89, 90, 92, 94, 95–96
Dersimis
  assimilation policies, 89, 92, 94, 95, 96, 97
  cultural diversity, 89
  distinct culture, 91, 203
  ethnocide, 89
  forced displacement, 89, 93, 94, 95, 97, 137
  HWH workshops, 98
  Kurdish identity, 87–89, 91, 96
  Ottoman Empire, 90, 91, 92, 99
  protection of Armenians, 47, 68
  resilience, 96, 97, 98
  Sheikh Said Rebellion, 85
  tribal disputes, 91, 93
  Turkish War of Independence, 92
  Turkishness, 94, 95, 98
diaspora *see* Armenian diaspora; Dersimi diaspora; Kurdish diaspora
Dikbaş, A., 24
Diken, S., 88
Dimitra, Giannuli, 78
Diner, C., 29
Dink, Hrant
  Armenians in the West, 190
  assassination of, 36, 110, 187–188, 189, 190, 197
Dirlik, Arif, 155
"dirty pain", 39, 41
disorganized attachment, 24
displacement, voluntary, 137, 138, 139, 140, 141, 142
displacement, forced, 31, 48
  Alevis, 137, 139
  "boomerang effect", 142–143
  children, 94–95, 140
  collective healing, 141
  Compensation Law, 141, 142
  Dersimis, 89, 93, 94, 95, 97, 137
  fall of the Ottoman Empire, 1
  Greco-Turkish War, 76–79
  internally displaced people (IDPs), 137–141
  Kurds, 32, 36, 88, 126, 127, 135, 137–143
  Muslims, 76–77, 78–79, 137
  recurring theme in human history, 137
  women, 94–95, 138
Dixon, Jennifer, 42, 183–184, 185–186, 187, 191
Diyarbakır
  craftsmanship center, 53–55
  Kurdish children study, 175
  Ottoman Empire, 55
  Sheikh Said Rebellion, 86, 87
  violence against Armenians, 68
Diyarbakır Military Prison
  deaths, 118
  DMP-TRIC report (2012), 114, 117, 118
  Kurds, 116, 117–118, 119–120, 121
  torture, 36, 114, 116–120, 174
Doğan, A., 27
Doğulu, C., 27, 28, 29, 31
domestic violence, 24, 29–31, 38
dönme (converts), 60, 69, 100, 101
Dosdoğru, M.H., 106
Dotson, K., 161
DP (Democratic Party), 104, 105, 107, 108, 112
drama therapy, 2, 32, 154–161, 172, 205*n*
Drinkwater, B.D., 27
drug abuse, 30, 38, 125, 128, 151
Dural, T.F., 145
Duran, Eduardo, 21, 38, 40
Düşğün, Umut, 79
Düzel, Neşe, 119–120

Eğin (Agn), 4–5, 6, 7, 16, 18, 194–195, 197–198
earthquakes
  in Armenia (1988), 33
  collective traumas, 24–29, 31
  Marmara (1999), 24–29, 34
  psychological trauma, 22, 24–29, 31
  in Van (2011), 26, 27
Ecevit, M., 27
Edirne, 179
Edremit earthquake, 26
education
  "Atatürk's Principles and Reforms", 181–182
  boarding schools, 87, 173, 180–181
  control of, 171, 172, 174–176, 181–183

high-school history textbooks, 185–186
  Kurds, 87, 173, 175–176
  mandatory, 173, 180
  national anthem, 183
  Student Oath, 182, 183
  Turkishness, 171, 172, 173, 174–176, 181–183
  village institutes, 178–180
Ekmekçioğlu, L., 69, 70
Ekopolitik, 43
Eksi, A., 27, 29
Elazığ, 90, 94
"empty chair conversation", 11, 98, 206n
En Son Haber, 129
Engdahl, B., 39
Ensaroğlu, Y., 127
Enver Pasha, 66, 67
epigenetics, 21
epistemologies of ignorance, 13–15, 153–199
  boarding schools, 180
  bystander behaviors, 171
  ethnic diversity, 191
  transgenerational experiences, 1, 153
  Turkish identity, 153, 154, 156
  Turkish state role, 1, 13–15, 77, 84–85, 202
  Turkishness, 14–15, 165, 200, 202
  understanding of, 161–170
Erat, Veysel, 135
Erbil, 53
Erdoğan, Recep Tayyip, 42, 125, 147, 148–149, 152, 184
Ergun, D., 140
Erkan, I., 30
Erman, T., 138, 140
Erol, Emre, 70, 71
Erzincan, 90, 94, 194, 197–198
Erzurum, 68
Eski Foça, 70
Eski, M., 178
Eskişehir, 16, 89, 179
ethnic engineering, 63
European Union
  PKK as a terrorist organization, 20, 122
  Turkey's interest in joining, 90, 143, 173
ever-present anger, 164
evil, banality of, 44
Evren, Kenan, 113, 116, 118, 119

Faroqhi, S., 49, 51, 52, 53, 75
Farrar, L.L. Jr., 62

Fatima (Muhammed the Prophet's daughter), 40
Fejto, François, 67
feminism, 170
feminist epistemology, 161
feudalism, 87, 122, 135
Figley, C.R., 22
Fındık, Özgür, 93
Fırat, Abdulmelik, 88
Firehammer, J., 40
Fiske, S.T., 45
fixity, 36–37
flow state, 32
Foçateyn, 70
Forero, J., 135
Fossion, P., 37
France
  Anatolia occupied zone, 83
  Arabic states, 74
  threat to Ottoman Empire, 49
Franco-Turco war, 74–75
Frankl, V.E., 28
Franz Ferdinand, Archduke of Austria, 67
Freire, Paolo, 161
French Revolution (1789), 49, 81
Freud, Sigmund, 205–206n
Friedman, M.J., 130
Friedrich, W.N., 23
Fuller, G.E., 125

Galip, Rasid, 178, 182
Garrard, P., 151
Gavrilis, G., 57
Gazi neighborhood massacre (1995), 144–145
generational trauma *see* transgenerational trauma
genocide
  history of the term, 207n
  see also Armenian Genocide (1915–1917)
George (HWH workshop participant), 3–4
Germany *see* Nazi Germany
Gestalt therapy, 206n
Gezi Park uprising, 148
Gezmiş, Deniz, 113
GöçDer, 135, 136
Göçek, Fatma Müge
  Armenian Genocide, 42, 70
  Committee of Union and Progress, 64
  Dink's assassination, 188
  emergence of nationalism, 49–50

Göçek, Fatma Müge *(continued)*
  Greek/Turkish population exchanges, 76, 78–79
  Hamidiye massacres, 60, 207*n*
  Hamidiye regiments, 59
  Istiklal Courts, 87
  justice for perpetrators, 150
  Muslim–Christian relations, 57
  non-Muslims exclusion, 168
  recognizing relationality, 164–165
  Turkish identities, 191
  Turkish Republic early assemblies, 169
  Turkish War of Independence, 75
  Workshop for Armenian-Turkish (WATS), 164–165
  Young Turk Revolution (1908), 61
Goenjian, A.K., 33
Gökçen, Sabiha, 93
Golcuk, 26
Goldblatt, H., 37, 132
Göle, N., 163
Gonzalez, J., 40
Gözde, I., 28, 31
Great Depression, 110–111
Greco-Turkish War (1920–1922), 7, 35, 50, 74, 76–81
Greece
  Balkan Wars, 62
  Cyprus dispute, 105, 109
  historical trauma, 77
  nation-building process, 77
  occupation of Izmir, 83
  Ottoman Greek refugees, 50, 76–78
Greek identity, emergence of, 77
Greek military coup, 109
Greek Muslims, 76–77, 78–79
Greek nationalism, 49, 105, 109
Greek Ottomans *see* Rum (Greek Ottoman) communities
Grier, William, 156
Grigorian, H., 73
Gülen, Fethullah, 149
Gülen movement, 149
Güloğlu, B., 128, 129, 130, 131
Gülşen, C., 140
Gülümser (Neyzi's study), 97
Günaydın, S., 29
Gündoğan, K., 94, 95, 96
Gündoğan, N., 94, 95, 96
Güneş, C., 119
Güneş, H., 31
Gurcan, M., 135
Gursel, Cemal, 113

Güven, Dilek, 104, 105, 106, 107, 108, 109

Haarer, Joanna, 44–45
Hafız Mehmed, 7, 8
hafir tax, 58
Hakan, A., 118
Hakyemez, S., 11, 116, 147–148
Halaçoğlu, Y., 70, 186
Halep, 68
Halil, Haji, 47
Halklarin Demokratik Partisi (HDP), 168, 209*n*
Hall, Richard, 62
Hamama-Raz, Y., 28
Hamidiye massacres (1893–1896), 35, 50, 58–61, 68, 190, 207*n*
Hamidiye regiments, 5, 59–60, 61, 86, 135, 151
Haney, C., 122
Harris, L.T., 45
Hartowicz, S.Z., 40–41
Hasan (Hüseyin's father), 5, 6–7, *6*, 8, 9, 10
Hasan Mazhar Bey, 68
Haslam, S.A., 45
Hatay, 91
Hatzivassiliou, Evanthis, 105
Hayat, 76
Haydaran tribe, 92
Hayreni, H., 5, 6, 195
HDP (*Halklarin Demokratik Partisi*), 168, 209*n*
healing, 39–43, 200–204
  at the collective level, 141, 150, 157
  at a personal level, 39–41, 150, 156, 198
  "context-centric healing", 40
  forced displacements, 141
  historical trauma, 41–42, 150, 205*n*
  ignorance, 162
  perpetrators, 42–43
  pre-Islamic and Islamic practices, 40
  psychological trauma, 39–41, 130, 150
  systemic trauma, 15, 41–43, 200
  transgenerational trauma, 16, 38–39
  see also psychological healing
Healing the Wounds of History (HWH) workshops, 154–161
  Ahmed's participation, 115–116
  Armenian Genocide, 155
  author's experience, 2, 154–158, 160
  Berna's participation, 3

Cem's participation, 123–124
Cevher's participation, 2–3
control of language, 171–172
creation of, 205n
Dersimis, 98
George's participation, 3–4
identity exploration, 115–116
Kurdish identity, 123–124
Kurdistan Workers' Party (PKK), 2–3, 116, 124, 171–172
military coup (1980) workshop, 115–116
recognition and apology stage, 198
reconciliation, 154, 205n
Rodin's participation, 171–172
Turkish military–PKK conflict, 155
Zoran's participation, 115–116
helper behaviors, 44, 47–48
Hennerbichler, F., 53
Herman, Judith, 22–23, 33, 41, 202–203
heroic helpers, 44, 47–48
Hesse-Biber, S.N., 161
hippocampus, 23
Hirschon, Renee, 77
historical trauma
  of Alevis, 143–147, 203
  in Anatolia, 11–13, 156, 188
  Armenians, 11–13, 188, 190
  definition, 37–38
  of Dersim, 97, 145
  diverse experiences of, 151
  examples, 3, 10–12, 171–172
  of Greece, 77
  healing from, 41–42, 150, 205n
  Healing the Wounds of History workshop, 3–4
  interlinked process, 32
  of Kurds in Anatolia, 11–13
  psychological consequences of, 12–13, 31
  study of symptoms, 151
  Turkish literature reviews, 31
  Turkish Republic, 8, 77, 80, 151, 153–157, 200, 203
  of Turks in Anatolia, 11–13
  Volkas' concept of, 36, 38
  Zaza Alevis, 203
  see also Armenian Genocide (1915–1917); slavery
Hoagland, Sarah Lucia, 164
Hobart, A., 40
Holocaust, 21, 38–39, 44–45, 71, 72, 73, 187, 205n, 207n

homelessness, 128
hope, 148, 160–161
hopelessness, 29
Hotel Madımak, 46, 144
Huffington Post, 121
Hunchakian, 60
Hüseyin (author's distant uncle), 4, 5, 6, 7–8, 9, 10–11

Ibrahim, I., 99, 100
İçöz, F., 22
identity
  anthropology, 21
  Armenians in Turkey, 14, 70, 72, 74, 109–110, 188–190
  author's personal background, 2, 15–20
  challenges to, 159
  collective, 55, 189, 201
  collective trauma, 189, 201
  formation of, 157
  Greek, 77
  historical trauma, 11
  HWH workshops, 115–116, 123–124
  Jewish, 156
  large group, 11, 13, 33, 36, 45–46, 65, 88
  loss of, 103
  Muslim, 63–64
  Ottoman Empire, 8, 13
  Turkish
  see also Kurdish identity; Turkish identity
identity based conflict, 19–20, 87, 126, 136, 143, 166, 201
identity exploration exercise (HWH), 115–116
ignorance, 161–168
  defined, 162
  and denial, 165–166, 184
  going against, 187
  HWH workshops, 154
  Kurdish displacement, 139
  neutral response, 197
  "not-knowing", 161, 162
  oppressed groups, 189
  of perpetrators or bystanders, 45
  of privilege, 154, 163, 193
  social construction of, 162
  see also epistemologies of ignorance
Ikizer, G., 27, 28, 31
Imset, Ismet, 114–115, 122, 123, 125
İnan, Hüseyin, 113
incest, 30

Inönü, Ismet, 179
Iran
　Kurdish community, 55, 88, 143, 165, 207n
　Safavids, 58, 91, 146–147
　Sheikh Said Rebellion, 87
　Twelver Shiism, 91
　World War I, 67
Iraq, Kurdish community, 88, 143, 165
Işık, A.S., 180, 181
Islam
　conversions to, 60, 69
　Ottoman Empire, 51
　patriarchal interpretations of, 170
　Shari'a law, 169
　Turkish Republic, 169
　see also Muslimness Contract; Muslims; Sunni Muslims; Twelver Shiism
Islamic fanaticism, 80
Ismael, Shah of Iran, 147
Istanbul
　Gazi neighborhood massacre (1995), 144–145
　Gezi Park uprising, 148
　Kurdish population, 139
　martial law, 108
　non-Muslims, 100, 104, 105–110
　pogroms, 104, 105–110
　Rum (Greek Ottoman) communities, 104
Istanbul Express, 105
Istiklal Courts, 36, 86, 87
Italy
　Anatolia occupied zone, 83
　Turkish War of Independence, 75
Itzkowitz, Norman, 77, 79–80
Izmir, 68, 74, 79, 83, 89, 108, 179
Izmit, 24, 25

Janoff-Bulman, R., 33
jazz musicians, 164
JCOAG (Justice Commandos for Armenian Genocide), 209n
JDP *see* Adalet ve Kalkınma Partisi (AKP)
Jenkins, R., 65
Jewish identity, 156
Jews
　Anatolia, 53
　labor camps, 101
　Ottoman Empire, 53, 58
　pogroms, 106, 107, 108
　Turkish recognition as minority, 175
　wealth and revenue taxes, 100, 101
　see also Holocaust
June Movement, 148
Jungian psychology, 40
Justice Commandos for Armenian Genocide (JCOAG), 209n
Justice and Development Party *see Adalet ve Kalkınma Partisi* (AKP)

Kadının Statüsü Genel Müdürlüğü (KSGM), 29
Kalan tribe, 92
Kalumenos, Dimitris, 107
Kamer, H., 119
Kamil Pasha, 66
Kapikian, Garabed, 185
Karabağlı, H., 129
Karaırmak, O., 128, 130, 131
Karakoyunlu, Y., 101
Karancı, A.N., 27, 31
Karaömeroğlu, A.M., 178, 179, 180
Karatay, G., 97
Karaveli, Halil Magnus, 148
Kardam, F., 30
Karenian, S., 73
Kasapoğlu, A., 27
Kasr-i Sirin Peace Treaty (1639), 146
Kastamonu, 179
Kay, A., 73
Kayi tribe, 51
Kaya, Ferzende, 88
Kaya, Furkan, 100
Kayra, Cahit, 102
KCK (*Koma Civakên Kurdistanê*), 126
Kehl-Bodrogi, K., 146, 147
Kellerman, N.P.F., 37
Kemalism, 155, 169, 172, 174
Kerimoğlu, H.T., 70
Keshgegian, Flora, 70, 71, 72
Keten, H.S., 128, 131
Kevorkian, R.H., 53, 55
Kharatyan-Araqelyan, H., 47, 68, 73, 109, 189, 195
Khmer Rouge, 46
Kıbrıs Türk Cemiyeti (KTC), 105–106
Kieser, H.-L, 47, 68, 89
Kirişci, K., 139, 191
Kısa, S., 29
Kısanak, Gültan, 118, 119
Kızılbaş, 146–147
Klein, J., 58
Klein, J.W., 156

Knipscheer, J., 140
knowledge creation, 161, 162
Koçan tribe, 92
Koçgiri resistance (*halk hareketi*), 91
Koma Civakên Kurdistanê (KCK), 126
Kongar, E., 148
Konya, 68, 74, 89
Köprülü, Mehmet Fuat, 108
Kopşa, Arzum, 188
Korucu, Serdar, 107
KSGM (*Kadının Statüsü Genel Müdürlüğü*), 29
KTC (*Kıbrıs Türk Cemiyeti*), 105–106
Küçükkaya, A., 148
Kupelian, D., 73
Kurdish diaspora, 142, 143, 192
Kurdish identity
  boarding schools, 181
  children, 181
  culture of fear, 134
  Dersimis, 87–89, 91, 96
  forced displacement issue, 141–142
  HWH workshop, 123–124
  intensification of, 173
  military coup (1980), 115
  multiple formations, 14, 85
  national differences, 165
  persecution of politicians, 174
  policies against, 96
  status in Turkish Republic, 20, 82, 167–168
  village guards, 136
Kurdish language, 87, 115, 117, 126, 171–172, 173, 174–178, 206–207n
Kurdish militias, 5
Kurdish nationalism
  Alevis, 143–144
  changing nature of, 143
  Diyarbakır Military Prison, 119
  emergence of, 83, 84, 85, 89, 95–96, 114–115, 119, 143, 165, 167, 207n
  forced displacements, 143
  political movements, 143
  Turkish language, 173
"Kurdish problem", 166
Kurdish rebellions (1925–1939), 36, 84, 85, 133
Kurdish *ulema*, 88
Kurdishness, 117, 165, 181
Kurdistan
  academic peace petition (2016), 149–150
  assimilation, 115
  boarding schools, 87, 173, 180–181
  children in, 32
  decades-long damage, 127
  government instability, 11–12
  independence demands, 122, 125, 209n
  location of, 55
  Ottoman Empire, 58
  rebellions, 36, 84, 85, 133
  state of emergency (1987), 124–125
  territorial extent, 143
  Turkification process, 115
  Turkish military–PKK conflict, 2, 20, 32, 36, 112, 116, 121, 122–128, 129, 131–137, 138, 141, 145, 155, 177, 203
  see also Dersim; village guards
Kurdistan Communities Union (KCK), 126
Kurdistan Workers' Party (PKK)
  aims and mission, 122, 125
  AKP designation as counterinsurgency, 126
  armed conflict with Turkish military, 2, 20, 32, 36, 112, 116, 121, 122–128, 129, 131–134, 135–136, 138, 141, 145, 155, 177, 203, 206n
  attack on Turkish military facilities (1984), 112
  cease-fire with Turkish military, 125, 135, 160
  considered a terrorist organization, 20, 122–123, 173–174
  Diyarbakır Military Prison, 119–120, 121
  early violent attacks, 122
  effect of armed conflict on family life, 123–124
  emergence of, 114–115, 173
  establishment of, 112, 122
  federalism demand, 125
  Healing the Wounds of History workshop, 2–3, 116, 124, 171–172
  history, 114, 119–120, 122–123
  peace talks, 125–128, 136, 148, 149, 160
  structural demands, 126
Kurds
  abuse and oppression of, 2, 32, 116, 149, 174
  academic peace petition (2016), 149–150
  in Anatolia, 53, 55, 112, 139, 140, 146–147, 180, 186

Kurds *(continued)*
  Armenian Genocide actions, 48, 68, 152, 196
  assimilation, 12, 84, 89, 115, 165, 167
  as asylum-seekers/immigrants, 142
  autonomous region expectation, 83, 84
  "boomerang effect", 142–143
  Citizen, Speak Turkish! campaign, 172
  collective identities, 55
  collective memory, 89
  collective wounding, 32
  conflicting political agendas, 167
  cultural experience, 3
  culture of fear, 123, 133–134
  diversity, 55, 163
  Diyarbakır Military Prison, 116, 117–118, 119–120, 121
  education, 87, 173, 175–176
  Eğin village attacks, 195
  ethnopolitical denial, 82, 84, 140, 142, 153, 165, 166, 167, 171, 181, 200, 201
  forced displacement, 32, 36, 88, 126, 127, 135, 137–143
  Hamidiye massacres, 59–60
  historical trauma, 11–13
  indigenous to Anatolia, 53
  in Istanbul, 139
  Lausanne Peace Treaty, 84
  left-wing movements, 113, 114
  local rebellions, 36, 84, 85, 133
  military coups, 112, 113, 114, 115–116
  Muslim identities, 82, 83, 91, 207*n*
  nomads, 55, 56, 58, 207*n*
  Ottoman Empire, 55, 58
  patriarchal system, 3
  political representation prohibited, 115
  "primordial loyalties", 65
  regional conflicts, 1, 12, 20
  relations with Armenians, 58
  resistance to Turkishness, 12
  revolts and uprisings (19th century), 207*n*
  Sèvres Treaty concerns, 84
  Sèvres Treaty ethnic recognition of, 83
  socio-political victimization, 32
  status in Turkish Republic, 20, 82, 167–168
  Sunni Muslims, 5, 82, 83, 85, 86, 91, 207*n*
  tribalism, 55, 61, 65, 92–93, 135
  Turkification process, 84, 165, 167, 177
  Turkish military–PKK conflict, 123–124, 132–137
  Turkish nationalism concerns, 84, 143, 192
  Turkish state perception of, 92, 166, 181
  Turks views on, 163
  see also "Dersim 38"; Hamidiye regiments; Sheikh Said Rebellion (1925); village guards
Kurmanji speakers, 88, 206*n*, 207*n*
Kuyucu, A.T., 105, 106–107
Kuzirian, K., 73

labor camps, 100–101
Laçiner, S., 70
Lang, B., 44
language
  control of, 171–178
  see also Kurdish language; Turkish language
"language wound", 175–177
Laufer, A., 28
Lausanne Peace Treaty (1923), 76, 83–84
Laz ethnic group, 159, 180
leadership, 66, 71
  reparative versus destructive, 46, 152
Leavy, Patricia, 205*n*
left-wing movements
  in the 1960s, 113, 114
  in the 1970s, 113, 114, 173
  in the 1980s, 114, 115
  Kurds, 113, 114
  third generation of Dersim 38 survivors, 98
leftist police force, 122, 146
Leveton, E., 154
Levine, P.A., 32, 128
Levine, S.Z., 28
liberation psychology, 40
Lifton, R.J., 33
Linzey, S., 139
Livanou, M., 27
Lobban, J., 128
London Tripartite Conference (1955), 105

McCarthy, Justin J., 59, 187
McDowall, D., 58, 89
Madımak Otel, 46, 144
Malatya, 86, 90, 144, 187
Malazgirt War (1071), 51
Mamluk Empire, 51
Mamuretulaziz, 68

Mango, Andrew, 53
Manoogian, J., 73
Manuk (Armenian interviewee), 103–104
Maraş Massacre (1978), 144
Marcus, A., 122
Marmara earthquake (1999), 24–29, 34
Marmaris, 3
Mater, Nadire, 130, 131
Mehmet II ("Fatih the Conqueror"), 51
Mehmet Nazim Bey, 66
Menakem, Resmaa, 39
Menderes, Adnan, 105, 107, 108, 109, 113
Meshorer, Sean, 121
methodology, 13–14
Mikhail, A., 51, 147
military coups
  Greece, 109
  Turkey (1960), 36, 108, 112–113, 114
  Turkey (1971), 36, 112, 113, 114, 119, 176, 192
  Turkey (1980), 36, 112, 113–116, 119, 122, 144, 146, 174, 176
  Turkey (2016 attempt), 149
military interventions, Dersim/Tunceli, 89–99, 145–146
military service, mandatory, 99–100, 108, 128–129, 130–132
Miller, D.E., 60, 68
Miller, L.T., 60, 68
Miller, P., 32
millet system, 56–58, 60, 84
Mills, Charles, 163, 164, 192
modernization policies
  Ottoman Empire, 14, 58
  Turkey, 14, 89, 91, 92, 95, 97
Montenegro, Balkan Wars, 62
Monterey Turkish Festival, 19
Montuori, Alfonso, 205n
Moreno, Jacob, 205n, 206n
Morin, Edgar, 205n
Morrill, B., 28
Mosul, 53
Mouhibian, R., 73
muhacirs, 16, 76, 79, 88, 196, 206n
Muhammed the Prophet, 40
Muhiddin, Nezihe, 170
Muller, M., 139
multi-generational trauma see transgenerational trauma
Muratyan, Nayan, 99, 103, 104, 189, 190
Muslim bandits, 8
Muslim Greeks, 76–77, 78–79

Muslim refugees, 4, 35, 57, 59, 63, 64, 76–77, 78–79, 152, 191
Muslimness Contract, 64–65, 81, 86, 163, 202
Muslims
  Anatolia, 35, 53, 57, 59, 63–65, 152, 163, 187, 191
  Balkan migrants, 15, 63, 191, 193, 196
  Balkan Wars, 63–64
  forced displacement, 76–77, 78–79, 137
  forced marriages, 9
  Ottoman Empire, 56–57, 59
  population exchange, 36, 50, 76–79, 104
  victimization of, 8–9
  see also Islam; Sunni Muslims
muteness, 74, 109
  "Conspiracy of Silence", 73
  Selective Mutism (SM), 102–103

Nadar, S., 181–182
Nagorno-Karabagh war, 189
nationalism
  Arab, 49, 143
  Armenian, 49
  fall of the Ottoman Empire, 1, 49–50
  Greek, 49, 105, 109
  historical trauma, 11
  Persian, 143
  rise of, 35
  see also Kurdish nationalism; Turkish nationalism
Native Americans, 21, 38, 40, 207n
NATO, PKK as a terrorist organization, 20, 122
natural disasters, 22, 24, 32–34, 203
  see also earthquakes
Nazi Germany
  child development, 44–45
  propaganda, 44, 45
  World War II, 99
  see also Holocaust
Necati, Mustafa, 178
neglect, childhood, 23, 30–31, 32, 44–45
Nesin, Aziz, 46, 144
neurofeedback, 128
Neyzi, Leyla
  Armenian collective trauma, 109–110
  Armenian Genocide, 47, 73, 195, 196
  Dersim massacres, 41, 97, 98
  oral history research project, 193
  Turkish identities, 191

Neyzi, Leyla *(continued)*
  Turkishness, 192, 196
NGOs (nongovernmental organizations), 139, 141, 170
Nichanian, M., 72
nomadism
  Anatolia, 56, 207*n*
  Kurds, 55, 56, 58, 207*n*
  Ottoman Empire, 56, 58
non-Muslim minorities
  economic place of, 110–111
  Istanbul, 100, 104, 105–110
  labor camps, 100–101
  as the "other", 99, 104, 107, 145
  Ottoman Empire, 3, 9, 58, 84, 104
  pogroms, 36, 46, 66, 104–111, 112, 152, 190, 201
  Turkish Republic, 83–84, 99, 104, 109–111, 168, 191, 201–202
  Twenty Kur'a Military Service, 36, 99–100, 110
  wealth and revenue taxes, 36, 99, 100–104, 110
  World War II, 110
  see also Armenians; Christians; Jews; Rum (Greek Ottoman) communities
non-Muslim women, 9, 10
nongovernmental organizations (NGOs), 139, 141, 170
Norris, F.H., 28, 39

Ocak, S., 56
Ocalan, Abdullah, 122, 125, 126
Occidental paradigm, 155
Oguz tribe, 50–51, 206*n*
Ökte, Faik, 101
Oliner, Pearl, 47
Oliner, Samuel, 47
Olson, E., 33
Olson, R., 58, 85, 93, 207*n*
Omer Naci Bey, 66
Oncu, E.C., 27
Önsüz, M.F., 27
oppressive societies, 43, 164
oral history
  anthropology, 21
  Armenian deportations and massacres, 47, 60, 68, 74, 109–110, 193–196
  Armenian Genocide, 47, 68, 193–194, 195–196
  Dersim massacres, 94, 97
  Eğin collective trauma, 194–195
  family story, 4–8, 15–16, 123–124

independence courts
  Istiklal Courts, 87
  population exchange, 78, 79
Oran, B., 83–84, 174
Orhan Gazi, Sultan of the Ottoman Empire, 51
Orhan, M., 88
Orientalism, 155
orphans, 47–48, 60, 68, 69, 89, 95
Osman I, Sultan of the Ottoman Empire, 51
Osman (Uzbek migrant), 4, 5, *6*
Ottoman Empire
  Alevi massacres, 143, 146–147
  Armenians, 53–55, 57–61, 72, 148, 185
  Chaldiran War, 146–147, 203
  Christians, 11, 53, 57, 58, 81
  collective brutalities, 46
  collective traumas, 35, 49–82, 203
  Committee of Union and Progress (CUP), 64–65
  Constitutional period (First – 1876–1878), 50, 61–62
  Constitutional period (Second – 1908–1918), 61–62, 64, 112
  Dersim, 90, 91, 92, 99
  diversity, 53, 157
  expansion, 50–51, *52*
  fall of, 1, 4–8, 14, 46, 49–82, 110, 148, 157, 168, 185, 201
  Great Eastern Crisis, 105
  identity, 8, 13
  Islam, 51
  Jews, 53, 58
  Kurdistan, 58
  Kurds, 55, 58
  military forces, 112
  millet system, 56–58, 60, 84
  modernization process, 14, 58
  Muslim communities, 56–57, 59
  nomadism, 56, 58
  non-Muslim minorities, 3, 9, 58, 84, 104
  opponents' threat, 49
  reforms, 50, 58, 59
  religious communities, 168
  Russo-Turkish wars (1828–1829), 59
  Russo-Turkish wars (1877–1878), 59, 93
  sürgün practices, 137
  Tanzimat era, 50, 58
  transgenerational trauma, 4–8
  ummet system, 56–57

Westernization policies, 172
women's rights, 170
World War I defeat, 6, 69, 74, 80, 83
Young Turk Revolution (1908), 61–62, 63, 64
see also Armenian Genocide (1915–1917); Balkan Wars (1912–1913); Greco-Turkish War (1920–1922); Hamidiye massacres (1893–1896); Hamidiye regiments; Rum (Greek Ottoman) communities; Sèvres, Treaty of (1920); Turkish War of Independence (1919–1923)
Ottoman Greeks see Rum (Greek Ottoman) communities
Özal, Turgut, 125, 173
Özcan, N.K., 29
Özdemir, B., 129
Özdoğan, G.G., 189, 195
Özerdem, A., 26, 27
Özmen, E., 120
Öztürkmen, Arzu, 170
Özücetin, Y., 181–182

Paboudjian, P.B., 53, 55
pain, healing transmission, 39, 41
Paker, M., 114, 117, 119, 120, 121
Paker, O., 120, 121
Papadopoulos, R.K., 28
parenting skills, 24, 30–31, 37
  Nazi Germany, 44–45
Partiya Karkerên Kurdistanê see Kurdistan Workers' Party (PKK)
patriarchal system, 3, 151, 170
Pattie, S.P., 70
Peace and Democracy Party (BDP), 118
Peker, Recep, 181–182
Peoples' Democratic Party (PDP), 168, 209*n*
People's Liberation Army of Turkey (THKO), 113
perpetrator energy, 38
perpetrators
  Armenian Genocide, 75
  and consequences of denial of actions, 73, 121, 151
  creation of, 45–48
  healing process, 42–43
  historical trauma symptoms, 151
  identification, 38
  and justice system, 42, 150, 151
  motives from psycho-social lens, 44–48
  trauma, 34, 71, 157
  Turkish Republic policies, 8
  and vampire metaphor, 38, 39
Persian nationalism, 143
Peru, *rondas campesinas*, 135
Pınar, R., 26, 27
Pir, Kemal, 118
Piraeus, 77
PKK *see* Kurdistan Workers' Party (PKK)
Platt, S., 27
playback theatre techniques, 2
pogroms, 36, 46, 66, 104–111, 112, 152, 190, 201
Polat, Hasan, 109
political activism, 98, 113, 119, 121, 124, 209*n*
political prisoners, 118, 121
political violence, 32, 46, 120
Pomian, Krzysztof, 67
population exchange, 36, 50, 76–79, 104
positive growth, 28
positivism, 63
post-traumatic growth, 28
post-traumatic slavery syndrome, 21
post-traumatic stress disorder (PTSD)
  Armenian–Azerbaijan ethnic violence, 33
  combat trauma, 10, 128, 129–130, 132
  earthquake survivors, 27, 28, 33
  forced displacements, 140, 201
  psychological trauma, 22–23
  torture survivors, 120
  transgenerational aspects of, 132
"primordial loyalties", 65
privilege *see* Turkish privilege; white privilege
Proctor, Robert, 162
Prophet Muhammed, 40
psychodrama, 2–3, 11, 19, 98, 154, 157–158, 160, 171, 205–206*n*
psychological healing, 40, 129, 130, 150, 151
psychological trauma, 21, 22–24
  academic research in Turkey, 31
  combat trauma, 130
  domestic violence, 29–31
  earthquakes, 22, 24–29, 31
  healing, 39–41, 130, 150
  Muslim migrants, 193
  political prisoners, 121
  public awareness of, 129
  rediscovering history, 202–203

252 | Index

psychological trauma *(continued)*
  resilience, 27, 28–29
  torture, 22, 24, 120–122, 140–141
  Turkey, 24–31
  wealth and revenue taxes, 102–103
psychotherapy, 21–22, 40, 41
PTSD *see* post-traumatic stress disorder (PTSD)

racial contract, 163, 192–193
racial dynamics, 163–164, 193
racism, 41–42, 162
racist socialization, 164
Radikal newspaper, 119–120
Rahmi Bey, 63, 68
rape, 60, 68, 106, 124
reconciliation
  efforts between PKK and Turkish military, 125, 127
  forced displacements, 142
  HWH workshops, 154, 205*n*
  mobilization of bystanders, 48
  needs in Turkey, 142, 150, 187, 201, 202
  South Africa, 41–42
Reicher, S., 45
Republican People's Party (RPP), 104
research methods, 13
  see also transdisciplinary research
research questions, 12
resilience
  Armenian Genocide, 73
  collective trauma, 32
  concept of hope, 161
  defined, 28
  Dersimis, 96, 97, 98
  earthquakes, 27, 28–29
  Holocaust survivors, 38
  presence in Turkey, 156
  psychological trauma, 27, 28–29
  transgenerational trauma, 38
  US immigrants, 3
  wealth and revenue taxes, 103
right-wing groups, 113, 114, 144, 148
right-wing police force, 122, 146
Robertson, R., 40–41
Robinson, G., 151
Rodin (HWH workshop participant), 171–172
Romano, S.J., 23
RPP (Republican People's Party), 104
Rum bandits, 7, 8, 75

"Rum bride" ("aunt from Samsun"), 6, 7, 8, 9–10
Rum (Greek Ottoman) communities
  Anatolia, 64, 70–71, 78, 206*n*
  labor camps, 101
  pogroms, 104, 105–106, 107, 108, 111
  population exchange, 36, 50, 76–78, 104
  Turkish recognition as minority, 175
  wealth and revenue taxes, 100, 101
Rum villages, Turkish raids on, 8, 9
Russia
  threat to Ottoman Empire, 49
  World War I, 5, 67
Russo-Turkish wars (1828–1829), 59
Russo-Turkish wars (1877–1878), 59, 93
Rwandan genocide, 207*n*
Rydelius, P. A., 120

Sabuncu, N., 26, 27
Safavids, 58, 91, 146–147
Said, Edward, 155
Said, Sheikh, 85, 86, 87, 208*n*
  see also Sheikh Said Rebellion (1925)
Salcıoğlu, E., 27
Salerian, A., 73
Salkim Hanim'in Taneleri (movie), 101
Samast, Ogün, 188
Samsun, 7, 8, 75, 79, 147
Sanandaj, 53
Saturday Mothers, 209*n*
schizophrenia, 129
Schützenberger, A.A., 37
Selahattin, O., 77
Selective Mutism (SM), 102–103
self-esteem, 24, 28, 156, 176
self-hatred, 38
self-Orientalism, 155
Selim I ("Grim Selim"), 52, 146, 147
Selin (oral history study participant), 109–110
Seljuk Empire, 51
Serbia, Balkan Wars, 62
Sergek Verim, E., 29
Seropyan, Sarkis, 197–198
Sèvres, Treaty of (1920), 69, 74, 83, 84
sexual abuse, 29, 30
Seyit Rıza, 92–94
shamanism, 40
Sheikh Said Rebellion (1925), 36, 82, 84, 85–89, 137, 167, 207*n*
Shorter, Frederic, 75–76
Sirman, Nüket, 170

Sivas, 53, 68, 75, 145, 147, 203
Sivas Massacre (1993), 46, 144
Siviş-Çetinkaya, R., 30
Skoglund, E., 120
Slater, Phillip, 204
slavery, 21, 42, 72, 164, 206n, 207n
Smelser, N.J., 111
Social Darwinism, 63
social trauma, 110–111, 203
socialization issues, 128
Sofuoğlu, Z., 30, 31
Solomon, Z., 28
somatic experiencing, 128
Sontag, Susan, 44
Soul Wound, 38, 39
South Africa, 41–42
Southwick, S.M., 128
Soviet Union
　collapse of, 186
　control of Armenia, 189, 190
Soyalp, Nermin, personal background, 15–20, 158–160, 177–178, 182–183
Stanford prison experiment, 121–122
Staub, Ervin, 44, 46, 47, 48
Stefanovic, D., 140, 141
Stein, E., 28
Stockholm Syndrome, 23, 95
stress-related symptoms, 11, 21, 73, 130
　see also post-traumatic stress disorder (PTSD)
Student Oath, 182, 183
substance abuse, 30, 38, 125, 128, 151
Sufism, 40, 146–147, 207n
suicide, 30, 68, 117, 129, 140
suicide bombings, 125
Suleiman, Sultan of the Ottoman Empire, 51
Sullivan, Shannon, 14–15, 153, 161–162
Sümer, N., 27, 28, 31
Sun-language theory, 173
Sunni Muslims
　Arabs, 85, 86, 207n
　Dersimi women, 95
　gender and hierarchy rules, 139
　Kurds, 5, 82, 83, 85, 86, 91, 207n
　Kurmanji speakers, 88
　Lausanne Peace Treaty, 84
　power in the Turkish state, 18, 82
　relations with Alevis, 85, 92, 143, 144, 146–147
　religious rights, 148
　Sivas Massacre, 46
　Turks, 207n

Suny, Ronald, 45–46, 57, 60, 66, 67, 70, 164–165
sürgün practices, 137
Suryanis, Anatolia, 206n
Sutker, P.B., 128
Syria, Kurdish community, 88, 143
Syrian civil war, 152
Sztompka, Piotr, 12, 32, 34–35, 43, 171

Tabanlı earthquake, 26
Talât Pasha, 63, 66, 67, 68, 69
talk therapy, 205–206n
Tapan, M., 26
taqsim, 164
Tas, L., 126, 127
Tawfiq, N., 120
Tekin, A., 27
Tekin, F., 140
Tekinoğlu, Devrim, 145, 166–167
Tevfik Pasha, 94
THKO (People's Liberation Army of Turkey), 113
Tobbell, J., 103
Tokat, 102, 147
Toktaş, S, 29
Tol, U.U., 167
Tonguç, Ismail Hakkı, 178, 179, 180
torture
　Diyarbakır Military Prison, 36, 114, 116–120, 174
　during military coups, 36, 113, 115
　and historical trauma, 151
　physical, 120
　as political violence, 32, 48, 67, 116–120, 133, 134, 150, 200
　psychological, 120
　and psychological trauma, 22, 24, 120–122, 140–141
　research studies, 31
　Stanford prison experiment, 121–122
Trabzon, 68
transdisciplinary research, 1–2, 13, 21–22, 34, 162, 205n
transgenerational trauma, 10–13, 14, 21–24, 37–39, 201–203
　Armenian Genocide, 71–74, 109–110
　catastrophes, 33
　cultural factors, 34
　defined, 11
　"Dersim 38", 96–99
　domestic violence, 30
　epistemologies of ignorance, 1, 153
　healing, 16, 38–39

transgenerational trauma *(continued)*
  Healing the Wounds of History workshop, 2–3
  interlinked process, 32
  Ottoman Empire, 4–8
  psychology studies, 21
  psychosocial consequences, 164, 193
  PTSD, 132
  resilience, 38
transhumance *see* nomadism
trauma, 21–48
  childhood, 23–24, 73
  chosen, 36, 46
  combat, 10, 128–132
  complexity, 22–23, 34
  epigenetics of, 21
  flow state of an individual, 32
  secondary/vicarious, 22
  social, 110–111, 203
  socio-cultural context, 31–32
  and war, 8
  see also collective trauma; cultural trauma; historical trauma; post-traumatic stress disorder (PTSD); psychological trauma; transgenerational trauma
trauma therapy, 29
traumatic sequences, 12, 35, 50, 81, 109, 152, 171
tribalism
  Dersimis, 91, 93
  Kurds, 55, 61, 65, 92–93, 135
  rebellion (1937), 92–93
  Turkic, 50–51, 56, 95, 190
TRT-6 Kurdish TV channel, 174
Tuana, Nancy, 14–15, 153, 161–162
Tüleylioğlu, O., 145
Tunceli, 90
turkeypurge.com, 149
Turkic tribes, 50–51, 56, 95, 190
Turkification process, 13, 36, 81–82
  Armenians, 168, 189
  control of language, 177
  dominant profile, 191
  Eastern Anatolia/Kurdistan, 115
  impact on business and trade, 100
  Kurds, 84, 165, 167, 177
  torture, 120
  tribal autonomy, 91
  Turkish nationalist identity, 165
  within schools, 94–95, 181
Turkish bandits, 7

Turkish bourgeoisie, 14, 64, 104, 152, 171
Turkish elite, 14, 79–80, 157, 178
Turkish historical thesis, 173
Turkish identity, 190–199
  Armenian Genocide, 184–185, 196
  of author, 2
  boarding schools, 181
  built from partial and selected truths, 167
  control of education, 183
  emergence of, 8–9, 14, 77, 79–82, 165, 171
  epistemologies of ignorance, 153, 154, 156
  forced displacements, 137
  identity crisis, 14
  Kurdish resistance, 87
  multiple formations, 14
  pogroms, 107
  secular emphasis, 13, 191
  village guards, 136
  Yörük Turks, 3
Turkish language, 169, 171–178
  Citizen, Speak Turkish! campaign, 99, 110, 172–173, 190, 201–202
Turkish military forces, 112–152
  armed conflict with PKK, 2, 20, 32, 36, 112, 116, 121, 122–128, 129, 131–137, 138, 141, 145, 155, 177, 203, 206*n*
  cease-fire with PKK, 125, 135, 160
  Cyprus crisis, 109
  Dersim/Tunceli interventions, 89–99, 145–146
  mandatory service, 99–100, 108, 128–129, 130–132
  pogroms, 108
  psychological treatment programs, 129
  Sheikh Said Rebellion, 86
  status in Turkish Republic, 112
  see also military coups
Turkish nationalism
  in the 19th century, 53
  amongst women, 93
  Armenian Genocide, 185, 186
  "Atatürk's Principles and Reforms", 181–182
  boarding schools, 180
  control of education, 183
  Dersimis, 92
  dominance in police force, 146
  emergence of, 49–50, 84–85, 207*n*

JDP–PKK peace talks, 126
Kurdish concerns, 84, 143, 192
laws and regulations, 87
pogroms, 107
Turkish language, 173
Turkish Republic, 169
village institutes, 180
Turkish paternalism, 116
Turkish privilege, 13–14, 154, 163, 193, 198
Turkish Republic
  abolition of the caliphate, 169
  abolition of the Sultanate, 169
  Armenian population, 11, 70, 72, 74, 109–110, 188–190
  Balkan Muslim migrants, 15, 191, 193, 196
  books banned, 185
  Christians, 11, 14, 148
  Citizen, Speak Turkish! campaign, 99, 110, 172–173, 190, 201–202
  collective trauma, 3, 80, 83–111, 203
  compulsory settlement law (1947), 88, 137
  Constitution (1924), 169, 172
  Constitution (1982), 115
  Constitution modified (1928), 169
  Cyprus dispute, 105, 109
  demographic engineering, 81, 137, 141, 147–148
  diversity, 81–82, 190–191, 193
  domestic violence, 29–31
  establishment of Republic (1923), 1, 4, 8, 14, 35–36, 50, 75, 81, 84, 112
  feminism, 170
  historical atrocities as taboo topic, 11
  historical trauma, 8, 77, 80, 151, 153–157, 200, 203
  industrialization era, 138
  Islam removed as state religion, 169
  Kemalist ideologies, 155, 169, 172, 174
  labor camps, 100–101
  militarism, 116
  military service mandatory, 99–100, 108, 128–129, 130–132
  modernization policies, 14, 89, 91, 92, 95, 97
  nation-building process, 77, 79, 85
  national ideology, 64, 116
  non-Muslim minorities, 83–84, 99, 104, 109–111, 168, 191, 201–202
  oppressive policies, 1, 98, 167
  Orient Reform Plan, 87
  PKK as a terrorist organization, 20, 122
  reforms, 169, 170, 171
  religious pluralism, 109
  secularism, 13, 80, 82, 85, 86, 87, 92, 168, 169, 191
  state of emergency (1987), 124–125
  Syrian refugees, 152
  women's rights, 170
  see also AKP/JDP; Committee of Union and Progress (CUP); "Dersim 38"; Greco-Turkish War (1920–1922); Lausanne Peace Treaty (1923); Marmara earthquake (1999); military coups; pogroms; Sheikh Said Rebellion (1925); Twenty Kur'a Military Service; wealth and revenue taxes
Turkish War of Independence (1919–1923), 7, 35, 50, 61, 74–76, 80, 83, 84, 92, 112, 168
Turkish Women's Union, 170
Turkishness
  Armenian Genocide, 69
  assimilation to, 191
  Atatürk as symbol of, 80
  control of education, 171, 172, 173, 174–176, 181–183
  control of language, 171–178
  in crisis, 192, 196
  Dersimis, 94, 95, 98
  Dink's misunderstood remark, 187
  epistemologies of ignorance, 14–15, 165, 200, 202
  heterogeneity, 193
  high-school history textbooks, 185–186
  Kemalist discourse, 191
  Kurdish resistance, 12
  non-Muslim women, 10
  power and privilege, 193
  secular emphasis, 13, 191
  shadow/negative sides, 192
  Turkish Republic strategy, 64, 137
  Ünlü's concept of, 163
  village guards, 136
  village institutes, 178–180
  willful ignorance, 200
Turkishness contract, 64–65, 163, 192, 193, 202
Turkmen tribes, 56, 146
Tüysüz, Nur, 135, 136
Tuzcu, A., 140
Twelver Shiism, 91, 207*n*

Twenty Kur'a Military Service, 36, 99–100, 110

Uçarlar, Nesrin, 175
Uddo, M., 128
ulema, 88
Uluğ, N.H., 92
ummet system, 56–57
Ünal, A.Z., 140
Ünal, M.C., 122, 126
Üngör, Uğur Ümit
  Armenian Genocide, 66, 67, 68, 69, 193–194, 195
  CUP coup d'état (1913), 66–67
  "Dersim 38", 89
  mass violence, 186
  Turkish identities, 191
  Turkish state repression of information, 185
  World War I, 67
Unionists *see* Committee of Union and Progress (CUP)
United States
  African Americans, 21, 72, 164
  disenfranchised communities, 21
  Great Depression, 110–111
  PKK as a terrorist organization, 20, 122
  slavery, 21, 42, 72, 164
  Turkish military coup attempt (2016), 149
  Vietnam Syndrome, 130
"unknowledges", 13, 162
Ünlü, B.
  Muslim–Christian relations, 63
  Muslimness Contract, 81
  Turkification process, 81
  Turkish–Kurd relations, 197
  Turkishness, 64–65, 163, 191, 192, 193, 202
Ünlü, M., 116
us-versus-them mentality, 11, 37, 48, 57, 65, 127, 146, 171, 201

vacant esteem, 164
vampire bite metaphor, 38, 39
Van, 53, 68, 70
  earthquake (2011), 26, 27
Van Bruinessen, M.
  Alevi groups, 91
  Beşikçi's imprisonment, 192
  Chaldiran War, 146, 147
  "Dersim 38", 89, 93, 96
  Dersim culture destroyed, 99

Dersimi tribes, 91, 93
Gazi neighborhood massacre, 145
Hamidiye regiments, 59–60, 61
Kurd-Armenian relations, 58
Kurdish displacement, 139, 142
Kurdish identity, 165
Kurdish Muslim solidarity, 83
Kurdish nationalism, 143
Kurdish nomads, 55
Kurdish primordial loyalties, 65
Kurdish rebellions, 85
Kurds in Ottoman Empire, 58
military coup (1980), 114, 122
military intervention in Dersim (1994–1995), 145–146
PKK activities, 122
PKK aims and mission, 122
PKK's independence demands, 125
Seyit Riza's surrender, 94
Sheikh Said Rebellion, 82, 85, 86, 87, 88
state violence toward Alevis, 144
Sunni Muslims and Alevis conflict, 143
Turkish military-PKK conflict, 125
van der Kolk, B.A., 23, 128
Van Hasselt, V.B., 23
Van, I., 193
Vasterling, J.J., 128
Vecchi, G.M., 23
victim identification, 38–39
victimization, 3, 8–9, 32, 70, 71–72
Vietnam syndrome, 130
Vietnam War, 125
village guards, 126, 133, 134–137, 139, 141, 203
village institutes, 178–180
violence *see* abuse; child abuse; domestic violence; witnessing violence
Volkan, V.
  Balkan Wars, 62
  blind trust, 44
  child development in Nazi Germany, 44–45
  "chosen" traumas, 36, 46
  large-group identity, 33, 45, 46
  national identity evolution, 77, 79–80
  tent metaphor, 45
  transgenerational trauma, 37
  tree model, 43
  Turks' idealization of Atatürk, 80
Volkas, Armand
  group dialogue, 40

Healing the Wounds of History
  (HWH), 154–155, 156, 160, 205n
  historical traumas, 36, 38
  potential perpetrators, 44
  white privilege, 193
volunteerism, 179
vorpahavak, 69

Wahlbeck, Ö., 142
Walker, A.S., 103
Walker, C.J., 58
Watts, N., 89, 94
wealth and revenue taxes, 36, 99,
  100–104, 110, 203
Wells, Jennifer, 205n
Werfel, Franz, 185
Western Armenia, 65–66, 205n
Wheat, Arianna, 192–193
white privilege, 162, 193
white supremacy, 164, 192–193
Whiteness Studies, 163
Wilson, J., 28
Wise, A., 27
witnessing violence
  active bystanders, 48
  Anatolians, 50
  Armenian experience in Turkey, 109
  children's trauma of, 88
  domestic violence, 24, 29–31, 38
  Eğin collective trauma, 194–195
  Hamidiye massacres, 61
  large-scale atrocities, 34
  psychological trauma, 24
  Turkish military abuse of Kurds, 116
  see also Armenian Genocide (1915–
     1917)
women
  Dersim massacres, 94–95
  forced displacement, 94–95, 138
  Marmara earthquake (1999), 27
  non-Muslims, 9, 10
  rape, 60, 68, 106, 124
  violence against, 24, 29–31, 38
women's rights, Turkish Republic, 170
World War I, 50
  Armenian deportations, 185
  catastrophic experience of, 128
  CUP participation, 5, 63, 67, 75
  Hamidiye regiments, 61
  Ottoman defeat, 6, 69, 74, 80, 83
  outbreak of (1914), 5, 66, 67
  see also Lausanne Peace Treaty (1923);
     Sèvres, Treaty of (1920)

World War II, 99, 100, 105, 110
  see also Holocaust
wounded healer, 40–41

Yalova, 25, 26
yanılma, 166
Yavuz, M.H., 122, 165, 167
Yeğen, M., 163, 166, 167, 202, 209n
Yehuda, Rachel, 22
Yıldırım, Onur, 77, 90
Yıldıran, Esat Oktay, 116–117, 118
Yıldız, M., 89
Yılmaz, Deniz, 130, 131
Yılmaz, Ismet, 129
Yonucu, D., 145, 173–174
Yorbik, O., 27
Yörük Turks, 3, 206n
Young Turk Revolution (1908), 61–62,
  63, 64
Young Turks
  Armenian Genocide, 66, 70
  relations to CUP, 64
  state violence, 188
  see also Committee of Union and
     Progress (CUP)
Yozgat, 147
Yücel, Hasan Ali, 179
Yükseker, D., 140, 141, 142
Yüksel, R., 29
Yurtlu, F., 133

Zalta, A., 149
Zana, Layla, 119, 174
Zana, Mehdi, 117–118, 119, 174
Zara, A., 22
Zarcone, T., 40
Zaza Alevis
  Armenian Genocide, 68
  assimilation, 137
  in Dersim, 68, 90–91, 137
  historical trauma, 203
  military intervention (1994–1995),
     145–146
Zaza language, 88, 91, 206n, 207n
Zelyut, R., 90
Zengin, S., 166
Zeydanlıoğlu, W., 115, 119–120, 172, 173,
  174
Zcyneloğlu, S., 29
Zimbardo, P., 122
Zoran (HWH workshop participant),
  115–116
Zorlu, Fatin Rüştü, 108, 109

Zoroğlu, S.S., 30
Zotev, V., 128

Zürcher, Erik-Jan, 62, 63, 77, 79